G. D. H. COLE
and Socialist Democracy

This drawing of G. D. H. Cole was made by the cartoonist Will Dyson in Cole's rooms in Magdalen College, Oxford, *circa* 1912.

G. D. H. COLE
and Socialist
Democracy

A. W. WRIGHT

HD
8393
·C57
W74

Clarendon Press · Oxford
1979

Oxford University Press, Walton Street, Oxford OX2 6DP

OXFORD LONDON GLASGOW
NEW YORK TORONTO MELBOURNE WELLINGTON
NAIROBI DAR ES SALAAM CAPE TOWN
KUALA LUMPUR SINGAPORE JAKARTA HONG KONG TOKYO
DELHI BOMBAY CALCUTTA MADRAS KARACHI

British Library Cataloguing in Publication Data

Wright, A W
G. D. H. Cole and socialist democracy.
1. Cole, George Douglas Howard
I. Title
335′.0092′4   HX243.C/   78–40644
ISBN 0–19–827421–1

*Printed in Great Britain by
Cox & Wyman Ltd, London, Fakenham and Reading*

To my parents;
and the memory
of my grandparents

Preface

MANY PEOPLE kindly offered information, advice, and opinion during the preparation of this work. In particular, I would like to place on record the generous assistance given by H. L. Beales, Colin Clark, Sir George Clark (who also allowed me to reproduce here an original Will Dyson sketch of Cole which he possesses), John Parker M.P., John Plamenatz, E. A. Radice, W. A. Robson, A. L. Rowse and Philip Williams. Special thanks are owed to Dame Margaret Cole, not merely for allowing me to use the material in the vast collection of Cole papers at Nuffield College, Oxford, nor even for making available to me a set of private papers which do not form part of this collection; but for her critical and generous assistance over several years. Special thanks, too, must be given to Steven Lukes, who nursed this project at Balliol and sustained it (and me) with unfailing support and encouragement thereafter; and to my typist, Kitty Stevens, who gave help far beyond the call of duty, as did Audrey Elliott at a later stage. Finally, there is Moira, my wife, without whom this work might have been finished either much sooner or not at all; little Ben, who arrived too late to stop it; and Nye, who made sure I had plenty of fresh air along the way.

Contents

I

The Sensible Extremist

'One can have democracy without socialism, and vice
versa. Whether the two can be effectively combined is the
prime question of our age.'
(George Lichtheim, *A Short History of Socialism*, 1970,
p. 281.)

THIS BOOK attempts to provide a comprehensive account and critical
assessment of the socialist thought of a man who occupies a central
position in the intellectual history of British socialism. The young
Oxford academic G. D. H. Cole came to prominence on the eve of the
First World War as an enthusiastic commentator on the pre-war labour
unrest. Almost half a century later he remained influential as an
inspirational force behind the nascent New Left. During the intervening decades he had established himself as the leading theorist of a
school of participatory democracy and socialist pluralism (known as
Guild Socialism) and as the mentor of a whole generation of British
socialists as they confronted the developing complexities of the
twentieth century. For a long time Cole's continuing commitment to a
decentralized and pluralistic socialism seemed out of tune with the
times, a hangover from a romantic and utopian phase of early century
socialism. In recent years, however, the renewal of interest in issues of
organizational size, democratic participation and self-management has
occasioned a rediscovery of Cole and his concerns, making it necessary
to attempt a critical evaluation of his contribution to socialist and
democratic thought.

Introducing the interesting *Life* of her husband,[1] Margaret Cole
issues a fashionable warning against the prospect of a new piece of
intellectual territory falling to the arid conquest of a growing army of
academic dissectors. In this case, the warning is directed against the
prospective creation of a 'Cole industry' by eager students of 'ideas'
armed with the instruments of dissection. There is clearly some justice
in this sort of warning. Intellectual biography seems prone to two (at

[1] Margaret Cole, *The Life of G. D. H. Cole*, 1971, Preface.

2   *The Sensible Extremist*

least) kinds of danger; either it tries to tell us everything about its subject, with sheer intellectual narrative triumphing over wider meanings, or the analysis is so tightly drawn that it seems to hang in an intellectual vacuum, again at the expense of a wider understanding. British socialists seem to have suffered particularly badly in these respects. Laski was skilfully demolished as a political thinker, but at the expense of an understanding of his role as something other than an academic political theorist. Tawney's thought has been intelligently analysed, but in a non-chronological form which makes it needlessly abstract and timeless. Strachey has been the subject of a biographical narrative, but with scant attention to his theoretical importance. Cole has received diligent American treatment, but treatment which suspends him in a pious vacuum and gives little sense of the nature of his socialist thought or of the tradition within which it worked.[2] Doubtless, at some points in what follows both, and more, of these dangers will rise to snare the narrative; though there is reason to believe that the very nature of G. D. H. Cole's intellectual enterprise and position should work to diminish dangers of this kind. Why should this be so?

Above all, because though always and essentially an intellectual, Cole was highly distinctive in his intellectualism. His constant purpose was to be relevant, even at the cost of much wearisome toil and involving at least the partial sacrifice of intellectual nicety. In this commitment to relevancy, he was to develop a theoretical stance which was firmly relativist in its impatience with philosophic absolutes and even with philosophy itself, and which had interesting and important political consequences. Quite simply, for Cole theoretical impurity was the price of relevance in the real world, and he often regretted when others seemed unwilling to pay this same price. His advocacy of a 'sensible extremism' or of 'loyal grousing' as the appropriate socialist perspective exemplifies this approach. There is clearly some difference between the early and later Cole in this respect, but even at the height of the Guild Socialist period the nature of Cole's theoretical leadership of the Guild movement can be fully understood only in terms of this determination to be relevant. But relevant to what? To the working class of course, which meant in fact to its organized industrial and political movement. But with Cole this global statement requires instant modification; for it is with the British working-class movement,

[2] H. Deane, *The Political Ideas of Harold J. Laski*, 1955; R. Terrill, *R. H. Tawney and His Times*, 1973; H. Thomas, *John Strachey*, 1973; L. P. Carpenter, *G. D. H. Cole: An Intellectual Biography*, 1973.

in particular phases of its development, that the imperative to relevancy especially applied. This does not mean that there is no wider relevance for his ideas and analysis; but it does mean that Cole's own particular focus was clear. After all, is there not something quintessentially English about a 'sensible extremism'?

It is this which makes it necessary, and perhaps easier, to put Cole's intellectual enterprise into context, for it is the context which effectively shaped the design and direction of the enterprise itself. In other words, Cole as theorist can be fully understood only in terms of the development of the British working-class movement as a whole. Indeed, it is as an exploration of this relationship between the British Labour movement and perhaps its leading socialist intellectual over a period of almost half a century that a study of this kind acquires a central part of its interest and justification. It should tell us much about the general ideological climate of the British Labour movement during a crucial period of its development. British socialism has been poorly served in this respect. Its theorists have been lightly dismissed with a word about the British incapacity for high theory: Cole is too utopian, Tawney too sentimental, Laski too vulgar, Strachey too derivative. What is missed in this approach is the opportunity for a wider intellectual inquiry into the theoretical climate in which these figures operated. G. D. H. Cole and Harold Laski are particularly interesting in this respect, and their treatment has been broadly similar. Here, it is said, were two young men of exceptional early promise; both were engaged in interesting theoretical work on the nature of the state and of democracy; and their efforts seemed to portend a theory of socialist pluralism which would have decisive consequences for the future development of British socialism. Yet it was to be a case of promise unfulfilled. At the moment of their most interesting theoretical work in the 1920s—Cole's *Social Theory* period, Laski's *Grammar of Politics*—they seemed to burn themselves out and to fall back into varieties of disillusionment. For Laski it was a windy Marxism; for Cole a temporizing Fabianism: both men had 'died' intellectually almost before their mature life had started.[3]

This sort of account is not so much inaccurate as inadequate. It tends

[3] With Laski, this is the tone of Deane's account; and Zylstra organizes his treatment of Laski's early thought around exactly this theme. (B. Zylstra, *From Pluralism to Collectivism: The Development of Harold Laski's Political Thought*, 1968.) With Cole, the verdict has been uniform: usually his theoretical disintegration is located in the 1920s, though one writer has sought, inaccurately, to find its origins in the First World War. (J. M. Winter, *Socialism and the Challenge of War 1912–18*, 1974, chapter 5.)

to abstract theories from the conditions which help to shape them, and to treat as static that which is essentially dynamic. It misses a whole developmental process rich in insights and understanding. Cole's life began amidst the renaissance of socialist theory and trade union practice at the end of the nineteenth century, and ended in the middle of the twentieth century with an official party of Labour established as a major governing party. He was active in, and brought a distinctive approach to, this whole long record of British socialist development. It was this distinctive approach which found expression in Guild Socialism during a decade which had the First World War at its centre, and any understanding of Cole's brand of socialism and of its relationship to the wider socialist tradition in Britain certainly requires a considerable exploration of this period. But we miss much if we stop there; for there remains the interesting and significant problem of the fate of Cole's version of socialist democracy in the world that followed the formal eclipse of the Guild movement. In some ways this is the most suggestive area of all, for whilst it is not difficult to trace the 'makings' of Guild Socialism and to account for its development at a particular historical moment, it is much less easy to predict how the leading exponent of the Guild Socialist doctrine would work out his responses to a post (or pre-) Guild world. What would be the response to Marxism? To Russia? To fascism? To economic depression? To the development of British socialism itself? The response would often be complex, for Cole himself was complex. He did not abandon Guild Socialism, but nor would he merely go on repeating its hallowed formulae in a changing world. The need for relevance demanded attention to one thing when instinct and preference inclined to another. Cole wanted to be of service to the world of labour; and an examination of the nature of that service should, therefore, make some contribution to an understanding of the development of the British socialist tradition.

This character of Cole's thought demands a particular treatment. It demands, on the one hand, that his Guild Socialism be treated as a theoretical unity; for it was developed and presented as such and so requires analysis in its own terms. This does not mean that the environment in which it was developed can be ignored, or that it can be divorced from Cole's later thought; but it does mean a treatment which recognizes Guild Socialism as a distinctive theoretical enterprise. Its distinctiveness is also chronological, for it was the collapse of Guild Socialism as both theory and movement in the early 1920s which rendered Cole theoretically and organizationally homeless, a condition which provided the essential framework for his later thought. Thus both theory and chronology combine to enforce a separate consideration of the Guild Socialist period: this is the purpose of Part One of this book. On the other hand, a rather different treatment is required for Cole's subsequent thought. No longer was he engaged in the elaboration of a coherent theoretical system, but in developing a theoretical response to a range of events and ideas in a complex environment. This response requires a thematic treatment, in order that the development of Cole's thought on central issues can be clearly followed through the complexities of four decades. This should illuminate the circumstances in which theoretical development took place and facilitate comparison with the Guild period on significant problems. Thus, in Part Two, one chapter (chapter VI) examines his continued treatment of Guild democratic theory, particularly industrial democracy; and another (chapter VII) discusses his developing conception of the respective merits of political and industrial action, including the role of the state. Other chapters in Part Two trace the new directions in Cole's thought in the post-Guild period: his immersion in the problems of the economy (chapter VIII), his critique of Marxism and formulation of a distinctive democratic socialism (chapter IX) and his increasing international preoccupation (chapter X). At the same time, however, a thematic approach has to avoid mere intellectual abstraction if it is to make good historical sense. This is especially important in Cole's case, for his determination to offer relevant analysis on contemporary problems gives his thought a firm historical grounding. Thus a thematic treatment must build upon chronology, not dissolve it.

The chapters in Part Two also focus particular attention on a central feature of Cole's intellectual activity which has already been identified; namely, his commitment to a practical relevancy. He was not content with the role of abstract theorist and was ever anxious to service the policy needs of the labour movement. This has a number of important consequences for the treatment of his thought. For example, it makes it necessary to relate the development of his thought to his analysis of contemporary events and tendencies (economic depression, the General Strike, fascism, etc.), for it was out of such analysis that theoretical development frequently took place. Thus, in the context of a thematic treatment, this work attempts to ground its account of theoretical development in an analysis of Cole's response to concrete problems. In doing this, it claims to provide an authentic portrait of the style and purpose (as well as content) of his thought. This also makes it necessary to relate Cole's own theoretical activity to its immediate intellectual environment, to the intellectual history of British socialism and, particularly, to the contemporary theoretical activity of comparable figures (such as Laski, Tawney and Strachey). Thus, where appropriate, this is attempted too. Another major consequence of this commitment to a practical relevancy was to introduce considerable tension and ambiguity into Cole's thought. Indeed, this is a central theme of the book. If it enabled him to provide sensible analysis of concrete problems (of unemployment, or the rise of fascism), it also produced tension between this sort of particular analysis (and prescription) and his wider socialist position. At various points, this study explores the difficulties inherent in this tendency to operate at two levels. It is central to the discussion of his economic thought (in chapter VIII) and of his continuing treatment of industrial democracy (in chapter VI). It is variously referred to as dualism or bifocalism; and is presented here as a leading and distinctive feature of his thought. These, then, are some of the considerations which govern the organization and treatment of what follows.

Cole's role was that of a relentlessly energetic intellectual who was literally full of ideas, often to the despair of official Labour. His formation of a socialist ginger group at the time of the second Labour Government, for example, was greeted by Ramsay MacDonald with instructions to Labour's National Executive Committee to 'ascertain the intention' behind Cole's activities,[4] which aptly summarizes the suspicions and difficulties involved in a 'loyal grouser' position. Unlike Laski, Cole's intellectualism was never that of a politician manqué or aspirant confidant of the mighty: both personal temperament (a stubborn integrity) and political persuasion (a radical anti-parliamentarism) conspired to prevent this. But these same qualities produced many of official Labour's doubts about Cole: somehow he was not quite sound, prone to reckless irresponsibility, a 'permanent undergraduate' in Attlee's telling phrase. Hence a study of Cole will add little to the official history of Labour: his exclusion and self-exclusion from the corridors of power ensure that. Instead, from his vantage point of critical loyalty, and armed with a distinctive socialism, Cole provides a particularly suggestive point of entry into the wider

---

[4] Labour Party N.E.C. Minutes, 23 June 1931, Transport House. Similarly, Herbert Morrison wished that Cole 'might do a little less research and lecturing and a little more of the rough and tumble work of the Labour Movement'. (Quoted in B. Donoughue and G. W. Jones, *Herbert Morrison, Portrait of a Politician*, 1973, p. 71.)

history of the British working class movement in this century, a history of which his own life and work form an essential part.

It is the 'work' which is the concern here, and which takes the form of what is surely the most prodigious output of any serious writer this century. 'Mr. Cole's whole life would appear to be a protest against the doctrine of restriction of output' was one early reviewer's comment,[5] typical of many others. Not only is the sheer volume remarkable, but also the massive spread. Philosophy, economics, social theory, politics, sociology, history, literature: in books, articles, journalism and teaching Cole defied, and denied, the academic boundary posts. He was a genuine encyclopaedist, in a world increasingly hostile to that art. The fact that he could hold, at different periods, academic posts in three disciplines (philosophy, economics, social and political theory)—and could well have held posts in at least two others—is sufficient indication of this. Of course a good deal of Cole's work suffers with time, whilst other parts are frankly ephemeral; but that is the price of diversity, especially in someone who was always a working journalist. The very spread of Cole's work is an important clue to its understanding. The perennial search for relevance implied a shifting focus, a constant willingness to respond to the preoccupations of the time. This reveals itself in the broad lines of Cole's intellectual life-cycle: the early emphasis on problems of social theory, followed by a long period in which economic concerns predominate, itself followed by a return to the very earliest interest in problems of social theory and organization. This cycle, though crudely drawn, tells us much about Cole's perceptions of the world in which he was operating, and of his place in it. It will be argued here that an understanding of Cole's socialism involves a recognition of the significance of the sheer range of his interests, and of their development over time. To put this in a nutshell: Cole as adventurous social theorist, as laborious economic analyst for the Intelligent Man, as historian and biographer, even as poet, all contribute to, and reflect, a consistent and unified conception of socialism. It will be the purpose of this study to elicit the nature of that conception from source material formidable in both volume and diversity.

Does Cole's standing as a theorist of socialism warrant a study of this kind? This is a difficult question, properly answerable only in terms of

[5] D. H. Robertson, *Economic Journal*, June 1920. Cole had scarcely begun to write at this stage, of course. In 1925 a *New Statesman* reviewer suggested, not implausibly, that the much-initialled Cole should be regarded as the collective pseudonym of a writers' syndicate.

what follows, but a few preliminary observations can usefully be ventured at this stage. In any strict sense, Cole was not an original thinker, even in the more limited sense of initiating an intellectual advance whose historical antecedents and ingredients become discernible only much later. With Cole, the ingredients and antecedents were usually both near and clear. This is true of his early discovery of socialism, of his formulation of Guild Socialism, of his economic doctrines and much else besides. In writing about Cole it is words like catalyst and synthesis which come most readily to mind, for he sucked in ideas and information with voracious if selective appetite and sent them forth again in developed and distinctive form. This will become clear when particular aspects of this thought are examined. What Cole's thought does exhibit, therefore, is a remarkable, often brilliant, eclecticism which produced, not an intellectual system, but a body of thought full of internal tension but rooted in a distinct perspective. The tensions were profound—between Morris and Marx, between direct democracy and centralization, between individualism and mass action, between reform and revolution; but they were also suggestive in their reflection of the tensions inside the wider tradition of which Cole was part. If Cole's socialism was idiosyncratic, its eclecticism also made it representative of much that is basic to British socialism as a whole. His tensions were the tensions of a whole tradition, almost of social democracy itself. When he was the critic of that tradition he was also its product and intellectual barometer. Much of the justification for this sort of study derives from just this.

But the idiosyncrasy is important too. In a very real sense Cole was the most democratic and most 'radical' of the British socialists. His instincts were rooted in a radical tradition which was firmly pre-socialist, and his version of socialism was decisively shaped by this tradition. It reflected itself in a radical view of power, sharply different from the collectivism of left or right.[6] Its expression was a creed of radical democracy which was at the heart of Guild Socialism and which continued to be basic to Cole's politics thereafter. In any historical perspective this infusion of radical democracy must be reckoned Cole's chief theoretical contribution to socialism in Britain. It is this, too, which made Cole something other than a conventional social democrat; and which makes it necessary to write not just of democratic socialism but of socialist democracy. The emphasis is important.

[6] See S. Beer, *Modern British Politics*, 1965, for a good discussion of the dominant collectivism of the modern British political tradition.

A further main ground upon which an extended treatment of Cole's thought is justified is his attempt (largely in the post-Guild period) to develop a coherent philosophy and strategy for West European (particularly British) socialism. This enterprise involved a critique of Marxism, an analysis of fascism, an attitude to liberalism, a particular sociology and political economy, an international perspective—and much else besides: these matters are the stuff of Part Two. Here the strengths and weaknesses of these particular items of analysis are discussed; but it is also suggested that from this Cole forged a general conception of the nature, constraints and potentialities of the environment within which a democratic socialism had to operate which merits serious treatment. Hence, in Cole's own shorthand, the strategy of 'sensible extremism'.

At the time of his death in 1959, there seemed little interest in Cole's distinctive theoretical concerns. Affluence seemed to have worked its soporific effects, whilst the Labour movement was still much too busy waging the old battle of public ownership to worry about the 'democratic control' which also had found its way into the Party's constitution in 1918 at the height of Guild Socialist propaganda. Cole's work remained influential but without its early bite. It was his pioneering work in labour history which found most recognition at this time—and for some years after.[7] Recent interest in 'participatory' democracy, with renewed attention to problems of workers' control, has done much to change this situation. In these circumstances it is unsurprising that there should develop fresh interest in a period of labour history which had these issues at its centre,[8] and in the ideas of the leading theorist of socialist democracy at that time. In a sense, then, Cole has been rediscovered and re-assessed. He could now be regarded as 'Britain's outstanding twentieth-century socialist theorist', as the 'outstanding Fabian of the post-Webb generation' and as 'one of the greatest of Red Professors'.[9] In both life and work Cole was a curiously complex and elusive figure. Margaret Cole, challenging her husband's

[7] Thus Carpenter (p. 251) could write that Cole's reputation 'currently survives most strongly in circles where his books on Labour history are still widely used'.

[8] See J. Hinton, *The First Shop Stewards' Movement*, 1973; Winter, op. cit.; W. Kendall, *The Revolutionary Movement in Britain 1900–21*, 1969: and the historical reader, *Workers' Control*, ed. Coates and Topham (1970). The rediscovery of these issues within the Labour movement has also been significant, of course: See R. Barker, 'Guild Socialism Revisited?', *Political Quarterly*, July–August 1975.

[9] Asa Briggs, 'G. D. H. Cole', *Listener*, 20 Oct. 1960; A. J. P. Taylor, 'A Bolshevik Soul in a Fabian Muzzle', *New Statesman*, 1 Oct. 1971; Royden Harrison, 'Stock-Bolshy', *New Society*, 30 Sept. 1971.

own claim that his life was to be found in his books, has done much to clarify, if not to resolve, this human elusiveness. But the wider intellectual and political elusiveness remains. Here Cole's claim will be largely accepted; for, to parody Feuerbach, in Cole's case man is very much what he writes.

PART ONE

Guild Socialism

II
Towards Guild Socialism

G. D. H. COLE WAS born in 1889, the year of the original *Fabian Essays*. This is an interesting coincidence, since Cole's early political outlook and activity was above all else a response to the Fabian tradition of socialist collectivism. He inherited this tradition; developed into its *enfant terrible*; then became its leading theoretical and organizational opponent. It is the intellectual process which underlies these bald statements that is the concern here. Cole's political and intellectual 'arrival' came in 1913, with the appearance of his first major book, *The World of Labour*, which seemed graphically to capture the mood of that world and to chart its future in new and attractive directions. With this book Cole's distance from Fabianism became clear, and the beginnings of an alternative were sketched. It was this alternative, in that version of socialist democracy known as Guild Socialism, which was to be Cole's preoccupation for the next decade, during which time it was to stake its claim for the loyalties of the labour movement. But to begin in 1913 is to miss much.

What is missed especially is any account of the intellectual and political development which made 1913 an end as well as a beginning. Such an account is useful not merely as a personal history, but as an illustration of some of the elements in the wider climate of ideas at the time. In Cole's case, it is interesting to trace the emergence of a particular brand of socialism in the intellectual and political environment of the world before 1914. It was a very Fabian world, not only in terms of the consolidation of Fabian ideas, but also in the apparent triumph of permeation via the New Liberalism. It was also a very secure world, or seemed so from these shores, and this allowed free exercise of the speculative imagination in the creation of many New Things. It was a world which, as Maurice Reckitt recalled, encouraged the belief that 'there were no problems to which man could not find the right answer if he looked in the right direction and worked on the right lines'.[1] Defying the requirements of socialization theory, Cole

[1] M. B. Reckitt, *As It Happened*, 1941, p. 112. In similar vein, the Webbs wrote that: 'In this making of plans for reform, we are apt, in the twentieth century, when no change seems out of the question, to be a little misled by our speculative freedom.' (*What Syndicalism Means*, 1912, p. 17.)

encountered this world already a socialist. As he never tired of saying, it was a schoolboy encounter with the verse and prose of William Morris which was decisive. 'It was Morris who made me a socialist'[2] was Cole's constant, and truthful, explanation. In Cole's case, then, 'conversion' is the appropriate word. This fact is more than a curio of intellectual history, for the prospect of life under socialism glimpsed in Morris's work was to provide the motive, goal and yardstick for Cole's own conception of socialism. It was Morris's insistence on socialism as fellowship which was to make Cole a permanent 'utopian', even when his more immediate concerns were severely practical. This gave a certain dualism to his work, a sense of operating at two levels, reflected in a considerable flexibility coupled with a deep rigidity. As we shall see, often Cole wanted to make it clear at which level he was operating, thus drawing the line between the negotiable and the non-negotiable. The lineage from Morris imposed this necessity.

This same lineage was clearly decisive in bringing Cole to Guild Socialism, and in distinguishing his version of that theory from some others. Here, as elsewhere, a comparison with Harold Laski is instructive. Although Laski never called himself a Guild Socialist, his own radical anti-statism put him very much under the same theoretical umbrella. Yet the distance between Cole's Guild Socialism and Laski's pluralism was the difference in intellectual and political ancestry between the two men. Nourished by Morris, Cole was romantic, poet, dreamer, excited by the new labour militancy and determined to give it a theory of industrial control. By contrast, Laski's theoretical development was heavily academic, and his pluralism emerged as the product of historical jurisprudence. Laski attacked the state to discredit sovereignty; Cole attacked both to install workers' control. The difference is obvious and important, with significant practical consequences. With his political home in progressive liberalism and his intellectual home in political and legal pluralism, Laski summoned events to the test of theory. What this meant, for example, was that the legal status of trade unions must comply with the requirements of corporate responsibility entailed in the pluralist position; and it was this approach which determined Laski's response to those contemporary judicial decisions which undermined the legal protection

---

[2] 'I was converted, quite simply, by reading William Morris's *News From Nowhere*, which made me feel, suddenly and irrevocably, that there was nothing except a Socialist that it was possible for me to be.' This was in 1905, at the age of sixteen. (*British Labour Movement—Retrospect and Prospect*, Ralph Fox Memorial Lecture, Fabian Special, 1951, p. 3.)

given to trade unions. Hence the Taff Vale case marked 'a vital advance', just as surely as the Osborne decision was regressive. 'The Taff Vale case decided, as it appears to us, quite simply and reasonably, that a trade union must be responsible for the wrongs it commits.'[3] If Cole and Laski arrived at a broadly similar political theory it was clearly as a result of very different intellectual and political experiences, and designed to serve substantially different social purposes. Thus in writing of a 'challenge to the state' at the level of theory in the years immediately prior to 1914, it will be important to distinguish between the types of challenge.

The immediate point, however, is that intellectual ancestry offers an important clue to the understanding of mature theory. Yet it is always difficult to trace intellectual development before it takes a formal shape, simply because of the absence of useful source material. In Cole's case this difficulty can be largely overcome, not least because Cole was a compulsive writer from youth, thus enabling the broad lines of his intellectual development to be pieced together from a variety of sources. In this way it is possible to get a much fuller picture of the Edwardian climate of ideas which confronted a young socialist, and from which he could develop his own brand of theory. Some of this source material is irrelevant for present purposes, though useful to a biographer. Cole's editorship of a school magazine, for example, provides little of political interest beyond evidence of a considerable distaste for games and prefects, and a certain consciousness of rebel status. There is much schoolboyish striving after satirical effects and some atrocious verse.[4] Subsequent journalistic forays were to prove more revealing.

If Morris was the inspiration behind Cole's socialism, he also stimulated much else in the youthful Cole. Indeed, at this time it was the impact of Morris's romantic verse which was decisive, leading Cole towards literary criticism and poetic creation. As we shall see, some of this literary activity well illustrates the mood in which political theories were rooted; but much of it simply reveals a painfully self-conscious romanticism liberally sprinkled with 'thees' and 'thous'.[5] Later in life

---

[3] H. J. Laski, 'The Personality of Associations', *Harvard Law Review*, Feb. 1916, p. 422. Similarly, Laski wrote of 'the great judgment . . . in the Taff Vale case', for with trade unions as with other bodies it was 'socially necessary to make them bear the burden of a policy for which they are at bottom responsible' ('The Basis of Vicarious Liability', *Yale Law Journal*, Dec. 1916, p. 125).

[4] *The Octopus* (St. Paul's School, 1906–7) reveals all. An article on 'Turnips and their Moral Import' is not untypical.

[5] Grim examples appear in 'The Record, An Occasional Diary in Verse 1910–12' (in *New Beginnings and The Record*, Oxford, 1914).

Cole was to master a form of honest doggerel with considerably more bite.[6] Yet Cole's early poetic pretensions *are* significant, for they are central to the link between socialism and aesthetics which Cole had firmly established. It is scarcely too much to say that at this time the former was conceived essentially as a branch of the latter. It was this sort of conception that accompanied Cole to Oxford in 1908, and which structured his early political outlook there.

It reflected itself in the journal founded and edited by Cole in his very first term at Oxford, *The Oxford Socialist*, the appearance of which caused some little stir.[7] In fact, it was not really very angry at all. If it conveyed a spirit of missionary zeal, this was because socialism was still an 'adventure' in Edwardian Oxford, even when preached in a tone of such sonorous sobriety as that of the *Oxford Socialist*. Cole's own contributions are particularly revealing, for they were essentially lyrical and romantic in vein, concerned with the nature of art, life and the universe. When socialism appeared, it was described in these same terms. Socialism was not a particular organizational or economic form but rather it 'depends upon an emotion, an impulse to Brotherhood', which was 'essentially an artist's impulse'.[8] Therefore, although there would be societies and parties engaged in socialist organization and propaganda, 'it is not so much through them as through a great general impulse that the revolution will be effected'.[9] Here was the romantic language of impulse, emotion and artistry in its clearest form. It had important consequences for day-to-day political practice too.

The political world of 1908–9 seemed full of promise to many socialists. Liberalism appeared to have taken a radical leftward turn as it confronted the establishment over successive instalments of social reform. Was this not clear validation of the inevitability of gradualness, the triumph of permeation? At the same time, the consolidation of Labour's own political organization seemed to be proceeding apace. Cole's early socialism reflected these prevailing assumptions. The opening editorial of the *Oxford Socialist* proclaimed: 'we have brought forth into the light of day the germ that is maturing everywhere',[10] the

---

[6] Cf. his *The Crooked World*, 1933. One of these poems even won recognition in Philip Larkin's *Oxford Book of Twentieth-Century English Verse*, 1973.

[7] Aided by G. K. Chesterton's friendly notice of this 'angry little red paper'. (*Illustrated London News*, 5 Dec. 1908.)

[8] 'The Crime of Silence', *Oxford Socialist*, No. 2, 1909.

[9] Ibid.

[10] *Oxford Socialist*, No. 1, 1908 (F. K. Griffith was Cole's co-editor).

germ of socialism. But it was a vague, uncritical socialism which was to be the keynote of Cole's Oxford, for the same editorial announced that 'in the present contentions of the various branches of the Socialist and Labour parties in England, we shall attach ourselves to no faction in especial', for they all have 'one real aim at heart, however different the methods they advocate for its attainment'.[11] Cole often insisted on this unity theme, treating such contemporary instances of dissension as the Grayson episode as mere excess of zeal in a growing and vigorous movement, which did nothing to undermine the fact that 'we are all brothers in one cause ...'.[12]

At no time was the exact nature of that cause defined. This is unsurprising, since it was essentially a movement of the spirit which deserved to be lyricized rather than defined. There was no discussion of socialism as theory and very little as practice. There was, of course, no hint of the existence of institutions so sordid as trade unions or of subjects so mundane as economics. Instead, the dominant note was ethereal, far distant from the industrial struggle of labour. The only explicit political orientation was towards an uncritical Fabianism.[13] If Cole's socialism was rooted in Morris, it could as yet find no more tangible expression than that offered by the Webbs.

This was clearly revealed during 1909–10 in the pages of *The Oxford Reformer*, Cole's successor to the *Oxford Socialist*. The change of name would be significant if the stamp of reformism did not run so deeply throughout both publications. Still the philosophy was that of spiritual humanism, of a spirit which gave meaning to aspirations. There was no creative power in reason, and no refuge in materialism, for 'however much we may strive to give all things a materialistic explanation, some will always recede from our grasp into an unfathomed track whither the reason cannot follow them'.[14] Reason can destroy, but only instinct and emotion can create. This carried with it an explicit conception of the method of human and social change. 'What then can give to an idea the motive power to change men and worlds?' asked Cole. 'It is when the idea becomes an emotion; when it appeals not only to the head, but to the heart also; to the instinct as well as the reason, that it has the

[11] Ibid.
[12] 'Socialist Policy', *Oxford Socialist*, No. 1, 1908.
[13] For example, Cole's co-editor attacked the attempt to disaffiliate the Fabian Society from the Labour Party in the cause of a more definite socialist policy, arguing that for a long time to come Labour's programme would provide 'the grand reservoir of reforms upon which Conservatives and Liberals will draw alternately'. (F. K. Griffith, 'Fabian Policy', *Oxford Socialist*, No. 2, 1909.)
[14] Cole, 'Faith-Making', *Oxford Reformer*, Nov. 1909.

power to stir men'.[15] The irony is, of course, that Cole's early attempt to fuse religion and philosophy into an emotional unity powered by spirit and imagination should find its first political expression in a tepid Fabianism.

The *Oxford Reformer* thus announced its intention to identify itself 'with the Progressive movement in all its sections in Oxford' and thereby to 'take as broad an outlook upon social reform as can be secured'.[16] This progressivist stance reflected itself in a general identification with the Minority Report of the Poor Law Commission, and with the Webbs in particular. Warm references to the Webbs and their work litter the pages of Cole's journal, and Sidney Webb himself contributed an article on the Minority Report campaign. On the occasion of the Marxist split from Ruskin College, the *Oxford Reformer* was on hand to denounce the seceders as ideological malcontents who forgot that 'the best interests of the student are served not by deliberate instruction in party propaganda, but by fair and unbiassed economic education'.[17] On the occasion of the Osborne Judgement, Cole warned that its most dangerous effect would be to shift labour agitation from the political to the industrial arena: 'Some Socialists, seeing this clearly, have wished to maintain the status quo, in the belief that a few years of persistent industrial agitation will do more for the cause of labour than a long period of parliamentary struggle; but, if we have any care for the interests of peace, we must at all costs strive to arrest this development before it is too late. Perhaps, labour would gain by it more quickly, but the price is greater than we can afford to bear, and it is better to reach the same goal by a more roundabout and peaceful road. Industrial activity cannot be dispensed with altogether, but we must contrive to keep it merely as the complement of parliamentary progress.'[18] Strange words indeed from the imminent apostle of the industrial gospel of Guild Socialism.

The year 1910 marked the high water mark of Cole's Fabianism. The final issue of the *Oxford Reformer* proclaimed that 'the prospects of Fabianism seem brighter than usual ...'[19] and the successes of permeation were charted. As both policy and method Fabianism stood vindicated. In a long and lucid critique of the Poor Law Commission, for example, Cole contrasted the efficient and scientific approach of the

[15] Ibid.
[16] Editorial, *Oxford Reformer*, Feb. 1910. (Cole was now sole editor.)
[17] Ibid.
[18] 'The Osborne Judgement: A Symposium', *Oxford Reformer*, Nov. 1910.
[19] Editorial, *Oxford Reformer*, Nov. 1910.

Minority Report with the muddle of the Majority. Here was all the Fabian vocabulary of efficiency, wastefulness, expertise and science as Cole contrasted 'the complicated unproductive and wasteful inefficiency of the Majority' with the 'curative and businesslike final economy of the Minority Report'.[20] In terms of strategy too, Cole's commitment to permeation seemed total. Thus in a revealing account of Oxford socialism written for the I.L.P., Cole described how the Fabian Society managed to 'absorb' Oxford progressives, as it 'leavens' the colleges with its method of 'permeation', and its success in 'assimilating' Liberals through its activities on particular issues. Hence 'we find ourselves in many cases treating the "New Liberalism" as an embryonic stage of Socialist ideas leading deviously to our own goal by way of Radical Collectivism. Certainly Oxford Liberals are becoming almost unrecognizably Socialistic'.[21] The chief threat to this strategy was seen as a tendency to class sectionalism in the Labour Party, which could only find an unfavourable response in the progressive middle-class Oxford world. 'It is one of the disadvantages of an otherwise admirable Labour Party that, even on account of its efficiency in labour disputes, it has little to offer the middle classes by way of inducement... it does not present a policy which appeals with any particular cogency to the middle class mind ... The call that the universities make on Socialism is for a truly national programme.'[22] The picture was of open and receptive middle-class minds, attracted by the essential rectitude and sense of the socialist argument, but deterred by its unpleasant class associations.[23] The attachment to permeation and its possibilities was clearly both touching and complete.

There was a basic paradox in Cole's early socialism. At one level, there was the vision of the society of fellowship which would be truly anarchist in its final form, and which nourished the spirit and the poetic imagination. Yet at a political and theoretical level there was a vacuum, filled only by a prevailing Fabianism. There was no attempt to establish the nature of the relationship between the two levels. In many ways this omission would be a continuing Cole characteristic, but at this stage it was especially acute. Partly it was due, as has been seen, to an undifferentiated conception of socialism which made concern for

---

[20] 'The Reform of the Poor Law', *Middlesex County Times*, Jan.–Feb. 1910.
[21] 'Oxford Socialism From Within', *Socialist Review*, Dec. 1910.
[22] Ibid.
[23] 'If Oxford and Cambridge can be won largely for Socialism, the conversion of the middle classes is only a matter of time.' (ibid.)

organizational forms and policy largely unnecessary. But it remained an omission nevertheless. What still had to be established, or refuted, was the connection between the assumptions of the Minority Report and the achievement of the sort of socialist society envisaged by Cole. In one sense, then, Cole was never a Fabian, for he held an essentially un-Fabian view of life under socialism; and it was this very fact which made the need to investigate the connection just mentioned ultimately so important.

It was this investigation which effectively began in 1911, and which produced its first mature conclusions two years later. Of course, this was the period of a new militancy as Irish, feminist and labour agitation seemed to threaten the stability and confidence of an established social and political order. For Halévy, here was the prelude to the era of tyrannies, a period of 'domestic anarchy'; for Dangerfield, here was the demise of Liberal England, for the combined assaults on parliamentary democracy had 'something profoundly in common'.[24] It was difficult to be precise about this common element; perhaps it was simply the spirit of revolt itself, a new temper which could flourish in the seemingly secure atmosphere of late Edwardian Britain. In G. D. H. Cole, this new spirit found a ready disciple, for it found him already emotionally, if not intellectually, prepared. It seemed to represent just the sort of activism of the spirit, the movement of a great emotional idea, which had long been his credo. In politics, philosophy, art, literature and education the new spirit seemed to reveal itself, for in each area the dominant note was of a spontaneous and confident experimentalism. Taken together, Cole hailed this new mood as the dawn of a 'new romantic movement', which found its surest confirmation in the fact that 'we recognise in ourselves the equivalent of what we see stirring around us'.[25] Cole's own recognition of this identification was complete. He celebrated it in verse and analysed it in prose.[26] Thus Henry James was seen as important for his refusal to lapse into a mechanistic psychology, but instead to give an authentic account of personality rooted in the perception 'that human action moves forward by continuous spontaneity', thereby presenting characters 'as they spon-

---

[24] Quoted in H. Pelling, *Popular Politics and Society in Late Victorian Britain*, 1968, p. 148. Pelling's essay on 'The Labour Unrest, 1911–14' (ibid., ch. 9) offers a more cautionary view of this period.

[25] 'The New Romantic Movement', handwritten MS, Dec. 1912–Jan. 1913, Cole Collection, Nuffield College, Oxford (hereafter 'Cole Collection').

[26] See *New Beginnings and the Record* (Oxford, 1914), in which verse written in 1912 and 1913 (e.g. 'Spring Song', 'Fool Youth', 'Making and Breaking') reflects the confidence and zest of a youthful romanticism.

taneously will to act when real alternatives are present'.[27] So too with
Wells, Bennett and Galsworthy, who certainly portrayed the individual
as confronted with the powerful complexities of modern life, but at the
same time presented him as 'at least trying to stand up to the environment, not basely lying down and yielding to the gigantic forces of
evolution'; for their essential picture was of 'man the insurgent',[28] a key
phrase. This attachment to spontaneity and to the creative exercise of
will was to have profound implications for Cole's political development.

In political terms, the new insurgency presented itself as the 'labour
unrest' of contemporary euphemism. As wage advance was checked,
and as the official Labour movement itself seemed increasingly to be
'drifting into futility',[29] a new militancy appeared in the world of labour
to cause a flurry of official and popular consternation. Much of this
consternation arose from the discovery that the strike wave was
allegedly infected with a new and sinister ideology of foreign origin
which called itself syndicalism, and which seemed to challenge both the
collectivism and the parliamentarism of orthodox Labour theory and
practice. Labour spokesmen hurried to denounce and refute this
dangerous foreign import.[30] For Cole, however, the spirit of syndicalism provoked a sympathetic emotional response, which made it
the occasion for a first critical examination of the amorphous Fabianism which hitherto had provided the practical content of his socialist
theory. Inevitably so, for syndicalism raised in acute form the possibility of contradiction between his socialist society of the future and the
prevailing socialist theory and method of the present. So Cole began to
put Fabianism under the theoretical microscope, an exercise which
soon produced some interesting findings.

In a suggestive paper read before Oxford Fabians in the spring of
1912, Cole described his purpose as 'an attempt to define the relation of
Collectivism to the good life', an attempt at definition which previously
it had never seemed necessary to make. Fabianism and collectivism had
triumphed hitherto because they offered something essentially tangible, but 'now, when we are threatened with the rise of a new great force
of revolt in Syndicalism, we begin to perceive, in the difficulties we
experience in combating it, that we have, to some extent, sacrificed

[27] 'Henry James', *The Blue Book*, No. 1, May 1912 (Oxford).
[28] 'The Revival of Poetry', *Caledonian Jottings*, 1913.
[29] *Beatrice Webb's Diaries 1912–24* (ed. M. I. Cole), 1952, p. 6 (entry dated 11 Oct. 1912).
[30] See MacDonald's *Syndicalism*, 1912; Snowden's *Socialism and Syndicalism*, 1913; and the Webbs'
What Syndicalism Means, 1912.

breadth of outlook for the sake of completeness and practicality, and that we must at least re-examine our theory, if not amend our practice'.[31] Fabianism had concentrated on the problem of distribution to the neglect of the conditions of production. Hence it had forgotten the need to make the workplace the arena of a joyful creativity, or the need to erect bulwarks against the development of servility and bureaucracy. Cole invoked Ruskin and Morris, Belloc[32] and Chesterton, to press his points home. The essential meaning of Morris, for example, was now seen no longer in terms of an epic romanticism but crucially in terms of the recognition that freedom and self-determination in the workplace were the key to a wider self-expression.[33] It was the task of socialism to understand and embrace this fact, for it meant that 'a trade should be, as much as is possible without detriment to the larger whole of the state, an individual, a social democracy in itself'.[34] Cole was now adamant that 'so long as Socialism remains mere bureaucratic monopoly it will be impotent'.[35]

If all this clearly marked a decisive breach in Cole's attachment to Fabianism, it was not yet intended or presented as a formal break. Instead, Cole wanted a modification of orthodox Fabianism in the direction of the new tendencies and requirements. Such a theoretical accommodation was seen as eminently possible, not least because the Fabian position was still essentially correct on important elements of future goals and present strategy. For example, although the goal was a society of self-governing associations, state socialism was still more perceptive than syndicalism in its recognition of the need for 'a strong central state to keep the associations in order'.[36] Furthermore, in terms of strategy it remained true that 'the only way of securing such an industrial system is by way of State Socialism'.[37] What was needed, therefore, was a revised version of Fabianism which would effectively accomplish this theoretical accommodation. It was when Fabianism displayed little inclination to contemplate this sort of theoretical self-

[31] 'Means and Ends: A Paper for Socialists', handwritten MS, Apr. 1912, read before Oxford University Fabian Society. (Cole Collection.) See also M. P. Ashley and C. T. Saunders, *Red Oxford* (1933) for a description of Oxford socialism at this time.
[32] Belloc's *The Servile State* (1912) had an important impact on the argument and vocabulary of various schools of contemporary thought, despite its distinctive distributivist perspective. For its importance to Guild Socialism, see A. W. Wright, 'Guild Socialism Revisited', *Journal of Contemporary History*, ix (1974), pp. 167–8.
[33] See Cole, 'William Morris', *The Blue Book*, No. 5, Jan. 1913 (Oxford).
[34] 'Means and Ends: A Paper for Socialists.'
[35] Ibid.
[36] Ibid.
[37] Ibid.

examination that Cole became sharply more critical. This more critical stance clearly revealed itself in another paper which Cole delivered to the same Oxford.Fabians in the autumn of 1912. After damning Fabianism for its failure to understand the centrality of working-class education for the development of consciousness, Cole conceded that he would doubtless be charged with exhibiting 'a morbid tendency to be forever digging up the precious bulb of Fabianism to see if the roots are sprouting', but his desire was 'less to set the Fabian house in order ... than to suggest that the present house is lamentably insufficient for the spiritual accommodation of youth, and to recommend the building of several new and palatial wings, and possibly the relegation of the present structure to the useful, if homely function, of "kitchens and offices"'.[38] The nature of the indictment was crucial, for what was being alleged was not merely a theoretical deficiency but a general failure of spirit and imagination. Even when the Fabians were correct, it was being said, it was often for the wrong reasons. There is a striking similarity here with J. S. Mill's early attack on the limitations of Benthamism. For Mill orthodox utilitarianism could properly apply to 'the merely *business* part of the social arrangements';[39] whilst for Cole, orthodox Fabianism was now restricted in scope to the homely world of 'kitchens and offices'. In both cases what was alleged was a failure of imagination, a spiritual void, at the heart of an intellectual system; and in both cases the allegation came from a leading youthful disciple attracted by the pull of the spirit. The comparison could be pressed even further, for the utilitarian ancestry of Fabianism is evident. In both cases the challenge came from a new romanticism, whether in the form of a Coleridgean conservatism or a William Morris socialism. If the vocabulary of the challenge was similar it was because much of its substance was the same.

By 1913, then, Cole was ripe for the frontal battle with official Fabianism, to be waged in boisterous and ill-tempered meetings and summer schools, where Cole's Oxford brigade took great delight in shocking the Fabian Old Guard in word and deed.[40] By 1913, too, the essentials of Cole's emotional and philosophical position were established, even if its precise theoretical content remained vague. It was

[38] 'Socialism and Education', handwritten MS, 12 Aug. 1912, read before Oxford University Fabian Society (Cole Collection).

[39] Quoted in R. Williams, *Culture and Society 1780–1950*, Penguin Books 1963, p. 72.

[40] Beatrice Webb's *Diary* charts each new outrage perpetrated by the Rebels. From the other side, S. G. Hobson recalled 'a delightful group, gaily starting a revolution armed with split hairs'. (*Pilgrim to the Left*, 1938, p. 190.)

rooted in a powerful voluntarism, an emphasis on the creative energy of human will and imagination. This involved a repudiation of any doctrine that smacked of determinism, including that of Marx. 'Marx has left us in his heritage much that is valuable and great', declared Cole, 'but he has infected us with an economic fatalism, which, in the excess to which it is often carried, cannot but prove fatal.'[41] Cole's attachment to voluntarism reflected itself in his enthusiasm for the cause of working-class adult education, for here was the true road to consciousness.[42] It reflected itself, too, in Cole's enthusiasm for Rousseau, that paradoxical Romantic of the Enlightenment, who rooted his social theory in an activism of the will.[43] From Rousseau and Morris in their different ways, Cole developed his conception of a community founded upon the cooperation of self-governing associations, a cooperation which found its source in a genuine community consciousness, a real general will. If Fabianism could not provide the theory or method to fulfil this conception, it was not yet clear if there was an alternative which could. Certainly there were hints towards an alternative. Syndicalism, for example, was valuable in its emphasis on industrial activism, and Cole's library and papers reveal the extent to which he immersed himself in syndicalist literature at this time. Yet syndicalism itself was flawed by its refusal to recognize the necessity of a cooperative relationship between the state and the industrial associations in a socialist society. It was just such a recognition which was hinted at in the pages of the *New Age*, a journal of intellectual socialism under the brilliant editorship of A. R. Orage, and inspired by the 'Guild' ideas of an eccentric architect, A. J. Penty. In syndicalism, Cole found an industrial doctrine rooted in the conception of active self-emancipation; in the *New Age* he found the idea of a partnership between state and workers in the control of industry which promised to tap the spirit of syndicalism whilst avoiding its likely excesses. Here were the materials for a synthesis which could provide a genuine alternative to Fabianism for the developing labour movement. Cole's artistry at synthesis thus produced its first and most famous product—Guild Socialism.

This is not the place to attempt a full history of Guild Socialism, either as theory or movement. Its intellectual origins lie deep in the historical experience of the British labour movement over the preceding

[41] 'Means and Ends: A Paper for Socialists.'
[42] See Cole, 'An Oxford Summer School', *The Blue Book*, No. 5, Jan. 1913 (Oxford).
[43] See his Introduction to Rousseau, *The Social Contract and Discourses* (ed. Cole), 1913. Cole always planned to write a major study of Rousseau. He never did (one of the few things he managed not to write), though Rousseau, like Morris, is a constant point of reference in his work.

century,[44] when 'utopian' notions of industrial self-government and of the general strike for control first found concrete expression. Its more immediate ancestry may be located in the general challenge to the state which appeared in the years just before 1914, a reaction against collectivism which took both academic and political form. If syndicalism provided the most dramatic expression of this challenge in the world of labour, it was in thc *New Age* that Guild Socialism found its embryonic theoretical statement. When that statement became rather more sophisticated, not least in the hands of Cole, the *New Age* grew vociferous in its assertion of original parentage of the Guild idea.[45] That claim was amply justified; for if A. J. Penty reintroduced the language and concept of 'Gild' into political discussion[46] early in the century, it was in the *New Age* that A. R. Orage and S. G. Hobson provided the Guild concept with its distinctive political programme.

The columns of the *New Age* thus form a fascinating historical record of the genesis and evolution of an idea. In those columns a rather strident tone of intellectual socialism, critical but not constructive, gradually transformed itself into something more positive. By 1911, the central lesson of a decade of parliamentary and political action was seen to be 'the bankruptcy of political Labourism',[47] requiring a new strategy which would directly attack the wage system itself. At the same time, social reform measures like the Insurance Act so strengthened the power of the state that eventually 'the working classes will be the most intelligent, the most comfortable, the most valuable class of slaves that the world has ever seen'.[48] From his own distinct perspective, Penty proclaimed an aesthetic decline and emphasized the perils of sheer organizational size.[49] The labour unrest testified to the force of this analysis, and its essence was detected as the working-class demand for a new status and self-respect. By early 1912, the *New Age* writers were able to give constructive statement to the choice between freedom and slavery, itself defined as the key choice for labour, in a formula which was claimed both to incorporate and to transcend syndicalism. It incorporated it in its recognition that industrial unrest was rooted in an

[44] N. Carpenter, presenting Guild Socialism as 'peculiarly the product of English social and economic history', provides a succinct account of its historical ancestry. (*Guild Socialism*, 1922.)
[45] So too did S. G. Hobson, who later complained that: 'Gradually Cole ignored us, then forgot us. To the outside world he had become the personification of the Guild idea'. (*Pilgrim to the Left*, p. 188).
[46] A. J. Penty, *The Restoration of the Gild System*, 1906.
[47] S. G. Hobson, Letter, *New Age*, 30 Nov. 1911.
[48] Editorial, *New Age*, 14 Dec. 1911.
[49] See Penty, 'The Peril of Large Organisation', *New Age*, 11 Jan. 1912.

instinct for participation; but it transcended it in its conception of a 'co-partnery' between the state and the trade unions, in which the unions became 'responsible bodies, approximating in spirit to the ancient gilds'.[50] This was the analysis and prescription which the *New Age* never tired of presenting throughout 1912 and 1913, attacking the sterility of a labourism which failed to understand the true character of industrial militancy, and proclaiming an alternative to capitalism which was neither syndicalism nor state collectivism, but 'what we may call a system of National Guilds, under which the State enters into partnership with the organized craftspeople and manages the industry jointly with them'.[51]

Against this background, it was scarcely surprising that in later years the *New Age* should have wanted to put straight the historical record when the intellectual parentage of Guild Socialism seemed to be appropriated by many of its eager offspring. Cole never attempted this sort of appropriation, but instead made frequent and friendly recognition of the place of the *New Age*'s Guild idea in his own early development.[52] In that early period, the *New Age* and 'Guild Socialism' (it soon lost its inverted commas) were synonymous. Yet in that period, too, Guild Socialism largely remained an idea without a theory, distinguished as much by what it was not as by what it was, and not yet subject to any serious critical investigation. To observers like Belfort Bax, the Guild idea was not yet sufficiently differentiated from syndicalist and collectivist versions of socialism, nor had it squarely faced the problems posed by a dual control of industry.[53] This was the setting against which Cole's contribution to Guild Socialism can best be assessed. The idea he found, but did not originate; but having found it, he effectively transformed it into both a theory and a movement.

Cole announced his discovery in 1913 in *The World of Labour*, a book which seemed exactly to capture a contemporary mood.[54] Describing it as 'both a compendium and a manifesto',[55] the *New Age* thereby per-

---

[50] Editorial, *New Age*, 18 Jan. 1912. This was the first full statement of the Guild position.

[51] Editorial, *New Age*, 2 May 1912.

[52] See *The World of Labour*, 1913, p. 52; and his deferential letter to *New Age* (4 Dec. 1913) in reply to a review of his book. Elsewhere he wrote: 'I was a regular reader of the *New Age* from 1906 onwards, and followed with keen interest the successive developments of the Guild idea.' (*Chaos and Order in Industry*, 1920, p. 51.)

[53] E. Belfort Bax, 'The Guild System and its Implications', *New Age*, 30 Oct. 1913.

[54] Barbara Wootton has described the impact on her, as a girl of seventeen, of Cole's book: 'My delight was boundless.... The day that I brought this home seemed to mark my first real emancipation....' (*In A World I Never Made*, 1967, p. 40.)

[55] 'Survey and Strategy', *New Age*, 20 Nov. 1913.

ceived what was to be the essential nature of Cole's future intellectual enterprise. In this instance, the compendium took the form of a comparative study of labour movements; the manifesto drew some lessons for contemporary British theory and practice. The book as a whole is so rich in the ingredients which went into the making of Cole's developed version of Guild Socialism that it is worth recording some of its central features before a more systematic discussion of that developed theory is attempted.

Cole asked a question at the very beginning of *The World of Labour* which all his later work was really an attempt to answer: 'What is the Labour movement *capable* of making of itself?'[56] By 1913 Cole was clear that Fabian collectivism was not a doctrine which could help labour to realize this developmental potential, for it was merely an arid theory of distribution. Syndicalism was a valuable corrective, an assertion of the producer's point of view, but it too was inadequate as a theory of, and for, the labour movement. There could be no refuge in organic theories of class harmony beloved by MacDonald and the I.L.P. tradition, for the class-struggle must be preached 'not on the ground that it is desirable, but on the ground that it is a monstrous and irrefutable fact'.[57] There could be no refuge, either, in the sort of 'false medievalism'[58] which sought to construct a new system of Guilds outside the existing structure of the organized labour movement. What was needed was a theory which started with the recognition that the labour movement was capable of making itself the agency whereby work could again become the arena for self-expression: 'There is a great difference between the common-sense ideal of high wages, and the other ideal of enabling men somehow to express, in the daily work of their hands, some part of that infinitely subtle and various personality which lives in each one of them, if we can but call it out.'[59]

So the end to be achieved was still very much that liberation of the human spirit and imagination which was Cole's earliest political objective, a liberation now seen to require fundamental changes in workshop organization and control. If William Morris was the grand 'diagnostician of alienation' as described by E. P. Thompson, then Cole could be said to carry further the same diagnosis, captured in Cole's telling phrase that 'the sense of being owned is deadening',[60] and to

[56] *The World of Labour*, 1913, p. 2.
[57] Ibid., p. 21.   [58] Ibid., p. 10.
[59] Ibid., p. 9.
[60] Ibid., p. 419. See E. P. Thompson, *The Communism of William Morris*, William Morris Society, 1965, p. 13, and his *William Morris: Romantic to Revolutionary*, 2nd ed., 1977.

break new ground in the search for remedies. The aim must be to create a sense of freedom in the workplace, not by an attack on machine production itself, but by a fundamental change in authority relationships at work. The exploitation characteristic of capitalism was not primarily economic, but human, even spiritual. 'It is too little realised', wrote Cole, 'even by Socialists—and especially by Marxists—that the whole question of the control of industry is not economic but ethical. The attempt to found "justice" on the theory of value merely revives the old conception of individual natural right in its least defensible form. The right of Labour to a life of comfort and self-expression is quite independent of whether it creates all wealth or not'.[61] Self-expression implied a share in control, in turn implying a conception of industrial democracy which challenged the assumptions of traditional parliamentary democracy. Much of Cole's later work was to be an attempt to demonstrate the need for a revision of orthodox democratic theory if participation and control by the mass of people was to be more than fictional. The workshop was crucial in this, because 'for the ordinary individual, the State is so far, and the workshop so near. . . . A man cannot miss the governing class in the workshop, while few even realise its existence in the state'.[62]

What was required, and the labour unrest was seen to reflect this, was a social theory which combined an ultimate social control by the whole community with real producer control in industry. A genuine community theory was needed, embracing the legitimate claims of both producers and consumers, of both collectivism and syndicalism. Such a theory would not eject the state, but would instead free it from its present sectional attachments and sordid preoccupations, allowing it to find its true role as 'the first expression of the national will and the depository of the national greatness'.[63] Socialists should realize that 'the State is not, through and through, the capitalist dodge they are apt to represent it as being',[64] for it existed now only in perverted form, unable to perform its true role as embodiment of a community consciousness and instrument of a general will in a reformed society. Moreover, the state would have a crucial role in the achievement of socialism, for nationalization 'retains all the importance assigned to it in Socialist theory',[65] except that its place was now firmly that of means rather than end. The state must be used for the creation of socialism, but without thereby creating a system of State Socialism.

[61] Ibid., p. 350.   [62] Ibid., p. 360.   [63] Ibid., p. 26.
[64] Ibid., p. 389.   [65] Ibid., p. 391.

Cole's grand discovery in the *World of Labour* was that the trade unions were the key agency both in the achievement of socialism and in the industrial organization of a socialist society. Thus trade union activity always had a dual purpose. On the one hand, it worked to secure better wages and conditions; but at the same time it was the harbinger of a new industrial order rooted in worker control. This was Cole's essential message at this time, and his central explanation of the labour unrest. The Webbs were wrong in their definition of trade unionism, for 'the first purpose of the trade unions is to fight the employers'.[66] Cole was unequivocal about the implications of this position. It meant that all trade union activity was essentially right, for the cause was just; therefore any criticism could only be at the level of tactics.[67] It meant, too, that trade union structure and organization must reflect the demands of a fighting organization, involving considerable re-organization and amalgamation on the industrial lines of the 'greater unionism'. If Cole was severely critical of trade union organization and leadership, it was because of a belief in the pivotal role of trade unionism in the creation and operation of a socialist society. The trade unions must be fitted out both for present combat and for future control. Trade unionism was simply too important to be left to the trade unions.

If this was Cole's broad conception of social change at this time, it did have one or two distinctive features. There was, for example, the continuing emphasis on the sheer power of human will, and the rejection of determinism. Change could only issue from the possibilities of the present, not from mere constructions of the mind or imagination; but inside this possibilist framework social change was essentially the product of the exercise of will and of the quality of human material available. Hence education and the greater unionism were alike crucial in fostering a more determined will and a quickening of the intellect, themselves central because 'the slave can only throw off his chains by showing himself a better man than his master'.[68] There was, too, a continuing relativist emphasis in Cole's discussion of social change in general and of the labour movement in particular. It seemed almost as

[66] Ibid., p. 259. The Webbs, by contrast, began their study of trade union history by defining a trade union as 'a continuous association of wage-earners for the purpose of maintaining or improving the conditions of their employment'. (*The History of Trade Unionism*, 1894.)

[67] Thus, in relation to the use of violence by strikers, 'the only argument against it, and also against militancy of other sorts, is that they do not pay'. (*World of Labour*, p. 377.)

[68] Ibid., p. 425. Cole was emphatic that: 'Will is, in the last resort, the basis of the State....' (ibid., p. 414.)

if the central purpose of Cole's lengthy comparative analysis of the European and American labour movements was to demonstrate the essential irrelevance of these movements to the British situation and experience. The analysis of syndicalism, for example, was concerned to stress its nature and development as being a response to specifically French industrial and labour conditions, which made it a futile exercise just 'to copy M. Sorel's opinions out of one book into another'.[69] The uniqueness of different national experiences was emphasized, as was the consequence of these differences for strategies of social action. 'The greatest service that can be done us by the intelligent study of foreign Labour movements', declared Cole, 'is to save us at least from becoming internationalists.'[70] Cole's 'Little Englander' tag finds its source in observations of this kind, often deservedly so; yet it is important to note that it was a general conception of the uniqueness of different national experiences which was being claimed, not the assertion of a merely parochial reflex. It was a conception which had important effects on Cole's later political thinking, particularly in relation to the Soviet Union. In 1913 it led Cole to contrast a genuine internationalism with a spurious cosmopolitanism, and to predict that in the event of war the behaviour of the European working class would amply demonstrate the power of national loyalties and the limits of internationalism. It led him, also, to emphasize the need for a social theory which was consonant with the historical experience and contemporary requirements of the British labour movement. 'We want more revolutionary feeling in this country'; wrote Cole, 'but we must make our own revolutionary conceptions, and not import the less successful of French ideas.'[71]

In the *World of Labour* Cole was feeling his way towards a revolutionary theory appropriate to British conditions. It would be a theory which aimed to transform the status of the worker by transforming authority relationships at work. It would abolish the capitalist, but would be alive to the dangers of a socialist bureaucracy. It must therefore be a democratic theory, ensuring real participation and control inside socialized industry. It must be a theory which was rooted in the trade unions, both as the agency of change and the embryonic industrial unit of the future. In the search for a theory which met these

[69] Ibid., p. 127.
[70] Ibid., p. 165.
[71] Ibid., p. 202. He announced that: 'On the whole, imported ideas do not pay. If we are to have a gospel of revolt, we must create it for ourselves, out of the materials in our hands. Neither pure Marxism nor pure Syndicalism will suit us; and it is a sign that we are beginning to struggle for ideas of our own that the recent intellectual unrest is hopeful.' (ibid., p. 204.)

requirements, the Guild ideas of the *New Age* seemed the most interesting development; for 'in its policy of ultimate co-operation between the State and the Unions, which it names "Guild Socialism", it has hold, possibly rather in the wrong way, of the only possible solution',[72] even if as yet 'it does little to teach us how to build the New Jerusalem, of which it has seized the general idea'.[73] It was out of the meeting of this general idea with the particular approach indicated in the *World of Labour* that Cole's more systematic theory of Guild Socialism emerged. It is now possible to examine some of the central features of that theory.

[72] Ibid., p. 51.
[73] Ibid., p. 52.

III

The State: Pluralism and Community

REVIEWING THE position of English political thought on the outbreak of war in 1914, Ernest Barker announced that a 'certain tendency to discredit the State is now abroad'.[1] Yet if the years immediately before 1914 can be described in terms of a general challenge to the state, it was clearly a challenge which took various forms. It took urgent political form, of course, as the place of Ireland, female suffrage and industrial militancy in the domestic history of the period amply demonstrates. Yet behind the political and industrial turmoil a more theoretical challenge to the supremacy of the state was also taking place. This challenge itself took both explicitly political and more narrowly academic form. Politically, syndicalism was its chief product of course, and collectivism its chief victim. No sooner had the victory of Fabian collectivism over Liberal individualism seemed assured, both theoretically and politically, than collectivism itself seemed in danger of losing its inheritance. A. D. Lindsay exactly captured this contemporary mood: 'Just when the collectivist theory of the State seems assured of its triumph, if we listen we can hear growing notes of discontent', he wrote in 1914; 'suddenly we realise that in some quarters the State itself is on trial. ... The men who five years ago would have called themselves Socialists and given everything to the State, now call themselves Syndicalists and can find no place for it.'[2] If syndicalism was the most significant challenge to collectivism, it was not the only one. Belloc's distributivist school, for example, was forceful in its assault on a collectivism which claimed to pursue socialism but which necessarily could only create Servility, 'a society wherein the owners remain few and wherein the

[1] E. Barker, *Political Thought in England 1848 to 1914*, 1915, p. 249.
[2] A. D. Lindsay, 'The State in Recent Political Theory', *Political Quarterly* (Oxford), No. 1, Feb. 1914. Beatrice Webb recorded this same tendency: 'Syndicalism has taken the place of the old-fashioned Marxism ... the glib young workman whose tongue runs away with him to-day mouths the phrases of French Syndicalism instead of those of German Social Democracy. The inexperienced middle-class idealist has accepted with avidity the ideal of the Syndicalist as a new and exciting Utopia. ...' (*Beatrice Webb's Diaries 1912–24*, (ed. M. I. Cole), 1952, p. 7, entry for 1 Dec. 1912.)

proletariat mass accepts security at the expense of servitude'.[3] If Belloc's own alternative, a diffusion of property ownership, had little general appeal, his powerful invocation of the Servile State contributed much to the armoury, and vocabulary, of those opponents of state collectivism who had their own alternatives. A common antipathy to bureaucracy and regimentation brought together conservative individualists and radical socialists in a united crusade against statism as both theory and practice.

At the same time, the philosophical integrity of the state came under an increasingly successful assault from varieties of pluralist doctrine, all of which insisted on the unreality and danger of the state's claim to sovereignty, and on the status of associational life. The work of Maitland, Figgis and others set out to challenge the historical and legal credentials of state sovereignty and to establish instead the credentials of corporate personality and self-government, the foundations for a true pluralism. The enemy was variously called Hegelianism, Idealism, Austinianism and monism; and all were proclaimed defective in their attempt to give meaning and status to group life only in relation to an all-embracing state. The state had often been challenged, noted Barker, but 'the challengers are now groups, challenging in the name of groups',[4] insisting on the reality of a social and political federalism. The early writings of Harold Laski provide an extensive commentary on this challenge, as he mounted a vigorous offensive against the dangerous fiction of state sovereignty, as a prelude to offering a positive theory of the state himself. His central weapons were those of constitutional history and legal theory, as he argued that state sovereignty was neither good history nor good law. Instead, it was will and personality which formed the real basis of the state, and which found their expression in a whole range of associations and loyalties, including a state which was therefore 'but one of the groups to which the individual belongs',[5] without any prior claim to supremacy.

Guild Socialism is interesting in its synthesis of the major ingredients in this general challenge to the state. It was intellectual enough to be sensitive to the philosophical argument, but worldly enough to

[3] H. Belloc, *The Servile State*, 1912, p. 101. Belloc has a powerful discussion of collectivism as 'the line of least resistance' (p. 105) for reformers of capitalism.
[4] E. Barker, 'The Discredited State', *Political Quarterly*, No. 5, Feb. 1915. A good and succinct account of the nature of pluralist thought at this time is provided by D. Nicholls, *The Pluralist State*, 1975, and *Three Varieties of Pluralism*, 1975.
[5] H. J. Laski, *Studies in the Problem of Sovereignty*, 1917, p. 11. Also his *Authority in the Modern State*, 1919, and his copious writings in American legal journals at this period.

emphasize the centrality of industrial action. The intellectual appeal of
Guild Socialism was strengthened by its consonance with a prevailing
academic temper, yet it was not itself academic. It entered the
academic argument only in order to demonstrate its philosophical
credentials. But its synthetic character did make it appear as the
essential political expression of a wider current of thought. 'The idea of
the guild ... is the idea of the hour', wrote Barker, for it offered a
critique of state socialism 'likely to lead to a new adjustment of Socialist
theory',[6] in the form of a reconciliation of the state with the new group
principle. It was the search for this reconciliation—of state and group,
of high theory and political practice—which absorbed much of the
intellectual energy of G. D. H. Cole at this time.

There are certain problems which present themselves in an examination of Cole's view of the state. Not the least of these is that the
viewpoint was not static, but evolved with the development of Guild
Socialist theory and with the changing conditions which shaped that
theory. In Cole's hands both the definition of the state and its place in a
Guild Socialist society changed substantially over time, even if a constant approach and perspective can be detected. For example, he
initially wanted to give an elevated status to the state, conceived as an
ideal type, but was obliged to withhold that status because at present
the state existed only in perverted form. In operational terms, too, his
early treatment of the state as the representative of the consumers was
substantially modified in his mature Guild theory, to be replaced by
new agencies of consumer representation. As state theory changed, so
too did Cole's version of social and political structure. Indeed, that
structure suffered strenuous elaboration as he constantly endeavoured
to give structural expression to a changing conception of state purpose
(notably in *Guild Socialism Re-Stated*, his last major Guild Socialist
book). A task here will be to elicit the purpose behind the elaboration.
In doing this, important help is provided by the fact that in Cole's case
changing theories *of* the state were decisively affected by changing
attitudes *to* the state during this period. In other words, state theory
became very much a response to state practice.

If Cole had ditched Fabianism by 1913, he had not yet ditched the
state itself. Indeed, he argued that where Fabianism went wrong was in
its confusion of the present state with the state as it might and should
become. The central mistake of the Fabians was 'to identify their ideal
State and their ideal citizen with the State and the citizen of the

[6] Barker, op. cit., p. 233.

present', a carelessness which would necessarily produce 'merely a transference of authority from the capitalist to the bureaucrat'.[7] For their part, the syndicalists made a similar error in their insistence on an essentialist definition of the state in terms of class coercion. This was to mistake essence for present manifestation. Against the syndicalists, Cole argued that 'the State is not, through and through, the capitalist dodge they are apt to represent it as being'; for even if at present the state existed 'only in the distorting-mirror of a powerful governing class ... it has, at least sometimes, to act up to the standards of the community as a whole.'[8]

This last sentence is the key to Cole's early attitude to the state—and to a permanent element in his social thought. Its foundation was the distinction between present and future, between actuality and potentiality. Above all else, Cole was a theorist of community, as an expression of fellowship, and the community would need its appropriate instruments of common purpose and self-expression. It was in such a community setting, therefore, that the state would find its true and proper role as the instrument of community consciousness, 'the alert and flexible instrument of the General Will'.[9] The influence of Rousseau here was central and explicit, for at this time Cole openly proclaimed him as the most important of the political philosophers, planned to write a big book on him, and introduced his *Contrat Social* as 'still by far the best of all text books of political philosophy'.[10] The basis for judgements of this kind was the belief that Rousseau provided the ingredients for a reconstructed political and social theory, which took the General Will as its master conception and endeavoured to give it modern expression through a democratized social structure which would mitigate the difficulties of size delineated by Rousseau himself. For Cole, the General Will was no abstraction, even if elusive, for it rightly sought the universal and moral basis of society in an active and popular will. As such, it gave meaning to the state and resolved the problem of political obligation. State and society must be seen as expressions of a natural human fellowship rooted in will. 'If it means anything', wrote Cole, 'the theory of the General Will means that the State is natural, and the "state of nature" an abstraction. Without this basis of will and natural need, no society could for a moment subsist;

[7] *The World of Labour*, p. 347.
[8] Ibid., pp. 389–90.
[9] Ibid., p. 421.
[10] Introduction to his edition of Rousseau's *Social Contract and Discourses*, (1913), p. 41.

the State exists and claims our obedience because it is a natural extension of our personality.'[11]

If we discover an important dualism in Cole's attitude to the state, here then is part of the explanation for it. Instead of a simple anti-statism, Cole regarded the present state largely as a distortion of its true role in a community environment. In such an environment, the state would emerge in purified form as an agency of expression for the organized will of the community. At present, the state was distorted by industrialism in general and by capitalism in particular. The state's preoccupation with industry and economics was merely a sordid and stultifying phase in its development, for 'if once the incubus of indus-trialism could be removed, the State would recover its health, and begin once again to give expression to the spirit of community and nationality which pervades every people whose national life is sound'.[12] The Marxists were correct in regarding the present state as essentially the servant of capitalism (though even here 'perversion of function is not carried so far as to obliterate all signs and traces of its real function')[13] but wrong to suggest both that the state was necessarily an agency of class domination and that its functions would disappear with the end of capitalism. Cole's central point was that 'what occurs under Cap-italism is a perversion of the true function of the State',[14] which led the Marxists to confuse temporary perversion with permanent domination. It also led them to deny a role for the state in a socialist society, whereas it was abundantly clear that 'under any economic system the State will continue to exercise functions which are not economic'.[15] Moreover, it was only in a community setting, with its function as the instrument of a communitarian general will, that the state might justifiably assume a more positive, even coercive, role.[16]

But if the state should not be abandoned, nor should it occupy an exclusive position in political theory and practice. Traditional political theory had taken force rather than will as its basis, producing an excessive emphasis on the role of the state. The need now, according to

[11] Ibid., p. 39.
[12] *The World of Labour*, p. 410.
[13] *Social Theory*, 1920, p. 149.
[14] Ibid., p. 148.
[15] Ibid., p. 149. Thus the state would not die with capitalism, for it was 'in its true nature an organization adapted to the carrying out of certain specific functions which must to some extent be performed in any social system'. (*Labour in the Commonwealth*, 1918, p. 185.)
[16] Cole wrote that 'coercion is only justifiable in a real democracy' (*World of Labour*, p. 288); and that 'when inequality has been swept away, we may begin penal legislation in favour of industrial peace—if we then need to do so'. (ibid., p. 318.)

Cole, was to develop a will-based theory which would be genuinely social rather than narrowly political. If the state was to be challenged in practice, then its theoretical primacy must be challenged too. Just as collectivism found its equivalent political theory in the doctrine of state sovereignty, Guild Socialism must evolve an alternative political theory of its own. Cole was emphatic on this need for Guild Socialists not merely to attack or reject traditional theories of state sovereignty but also to develop 'a new and positive theory of sovereignty'.[17] It was this theoretical quest which provided the basis for Cole's pluralism. The emphasis was important: his concern at this time was less with the political implications of a theory of politics than with the implications *for* theory of a political programme. To misunderstand this, to treat him as simply one protagonist in the debate inside political theory between pluralism and monism, is to miss much.[18] If Cole was a pluralist, it was because pluralism provided a political theory for Guild Socialism.

The essence of Cole's pluralism is best located in a paper read before the Aristotelian Society in 1915. Here Cole attempted to provide an approach to the problem of social obligation which avoided the snare of state sovereignty. Inevitably, it was Rousseau who provided the starting point, with his perception that all social machinery was necessarily the organization of human will, involving the recognition that particular associations gave rise to corporate wills of their own. If this was Rousseau's insight, however, his 'fundamental error'[19] was to misunderstand the true nature of these associations, regarding them essentially as conspiracies against the public, and therefore wanting to eliminate the competition of wills inherent in such a situation. For Cole, it was Rousseau's failure to grasp the concept of function as the differentiating principle of corporate wills which led him to his erroneous declaration against every form of particular association. Certainly as far as modern associational life was concerned, 'speciality of function'[20] was its key distinguishing feature, and provided the theoretical basis for a resolution of the problem of conflicting social obligations. The prevailing tendency to find such a resolution in a doctrine of state sovereignty, even amongst men who wanted to preserve something akin to a communal value (a swipe at Green and Bosanquet), was seen by Cole as a retreat from social philosophy into a constricting politics.

[17] 'State Sovereignty and the Guilds', *New Age*, 15 Apr. 1915.
[18] Hence the limitation of otherwise good accounts such as K. C. Hsiao, *Political Pluralism*, 1927.
[19] 'Conflicting Social Obligations', *Proceedings of the Aristotelian Society*, Vol. xv, 1914–15, p. 143.
[20] Ibid., p. 144.

What was required was not a philosophical theory of the State, but of Society itself. This involved a recognition that a single obligation to the state could not contain the full range of social obligation; and that will and personality sustained the whole complex of social life, of which the state was merely a part. Ultimate social obligation could only be to the general will which sustained all social machinery, not merely to a part—even if that part was called the state. What this meant was that the state had no claim to first allegiance or superior obligation, for it was 'still only an association among others',[21] organized on a geographical basis for the performance of certain common purposes.

But if the state was to be dethroned, the aim was not to install a rival incumbent. Cole was emphatic that his object was 'not to generalize the association, but to particularize the State'.[22] The state became simply one functional association, but if this entailed the rejection of state sovereignty it also meant a rejection of syndicalism, theocracy and all other theories which mistook the part for the whole. What was demanded was not a recognition by the state of groups and associations but a real functional devolution which regarded the state itself as an association, 'elder brother, if you will, but certainly in no sense father of the rest'.[23] As a geographical grouping for purposes in common, the state could claim no dominance over, though interest in, other distinct functional areas. For Cole, this was the meaning of the theoretical movement in religion ('a disease which takes people in different ways'[24]) headed by Dr. Figgis and of the industrial theorists of National Guilds. In both cases special forms of control were being claimed on the basis of a distinct functional integrity. Against those who maintained that such an abandonment of state sovereignty would produce an anarchic conflict of functional authorities, Cole had two main answers. In the first place, some conflict was inevitable, and attempts to avoid it by making one party supreme were self-defeating; and in the second place, a well-organized society would at least manage to reduce such conflict to a minimum. Once it was recognized that sovereignty was not a state prerogative but was instead diffused throughout the whole complex of social arrangements, then there was no alternative to the creation of the social machinery which would embody this recognition.

[21] Ibid., p. 154. The state was 'one among a number of forms of association in which men are grouped according to the purposes which they have in common'. (*Self-Government in Industry*, 1917, p. 129.)

[22] 'Conflicting Social Obligations', p. 154.

[23] Ibid., p. 157.

[24] Ibid., p. 152.

It was at this point that social philosophy had to turn to social and political science. Once the sovereignty of society was established at the level of theory, it became the task of the practical man to devise the appropriate social machinery, for 'the devising of such machinery is not philosophy, but science'.[25] Cole was emphatic on this distinction. The fact that the sovereignty of society was an amorphous conception, or that it was a complex task to devise a federal structure embracing the state and other functional associations, was a problem not for social philosophy but for social engineering. Sovereignty was not less real for being indeterminate, nor obligation removed for being individually determined between groups and associations with ultimate reference to a general will which was 'something greater than all these',[26] greater even than society itself. Much of Cole's Guild Socialist system-building was an explicit attempt to give practical form to this approach to social philosophy. In making this attempt he exposed himself to the charge of having created impossibly Byzantine forms of social organization,[27] despite his constant insistence that his organizational suggestions were necessarily tentative and experimental, destined to be radically amended in practice and whose defects did nothing to impair the essential correctness of the social philosophy which sustained them.

The pluralism sketched by Cole in his 1915 paper provided the constant theoretical underpinning for his Guild Socialism. Its key features were an awareness of groups and associations as the repositories of loyalties and obligations; of the principle of function as the central differentiating criterion in society; of the state as one functional association amongst others; and of the need to create an organizational structure which recognized the right of associations to substantial self-government whilst harmonizing the relationship between the associations themselves to meet the requirements of the community as a whole. Specifically, of course, it was the place of the Guild idea inside this pluralist framework with which Cole was centrally concerned. In

[25] Ibid., p. 159.
[26] Ibid., p. 159. Greater than the state certainly, so 'it is not necessarily any worse to be unpatriotic, in the sense of being unwilling to side with the State in its external relations, than it is to be false to a Church or a Trade Union or an idea'. ('The Nature of the State in View of its External Relations', *Proceedings of the Aristotelian Society*, Vol. xvi, 1915–16, pp. 318–19.) Laski made the same point: 'Whether we will or no, we are bundles of hyphens. When the centres of linkage conflict a choice must be made.' ('The Personality of Associations', *Harvard Law Review*, Feb. 1916, p. 425.) Cole's argument on this point had particular relevance in the context of war and conscientious objection of course.
[27] Thus the Guild scheme has been pronounced 'too ambitious' (S. T. Glass, *The Responsible Society*, 1966, p. 69) and hopelessly impractical. (G. C. Field, *Guild Socialism*, 1920.)

an important sense, Cole embraced pluralism—though he used the term only rarely—because it provided Guild Socialism with a legitimating theoretical framework. The claim for industrial self-government, the conception of community ownership coupled with worker control, could be presented as a natural application of pluralist principles. Pluralism provided Guild Socialism with a political theory which could illuminate the errors of Fabians and syndicalists alike. If pluralism was 'natural' to Cole (as it was), it was certainly useful too. Initially he was reluctant to throw off the state, preferring instead to talk in terms of a temporary perversion of function, because of his attachment to the communitarian ideal. What pluralism came to provide, however, was a downgrading of the state coupled with the retention of a community consciousness to be expressed in new organizational forms. No longer could there be any 'facile identification of the community and the State'.[28]

Inside this general theory of the state, many questions remained unanswered and many problems unsolved, not least for Guild Socialism. For example, if the state was simply one type of functional association what exactly was its particular function? How were the present activities of the state to be performed in a Guild Socialist society? Where exactly did the state now stand in the struggle of social classes? What role, if any, could the state be expected to play in the achievement of socialism? Cole's answers to these questions were central to the development of Guild Socialist theory.

The problem of the state's proper functional role was something to which Cole devoted a good deal of attention, producing significant shifts in his thinking. The starting point was the idea that the state represented people in the purposes they have in common, particularly in respect of their common status as consumers.[29] It was this conception which provided the foundation for Guild Socialism's key demand for a partnership in industry between state and guilds, the former to own and the latter to control.[30] For Cole, this position succeeded in thwarting any state claim to general sovereignty, whilst recognizing the need of

---

[28] *Self-Government in Industry*, 1917, p. 120.

[29] See the 'Storrington Document' (the Guild 'manifesto' drawn up in December 1914 and slightly revised in 1915) which described the state as existing to deal with things 'which affect all the citizens equally and in the same way', so that, in economic terms, it was 'an organisation of consumers on a geographical basis'. (The Document has been published in A. Briggs and J. Saville (eds.), *Essays in Labour History*, Vol. II, 1971.)

[30] Thus the object of the National Guilds League, formed in April 1915, was stated as: 'The abolition of the wage-system and the establishment of self-government in industry through a system of National Guilds working in conjunction with the State.'

the community as consumers to be represented in industry. So enthusiastic was Cole's attachment to such a neat synthesis that it brought him into dispute with another wing of the Guild movement, headed by S. G. Hobson, which was quick to brand him with the taint of Fabianism for suggesting that the Guilds would be so careless of consumer interests that these interests would require the guardianship of the state. Thus the *New Age* reviewer of *The World of Labour* noted Cole's error in believing that the state would retain an economic role in relation to the Guilds, so that despite it being 'logically clear' that there could be no question of consumer exploitation Cole 'actually fears "Guild profiteering". This is really heart-breaking'.[31] This initial difference of approach towards the economic role of the state between Cole and the *New Age* group was never resolved, with Cole continuing to insist on a functional differentiation between production and consumption whilst Hobson consistently endeavoured both to deny such a differentiation and to deny the state any economic functions. At the root of this disagreement was a dispute about the nature of the state itself. For Hobson, the state had to be removed from any sordid economic preoccupation so that it was free to perform its spiritual role as the expression of a national will. Instead of having simply a functional task, the state had 'a mission, a responsibility, a continuing task to interpret faithfully the citizen will',[32] whereas Cole wanted to treat it as no more than one piece of functional machinery. In essence, the Hobson-*New Age* school wanted to retain the sovereignty of the citizen state whilst Cole wanted 'above everything else, to destroy the conception of the Sovereign State, without at the same time destroying the State itself'.[33] Cole's notion of a communal sovereignty finding its expression through a system of functional coordination struck Hobson as both excessively mechanical and a denial of the fact of common citizenship.

There was a certain paradox in this clash of theory inside Guild Socialism, above all in its practical implications. Hobson's assertion of the sovereign supremacy of the state turned out to mean *less* role for the state, because its concern was spiritual rather than economic, than did Cole's denial of such sovereignty. To allow the state the job of consumer

[31] *New Age*, 20 Nov. 1913. In reply (4 Dec. 1913) Cole said he was 'not clear that the future will be as logical as you would rightly wish it to be', though on the question of consumer representation he conceded that he had 'perhaps been led to insist on it too much from living in the atmosphere of Fabianism.'
[32] S. G. Hobson, *National Guilds and the State*, 1920, pp. 105–6. This book contains Hobson's version of his dispute with Cole.
[33] 'A Second Round with Mr. Hobson', *New Age*, 21 Feb. 1918.

representative would, for Hobson, not only be a distortion of its true role but would 'subject the producer to a supervision almost as galling as under capitalism',[34] whereas to allow the guilds the responsibility for consumption as well as for production would, for Cole, mean a failure to recognize that these functions were distinct, albeit complementary. In large measure, this sort of dispute reflected the disparate nature of the Guild movement and the different avenues of attraction to it.[35]

It was when Cole ceased to accept some of his own assumptions in this dispute with Hobson that complications arose in his attempt to work out the framework of a Guild Socialist society. As long as the state could be charged with the job of consumer representation, it remained relatively easy, at least conceptually, to present the structural form of a Guild society in terms of the functional co-ordination of the producer guilds and the consumer state. Once Cole ceased to identify the state with the consumer it became necessary to construct ever more elaborate forms of consumer representation and functional co-ordination, an enterprise which absorbed the energies of Guild Socialism in its later stages. Just as he had earlier insisted on the need to distinguish the state from society (and to distinguish both from community), by the 1919 edition of his *Self-Government in Industry*, Cole declared himself 'no longer satisfied with the State as the final and only representative of the consumers'.[36] The need for a distinct representation of the consumer interest was still emphasized but now this was said to require new functional agencies at every level. Indeed, consumption itself was now discovered to be not a single undifferentiated activity but something requiring a functional breakdown of its own. The implications of this for the organization of a Guild Socialist society were revealed in the pages of Cole's *Guild Socialism Re-Stated*, his final and most intricate essay in system-building. Here a scheme was sketched in which various agencies of consumer representation (Co-operative Councils, Collective Utility Councils, Cultural and Health Councils) exist parallel to the structure of Guild organization at local, regional and national level, bringing production and consumption into harmony. The state found no place in this organizational structure; indeed, in its present form it could be expected to 'wither away'.[37] It could claim for itself no coercive

[34] Hobson, op. cit., p. 126.
[35] Thus Bechhofer and Reckitt: 'Mr. Hobson was seeking to release statesmanship by subtracting industry from it; Mr. Cole was seeking to rationalise Syndicalism by adding the consumer's outlook to it.' (*The Meaning of National Guilds*, 1918, p. 356.)
[36] *Self-Government in Industry* (1919 edn.), p. 6.
[37] *Guild Socialism Re-Stated*, 1920, p. 123.

or coordinating role, for it was simply one association amongst others which, when stripped of its claim to represent the consumer, was left only with an ill-defined 'politics'. But if the state was dispensable, coercion and coordination were not, though the extent of these functions would be much reduced since all that would be required were 'a few fundamental decisions on policy'.[38] These fundamental decisions would relate to general questions of resource allocation and economic policy, policy and demarcation differences between functional bodies, general policy outside the scope of the functional associations, and to the task of coercion. A federal body was required for these tasks which would be drawn from the essential functional groups in society. In his *Social Theory*, Cole suggested a 'democratic Supreme Court of Functional Equity'[39] for this purpose (a name whose unwieldiness was designed to emphasize its essentially appellate and coordinating role), but by *Guild Socialism Re-Stated* the nomenclature had simplified to 'National Commune', though its functions remained the same.

There was ample scope for argument about the content and meaning of this elaborate structure. Above all, did it mark the final extinction of a recognizable state, or was Cole's commune 'merely a new political leviathan with a different name', whose title alone obscured the fact that it was 'a perfect example of a monistic state'?[40] In an important sense it was both these things—but more of that in a moment. What was immediately clear, however, was that Cole had become increasingly unwilling to accept a continuing role for the present state. Contemporary experience, particularly of the state at war, was a decisive factor in this theoretical shift. Between 1914 and 1918 Cole's war was waged against a regulatory state which seemed determined to break the power of organized labour in the service of capitalism. A state which preferred to shackle the trade unions rather than to devolve responsibility to them for wartime production seemed amply to confirm the diagnosis of the state as 'the expression of the dominant power of the capitalist class'.[41] The state had not merely grown in strength under the impact of war, but had openly used this new strength as a buttress for an ailing capitalism. For Cole, here was the chief lesson of the war

[38] Ibid., p. 136.
[39] *Social Theory*, 1920, p. 137.
[40] Hsiao, op. cit., p. 123.
[41] 'National Guilds and the State', *Socialist Review*, Jan.–Mar. 1919. During the war Cole worked for the engineering union (A.S.E.) and was much concerned with the effects of the Munitions Act and other restrictive legislation.

when it came to framing a policy for post-war reconstruction. Addressing the 1917 conference of the National Guilds League, Cole confessed an 'intense hostility to the state', so intense that he could add: 'I feel at the moment that the State is more dangerous than the employer.'[42] The state seemed likely to assume a vast new role in industrial control in alliance with capitalism, making it necessary for Guild Socialists not merely to attack capitalism as the employer, but to 'concentrate our hostility on State Capitalism'.[43] During the war, this meant a demand that the trade union movement should assume control of the industrial relief agencies and win a footing in industrial control itself. After the war, it meant a concerted bid by organized labour to break the newly powerful unholy alliance of state and capitalism. If the state disappeared from Cole's developing version of a Guild Socialist society at this period, at least part of the explanation was to be found in a desire to 'dish the state' born out of contemporary experience of that state's response to war.

It is important to be clear about the exact nature of the war's impact on Cole's thought, particularly in relation to the state, nationalization and political action. It has been claimed that his theory of industrial action 'broke down under the stress of the First World War' and that 'the socialist position which he had begun to build before August 1914 was scarcely recognizable four years later'.[44] This view is profoundly inaccurate; partly, because it exaggerates the place of the war in the development of Cole's thought and, partly, because it suggests that there was a fundamental transformation in his theoretical position during the war years. In fact, the extent to which Cole managed to ignore the substantive issues of the war and to concentrate his attention on the 'other war' is remarkable.[45] His chief practical concern was with the effects of wartime industrial regulation on the spirit and organization of the labour movement; but his main theoretical preoccupation continued to be the further development of Guild Socialist doctrine,

[42] N. G. L. Annual Conference report, 1917 (Cole Collection).
[43] Ibid.
[44] J. M. Winter, *Socialism and the Challenge of War*, 1912–18, 1974, pp. 121, 143. Later, however, Winter writes of the 'continuity' in Cole's thought during the war, so that 'the case for guild socialism which he argued in the four years which followed the armistice varied only slightly from the one he presented in his earlier work'. (P. 281.) Winter fails to reconcile these contradictory interpretations.
[45] R. P. Arnot's description of the Guildsmen's 'personal boycott' of the war applies especially to Cole. (*History of the Labour Research Department*, 1926, p. 9.) Even Winter (loc. cit., p. 143) concedes that 'it is impossible to deal with his attitude to the war in the same way that one would approach Tawney's views or the Webbs''.

with an eye on the situation which would exist once the interruption of war had passed. The war itself did little damage to the essentials of Cole's theoretical position.

Yet the experience of the capitalist state at war did produce some change in his conception of Guild Socialist strategy in relation to nationalization and political action, even if the effect of this change was to return his thought to its earliest position on this issue. In 1913 he had envisaged a large role for a nationalizing state in the achievement of Guild Socialism,[46] involving at least a partial embrace of political action. At the same time, however, he came to believe that nationalization was increasingly likely anyway ('whether the Fabian Society and the Labour Party choose to welcome it as a triumph for Socialism or not'),[47] which meant that Guild Socialism should concentrate on pressing its demands in relation to nationalization rather than take a positive stand on the issue itself. This approach inevitably involved a devaluation of political action and an increased emphasis on industrial action in Cole's thought. The effect of the war was to reverse this tendency. The nature and consequences of this reversal were clearly revealed in Cole's contribution to the Industrial Symposium on post-war reconstruction conducted by the *New Age* in January 1917,[48] in which the character of wartime industrial organization was evaluated and the implications for labour strategy were discussed.

The war had produced both more recognition and more restriction for labour; and the state had intervened extensively in industry but without interfering with the structure of capitalist ownership or management. Pre-war capitalism had been dealt a decisive blow by the war, but—and this was Cole's essential point—it had been 'replaced by none of the alternative systems which, before the war, seemed its only serious rivals'.[49] Instead of an advance towards either collectivism or Guild Socialism, the war had produced 'the beginnings of a new industrial system, properly to be called State Capitalism, under which private capitalism and profiteering continue with the moral and physical support of the State'.[50] Cole offered a perceptive account of the

[46] 'If the State has no business in industry, neither has the capitalist—and only the State can turn him out.' (*The World of Labour*, 1913, p. 409.)
[47] *New Age*, 4 Dec. 1913. Cf. his articles on 'Nationalization and the Guilds', *New Age*, Sept.–Oct. 1914.
[48] Cole's article, 'Labour Policy After The War', was reprinted as Appendix B to his *Self-Government in Industry*, from which the following quotations are taken.
[49] *Self-Government in Industry*, p. 278.
[50] Ibid.

nature of this emerging industrial system which combined state control with private ownership, a system which it has now become fashionable to describe as 'corporatism'.[51] The greatest post-war danger was that such a system might be established on a permanent basis, with labour accepting incorporation as a junior partner in industry. Labour's behaviour during the war, both politically and industrially, gave Cole little hope that incorporation would be resisted; so that 'only the folly of Capitalism, or a new-found wisdom in the ranks of Labour . . . can save us from the regime of State Capitalism after the war'.[52]

It was this analysis which provided the foundation for his reconsideration of Guild Socialist strategy during the closing stages of the war. Above all, it involved a new attitude towards nationalization, for it was a problem which had 'radically altered as a result of the war'.[53] Describing his previous attitude, correctly, as that of 'half-benevolent neutrality', Cole now presented the immediate post-war situation in terms of only two alternatives: state capitalism or nationalization. Although Guild Socialism was antagonistic to both these alternatives, its prospects were much better under the latter system—which should, therefore, be supported. It remained necessary to press the Guild demand for control in connection with all nationalization proposals, but 'even without that, Collectivism is to be preferred to State Capitalism'.[54] At the same time, the need to resist incorporation meant that the labour movement should seek and accept only those forms of workshop control which gave increased interference in industrial control without increased responsibility. This was the principle which Cole applied to all proposals on the form of joint consultation and works committees. Interference by labour was necessary as a training ground for future control; yet such interference had to remain ultimately irresponsible if the labour movement was to avoid entanglement in the corporatist net of an emerging state capitalism.

Here, then, was the real nature and significance of the war's impact on the development of Cole's thought. His elaboration of Guild theory proceeded largely irrespective of the war, as evidenced by its massive continuity during this period. An increasing antipathy to the state did lead (as was noted) to its replacement by new organizational forms as the consumer partner of the Guilds in Cole's scheme, but that was the

[51] See N. Harris, *Competition and the Corporate Society*, 1972; and R. E. Pahl and J. T. Winkler, 'The Coming Corporatism', *New Society*, 10 Oct. 1974.

[52] *Self-Government in Industry*, p. 279.

[53] Ibid., p. 280.

[54] Ibid.

only substantive change. The most significant development was in the realm of strategy, where the analysis of wartime state capitalism produced the modified attitude to nationalization which has just been noticed. It is this, too, which provides the explanation for Cole's involvement in the research and policy activity of the Labour Party at the end of the war. A political programme of Fabian collectivism, however defective from a Guild point of view, did at least offer a preferable alternative to state capitalism as the course of post-war industrial development. Cole had not entered 'the political mainstream',[55] but nor is it true to say that he 'barely noticed the emergence of the 1918 Labour Party'.[56] The truth lies elsewhere: that he was prepared to modify his strategy for the achievement of Guild Socialism in the light of his analysis of the state at war and the developing shape of the post-war industrial and political situation. As ever, his thought showed itself responsive to the pressure of events.

It would be possible simply to register the contradictions in Cole's treatment of the state, with considerable supportive evidence. There was, for example, that view of the state as a body only temporarily perverted from its true function, which stood alongside a conception of the state as a necessarily coercive agency of capitalism. There was the denunciation of collectivism for its reliance on the state to create socialism, a process which could only produce a bureaucratic leviathan, which coexisted with a re-affirmation of the central role of the state in the building of socialism. In relation to nationalization, in particular, there was the insistence that the issue was irrelevant to the demand for industrial freedom, coupled with an assertion not merely that nationalization would ease the path to a Guild society but that such action by the state was imperative if the grip of capitalism was to be broken and corporatism avoided. There was the paper model of a Guild Socialist society in which the state disappeared, yet which provided for state functions to continue under a different name.

It was clearly a confusing picture, involving formal contradictions which were both real and evident. If Cole could justly detect 'a revolution in Socialist thought on the subject of the State',[57] it was a revolution whose outcome remained elusive, not least in his own case. On the one

[55] J. M. Winter, op. cit., p. 143.
[56] Margaret Cole, 'Guild Socialism and the Labour Research Department', in Briggs and Saville (eds.), *Essays in Labour History*, Vol. II, 1971, p. 279. Cole's involvement in the research and advisory work of the Labour Party at this time is documented by R. McKibbin, *The Evolution of the Labour Party 1910–1924*, 1974.
[57] *Guild Socialism Re-Stated*, p. 30.

hand, his position could be described as reflecting 'the typical view-point of anarchism';[58] on the other hand, it could be seen to involve 'a legal monism of the most absolute sort',[59] which sought to kick sovereignty out of the front door only to smuggle it in again at the back. Yet there did exist a unity in his thought which, if it could not resolve the contradictions and tensions in his treatment of the state, can do much to explain them. At the centre of such an explanation must be Cole's attachment to the idea of community. It was the continuing search for the appropriate organizational expression of this communitarian ideal which informed all his attempts at system-building. Even when the existing state was deemed to be discredited and beyond redemption for any role in a community setting, new organs of community control had to be created. Nor was Cole unwilling to continue to present this idea in terms of the difference between the state of the present and a state of the future. Guildsmen refused to accept the view that the state would disappear with capitalism, for a democratic state would have important functions in a socialist society, not least because 'man's nature and capacity for civic organization are not exhausted by the industrial groupings of which he forms a part'.[60] Whilst accepting that the existing state was vitiated by its association with capitalism, Cole never relinquished a conception of the potential role of the body politic, declaring himself 'not convinced that the State must be, under all social conditions, merely a pale reflexion of the economic structure of Society'.[61] But if it was an attachment to the concept of community which was vital in welding Cole to the permanency of politics, that concept was of a distinctive kind. Merely to be a communitarian would be to range oneself with Hegelians, idealists and other assorted species who provided a ready home for an unwary traveller.[62] Cole's community, by contrast, was rooted in both democracy and decentralization, and the state had to find its place inside this framework.

Cole began by attacking the State whilst preserving the state. Even when the existing state was seemingly abandoned, the state in a functional sense still survived. What mattered throughout was the existence of a range of coordinated functional bodies which together could

[58] A. Ulam, *Philosophical Foundations of English Socialism*, 1951, p. 88.
[59] Hsiao, op. cit., p. 138. For a similar view of Cole as having led Guild Socialism along a 'devious' path back to collectivism see N. Carpenter, op. cit., 1922, p. 268.
[60] 'National Guilds and the State', *Socialist Review*, Jan.–Mar., 1919.
[61] *Self-Government in Industry*, p. 137.
[62] See B. Bosanquet, 'Note on Mr. Cole's Paper', *Proceedings of the Aristotelian Society*, Vol. xv, 1914–15, for an example of the Hegelian embrace.

provide the means of expression for a community will. Once it was established that the state alone could not claim identity with this communal will, it became a matter not for philosophy but for social engineering to provide the organizational structure for a diffused sovereignty. At present the state was both supported by an erroneous theory and partial in its daily practice; thus the task of reform was likewise both theoretical and practical. At bottom, however, it *was* a question of reform rather than abolition, for society required its agencies of community control, albeit in a changed social and economic setting. The stronger the sense of community, then the task of coercion and coordination would be correspondingly diminished. For example, Lenin's conception of government replaced by universal administration 'fails to make plain the extent to which his Communist hopes depend on the existence of a "community" underlying class differences, though unable to express itself because of them.'[63] For Cole, this spirit of community was a fact; the task was to give it organizational expression.

What emerged, therefore, was a synthesis. From Marx, there was the analysis of the state as an agent of capitalism; but from liberalism there was the recognition of an autonomy and permanency for the activity of politics. From the pluralists there was the denial of the sovereign state and the assertion of the independence of groups and associations; but from Rousseau and the theorists of community there was the recognition of the essential interdependence of the group universe. When compounded with changing contemporary perceptions of the state in action, it is scarcely surprising that there should have been important tensions in Cole's treatment of the state, both in a theoretical and strategical sense. In academic terms, as a theorist of the state Cole was often both confusing and logically careless. In political terms, as a community theorist of socialism, his approach to the state exhibited a striking consistency. Its outcome was a delicate balancing operation, the perils and attractions of which become clearer in the context of Cole's wider theoretical position.

[63] 'What is the State?', *The Venturer*, Aug. 1921. Cole's conception of 'community' at this time was influenced by R. M. Maciver's, *Community: A Sociological Study*, 1917; while Maciver (pp. 46–7) indicated his general approval of the approach adopted by the Guild Socialists.

IV

Democracy and Participation

POLITICAL PLURALISM is democratic in its claim for group self-government; yet it is not primarily a theory of democracy. Group autonomy is clearly compatible with many varieties of internal group government, even for socialists. For Harold Laski, for example, the attraction of pluralism consisted almost wholly in its assertion of the integrity of associational life independent of the state. This assertion had both academic and political importance, and Laski may accurately be called pluralist at this time because here was the defining principle of his general theoretical position. With Cole, however, the emphasis was very different. Indeed, it may be said that Cole came to pluralism because he was already a democrat of a special kind. It was a democracy which claimed self-government both *for* the group and *within* it, crucially in relation to industry; and pluralism could usefully give theoretical support to at least half this general claim. In simplest form, Cole's earliest and central commitments were to industrial democracy in particular and to a decentralized social and political structure in general. Pluralism was valid in so far as it could usefully serve this wider democratic purpose.

In Cole's hands, Guild Socialism was essentially a theory of democracy. As such, one of its chief values was its attempt to delineate a democratic theory uniquely appropriate to a modern industrial society. It claimed to have discovered an antidote to the problem of size which prevented Rousseau from carrying his participatory theory beyond city-state limits. It was Rousseau's failure to grasp the real nature of group life which prevented him from discovering the sectional and functional principles which would sustain democracy in the setting of the great state.[1] But if Rousseau erred in perception, the collectivists of contemporary socialism were more fundamentally in error. To Cole, they seemed to have forgotten that the social order was rooted in a set of power relationships and that socialism was essentially a statement

[1] With industrial democracy 'we may hope to improve upon Rousseau's ideal, and even in the great State, to secure the realisation, in large measure, of that elusive but fundamental reality which he named the General Will'. (*World of Labour*, p. 29.)

about the ordering of those relationships. So widespread was the collectivist misconception on this point that, in Cole's classic formulation, when asked what was the 'fundamental evil' requiring eradication in society most people would answer wrongly: 'They would answer POVERTY, when they ought to answer SLAVERY.'[2] The former was the symptom; the latter the disease. It was, therefore, a radical view of power which Cole sought to inject into the British socialist tradition—a tradition which, as Samuel Beer has nicely demonstrated, had embraced a paternal governmentalism rooted in a view of power common to much of British political life.[3] The radical approach to power often reflects itself in a vigorous liberal individualism, centrally concerned with the protection of the individual from a powerful state. In Cole's case, it reflected itself much less in the claim for freedom *from* government than in the demand for access *to* social power. In modern conditions of capitalist industrialism, for most people power was something remote and external, crucially in industry itself. Hence Cole's attraction to a Guild Socialism which embraced democracy in industry as its central tenet. Hence, too, his antipathy to a socialist collectivism so neglectful of the problem of social power that it failed to understand that even if the class character of existing society was abolished there would remain a social structure which 'still fails to satisfy the conditions of reasonable human association and government'.[4] Indeed, far from contributing to a democratic solution to the problem of social power, the structural consequences of collectivism would really mean 'the completion of the present tendency towards State Sovereignty by the piling of fresh powers and duties on the great Leviathan'.[5]

It was on this issue of democracy that much of the antagonism between Fabianism and Guild Socialism turned, revealing the existence of fundamentally different approaches to social analysis and to social action. Inside the British socialist tradition it is rare to find sustained internal debate on an item of theoretical vocabulary, yet much of the controversy between Cole and the Webbs on the meaning and content of democracy provided just this. It was a moment of genuine theoretical debate, with Cole launching a sustained

---

[2] *Self-Government in Industry*, p. 34. Notice Tawney's similar formulation: 'The supreme evil of modern industrial society is not poverty. It is the absence of liberty, i.e. of the opportunity for self-direction.' (*R. H. Tawney's Commonplace Book*, ed. J. M. Winter and D. M. Joslin, *Economic History Review Supplement*, 1972, p. 34, entry for 6 Oct. 1912.)

[3] S. Beer, *Modern British Politics*, 1965.

[4] *Guild Socialism Re-Stated*, p. 27.

[5] Ibid., p. 31.

intellectual critique of Fabian democracy which forced Fabianism back to fundamentals in a search for a satisfactory formulation of its position. Theoretical battle was waged, involving a discussion about the meaning and nature of democracy which in many ways seems strikingly modern. Both sides had to lay bare their assumptions about the place of man in the social system, thereby also revealing assumptions about the nature of man and of social systems. Both sides invoked the teachings of theory and the lessons of experience. Almost simultaneously, in 1920, both sides produced paper models of their preferred societies (the Webbs' *Constitution for the Socialist Commonwealth of Great Britain* and Cole's *Guild Socialism Re-Stated*) which, taken together, perhaps represent the high water mark of optimistic social engineering in a modern context. For these reasons, it is both theoretically revealing and historically accurate to locate Cole's democratic theory in the context of this debate with Fabianism—and an attempt will be made to do just this.

The debate was more complex than is often suggested by those people who see the Webbs merely as stubborn old bureaucrats and the Guild Socialists as utopian dreamers with one foot in the Middle Ages.[6] Its origin was the Guild attack on the easy Fabian identification of collectivism with socialism, coupled with a denial that efficiency of production and justice of distribution were the twin foundations of the socialist position. In essence, the Guild Socialists—like Belloc, the syndicalists and the academic pluralists in their different ways—discovered that the Fabian state might succeed only in replacing the capitalist by the bureaucrat, producing a regime of distributive justice certainly, but with deadening consequences for the whole social world, in which the individual, as both worker and citizen, would be a passive recipient rather than active participant. It would be the Servile State predicted by Belloc, or the Selfridge State anticipated by Cole. Such a state found its essential theoretical statement in Shaw's contribution to the original *Fabian Essays*. 'We have the distinctive term Social Democrat', he wrote, 'indicating the man or woman who desires through Democracy to gather the whole people into the State, so that the State may be trusted with the rent of the country, and finally with the land, the capital, and the organisation of the national industry—with all the

---

[6] For example, in his excellent little book on *The Theory of Democratic Elitism*, 1969, Peter Bachrach is wrong about both Cole and the Fabians: Cole did not exclude government and consumers from all control over industry, nor did he maintain that workers represented the interests of the entire society; while the Fabians did not hold a merely one-dimensional view of man's political interests (pp. 104–5).

sources of production, which are now abandoned to the cupidity of irresponsible private individuals.'[7] Here stood revealed some of the most distinctive assumptions of classical Fabianism. Individualism was the enemy; democracy was merely the method of change; the aim was to 'gather the whole people into the State'; the State (not 'state'!) would own, efficiently control and justly distribute. If this scenario seemed to leave little role for the individual worker and citizen in the making of social decisions, the reason was quickly supplied by Sidney Webb: 'The objection to authority is a radical not a socialist objection.'[8] To the Guild Socialists, the Fabians stood for nationalization without socialization, a grim prospect. In a rare burst of extravagant prose, Cole described the Fabian future: 'If, after a voyage almost as lasting as that of the Flying Dutchman', he wrote in the *New Age*, 'we round in the end the Cape of State Capitalism, we shall only find ourselves on the other side in a Sargossa Sea of State Socialism, which will continue to repress all initiative, clog all endeavour, and deny all freedom to the worker.'[9] The Guild Socialists thought they would not like to live in that sort of world, and that the worker would not like it either. They therefore developed a scheme of socialist democracy, which sought to transform every area of social activity—most immediately and crucially, the workplace—into an arena of democracy. The aim was to prevent that loss of individuality and citizenship inherent alike in capitalism and state socialism.

Here was a challenge to Fabianism which was not simply a matter of different views about the appropriate constitutional machinery for a socialist state, but of fundamentally different conceptions about both socialism and democracy, and of their relationship. Fabian and Guild Socialist could agree that political democracy implied (and was largely nullified without) economic democracy, and that democracy and socialism were thus two sides of the same coin. But this agreement on terms barely disguised the deep disagreement on their content. During its formative period, Fabian Socialism never had to confront the problem of democracy in any fundamental way, except to brush aside the claims of anarchists or Marxists. As Sidney Webb conceded in 1919, 'Socialists have contributed so far very little to the theory or practice of Democracy'; they have been 'accepting uncritically the ordinary

---

[7] *Fabian Essays*, 1889 (6th edn, 1962, p. 216).
[8] S. Webb, 'A Stratified Democracy', p. 8 (a Fabian lecture on 14 Nov. 1919, published as supplement to the *New Commonwealth*, 28 Nov. 1919).
[9] 'Nationalisation and the Guilds', *New Age*, 10 Sept. 1914.

Radical idea of democracy.'[10] It was this uncritical acceptance which Guild Socialism destroyed, leading the Webbs to point out in their *Socialist Constitution* that in the early twentieth century there occurred 'a revolution in thought with regard to the nature of Democracy'.[11] The aim here is not to give a full account of Fabian or Guild doctrine, but to focus on those aspects of Cole's democratic theory of Guild Socialism which seemed to conflict most fundamentally with the assumptions of Fabianism, and which raised some of the permanent problems of democratic theory.

For example, it is clear that the conception we have of the nature and development of a social system will have important consequences for our view of democracy. For the Webbs, society was an evolving organism, and a key aspect of this evolution was the 'organic differentiation of function'. This differentiation was both political and economic. In the one case, it was seen in the development of representative government, alike in the political and industrial world, instead of the old 'primitive' democracy which encouraged legislative instability and administrative weakness. The Webbs conceded that this professionalization of the representative function did mean that the representative lost 'that vivid appreciation of the feelings of the man at the bench or the forge', but this was the 'cruel irony'.[12] In the other case, differentiation appeared as the increasing specialization and division of labour of modern production. So here was an argument 'from the centre' (of the kind which has become more familiar in recent years, but which is as old as Plato): activities and individuals were defined in terms of the needs of a developing social system. Of course these 'needs' could be many and various. For example, the defining principle could be military power or social stability, or—with the Webbs—social efficiency and distributive justice; but in each case the argument began at the centre and moved outwards to embrace institutions, groups and individuals.

The Guild Socialists, especially Cole, sought to challenge this whole approach to social theory. Society was not like anything else, not organism or mechanism or any other analogy. It had to be analysed in its own terms, and especially in terms of the needs and wills of the individuals who composed it. Cole expressly declared himself to be engaged in normative social philosophy, and Guild theory was heavily idealist and voluntarist. For instance, Cole spoke of the 'deadening

[10] S. Webb, 'A Stratified Democracy', p. 2.
[11] S. and B. Webb, *A Constitution for the Socialist Commonwealth of Great Britain*, 1920, p. xiv.
[12] S. and B. Webb, *Industrial Democracy*, 1897, p. 56.

determinism' of Marx, and was powerful in his insistence on the role of ideas and theory. 'Only an idea can slay an idea', he wrote: 'until the workers are animated with the desire to be their own masters they cannot supplant the idea that their class is born for wage slavery.'[13] In contrast to Fabian theory, the Guild Socialist man had considerably more power to construct his own social world. The divorce of work from art, the division of labour, the wage system, industrial autocracy—these were not to be seen as inevitable (let alone progressive) aspects of modern social organization, but as obstacles to personal development and social fellowship which could and should be removed by a democratic social and industrial structure. This view struck at the roots of a Fabianism which embraced all these developments as necessary and welcome ingredients of a progressive social organism, and which therefore saw Guild Socialism as not merely undesirable or impracticable but as historically regressive.

But the organic evolutionism of the Fabians was itself rooted in a complex of beliefs and assumptions—about work, discipline, authority, moral character, and crucially about the nature of man himself—which had decisive consequences for their view of the desirability or possibility of a democratic social order. A basic and constant charge made by Guild Socialism against the Fabians was that they had a fundamental distrust of ordinary people and little understanding of their aspirations. The Webbs certainly devoted vast volumes to the study of working class organizations, but rather in the manner of anthropologists investigating an interesting tribe. In 1894 Beatrice had noted in her diary: 'we have little faith in the "average sensual man", we do not believe that he can do much more than describe his grievances, we do not think he can prescribe his remedies.'[14] When the syndicalist movement did announce a prescription by the average sensual worker of his own remedies, the Webbs—very much in the tradition of Tocqueville, Mill and more modern theorists—raised the spectre of 'small minorities' of workers with special needs being 'swamped' by the 'mass' of workers who exerted a majoritarian tyranny. It was the manual worker who was particularly to be feared. 'I often wonder', wrote Sidney Webb, 'when I hear my Guild Socialist friend talk about the right of the workman to control his own work, to

[13] *Self-Government in Industry*, p. 162. There is no evidence for the view that Cole succumbed to an 'optimistic determinism' or 'believed that shifts in ideas were caused by shifts in social structure' (J. M. Winter, *Socialism and the Challenge of War 1912–1918*, 1974, p. 111—emphatically the opposite, in fact.
[14] Beatrice Webb, *Our Partnership*, 1948, p. 120 (entry for 29 Dec. 1894).

exercise authority over his own sphere, when we shall have a revolt of the technician, the electrician, the chemist, the artist, the designer, the manager. We, too, want to have self-determination; we want to have control over our working life.'[15] It would be easy to document countless instances of Webbian fear and suspicion of workers in the aggregate, and of the need to discipline workers in the interest of social order. For example, syndicalism was indicted for preaching to the workers 'a deliberate disregard of the duties of citizenship', while the methods of syndicalism could only mean 'a serious deterioration of moral character in those who consent to take part in it'.[16] Even much later, when the Webbs—under the Guild challenge—had moved to a position much more critical of merely geographical or consumer democracy, this shift did not mark any significant change in their opinion of the ordinary man's democratic possibilities. For example, in his interesting and important lecture in 1919 on 'A Stratified Democracy', Sidney Webb declared that democracy of the geographical variety 'inevitably means the submerging of the active spirits in what the French call the apathetic mass. The great mass of people will always be found apathetic, dense, unreceptive to any unfamiliar ideas, and your eager active spirit with the unfamiliar idea . . . frets and fumes at being held in check by this apathetic mass. But, after all, the apathetic mass are individually God's creatures, and entitled to have a vote, and it is no use kicking against their apathy and denseness; you have got to work your governmental machine in some way that will enable you to get on notwithstanding their denseness.'[17] Here was a splendid glimpse into Webbian sensibility, not least in its suggestion that the entitlement to a vote was the hallmark of divine pedigree.

Denouncing what they called this 'Fabian heresy of distrust', the Guild Socialists were loud in proclaiming their trust in both the capacity and the character of the average sensual man. The Fabian assumption was always that men were likely to exploit each other unless there were firm institutional safeguards provided by the community at large. The Webbs wrote constantly of the dangers presented by sectional selfishness and exclusiveness, above all the selfishness of groups of manual workers; and they offered this insight into the selfishness of organized groups as a lesson of history, revealed in ancient castes and medieval gilds no less than in the modern world. Industrial self-

---

[15] S. Webb, 'A Stratified Democracy', p. 7.
[16] S. and B. Webb, 'What Syndicalism Means', 1912, p. 11 (supplement to *The Crusade*).
[17] S. Webb, 'A Stratified Democracy', p. 5.

government would therefore give a blank cheque to producer groups to exploit each other and the community of consumers. The golden rule in this respect was to be found in 'the homely adage that no man can be trusted to be judge in his own case'.[18] At present (they believed) the sectional selfishness of groups of workers was only held in check by the need to unite against the common capitalist enemy, though even now demarcation disputes gave some indication of what would happen if the trade union developed into an organ of government.

In fact, the Guild Socialists did not propose to dispense with institutional safeguards against possible sectional exploitation. They were especially anxious to remove fears about the fate of the consumer under a system of industrial democracy. Much of Guild Socialist system-building, as has been noted, was centrally concerned with the elaboration of the proper balance in each sphere and at every level between legitimate social interests, particularly the interests of producers and consumers. Cole's *Guild Socialism Re-Stated* stands as a monument to this concern. But it was always insisted that the purpose of such elaborate social machinery was not to protect the consumer from the producer—for that would imply a natural tendency to exploit—but simply to provide machinery whereby consumer needs and desires could be communicated to the Guilds of producers. The effect might be the same, but the difference of approach was surely important. The Guild Socialist man was seen as having a natural tendency towards fellowship, thwarted only by a divisive social environment: Fabian men needed protection from each other.

The Guild Socialist man was also a natural democrat, in the sense both that he was fit to control his own social environment and that he demanded those personal and social benefits—dignity, creativity, self-development and the rest—which were the fruits of an actively democratic social world. By contrast, as we have seen, the Fabian man—not the expert or the professional representative, but the average sensual man—was fitted only to express his demands and grievances. This argument, classically developed by Aristotle, was that even the simplest men know where the shoe pinches (they can feel if not think); from which could be derived the position that men should have a 'say' in government (in modern times, a vote), but that they should have no more than this. They expressed their needs by passing retrospective verdicts on external prescriptions. The implications for democratic theory were clear, and were spelled out by the Webbs in their critical

[18] S. and B. Webb, *The Consumers' Co-operative Movement*, 1921, p. 465.

analysis of various devices for making democracy more directly participatory. 'What Democracy requires is assent to results', they wrote; 'what the Referendum gives is assent to projects.'[19] To the Guild Socialist, democracy was about process as much as product: it was both natural and necessary that men were actively engaged in the making of social decisions, or they lost part of themselves. Especially was this true of industry, where for the mass of workers the enervating consequences of their divorce from control were both apparent and acute. Guild Socialists always insisted on the benefits of industrial democracy in terms of 'product' too, especially efficiency—denying that men would do good work in the absence of conditions of self-government—but it was democracy as process that remained central.

The foundation of the democratic theory of Guild Socialism—perhaps its greatest contribution to that theory—was its analysis of the concept of representation, particularly as developed by Cole. The democratic idea, it was alleged, had got lost over time in a false theory of representation, which claimed that one man could 'represent' another. It was a false and dangerous theory which said that man as a 'whole' could be represented, when all that could really be represented were particular functions and purposes which men had in common. The concept of function was 'the real and vital principle of democracy',[20] not to be confused with the sort of functionalist social theory, stretching from Plato to the Webbs (and now familiar in much contemporary theory), which defined individuals and institutions in terms of the requirements of a particular social system and which therefore served as an agency of social control. Guild theory made nonsense of any theory of state sovereignty, for the state was simply a functional association like any other, formed for a particular purpose, and belonging to the same category as trade unions, churches, football clubs and the host of other associations which commanded our membership and loyalties. The state was not universally sovereign, nor did we derive our rights from it; for sovereignty was diffused throughout the entire community, which was the locus of our rights and obligations. Genuine democracy would only be realized in a system of coordinated functional representation. The Guild argument was not an anarchic attack on the concept of representation itself, but an attack on the current misuse of the concept contained in the doctrine that in one single and general act man as a whole could be 'represented'. In fact, men should be rep-

[19] S. and B. Webb, *Industrial Democracy*, p. 61.
[20] *Labour in the Commonwealth*, p. 201.

resented in all their multiple functional associations and loyalties, requiring an elaborate and coordinated representational structure throughout society. It should be noted that Guild Socialism did explicitly claim to embody a general social theory, of which its industrial doctrine was merely its most urgent expression. Just as democracy could not be confined to politics, nor could it end with industry: it was a general theory of social organization. In Cole's words, the democratic principle applied 'not only or mainly to some special sphere of social action known as "politics", but to any and every form of social action.'[21] Much of Cole's work at this time was therefore an attempt to indicate not merely what a democratic industrial structure would look like but what a whole society which took participatory democracy as its central organizing principle might look like too.

The conception of representation developed by Cole carried with it a view of the *conditions* in which representation would be genuinely effective and of those in which misrepresentation would necessarily result. The golden rule in this matter, laid down by Cole, was that representation must be 'specific and functional', not 'general and inclusive'. Misrepresentation occurred when the purposes for which the representative was chosen lost clarity and precision. In this matter parliament was the worst offender for, as Cole said, it 'professes to represent all the citizens in all things, and therefore as a rule represents none of them in anything'.[22] Its claim to omnibus representation was a denial of the functional principle basic to a real democracy. Cole was consistently bitter about the parliamentary perversion of democracy, a bitterness which was rooted in a deep personal antipathy.[23] Men could best control those things which they were most closely involved in and which they best understood: here was the arena for effective representation. (It is interesting that Schumpeter makes a very similar point, though of course without arriving at similar conclusions about the need to 'socialize' the representative function.)[24] A comparison with

[21] *Guild Socialism Re-Stated*, p. 12.
[22] *Social Theory*, p. 108. For a recent attempt to reconstruct parliamentary representation on a multi-voting basis in line with Cole's argument, see L. Shaskolsky Sheleff and B. Susser, 'The Referendum-Election: One Person, Several Votes', *Parliamentary Affairs*, xxviii, 1975. The authors argue that the decline of Guild Socialism produced an 'unwarranted neglect of Cole's fundamental insight regarding the electoral functions'.
[23] Offered a parliamentary nomination, Cole replied: 'I loathe Parliament and everything connected with it. ... Why not stand yourself, unless you hate it as much as I do?' (Letter to A. Wiltshire, 18 Mar. 1920; in possession of Margaret Cole.)
[24] According to Schumpeter, a man's judgement will be best in relation to 'the things which are familiar to him independently of what his newspaper tells him, which he can directly influence or

the Webbs at this point is very revealing, for they were concerned to argue a directly contrary position about the conditions for democratic representation. It was 'the supreme paradox of democracy', they wrote, 'that every man is a servant in respect of the matters of which he possesses the most intimate knowledge, and for which he shows the most expert proficiency, namely, the professional craft to which he devotes his working hours; and he is a master over that on which he knows no more than anybody else, namely, the general interests of the community as a whole. In this paradox ... lies at once the justification and the strength of democracy.'[25] To which the Guild Socialist reply was that democracy of this type had become generally acceptable to all classes simply because it had so obviously failed, serving only to deprive the ordinary worker and citizen of any effective role in the determination of his social environment. The need now, said the Guild Socialists, was to inject democracy into the workplace, which would then become a laboratory and base from which men would learn to control the wider society (the individual 'in learning to control his own industry ... would learn also to control the political machine'[26])— which would be a black day indeed for those described by Cole as 'the bureaucratic jugglers in human lives whom we still call statesmen—or sometimes New Statesmen'.[27]

It is interesting to notice how this whole controversy between Guild Socialism and the Fabians over the question of democracy was an intricate mixture of values and potentially testable empirical judgements. Even Cole's explicitly normative position was affected, as he pointed out himself, by such things as the findings of social psychology. The Webbs declared an impossible relationship between manager and workers in a democratic factory: 'the relationship set up between a manager who has to give orders all day to his staff, and the members of that staff who, sitting as a committee of management, criticise his

manage and for which he develops the kind of responsibility that is induced by a direct relation to the favourable or unfavourable effects of a course of action'. (P. 259.) Lest this should be construed as an argument favourable to radical democracy, Schumpeter later declares that 'no responsible person can view with equanimity the consequences of extending the democratic method, that is to say the sphere of "politics", to all economic affairs'. (P. 299.) (J. Schumpeter, *Capitalism, Socialism and Democracy*, 1942.)

---

[25] S. and B. Webb, *Industrial Democracy*, p. 844.
[26] *Self-Government in Industry*, p. 185. Cole always made the workshop central, 'for the conditions which prevail in the workshop inevitably condition and govern the conditions which prevail in men's social relationships'. (*The Payment of Wages*, 1918, p. 115.)
[27] 'Freedom in the Guild', *New Age*, 5 Nov. 1914.

action in the evening, with the power of dismissing him if he fails to conform to their wishes, has been found by experience to be an impossible one.'[28] It was all said to be 'a matter of psychology'; but we might well want to look a little more closely at the exact nature of this psychological impossibility before accepting it as axiomatic. The Webbs also invoked the teaching of history to suggest a terrible inevitability about the failure of all 'self-governing workshops' (of which they believed Guild Socialism to be merely the latest variant). Beatrice had written off the idea of the self-governing workshop as 'that "charmer" within the order of thought but gay deceiver within the "order of things"', and she and Sidney set out to document this early verdict.[29] Cole's reading of history was rather different, leading him to deny that the self-governing feature of the self-governing workshops was the decisive factor in their demise, and to emphasize instead the capitalist environment in which they operated. So here, too, was an area in which it might be possible to furnish some evidence which would have some bearing on the argument.

There were many other propositions of both the Guild and the Fabian position which might be open to some form of empirical investigation. For example, was it true, as the Webbs maintained, that the vocational tie was stronger than that of an industry as a whole, so that it was 'for his vocation that every worker intuitively aspires to all the self-determination that can be attained?'[30] Would a vocation or craft rather be subject to the decisions of the whole community than be part of a single industry democracy, so that 'paradoxically' Guild Socialism turned out to be 'actually incompatible with "workers' control" in its most legitimate and . . . highest sense?'[31] On the other hand, was it true, as the Guild Socialists maintained, that democracy in industry would release a democratic vitality in the wider society? What of Cole's oft-repeated adage that 'a taste of control will produce a taste for control'? Can we properly attribute apathy about politics to the lack of democracy in industry? Was it true that 'over the vast mechanism of modern politics the individual has no control, not because the state is too big, but because he is given no chance of learning the rudiments of self-government within a smaller unit'?[32] Would democracy in industry

[28] S. and B. Webb, *A Constitution for the Socialist Commonwealth*, p. 161.
[29] Beatrice Webb, *My Apprenticeship*, 1926, p. 377. Also Appendix E (ibid.) on 'Why The Self-Governing Workshop Has Failed'.
[30] S. and B. Webb, *The Consumers' Co-operative Movement*, p. 471.
[31] Ibid., p. 472.
[32] 'Freedom in the Guild', *New Age*, 12 Nov. 1914.

succeed in making the factory less of 'a mere prison of boredom and useless toil', or did the nature of modern production make democracy irrelevant in this respect? Would a system of functional democracy produce that flowering of art and science, taste and appreciation, predicted by the Guild Socialists? At a basic level, did men want to control the conditions of their working life and to assume the responsibilities which went with such control? Finally, Guild Socialists and the Webbs came to differ fundamentally on an even more basic issue: how important was the work situation anyway? It was a cardinal tenet of Guild Socialism that the lack of real industrial democracy induced in man a stultifying psychology of servility which went far beyond the factory gate. But the Webbs insisted that man's real enslavement was during his unproductive and non-producing years: 'it is not so much in the hours of work that a manual working man or woman . . . at present suffers; it is in the limitations which his present penury sets to his use of his hours of leisure'.[33] By concentrating on the conditions under which production was carried on, Guild Socialism was said to be a crudely materialist doctrine; whereas state socialism would provide the resources for a fuller and freer life for the whole community. It was clear from this that an analysis of the social and psychological significance of work would have important consequences for prescriptive theory. But these are all problems in this area which are easier to identify than resolve. Here it is suggested only that it might be possible to assemble evidence which would have some bearing on some of the arguments which were used by both sides in this debate about democracy.[34]

Indeed, this approach is true to Webbian methodology itself, and was used by the Webbs in 1920 to justify their shift to a position far more favourable to the general notion of trade union participation in the management of industry. The abolition of the wage system was now recognized as an abiding working-class aspiration, and a democracy of consumers was acknowledged to suffer from 'the outstanding defect to the manual-working producer that, so far as his own working life is concerned, he does not feel it to be Democracy at all!'[35] In an Appendix to the 1920 edition of their *History of Trade Unionism*, the Webbs identified three main factors causing them to modify their earlier

[33] S. and B. Webb, 'What Syndicalism Means', p. 18.
[34] See P. Blumberg, *Industrial Democracy: The Sociology of Participation*, 1968, and C. Pateman, *Participation and Democratic Theory*, 1970, as examples of the attempt to apply evidence to argument in this area. Other relevant evidence is succinctly presented, and interestingly interpreted, in M. Mann, *Consciousness and Action Among the Western Working Class*, 1973.
[35] S. and B. Webb, *The History of Trade Unionism*, 1920 edn., p. 711.

absolutist opposition to producer participation in industrial control.
These were: (i) the growth among manual and technical workers of
'corporate self-consciousness and public spirit' (rather than the corporate selfishness which the Webbs had previously laid down as
axiomatic) (ii) the diffusion of education (iii) further discoveries in the
technique of democratic institutions, above all the technique of devolv-
ing responsibility to organized groups. This last point was especially
important, for it marked a shift in the Webb position from the old
one-dimensional collectivism to a new group view of the political
process. This shift was clearly spelled out in Sidney Webb's lecture on
'A Stratified Democracy', where political decisions were seen increasingly to be the result of a process of 'going to the group' rather than
to the traditional channels of parliamentary and geographical democracy. Guild Socialism was seen as one expression of the group idea, but
defective because of its narrow focus on the industrial working class.
What was needed was a theory of democracy which combined an active
role for organized groups with the best elements of the traditional
geographical representation. In their *Socialist Constitution*, the Webbs
offered their own considered version of such a democracy. 'The condition of any genuine Democracy, of the wide diffusion of any effective
freedom', they wrote, 'is such a systematic complication of social
machinery as will negative alike the monarchical and the capitalist
dictatorships, and prevent the rise of any other. The price of liberty . . .
is the complication of a highly differentiated and systematically coordinated social order'.[36] So here was a Fabian pluralism, strikingly
similar—at least in spirit—to the 'democratic pluralism' of more
recent vintage.

It remains to say something about the extent to which Fabian and
Guild thinking on the problem of democracy arrived at some sort of
synthesis by around 1920. This was the Fabian claim—indeed Fabianism, not unlike Hinduism, liked to boast of an amorphousness which
enabled it to contain and embrace rival doctrines. Thus, according to
Shaw, the alleged antithesis between Guild Socialism and Fabian
collectivism was 'imaginary' and 'vanished at the first touch of the
skilled criticism the Fabians brought to bear on it'.[37] But did it?
Certainly the Webbs had travelled a considerable distance from their
Industrial Democracy of 1897 to their *Socialist Constitution* of 1920, but had

[36] S. and B. Webb, *A Constitution for the Socialist Commonwealth*, p. 202.
[37] G. B. Shaw, Appendix 'On Guild Socialism' (p. 266) to E. R. Pease, *The History of the Fabian Society*, 1916.

they really arrived at a different destination? It is true that in their later writings they did accept a Guild Socialist definition of the crucial issues to be tackled. Terminology reflected this change: there was less talk of efficiency, waste, anarchy, individualism, poverty and the rest of the Fabian stock-in-trade, and much more of power, status and authority. It was the distribution of power which was now accepted as central: 'the central wrong of the Capitalist System', wrote the Webbs, 'is neither the poverty of the poor nor the riches of the rich; it is the power which the mere ownership of the instruments of production gives to a relatively small section of the community over the actions of their fellow-citizens and over the mental and physical environment of successive generations.'[38] Accepted, too, was Cole's analysis of the nature of representation, and the Webbs devised schemes for representing men in each of their leading functional roles. They stressed the value to men of democratic participation. Democracy now was necessary, not merely for the expression of grievances or to check abuses of power, but crucially for 'that development of personality, and that enlargement of faculty and desire dependent on the assumption of responsibility and the exercise of will'[39]—in industry no less than in politics. The Webbs would now yield to no-one in their enthusiasm for the democratic cause.

But this acceptance by the Webbs of the basic categories of the Guild Socialist argument scarcely disguised the fact that they were as far as ever from accepting the implications of that argument. The old authority relationships, once thought indispensable to industrial efficiency, could now be largely abandoned—but only because decisions were now seen as emerging from a consultative process in which the stream of reports from disinterested experts would exercise decisive influence. Of course, the representatives of the workers would find a place in the decision-making process. Perhaps literally a place: 'It is a real social gain,' wrote the Webbs, 'that the General Secretary of the Swiss Railwaymen's Trade Union should sit as one of the five members of the supreme governing body of the Swiss railway administration.'[40] We might wonder how participation of this order would produce that

[38] S. and B. Webb, *A Constitution for the Socialist Commonwealth*, p. xii. Pease, the official Fabian historian, identified the elimination of poverty as the key Fabian objective. (Op. cit., p. 257.) Now the Webbs seemed closer to Cole's view that 'Socialists have all too often fixed their eyes upon the material misery of the poor without realising that it rests upon the spiritual degradation of the slave'. (*Self-Government in Industry*, p. 35.)

[39] S. and B. Webb, *A Constitution for the Socialist Commonwealth*, p. 100.

[40] S. and B. Webb, Appendix on 'The Relationship of Trade Unionism to the Government of Industry', in *The History of Trade Unionism*, 1920 edn., p. 760.

widespread 'development of personality . . . dependent on the assumption of responsibility and the exercise of will' which the Webbs now believed was so important. The truth was, it seems, that the harmony model of the Webbs was seen as making redundant most of the traditional arguments about democracy. Authority was to be transformed by being universalized: what would disappear would be *personal* authority, for we were all servants now. ('There is something rather fine in the heraldic motto of the Prince of Wales, "I serve"[41]—Sidney Webb.) The old problem of 'government from above' versus 'government from below' was now dissolved in a common subservience to the community and to facts. What this meant for authority relationships at work was delightfully expressed by Sidney: 'The manager, instead of saying to one man "Go", and he goeth, to another man "Do this", and he has to do it, will give him his job to do, tell him how to do it, and leave him to do it in his own way; just what a reasonable person does with his cook.'[42] Vocational self-determination turned out merely to be the right of a vocation to be consulted in matters which directly concerned that vocation; and the model of a vocation as conceived by the Webbs was much closer to the B.M.A. or even the Jockey Club than to an industrial trade. The community was still king; and organized democracy would simply allow and encourage functional groups to develop a professional ethic in the common interest. Instead of subverting social harmony, democracy turned out to reinforce it; and so we were all democrats now.

Of course, Guild Socialism was in many respects a harmony model too. If the Webbs largely managed to dispense with democracy, Cole perhaps managed to make it a little too easy. He offered a set of propositions about democracy (e.g. that men demand participation, that they must first participate at work, that industrial democracy would provide the stimulus for a wider democratic energy etc.) and an organizational model of a society which incorporated these propositions. Yet both the propositions and the model raised issues which Cole failed to handle satisfactorily. Some of these issues were perhaps necessarily elusive for a projected participatory society, but they did require serious treatment. The problem of the relationship between democracy and efficiency, for example, was something which Guild Socialism had to tackle, not least because this area was a natural target for Fabian critics. Yet Cole was both impatient and ambivalent on this point, seeming to vacillate between an insistence that industrial

---

[41] S. Webb, 'A Stratified Democracy', p. 8.
[42] Ibid.

democracy would be progressive and innovatory in its work practices because only free men could do good work, and a belief that the obsession with efficiency was the occupational hazard of unregenerate bureaucrats. Cole *knew* that industrial democracy would produce a workforce committed to experimentation and excellence, and if proof was demanded then the reply could only be that in such matters 'an ounce of belief is worth a ton of proof'.[43] A similar ambivalence was evident on the question of leadership in a democratic setting. On the one hand, Cole was loud in his assertion of the democratic capabilities of Beatrice Webb's 'average sensual man', yet was no less dogmatic about the necessity and integrity of the leadership function. Far from involving the extinction of a specific leadership role in social organization, Cole's democratic theory was deliberately designed to strengthen that role. In pursuit of that end, a distinction was made between those (supervisory) jobs where direct election was appropriate, and those (technical) jobs where an indirect, appointive system properly applied. The distinction was often difficult to make; nor was it less difficult to demonstrate how a direct sense of control would be engendered in industry (and elsewhere) if the democratic machinery was subject to an elaborate filtering process. Cole's attachment to leadership could not avoid this complexity, for he was still Fabian enough to insist that 'a factory administered by constant mass votes would be neither efficient nor at all a pleasant place to work in'.[44] Even when the necessity for leadership was established, it did not ensure that a democratic society would encourage a vigorous leadership of ability rather than a tepid mediocrity. Here again Cole did little more than repeat his articles of faith about a democracy which would 'afford full scope for its supermen'.[45] A participatory society might well be quick to recognize the value of good leadership, whilst leaders themselves might equally well prefer to exercise their art in a non-coercive democratic environment; but these were propositions which required something more than mere reiteration to sustain their validity.

There are other difficulties which go even more directly to the heart of Cole's theory. In his scheme of coordinated functional democracy both the coordination and the democracy came a little too easily. The functional principle integrated as well as separated, and there was a

[43] *Labour in the Commonwealth*, p. 126. Cole *knew* that 'the key to real efficiency is self-government....' (*Self-Government in Industry*, p. 181.)

[44] *Guild Socialism Re-Stated*, p. 50. Similarly, 'a mass vote on a matter of technique understood only by a few experts would be a manifest absurdity'. (idem.)

[45] *Labour in the Commonwealth*, p. 113.

tendency to *define* group activity in terms of the proper performance of social function, thereby producing a deceptively minimal amount of inter-group conflict and a deceptively easy process of social adjudication and coordination. A central regulatory body was therefore envisaged as doing little more than providing occasional oil for a social machine whose parts were in good and harmonious working order. In fact, of course, inter-group disagreement might be considerable, not least in the area of economic structure and allocation, and this might well reflect itself in the deliberations of the representative regulatory body itself. If inter-group coordination presented difficulties, so too did intra-group democracy. Cole was aware of the problems here, consistently pointing to the need to avoid the development of a Guild bureaucracy or a democratic oligarchy—'a new form of bureaucracy resulting in the ossification of the Guild'[46]—and introduced structural devices (e.g. the recall) to offset this sort of tendency. At the same time, however, the maintenance of intra-group democracy was not seen as dependent primarily upon a structured environment. Rather, there was a tendency to assume that because men shared a common *area* of interest they would also share a common *policy* position inside that area; whereas in fact proximity of interest and knowledge might well increase the scope for disagreement. This might be no bad thing, of course, but it does require some consideration of the mechanisms of opinion formation and policy formulation inside democratic organizations and within the wider society. Not only did Cole tend to assume that division by function would itself ease decision-making, but also that functional democracy would usher in such a spiritual revolution that structural provisions and mechanical safeguards would be rendered unnecessary or redundant. If the spirit was right, democracy would work; the functional scheme would produce this spirit, therefore it would work. In essence, it was these two propositions—both questionable of course—that Cole nailed to his mast. They provided his real answer to the alleged threat of bureaucracy, for 'the danger of bureaucracy in any system of organization varies inversely with the spirit of independence displayed by the individuals whom it governs.'[47] It was spirit and motive which explained the present alienation and lethargy under capitalism and which would provide the surest antidote to the ossification of Guild democracy. Indeed, the Guild organization of industry would produce such a spirit of cooperation in the factory that the

[46] *Guild Socialism Re-Stated*, p. 61.
[47] 'Freedom in the Guild', *New Age*, 12 Nov. 1914.

'mere machinery of democracy' might well remain 'nominally in the background'.[48] Cole's insistence on the motivational basis of social and economic systems was one of the major constants in his work.[49] However, it may seem an inadequate response to the problem of maintaining the reality of participatory democracy in an organizational setting.

Cole's treatment of the relationship between democracy and freedom was also unsatisfactory. He was clear that freedom was not merely the absence of constraint, but found it much more difficult to define its positive status and content. Indeed, far from feeling the need to defend a conception of freedom even against democracy itself, Cole seemed to want to deny the problem by making freedom and democracy synonymous. 'That community is most free', he wrote, 'in which all the individuals have the greatest share in the government of their common life.'[50] Equally, that individual was most free who most participated. This description of Cole's position needs instant qualification, of course, for he defended a realm of individual freedom outside the scope of all associational organization, and insisted on the ultimate right of the individual to impose his own loyalties and obligations irrespective of group affiliations and majority decisions. Yet this did more to defend the moral status of the individual when he was being coerced than to indicate the sort of organizational environment in which such coercion was more or less likely and the sort of structural constraints which gave a content to freedom which was more than just moral. The diffusion of power inherent in pluralism might plausibly be cited in this respect, yet it was not enough. It was not enough because Cole was wedded to a participatory definition of freedom which blurred the status of the individual in relation to the group.

The source of this definition was Cole's commitment to activism itself. It was this which provided the foundation for his democratic theory and which coloured his conception of the nature of freedom. It was this, too, which led him to insist on servility as the central product and evil of life under capitalism. In making authority external to men, capitalism stripped them of their democratic energies. To Cole, men were born active; it was capitalism which rendered them passive. This

[48] *Guild Socialism Re-Stated*, p. 58.

[49] 'A choice of system is always primarily and fundamentally a choice, not of the machinery to be created, but of the motives to which the principal appeal is to be made.' ('Motives in Industry', *The Venturer*, Mar. 1920.)

[50] *Self-Government in Industry*, p. 183. Cole also wrote that: 'Freedom is not simply the absence of restraint: it assumes a higher form when it becomes self-government.' ('Freedom in the Guild', *New Age*, 5 Nov. 1914.)

attachment to participation as a fundamental human good in its own right, as a school of political education and personal development, places Cole in the mainstream of participatory democratic theory. For example, his argument was strikingly similar to that of J. S. Mill.[51] The antithesis between activity and passivity as the key distinguishing feature of social systems was basic to Guild Socialism, providing the inspiration for the democratic development of that theory in Cole's hands. His emphasis on the centrality of human will in social action has already been noticed, and will have to be noticed again in various contexts. It appeared here as the foundation for a theory of participatory democracy designed to provide ample scope for that active exercise of will which was seen as intrinsic to the definition of a human being, and which was negated by capitalism and state socialism alike. It may well be, of course, that this whole conception was wrong, resulting in the construction of an intricate democratic model which grossly exaggerated men's participatory inclinations and capabilities. This is a frequent allegation;[52] and certainly Cole did little to refute it. The important point here, however, is that Cole's commitment to an activist social world does much to explain his development of a particular democratic theory. It also provided his essential justification of that theory against critics who charged it with inefficiency and much else. At bottom, democracy was right because 'the one thing in the world that supremely matters is the free exercise of human will', whatever its 'factual result', even if that result was 'a hopeless mess'.[53] Such a mess, the product of the active exercise of will, was infinitely preferable to an order imposed from without. Despite spending much effort in demonstrating that a democratic society would not have a messy outcome, this was ultimately Cole's answer. The possibility of chaos was the price of an active democracy; only 'Prussians and bureaucrats'[54] would think the price too high.

---

[51] Mill believed that: 'the only government which can fully satisfy all the exigencies of the social state is one in which the whole people participate; that any participation, even in the smallest public function, is useful.' (*Considerations on Representative Government*, 1861, in *Utilitarianism, Liberty and Representative Government*, Everyman, 1910, p. 217.) Mill's case for participation, however, seems to conflict sharply with his cautious scheme of representative government.

[52] For example, Margaret Cole suggests that it was a conception involving so much participatory activity that 'the interest of the ordinary man would lapse altogether, and the final result would be the not very exciting spectacle of a small handful of busybodies manning all the "functional" committees.' ('Guild Socialism and the Labour Research Department', in Briggs and Saville, (ed.), *Essays in Labour History*, Vol. II, p. 274.)

[53] *Labour in the Commonwealth*, p. 219.

[54] Ibid., p. 223.

If Cole made his democratic theory too easy, reflected in an inadequate treatment of both inter-group and intra-group relations, much of the explanation may be found in his belief in the essentially harmonious implications of the functional principle. It was this which tended to give Cole's democratic model the impression of an 'imposed pluralism'[55] in which roles were defined in relation to a central organizing principle which was essentially cooperative. In Cole's hands, functional democracy was separative yet integrative. The result was not quite harmony, for that was seen as a passive Fabian conception far removed from the sheer activism, even turbulence, of a Guild Socialist society. Rather, the result was community, alive with democratic activity yet rooted in a basic unity of purpose. It was this communitarian vision of a society of fellowship which ultimately informed Cole's theory of democracy, just as it provided the foundation for his theory of the state.

Against those who suggested that his democratic society was excessively mechanical in construction, Cole would concede the charge. The aim was not to develop a refined constitutional structure, but to suggest what a society which genuinely took democracy as its central organizing principle might in fact look like. This involved a number of important propositions that still seem relevant. For example, that even if the class character of existing society was abolished, it would still fail to meet the conditions of reasonable human association; that representative democracy must be a complex social process and not a single general act; that while everything may be everyone's concern, some things concern some people in special ways (it affects everyone how the coal mines are run, but it affects the miners in a special way); that unless a man felt a sense of freedom *at his work* he would not enjoy freedom in the wider society either; that the future of society was better trusted to an active social democracy than to a band of disinterested experts—and so on.

A final proposition, of course, was that Fabian collectivism would meet none of these conditions of the good life. Guild Socialism denied what Fabianism asserted—that in mass industrial society man necessarily lost control over his own life and immediate circumstances and found his own true freedom only in service to the wider community. A central problem for democratic and socialist theory was at issue here.

---

[55] E. Berg, *Democracy and the Majority Principle*, 1965, p. 100. Berg notes the definitional harmony in Cole's argument, which 'turns out to be largely a "non sequitur": his functional society by definition implies social harmony; his program aims at constructing such a society; the realization of this program will consequently inaugurate a state of social harmony'. (P. 99.)

What was to be the size of the democratic unit? Could a collective control compensate for the loss of a more direct control over social life? On this basic issue the Webbs never wavered. They shed no tears over the demise of the old direct or 'primitive' democracy, for it produced only anarchy and turbulence. The rise of socialism was important above all else because it suggested the possibility of regaining collectively what had been lost individually.[56] The real change involved in the transition to socialism had ultimately little to do with authority relationships or the nature of work, but with the expropriation of capitalist surplus value by a state which would then provide the material resources for a fuller life for the whole community. A whole definition of socialism was involved here, a definition challenged by the Guild Socialists in the name of democracy, thereby earning for themselves the castigation of the Webbs as 'those impatient democrats who will not take the trouble to understand the problem, and who petulantly demand, at the same time, the elaborations and refinements of civilisation and the anarchy and simplicity of the primitive age'.[57] In terms of the famous Webbian division of the world into the 'A's (anarchists) and the 'B's (bureaucrats), Cole seemed to belong so eminently to the former as the Webbs themselves so conspicuously to the latter. Cole would willingly assent to this classification, though giving it a rather different content. Thus of Sidney Webb: 'He still conceives the mass of men as persons who ought to be decently treated, not as persons who ought freely to organise their own conditions of life; in short, his conception of a new social order is still that of an order that is ordained from without, and not realised from within.'[58]

[56] 'The very fact that, in modern society, the individual thus necessarily loses control over his own life, makes him desire to regain collectively what has become individually impossible.' (S. and B. Webb, *Industrial Democracy*, p. 850.)

[57] S. and B. Webb, *A Constitution for the Socialist Commonwealth*, pp. 201–2.

[58] 'Recent Developments in the British Labour Movement', *American Economic Review*, Sept. 1918.

V

Socialism and Guild Socialism

'I WELCOME the gild movement,' announced R. H. Tawney, 'because it brings English socialism out of the backwaters and bypaths of government regulation, in which it was boring itself ten years ago, into the mainstream of the Socialist tradition...."[1] Yet if Guild Socialism did really provide, as Tawney suggested, a path along which a sterile domestic socialism could find its way back to a wider socialist tradition, it was a path of a rather distinctive kind. Indeed, much of Guild Socialist propaganda was explicitly designed to demonstrate just how domestic and distinctive it was. The particularity of the national context was emphasized, along with the need to develop native theories relevant to that context. Cole was consistently hostile to approaches which seemed to neglect this necessity, and equally consistent in his affirmation of respect for the boundaries of nation and culture. More is involved here than Cole's alleged status as a 'Little Englander',[2] though that is important too; rather, he wanted to state general propositions about the limiting factors relevant both to political theory and to political expectation. The central proposition was that 'the pure class-conscious cosmopolitan of some Socialist theory is as unnatural and as unreal as the pure "economic man" of the older economists.'[3] The collapse of socialist internationalism on the outbreak of war in 1914 had been predicted by Cole, whilst the war itself seemed to provide ample confirmation of the continuing strength of national loyalties. If the workers rallied to the capitalist state it was because that state was 'in some sense their own'.[4] Socialist theory had to recognize this fact, involving also a recognition that a real international socialism could

---

[1] R. H. Tawney, early 1920s: 'Speeches on various occasions', Tawney Papers, British Library of Political and Economic Science.

[2] 'He was not even a little Englander—really a little Southern Englander!' (Hugh Gaitskell, 'At Oxford in the Twenties', in A. Briggs and J. Saville (eds.), *Essays in Labour History*, 1960, p. 12.)

[3] *Labour in Wartime*, 1915, p. 21.

[4] Ibid., p. 3. It is quite wrong to say that during the war Cole 'discovered a national identity which superseded that of class'. (J. M. Winter, *Socialism and the Challenge of War 1912–1918*, 1974, p. 125.) The 'discovery' was made much earlier. (Cf. *World of Labour*, 1913, p. 196.)

come only as the product of a series of national socialisms, each appropriate to particular national settings and requirements.

The emphasis on national particularity, therefore, was basic to Guild Socialism, not least in the explanation of its own theoretical origins. This produced an insistence on its native credentials, often carried to quite eccentric lengths. As early as 1912, the *New Age* declared that: 'It should never be forgotten that the gild system was a genuine Saxon invention, as native to our genius as our language',[5] the clear implication of this being that a new guild system would itself have exemplary Saxon lineage. Especially was the need felt to distinguish Guild Socialism from that contemporary foreign import, syndicalism; so much so that the authors of *National Guilds*, the first statement of the *New Age* position, were proud to proclaim that 'not one of the writers of the book had ever read a single word by a French Syndicalist'.[6] In this statement it is tempting to regard 'French' as the crucial word. Cole was altogether distinct in this respect, for he had immersed himself in the literature of syndicalism before his formal adoption of a Guild Socialist position. Indeed, in the years before 1914 he was regarded, not least by himself, as a leading authority on the French movement.[7] He was at one with other Guild Socialists, however, in stressing the barriers to foreign importation (even should such importation be desirable) and in presenting Guild Socialism as a species of socialism uniquely appropriate to British tastes and conditions.

In essence, the claim made for Guild Socialism was that it offered a 'via media' between rival and defective brands of socialism which gave it not only an intrinsic theoretical superiority but also a special British relevance. The defective rivals were syndicalism and collectivism, the latter wanting to nationalize but not socialize, the former wanting to socialize but in a manner careless of wider interests. British socialism, it was claimed, had become too collectivist; syndicalism provided a valuable if ultimately misguided corrective to this; Guild Socialism represented a true synthesis which, by incorporating the insights of both collectivism and syndicalism, put socialism on a new and fruitful footing. Syndicalism was correct in emphasizing producer control in industry; collectivism was correct in stressing the need for economic

---

[5] *New Age*, 18 Jan. 1912.

[6] 'Towards National Guilds', *New Age*, 11 June 1914, which added that 'the whole conception of National Guilds is home-grown English'. Later the same authors declared: 'we are English nationalists even before we are Socialists and Trade Unionists'. (*New Age*, 13 May 1915.)

[7] His library reveals an extensive collection of syndicalist literature at this time, and he prepared MS notes for 'A Primer of Syndicalism' (Cole Collection).

ownership by the community as a whole; yet both were finally inadequate as theories of socialism for each denied what the other asserted.
In developing its central conception of a partnership between a state
which owns and a guild which controls, Guild Socialism claimed to
have discovered the only satisfactory foundation for a general theory of
socialism. Certainly this was Cole's central and consistent claim, for he
presented Guild Socialism in essentially synthetic terms, deploying the
language of balance and reconciliation. 'Socialism cannot afford to
neglect either producer or consumer', he wrote in 1913; 'if, as Collectivism, it forgets the one, it becomes a dead theory incapable of
inspiring enthusiasm or bringing about a change of heart; if, as Syndicalism, it forgets the other, it falls into sectional egoism and loses the
element of community and brotherhood in individualism and self-
assertion.'[8] The great virtue of Guild Socialism, by contrast, was that it
prevented the potentially exploitive control of either producer or consumer. In 1920 Cole was still insisting that the historic task of Guild
Socialism had been to 'hold the balance between these two schools of
thought'.[9] For Cole especially, its central value was its status as a theory
of community. As such, it offered the promise of a successful assault on
the hegemony of the state without the perils of a lapse into sectionalism.

If Marx figured little in this synthetic enterprise of Guild Socialism, it
was chiefly because he seemed largely irrelevant to it. In so far as Guild
theory had a specifically economic content, such as in the early work of
S. G. Hobson, it did reflect a tacit Marxism. Yet that economic analysis
was designed to provide a supportive framework within which the
central human meaning of the wage system could be examined.[10] When
Guild Socialists discussed exploitation, their prime concern was not
with the economic extraction of surplus value but with the human
implications of the treatment of labour as a commodity. At this stage,
Cole was little concerned with economics, often becoming impatient
with those who were so concerned. For example, in presenting its case
for producer control in industry, syndicalism 'can make a far more
reasonable demand, if, abandoning abstract economics and leaving the
theory of value to take care of itself, it adopts the standpoint of concrete
and commonsense ethics'.[11] The aim was to break the tyranny of
economics, not to perpetuate it. If syndicalism and collectivism pro-

[8] *World of Labour*, p. 368.
[9] *Guild Socialism Re-Stated*, p. 37.
[10] 'The Guildsmen have not so much tried to prove the Marxian doctrines of labour-value and surplus-value as they have assumed them.' (N. Carpenter, *Guild Socialism*, 1922, p. 19.)
[11] *World of Labour*, p. 350.

vided the decisive theoretical environment for Guild Socialists, it was because they were doctrines which made crucial statements about the power relationships in social and economic systems, defined by Guild Socialism as the central issue for social analysis and social action. By contrast, Marxism then—if not now—seemed to address itself primarily to the realm of 'abstract economics', thereby neglecting that primacy of slavery over poverty basic to the Guild Socialist position. The economic exploitation of capitalism was accepted as its defining characteristic, yet its central evil was less the production of surplus value than the status implications of a commodity theory of labour. To a world unversed in that industry of Marxian exegesis which has given us the 'early' Marx, it seemed that Marx had little to contribute to this human analysis of capitalism.

This is not to say that Cole ignored Marxism, or that he had slight regard for its theoretical accomplishments. Indeed, he insisted on its value to the working-class movement if properly presented and understood. What this required was much less attention to the Marxist theory of value ('If the question is raised whether Marx's theory of value is true or untrue, the answer must be that it is neither true nor untrue, that it was useful. . . . Neither it nor any other theory of value can be held to possess absolute truth. . . .')[12] and much more attention to its historical approach to economics. History, not economic science, was the key Marxist contribution to social analysis. Cole's consistent point at this time was that for Marx himself his theory of value was essentially 'a polemic, directed against the political economy of his day',[13] a fact obscured only by the errors of his latterday disciples. It was as a theory of capitalist development, as a philosophy of history, that Marxism had its great contribution to make. Even in this respect Cole, much versed in Sorel at this time, was less concerned to argue the validity of Marxian theory than to stress its usefulness to the labour movement in injecting it with a confidence rooted in a sense of its historical development. In general, Guild Socialism preferred its own description of this historical process, in terms of a shift from chattel slavery to wage slavery defined as a power relationship; but it shared with Marxism a conception of the future viewed as a culmination of a class-based historical evolution.[14] Cole's own belief in

[12] 'The Place of Marx in Economic Teaching', W.E.A. Tutors' Conference, Sept. 1919.

[13] 'A Philosopher on Marxism', *Highway*, Feb. 1915.

[14] 'We envisage National Guilds, as Marx envisaged his conception of Socialism, as the culmination and completion of this long process [of class struggle].' (Cole, 'National Guilds and the Balance of Powers', *New Age*, 16 Nov. 1916.)

the political value of historical analysis was to remain basic to his thought.

Cole's treatment of Marx provides an important clue to a central feature of Guild Socialism. As a theory of socialism, Guild theory was deeply rooted in voluntarism, spontaneity, even sheer activism. Thus, in discussing a theory of historical development, Cole was emphatic that it should be a theory of historic possibilities, not of materialist determination. There could be no 'science' of history, only an understanding of its possibilities. Marxism was valuable in so far as it was alive to the nature of historical opportunity; but harmful to the extent that its claim to scientific status smacked of determinism. Cole contrasted the moralism of the early socialists with the scientism of Marx, the latter inducing a 'decay of idealism'[15] which led the socialist movement into the path of reformism. The great advantage of Guild Socialism, it was claimed, was that it combined the material analysis and the moral demand, making it a ' "scientific Utopianism", a synthesis of all that is best in rival schools of Socialist thought'.[16] Just as Cole's synthetic appetite had swallowed up syndicalism and collectivism, now it claimed to have digested the best of Marx too. The same attitude which led Cole to criticize Marxism moved him to endorse the spirit of syndicalism. As a doctrine, syndicalism was fatally flawed, of course, for it was not the task of socialism, as Cole liked to put it, merely to entrench the coal-miners in the place of the coal-owners. Yet ultimately syndicalism was preferable to collectivism, for it was at least the mistake of men not automatons, the 'infirmity of noble minds'[17] which looked to active, willing men for the creation of their own social world. If Marxism was defective to the extent that it removed men from the driving seat of history, syndicalism was correct to the extent that it firmly put them back into it.

So central was this whole approach to Cole's Guild Socialist theory that it needs some emphasis. In one form, it appeared as the insistence on the role of ideas in the making of history, with a consequent denial of the power of the material world. 'No movement can be dangerous unless it is a movement of ideas,'[18] declared Cole, whilst social theories

---

[15] Cole and Mellor, 'Socialism Old and New', *Herald*, 3 Oct. 1914. Hence the paradox 'that Marx, himself a revolutionary, is largely responsible for the lapse of Socialism into a futile and self-destructive reformism'. (idem.)

[16] Ibid.

[17] *Self-Government in Industry*, p. 46.

[18] Ibid., p. 24.

were 'the stuff of which revolutions are made.'[19] A long catalogue of such statements could be assembled from Cole's writing at this period, all designed to support the same theme. The labour movement, especially its industrial wing, had become increasingly sterile precisely because it had abandoned its idealism for a tepid materialism. So antipathetic to such a position was Guild Socialism, that it frequently felt the need to apologize for its attention to the material world at all. It was simply a temporary and distasteful labour of necessity, a removal of the chief obstacle to the realm of freedom beyond. 'We ought to pay attention to industry', wrote Cole, 'not because we are materialists, but absolutely and precisely because we are spiritualists.'[20] The voluntarism of Guild Socialism was a natural consequence of its idealism, for it was men as the possessors of ideas who made history. That labour must be the agent of its own emancipation was for Guild Socialism not a slogan but a fact. Such emancipation could not merely be the product of a conjunction of material forces, nor could it be won *for* labour from outside. It could be won only by the active exercise of will on the part of men armed with an ideal; for 'are not we Guildsmen "industrial Lamarckians", fighting our battle against the "industrial Darwinians" or Marxian determinists?'[21] In simplest form, Guild Socialist man chose his ideal and willed its achievement. By contrast, Fabian man was the passive object of social engineering and Marxian man the actor in a historical drama the script of which was already written. The sheer virulence of Cole's attacks on Fabians and Fabianism, for example, was above all else his response to a creed which seemed so devoid of spirit and imagination that it denied the centrality of active human will in social action.[22]

Equally, his enthusiasm for the new industrial militancy sprang from a belief that it was a vitalizing impulse, a quickening of the sense of being alive, an expression of active will. The strike weapon was the

[19] Ibid., p. 131. Cole's MS 'Primer of Syndicalism' (n.d., 1912–13?) was lyrical in its account of the role of ideas in history: 'ultimately behind all revolt, and still more behind all attempts at reconstruction, will be found the volitional force of an idea. . . .' Similarly, his contemporary sketch for 'An Outline of Political Theory' (MS, n.d.), stretched, in a firmly idealist idiom, from Socrates to Orage, with no mention of Marx. (Cole Collection.)

[20] *Labour in the Commonwealth*, p. 32.

[21] 'Hussein' (Cole, pseud.), 'The Sign of the Book', *Guildsman*, Oct. 1919. He was always impatient with doctrines which suggested that 'the human race marches upon its belly'. (*Social Theory*, p. 146.)

[22] The Fabians 'know' said Cole; 'if they could but imagine, their souls might still be saved'. ('The New Statesmanship', *The University Socialist*, 1913.) A letter to Beatrice Webb captured his attitude: 'I believe this is a rude letter; but I cannot write temperately of Fabians.' (14 Mar. 1917; Passfield Papers, L.S.E.)

quintessential expression of the free will of labour, and Cole employed a Sorelian idiom in his discussion of it. Apathy and passivity were the enemy; activism and spontaneity the need. If history was useful, it was to fortify will in the present. Cole was emphatic that the mobilization of will among men armed with an ideal was the key to the emancipation of labour. 'If the workers want to destroy capitalism', he declared, 'and are ready to take its place and to assume its power, there is absolutely nothing to stop them from doing so'[23]—provided they wanted it enough. It will be necessary later to say something more about this 'absolutely nothing', but for the moment it stands as a clear illustration of Cole's general approach both to social theory and to social action. The particular application of this approach to the world of labour was no less clear: 'what is wrong with Labour today is not nearly so much lack of power as lack of will and imagination'.[24] Guild Socialism was presented as an ideal uniquely capable of inspiring the imagination and mobilizing the will of the labour movement.

If this says something about the distinctiveness of Cole's general approach to social theory, against which particular theories could be examined and assessed, it remains to say something more about the distinctiveness of his own particular theory of socialism. Certainly its 'Guild' prefix made it sound distinctive, and many of its adherents were anxious to define the exact content of that distinctiveness, often in different ways. Much internal discussion in the Guild movement turned on the extent of the aesthetic, medieval, localist content of the Guild idea, thereby revealing the range of ingredients which went into the making of that idea. Here, as elsewhere, Cole endeavoured to adopt a middle course designed to reconcile the irreconcilable, but which exposed him to heavy fire from the flanks. To A. J. Penty, the father of the Guild idea, Cole had got himself 'entangled in this net of Modernism', for he had failed to understand that there was 'ultimately no sure foothold anywhere between pure Collectivism and pure Medievalism'.[25] Penty was an uncompromising medievalist, firmly localist in orientation, with a deep hatred of machine production. Cole had much emotional sympathy with this position, stressing the valuable lessons of the medieval world and suggesting a revival of craftsmanship when machine production had done its job; yet his distance from the Penty

---

[23] *Workers' Control in Industry*, Independent Labour Party, 1919, p. 14.
[24] Ibid., p. 15.
[25] Penty, 'Medievalism and Modernism', *New Age*, 23 Apr. 1914. In reply to an earlier criticism of this kind Cole confessed that, because he had come to Guild Socialism via Morris, Penty had 'hit me in a very tender spot'. ('Aestheticism and History', *New Age*, 9 Apr. 1914.)

school was enormous. Penty's ideal was to be found in the past, to which he genuinely wanted to return; Cole's ideal lived in a future to which he wanted to proceed armed with the lessons of the past. Penty was correct in his assertion of the ultimate irreconcilability of the two positions. In one sense, Cole was too informed about the medieval world ever to become a good medievalist, and was full of warnings about the dangers of a false medievalism prone to the 'parrot-lessons of slavish imitation'.[26] Why then should Cole have accepted the Guild label at all?

There are two main answers to this. In the first place, it did serve to indicate the valuable spiritual inheritance of a medieval Guild system which united the worker with his work in a self-governing and decentralized social structure. Whilst it would be wrong to suggest any direct historical continuity between the medieval Guilds and the modern trade unions, 'it does not follow that, because there is no historical connection, there is not a spiritual connection, a common motive present in both forms of association'.[27] Cole always preferred to use the language of spirit in this context. The second and major reason for Cole's adoption of a Guild label is that he inherited it. For his own purposes he would neither have invented it nor needed it. He became a Guild Socialist because in the theoretical climate of 1913 the group which called itself by that name seemed to offer the most attractive and fruitful suggestions for the development of socialist theory. Their conception of a partnership between self-governing industrial associations and a democratic state seemed to provide the foundation for a socialism which incorporated the insights and avoided the defects of rival schools of socialist thought. The fact that these industrial associations were to be known as Guilds was, for Cole at least, both incidental and accidental. Indeed, despite his espousal of the spiritual heritage of the medieval Guild system, it is clear that Cole would consistently have preferred a different nomenclature. Even as early as 1913, newly arrived in the Guild camp, he pointed to the confusion and misunderstanding caused by the term itself, which 'raises the doubt whether it is wise nowadays to use the word "Guild" at all',[28] when what was really meant was 'Trade Union'.

Some years later he launched a more direct attack along these lines, designed to transform the National Guilds League, the organizational

[26] *Guild Socialism Re-Stated*, p. 46.
[27] Introduction (p. xi) to G. Renard, *Guilds in the Middle Ages* (ed. Cole, 1919).
[28] *World of Labour*, p. 362.

arm of the Guild movement, into the Guild Socialist League. Here again, the intention was partly to avoid confusion by giving the movement a more modernist ring. Above all, however, the aim was now to locate the Guild idea firmly in a wider socialist tradition, and to give the Guild movement a clearly left orientation. Against those who insisted on the distinctiveness of the Guild position, Cole argued that 'National Guildsmen did not invent the doctrine of wage-abolition. It is an essentially Marxian Socialist doctrine, though many political Socialists have forgotten it.'[29] Equally, against those who treated socialism as a narrowly political doctrine, which could claim status only as a subsidiary element in a much larger tradition, Cole declared: 'When I think of Socialism I think of a great tradition of revolutionary action and agitation—of Robert Owen, of Karl Marx, of William Morris, and of a record quite as full of industrial as of political effort and achievement.'[30] For Cole, Guild Socialism offered an opportunity for integration and synthesis of a larger socialist tradition; for others, National Guilds represented a separate and distinct tradition, of which socialism was itself no more than a part. This basic difference of conception does much to explain both the doctrinal disagreements and the organizational tensions which contributed to the eventual collapse of the Guild movement.

Yet it needed the impact of external events to transform tensions into fatal divisions. Until that time it seemed possible to maintain the identity of Guild Socialism in terms of its central tenets. There was its conception of the end to be achieved; namely, a union of industrial self-government and community control. Inside that conception, much scope remained for argument about structure and definition, yet the end itself was broadly agreed. There was, also, its conception of the means whereby this end could be achieved, no less central in Guild Socialist theory than the end itself. The golden rule here was that economic power preceded political power, a formulation so basic to Guild Socialism that it was sometimes even contracted to a formula, E.P.P.P. In so far as this sought to establish the derivative status of the body politic, it was scarcely original of course, as Cole was ever anxious to remind Guildsmen. Its real meaning was strategical, producing an insistence on the necessity of industrial action coupled with a

[29] 'Name and Substance', *New Age*, 13 Feb. 1919. Cole added that 'whatever the medieval guilds were, they were certainly not Socialist'. (idem.)
[30] Ibid. Cf. 'National Guilds—not "Cole Socialism"' (*Guildsman*, Feb. 1919) for the opposition to Cole on this.

deep hostility to the formal world of politics. In S. G. Hobson's early statement of the Guild position, the bankruptcy of official Labour was a central theme; for, in his nice phrase, the Labour movement had consistently displayed 'a soft head for economics and a soft heart for politics'.[31] Throughout Guild thinking the need was stressed for a direct attack on the wage-system, and for a repudiation by the labour movement of the futilities of parliamentary politics. The reluctance of many Guild Socialists to acknowledge their doctrine as a species of socialism sprang from a suspicion that socialism was primarily 'political' in orientation. The Labour movement was vigorously denounced for having succumbed to the political embrace; its Fabian creed was pronounced sterile; nationalization was irrelevant: these were the insistent themes of Guild propaganda. The antipathy to politics was basic to Guild Socialism. It produced a sharp reaction from George Lansbury at the 1917 Conference of the National Guilds League, where a proposal to allow socialist bodies to affiliate to the League met opposition from those who suggested that the effect would be a dilution of the movement, involving a shift towards political action. 'Any one would think that a socialist was a species of leper', was Lansbury's reply, adding, 'I don't understand all this holy horror of politics.'[32] The source of this horror was a belief that industrial emancipation could only be won directly by industrial action, not circuitously by a parliamentarism which seemed to offer a short cut but which was really a cul-de-sac. The expression of this belief was a concentration on the industrial world of labour coupled with a hostile indifference to the political movement.

Cole himself endorsed much of all this. He yielded to no one in his contempt for parliamentary politics, stressed the illusory nature of political democracy, and happily dismissed the infant Labour Party as 'that sad failure of Socialism'.[33] He was vigorous in his denial that Fabian nationalization could provide a path to socialism and no less vigorous in his assertion of the centrality of industrial action. Yet his position was also more complex than a mere catalogue of such attitudes would suggest. It has already been noticed that his treatment of the state was rendered ambivalent by his attachment to a continuing organ of community control; and that he was unable to concede that the abolition of the class basis of society would itself solve problems of

---

[31] S. G. Hobson, *National Guilds*, 1914, p. 217.
[32] N. G. L. Conference report, 1917 (Cole Collection).
[33] *World of Labour*, p. 242.

political organization and control. It was also noticed that his approach to these issues was sensitive to developments in the contemporary world. Similar tensions reflected themselves in his discussion of the respective roles of political and economic action in the achievement of a Guild Socialist society. For example, whilst stressing the basic irrelevance of political action to economic emancipation and castigating official Labour for its pursuit of a shadow and neglect of its substance, Cole nevertheless retained a conception of a useful role to be performed by a political party of labour, 'a party standing definitely for the dispossessed',[34] pledged to political and economic emancipation. Cole's wrath was directed against a Labour party which stood in a dependent–independent relationship to Liberalism; and against an attitude which produced an exclusive, and ultimately disillusioning, concentration on the parliamentary arena.

His estimation of the value of political action was crucially influenced, as was seen earlier, by his developing conception of the place of nationalization in the achievement of Guild Socialism. It was noticed that his early espousal of nationalization as the decisive first step towards subsequent Guild control involved a considerable role for socialist political action; but that this was followed by a period during which nationalization was pronounced as irrelevant from a Guild perspective, in turn involving a dramatic devaluation of political action. Yet it was also noticed that this position itself came to be modified during the closing stages of the war, as Cole detected a dangerous corporatist tendency at work which could only be combated by a reassertion of the traditional importance of nationalization—and, therefore, of a socialist politics. Thus, by the end of the war, with capitalism and the state seen as forging a new form of economic control, with the Labour Party acquiring a new independence and programme, and with the triumph of a revolutionary party in Russia, Cole's mature Guild Socialist conception of the proper balance between industrial and political action had been developed. The primacy of industrial action was still upheld, along with the belief that economic emancipation could only be won finally through the exercise of economic power, but now Cole warned against an exclusive reliance on the industrial weapon. Political action might be secondary but it remained important, not least because Guild Socialism was rooted in a con-

---

[34] Ibid., p. 394. Such a party was seen as having 'an immense role to play' (ibid., p. 400). All this complicates any simple attribution of 'economism' to Cole's thought at this time (cf. J. M. Winter, op. cit., p. 99).

ception of a transformed political body working in partnership with a
democratized industry. This meant that Guild Socialists had a direct
interest in the direction of political development, which made it
imperative that they 'work at the reorganization, and also at the
limitation in function and power, of the State from within by means of
political action'.[35] Even the hallowed Guild formula about the precedence of economic power was now attacked by Cole for its inadequate
conception of the usefulness of political activity.[36]

These shifts in his position on this issue again serve to indicate his
tendency to want to reconcile and integrate competing positions inside
a Guild Socialist framework. In terms of this particular issue, he always
envisaged a balance between industrial and political action, rather
than an alternative. The task was to get the correct balance, based upon
considerations both of theory and practice. His mature assessment of
this during the period of Guild Socialism established the continuing
primacy of the industrial arena but also emphasized the important
supportive role of political activity. Labour's 1918 programme was,
therefore, to be welcomed exactly to the extent that it was conceived as
providing such support, for 'it will be the task of the Labour Party in
Parliament to second the efforts of Labour's industrial army',[37] just as
the other parties performed such a supportive function for capitalism.
Cole continued to stress the futility of parliamentarism and the inevitability of future disillusionment if the labour movement pinned its hopes
to political success alone, but he wanted to reconcile this with an
affirmation of an important secondary and supportive role for political
action. In his own neat summation of this position, the correct function
of working-class political action was to 'ease and smooth a transition
which it is impotent actually to accomplish'.[38]

In general, therefore, Guild Socialism was emphatic not only in its
commitment to industrial transformation but also in its commitment to
the centrality of industrial action in the achievement of such a transformation. A body was required both to provide the organizational
foundation for a Guild society and to provide the agency whereby such

[35] 'Political Action and the N.G.L.', *Guildsman*, Feb. 1919.
[36] At the 1919 N.G.L. Conference Cole 'condemned the well-known slogan concerning
economic power as ambiguous ... and unduly narrowed our scope.' (Report in *Guildsman*,
July–Aug. 1919.)
[37] *Why Labour Left the Coalition*, *Herald* Pamphlet, 1918. For further reflections on Labour's 1918
programme, see Cole's 'Recent Developments in the British Labour Movement', *American
Economic Review*, Sept. 1918.
[38] *Guild Socialism Re-Stated*, p. 180.

a society could be created. Guild Socialism claimed to have discovered a body capable of performing both these tasks: the trade union movement. As S. G. Hobson declared, 'the English trade unions are the hope of the world'.[39] They may seem an unlikely vehicle for the aspirations and loyalties of a Guild Socialism usually regarded as essentially romantic and utopian. Certainly they found little place in the thinking of other contemporary 'utopian' critics of the social order. For example, in R. H. Tawney's personal record of the years before 1914, a record which closely reflects the atmosphere in which Guild Socialism was born, there was much emphasis on the need for a radical transformation in industry but a complete absence of any discussion of the labour movement.[40] Guild Socialism shared Tawney's social diagnosis, but attempted to give that diagnosis a concrete form and programme which hinged on the role of the trade unions. It was the trade unions who were cast as the embryonic Guilds and it was their industrial action which was destined to usher in the Guild society.

Here, then, was the setting in which Cole began his long association, as both friend and critic, with the trade union movement. For him, Guild Socialism was essentially a theory of trade unionism, above all because 'the problem of the transition to Guild Socialism is ... primarily a problem of Trade Union development'.[41] Thus he immersed himself in the world of the industrial labour movement, endeavouring to build a bridge between the industrial demands of labour and the ideas of Guild Socialism. He grew increasingly impatient with those adherents of Guild Socialism who preferred the language of lofty generality to any actual contact with the labour movement. 'It is admitted that the Guilds must grow out of the trade unions,' he wrote; 'is it not then, the business of any person who desires to play either a constructive or a critical part in the formulation of Guild Socialism to make himself reasonably familiar with the working of modern trade unionism.'[42] In this respect, the *New Age* seemed increasingly irrelevant, having the appearance of a journal written by superior men for

---

[39] S. G. Hobson, op. cit., p. 364 (Appendix III).

[40] *R. H. Tawney's Commonplace Book*, ed. J. M. Winter and D. M. Joslin, 1972. As J. M. Winter puts it, Tawney 'saw the labour unrest with the eyes of a platonic idealist'. ('R. H. Tawney's Early Political Thought', *Past and Present*, 47, May 1970, p. 77.)

[41] *Guild Socialism Re-Stated*, p. 191.

[42] 'Democracy and the Guilds', *New Age*, 25 Feb. 1914; and added: 'I am building on the practice of the workers themselves, and not upon a confused, if wide, reading of Nietzsche, Faguet, Dicey, and other indigestible persons.' (idem.) Similarly, Cole urged the *Daily Herald* (29 Nov. 1913) to reserve a 'corner' for the discussion of trade union and industrial problems: a corner which 'Coleandmellor' were soon to fill.

superior men, with high expectations of—but little contact with—the
organized labour movement. In moving outside the *New Age* orbit, Cole
set out to make Guild Socialism more directly relevant to the world of
labour. Thus his role in the formation of the National Guilds League,
his activity in the Labour Research Department, his wartime service to
the engineering union and his industrial journalism were all designed to
bring Guild Socialism into direct and useful contact with the trade
unions. To this activity he brought a conception of a labour movement
always performing two essential functions—one aimed at system-
improvement (wages, conditions etc.), the other at system-change (the
demand for control). It was this enlarged definition of trade unionism
which Cole consistently opposed to that Webbian definition which
restricted itself to the former function. Much of Cole's energy was
directed towards the detection and demonstration of the existence of
the latter function in the activities of the trade unions. Thus the
pre-1914 labour unrest was presented as evidence of the vitality of the
aspiration to control inside the labour movement, even if actual labour
demands suggested otherwise. The real meaning of labour's militancy
was that the trade unions were 'moving naturally and spontaneously in
the direction in which their theories, if they had any, would be bound to
lead them'.[43] Guild Socialism was presented as a theory which gave
concrete form to this natural movement within the world of labour.

All this was unexceptional, for it was the typical viewpoint of industrial theories of socialism. It became more exceptional in Cole's hands,
because he brought a distinctive approach to it. Moreover, this
approach revealed a good deal about his wider conception of socialism.
His central concern was with the capability of the trade unions to assume
their essential control function. If he had high hopes for the trade
unions, he also had a grim realism about their present state. In many
ways, his writings provided a depressing commentary on the infirmities
of the organized labour movement. It was 'an appalling chaos of
contending atoms';[44] it had become 'no less conservative than the
institutions which it is its mission to destroy and to supplant';[45]
episodes like 'Black Friday' indicated 'with startling clearness the
weakness and pitiful inadequacy of the British Labour movement'[46]—and so on. Not only did the trade union movement lack an

[43] *World of Labour*, p. 371.
[44] 'Recent Developments in the British Labour Movement', *American Economic Review*, Sept. 1918.
[45] *Self-Government in Industry*, p. 75.
[46] 'Black Friday and After', *Labour Monthly*, July 1921.

organizing idea and coherent structure, but Cole also missed no opportunity of telling it so. To people like Beatrice Webb, it seemed ironic that Cole should pin his hopes to a movement whose manifest deficiencies he spent so much time in cataloguing. Yet to identify the defects was also to suggest the remedies, and it was to this end that Cole's energies were directed. In so far as labour's inadequacies sprang from the lack of a theory, the task was to disseminate that ideology of control which was alone capable of transforming trade union consciousness into class consciousness. In so far as the defects were organizational, the task was to engineer an amalgamation movement among the trade unions on industrial lines. This 'greater unionism', of which Cole was chief advocate, was designed both to improve the trade unions as fighting organizations against capitalism and to prepare them for their control function in a Guild society.

It was this emphasis on preparation which gave to Cole's approach much of its distinctive character. Indeed, preparation for control was presented as the central issue for trade unionism. It was stated bluntly: 'the question which every active Trade Unionist ought to be asking himself to-day is not "How can I raise my wages under capitalism?" but "How can I help to fit my Trade Union, and the Trade Union Movement generally, for the function of replacing capitalism in the control of industry?"'[47] Two aspects of this position deserve special notice. On the one hand, there was the notion of fitness, a key word in the Cole vocabulary. On the other hand, there was the stress on replacement, another key word. Put together, Cole was arguing that the crucial task was not merely to displace capitalism but to replace it, something requiring considerable preparation on the part of the labour movement. There is, perhaps, some paradox in Cole's position here. He devoted much effort to the repudiation of the Fabian distrust of ordinary people and was almost lyrical in his embrace of will and spontaneity; yet he was equally insistent that without prior preparation the labour movement might succeed in destroying capitalism but would be quite unfit to replace it in the control of industry. It was in relation to this whole concept of preparation, in fact, that Cole's Guild Socialism not only earned the wrath of other industrial schools of socialism,[48] but also bore the traces of its author's Fabian parentage.

[47] *Workers' Control in Industry*, I.L.P., 1919, p. 10.
[48] *The Syndicalist* (Feb. 1914) saw Guild Socialism as 'the latest lucubration of the middle class mind'. (Quoted in B. Russell, *Roads to Freedom*, 1918, p. 91.) The class factor certainly coloured a Guild movement which 'spread its revolutionary gospel from the delightfully bourgeois neighbourhood of Acacia Road, Hampstead'. (M. P. Ashley and C. T. Saunders, *Red Oxford*, 1933, p. 22.)

The affinity with Fabianism was especially evident in two important respects. Firstly, there was Cole's constant emphasis on the need to bring the technical and professional salariat into a re-organized trade unionism if the objective of industrial control was to be seriously and successfully pursued. On the administrative needs of socialism Cole stood firmly beside Webb and against Lenin. The workers might destroy capitalism, but they would need a salaried staff to replace it. Thus Cole devoted much effort to the demonstration that an alliance of manual worker and brain worker was mutually advantageous. To the brain worker, Cole emphasized the scope for managerial initiative in a Guild society, so that 'there is no class of "industrious persons", as the Chartists would have said, to whom the Guild idea ought to have a stronger appeal than to the managers and technicians of industry'.[49] To the manual worker, Cole argued that the detachment of an important section of the technical and managerial class from capitalism would do much to tip the balance in the struggle for control and enormously ease the establishment of new forms of industrial control. In general, therefore, Cole suggested the need for 'an enlarged definition of the proletariat'[50] which, whilst recognizing the fundamental reality of the class struggle, would also embrace those intermediate groups 'upon whom the issue of the struggle may easily depend'.[51] This was a theme which informed much of Cole's treatment of Guild Socialism in general, and of trade unionism in particular. It also informed his response to the Labour Party's 1918 constitution, which he welcomed for its individual membership provision which would provide an opportunity for the entry of these intermediate social groups into the Labour movement. It was also a theme which, as will be seen, would continue to influence Cole's thought long after the formal demise of Guild Socialism.

A second main area in which the affinity with Fabianism persisted was Cole's emphasis on the centrality of the research function in the preparation for socialism. For all his denunciation of the triumph of the Blue Book over the imagination in the Fabian mind, he was both apostle and practitioner of a creed of factual analysis and detailed investigation as the basis for social action. In an important sense, Cole felt the need for Guild Socialists to match Fabianism in this respect if the Fabian ascendancy over the labour movement was to be effectively

[49] *Guild Socialism Re-Stated*, p. 57. As a reviewer wrote of Cole: 'No one has done more to explain to the manual workers what good and important fellows the "salariat"... really are.' (D. H. Robertson, 'Mr. Cole's Social Theories', *Economic Journal*, Dec. 1920.)
[50] *Chaos and Order in Industry*, 1920, p. 241.
[51] Ibid., p. 244.

challenged. At a personal level, Cole felt the need to be as good as the Webbs. Significantly, his first contribution to the *Daily Herald*, in 1913, contained a warning to the militants of the trade union movement that if they 'attempt to fight on mere spirit, and say that *no* statistics matter, they will come a cropper'.[52] Similarly, he defended his continued association with the Fabian Society at this time wholly in terms of the need for the labour movement to have its research staff and intelligence department, and 'no body in the Labour movement, except the Fabian Society, is making any concerted effort to collect the information, and do the hard thinking which are essential to the reconstruction of Socialist theory'.[53] Cole set out to make himself master of the facts about the labour world, to analyse the effects on the labour movement of government and employer action, and to provide the movement with facts, analysis—and interpretation. His immersion in the work of the Fabian (later Labour) Research Department was aimed directly at performing this research function for the labour movement on an organized basis.

An additional presumption was that Guild Socialism would make headway amongst trade unionists to the extent that it could first make itself useful to them in this way. The aim was not to meddle and interfere with the affairs of the trade unions, but to provide a service which was available to them if required. Equally, Cole was emphatic on the need for the trade unions themselves to incorporate research and expertise into the definition of their purpose. They must 'have in their possession as complete and scientific a method as the employers',[54] or they must certainly abandon all aspirations to the control of industry. Thus they must develop specialism in techniques of job evaluation and wage payment, to match an increasing specialism on the employers' side at both national and workshop level. In addition, they must not take up an exclusively obstructive and negative stance on matters relating to industrial efficiency and scientific management, for a democratic industry must be efficient too. The aim must not be to oppose the application of science to industry, but to break the class monopoly of science by the development of labour's own scientific expertise. It was this language of fact, knowledge and expertise which ran throughout Cole's discussion of the labour movement which indicated its strong

---

[52] 'Solemnity and Statistics', *Daily Herald*, 29 Nov. 1913.
[53] 'Fabian Excursions', *Daily Herald*, 10 Feb. 1914. The *New Statesman* recognized the affinity with Fabianism in this respect, writing of the Guildsmen that: 'They resemble the early Fabians (we fear they will resent the comparison!) in their desire to perfect administration and discover new facts....' ('The Guild Idea', 3 Mar. 1917.)
[54] *The Payment of Wages*, 1918, p. 114.

Fabian idiom. As he conceded himself: 'we are so old-fashioned as still to believe in thinking things out'.[55]

Above all, however, Cole's belief in preparation for control involved an educative process. Much of his Guild Socialist writing could be read as a commentary on one central statement: 'Before Labour can control, it must learn how to control.'[56] The emphasis on learning pervaded his whole approach to social action. Partly, it was education in a fairly formal sense that was meant, especially the adult education associated with the organized working-class movement, expressed through the W.E.A., Ruskin College, the Central Labour College and the Plebs League. Faced with the rivalry and hostility amongst these bodies, rooted in different conceptions of the nature and function of working-class education, Cole consistently argued for a unity which recognized diversity. Although himself committed to the view that working-class education should attempt to master the foundations of 'bourgeois' education before transcending it—a view reflected in his own commitment to the W.E.A.—he also defended the activities of the more directly propagandist schools. Faced with the miserable inadequacy of such educational provision in general, ideological division in this area seemed a luxury which the working-class movement could ill afford. Cole constantly urged a recognition by the trade unions of the central importance of education in the achievement of their wider aims. They must equip themselves 'with that educated rank and file through which alone the emancipation of Labour can be accomplished.'[57] Especially did the demand for industrial control require a diffusion of knowledge and capacity amongst the mass of trade unionists which the present educational system, essentially a training in servility, did not provide. The trade union movement was an ideal vehicle for meeting this deficiency through its own educational provision, if once the importance of the need was recognized. Cole suggested the unlimited possibilities for trade union development if this diffusion of knowledge was seriously undertaken; but also the limitations on development if it was not. Certainly it was central to the achievement of Guild Socialism, for 'the first question that always confronts the idealist who pins his faith to the Labour Movement is, how far this intelligence and knowledge exist, or can be called into being'.[58]

[55] 'Labour's Advisers', *New Statesman*, 10 Jan. 1914.
[56] *Self-Government in Industry*, p. 93.
[57] 'Trade Unionism and Education', *W.E.A. Education Yearbook*, 1918, p. 373.
[58] *An Introduction to Trade Unionism*, 1918, p. 100.

Yet when Cole urged the necessity of a 'learning' process before the control of industry by the workers could be realized, it was not primarily a process of formal education that was being suggested. Rather, it was a process of learning by doing, almost of socialism on the instalment plan. As instalments of control accumulated, with men both getting a taste for control and learning how to exercise it, the achievement of a full Guild Socialist society became progressively more likely and possible. In 'encroachment', Guild Socialism coined its distinctive term to describe this conception of social change. Its essential idea was that capitalism would be functionally expropriated in the workplace by the progressive assumption by the workers of new areas of control, wrested by the direct exercise of industrial power. Hence it was in this direction that Cole urged the trade unions to concentrate their demands. Two chief virtues were claimed for encroachment. In the first place, it attacked capitalism at its most critical point—its dependence upon the subordination of labour in the workplace. If that subordination could be ended, capitalism would be rendered increasingly functionless, its final collapse and overthrow much easier to accomplish. In the second place, encroachment was a strategy which recognized the necessity of a learning process in the achievement of control, thereby minimizing the transitional chaos which a bid for power without this sort of preparation would necessarily produce. Cole's concern with 'chaos' was to distinguish much of his later thought; indeed, it was almost a motif which ran throughout his work. He feared it, half expected it, and desperately wanted to avoid it. Thus the attraction of encroachment was that it was directed towards the minimization of chaos by founding the attack against capitalism on the prior exercise of control functions in industry by the workers themselves. '"Through terror to triumph" is a desperate remedy', wrote Cole, 'and if there is a chance, as I am sure there is, of rebuilding society without an intervening period of chaos, we should be fools and criminals to miss that chance.'[59] Encroachment seemed constructive, promising continuity instead of disruption, replacement as well as displacement. It was a programme of practical education for socialism.

The problem remained of defining the content and forms of encroachment, in order that it might perform the role assigned to it by Guild Socialism. Cole defined encroachment as a policy whereby the workers could 'increase their power under capitalist ownership, and place in their hands a measure of control without entangling them in

[59] *Chaos and Order in Industry*, p. 24.

the present system'.[60] The terms of this definition posed considerable difficulties for analysis and action, which Cole spent much effort in attempting to resolve. He warned the labour movement to steer clear of spurious avenues of involvement in the capitalist system, ranging from profit-sharing to Whitley Councils, which offered only entanglement without any advance in real control. Genuine control in a small area was to be preferred to entanglement in a larger one. Thus the key demand must be for worker control over part of the authority and reward structure of the workplace, involving responsibility for supervisory activities and work organization and allocation. Above all, the demand must be for a collective contract—described by Pribićević as Guild Socialism's 'distinctive contribution to the doctrine of workers' control'[61]—whereby the workers as a body received a lump sum payment for a work contract that was collectively undertaken and organized. The great merit of such a scheme was that it involved the complete transference of certain functions to the organized workers, rather than any joint control with the employers. Hence it was 'worth a hundred Whitley Reports'.[62] In Cole's mature Guild Socialist theory, it was the combined impact of economic expropriation by the state and functional expropriation in the workplace which would ensure the collapse of capitalism, whilst the process of steady encroachment would also have done much to ensure a smooth transition to new forms of control.

Encroachment found ready disciples and no less ready critics. To some, it seemed to offer, as did Fabianism, the prospect of a new society to be created without prolonged and messy conflict. When Cole employed the language of 'stable revolution'[63] it elicited a wide response amongst those critics of the social order who wanted the revolutionary product without the revolutionary process. A good example of this was provided by Kingsley Martin, who presented the case for Guild Socialism to a Cambridge audience in 1921 by saying that there would be 'some rough play, but no revolution', with the capitalist 'deprived of his power like a stranded starfish'.[64] There was clearly some unreality in a conception of social change which envisaged the withering away of capitalism as it was progressively denuded of its functions. Was it not more likely, to use Martin's imagery, that the

[60] Ibid., p. 116.
[61] B. Pribićević, *The Shop Stewards' Movement and Workers' Control*, 1959, p. 150.
[62] 'The Whitley Report', *Guildsman*, June 1918.
[63] 'Guilds at Home and Abroad', *Guildsman*, Nov. 1919.
[64] K. Martin, *Cambridge Press and News*, 2 Dec. 1921. (Quoted in C. H. Rolph, *Kingsley: The Life, Letters and Diaries of Kingsley Martin*, 1973, p. 70.)

starfish would struggle furiously for its life? Much criticism of Guild
Socialism has followed these lines, suggesting that capitalism would be
far from idle when faced with a decisive challenge to its functional
control. Thus Glass writes of Guild Socialism as flawed by its 'dreams
of easy victory',[65] ignoring the real obstacles to industrial action
presented by both government and employers. To the Marxist left,
Guild Socialism has seemed fatally flawed by its failure to confront the
question of power or the essential nature of the state, forcing it to lose
itself—in John Strachey's phrase—in 'a barren world of fantasy'.[66] The
origins of this type of criticism are to be found in the Guild Socialist
period itself, above all in the response of sections of the Guild movement
to the Bolshevik Revolution in Russia. The success of that revolution
raised the question of power in a direct and immediate form, causing
many Guild Socialists to grow impatient with an encroachment
strategy which seemed to neglect the need for an organized seizure of
state power. Thus Ellen Wilkinson urged Guild Socialism to 'range
itself with the revolutionaries throughout Europe who are working for
an immediate revolution, offering the Guild theory as its contribution
to the building of communist society after the transference of power has
taken place.'[67] On this view, Guild theory had lost all relevance to the
transfer of power itself, where encroachment had formerly been its
distinctive contribution to the theory of socialism.

Yet Cole's own conception of social change was much less narrow
and dogmatic than this account of encroachment might suggest. Certainly he expected no easy victory, but strenuous resistance. Nor did he
present encroachment as an alternative to other forms of social action,
but offered it as a valuable tactic in a wider strategy. Above all, he did
not present it as an evolutionary alternative to revolution. In one sense,
however, Cole was both evolutionist and gradualist, for he was wedded
to a view of social change as a process involving a series of stages,
certainly if it was a Guild Socialist society which was to be achieved.
For Cole, this fact was both necessary and desirable; and it was the
virtue of encroachment that it recognized and provided for it. 'We do
not believe that we are going to leap into the millenium without any
steps at all'[68] Cole reminded Guild Socialists in 1917, and much of his
own theoretical activity was an attempt to sketch a policy for the

[65] S. T. Glass, *The Responsible Society*, 1966, p. 59.
[66] J. Strachey, *What Are We To Do?*, 1938, p. 115. Margaret Cole also wrote that 'we had not really faced up at all to the problems of political power'. (*Growing Up Into Revolution*, 1949, p. 88.)
[67] E. Wilkinson, 'With the Revolutionaries', *Guildsman*, May 1920.
[68] N.G.L. Conference report, 1917 (Cole Collection).

transition in which the steps and stages were clearly marked. For a long time, however, the encroachment policy of Guild Socialism seemed to exist in a vacuum, without the need either to define itself with rigour or to defend itself with vigour. It seemed enough to recommend the active exercise of will in the workplace, directed towards the steady erosion and transference of capitalist functions, without confronting the implications of such a strategy in any serious way. It was the impact of the Russian Revolution which was decisive in forcing a more critical examination and statement of Cole's conception of social change, as he endeavoured to reconcile the evolutionary and revolutionary positions.

Far from abandoning the preparation policy of encroachment, he now defended it as integral to a successful revolutionary process. For Cole, encroachment was itself part of a continuing revolution, making the alleged antipathy between an evolutionary and revolutionary approach largely misleading. Yet he conceded the probability of a revolutionary moment, conceived as a sharp break, at some point in the encroachment process. What he denied, however, was that this breaking point deserved exclusive, or even primary, attention from Guild Socialists, for the nature and success of the break would be determined by the preparatory work that had preceded it. If encroachment could not avoid a revolutionary clash, it could and should precede it. It was not an alternative to revolution, but a necessary part of it. This was the essence of Cole's response to the Bolshevik seizure of power. Thus to those elements in the Guild movement who wanted to follow the Bolshevik example, Cole argued that there could and should be agreement on *present* action irrespective of different estimations of the course of future struggle. 'If early revolution is wanted', he told the revolutionaries of the Guild movement, 'the best way of ensuring its success is to get the army of Labour posted in the best possible strategic positions before it takes place.'[69] In other words, the pursuit of revolution made encroachment more rather than less necessary. Above all else, therefore, Cole dissented from the communist position because of its refusal to recognize the primacy of preparation and training in the pursuit of power, whereas he envisaged the form of transition from capitalism to socialism 'as one not merely of strength in aggression, but also at least as much of fitness for administration'.[70] It was not enough to destroy; it was also necessary to construct and replace.

[69] 'The Communist Party and the N.G.L.', *Guildsman*, Sept. 1920.
[70] *Guild Socialism and Communism* (no source; a copy, dated 1921, extracted from an unnamed Chinese periodical, is in the Cole Collection).

This was Cole's response to Lenin's *State and Revolution*, with its emphasis on the need to smash the capitalist state. Cole offered instead a policy of 'substitution', to be carried as far as possible before a direct and final clash with capitalism occurred.[71] Even if the Leninist definition of the state was accepted, the problem of strategy remained. It was here that the Guild policy of substitution was valuable for, although it might not do the whole job, it could do much to minimize the dislocation and suffering involved in the transfer of power. Thus Cole offered an 'evolution' which was not primarily parliamentary and a 'revolution' which was not primarily a conflict of arms. The revolution could succeed if it was rooted in a steady evolutionary encroachment into capitalist power on the part of the organized workers. At bottom, Cole was less concerned that such evolution might prove ultimately inadequate than that it would not be accepted as a necessary precursor to a revolution which should be 'as little as possible a civil war and as much as possible a registration of accomplished facts and a culmination of tendencies already in operation'.[72]

Cole's treatment of this question provides an important clue both to the strength and the weakness of his wider Guild Socialist position, above all in its attempt to unite and reconcile seemingly divergent viewpoints. The usual criticisms made of Guild Socialism are familiar: it was too schematic; too romantic; too intricate; too utopian; too optimistic; too harmonious. Some of these charges may be conceded at once, either in whole or in part. Certainly Guild Socialism paid little serious attention to the problems of order and coercion in a Guild society, producing a picture of deceptive harmony. It was clearly inadequate to suggest that social coercion, the product of social division, would 'speedily and progressively disappear'[73] as functional democracy was established. Functional devolution, as has already been said, is no guarantee of social harmony and coordination. At times, too, Guild Socialism did seem to lose itself in the details of future Guild organization at the expense of immediate concerns, making it vulnerable to charges of intellectualism and unreality. At other times, it did seem to evade the nature of social power in its invocation of the centrality of will in social change. At an institutional level, it is arguable that Guild Socialism made a fundamental mistake in expecting existing trade unions to develop into control bodies, instead of anticipating the

[71] See Cole, 'Lenin on Bolshevism', *Guildsman*, Mar. 1920
[72] *Guild Socialism Re-Stated*, p. 187.
[73] *Social Theory*, p. 140.

creation of new agencies of control independent of a trade union movement which should continue to perform its traditional functions. Even more fundamental, however, was the failure to confront the implications of a theory which made the trade unions central to the achievement of socialism. If the state was to be rejected, if political action could be no more than secondary, then a sustained analysis of the socialist potential (and limitations) of trade unionism was imperative. Such an analysis was never really provided by Cole. Instead, there were merely demands and suggestions for trade union reorganization and a belief in the power of spontaneity. As a result it is difficult to avoid the conclusion that there was an organizational vacuum at the heart of Cole's socialist theory.[74]

Yet if much of such criticism can be accepted, it is also necessary to reject the unacceptable criticism too. For example, it was plausible to expect the trade unions to provide the organizational vehicle for a control movement, even if such control should ultimately be realized and exercised by bodies created expressly for that purpose. Nor did Cole's enthusiasm for trade union reorganization on industrial lines betray an excessive faith in the importance of formal structures. Some versions of industrial unionism may rightly be criticized for proposing 'a purely *administrative* solution to fundamental problems of ideology and class consciousness',[75] a solution which tended to confuse causes with consequences. Cole avoided this difficulty through a sensitive appreciation of the inter-relationships of structure, ideology and consciousness—and between these and the external environment—in his discussion of trade union organization. In this, as in other matters, his position appeared almost *too* sensible; so that his call to action sat uneasily alongside his delineation of all the difficulties involved. Furthermore, it is misleading to present Cole's version of Guild Socialism as a labyrinthine structure which was inherently unworkable, for he was never so rigidly schematic as this would suggest. Indeed, he was emphatically tentative in his social engineering, defending his whole enterprise largely in terms of the power of a practical ideal. Far from presenting his Guild structure as a blueprint correct in every detail, he insisted that it was 'far too tidy to be true'.[76] It was a model outline,

[74] Thus J. Hinton has written that 'the greatest weakness of Cole's theoretical work was his failure to confront the analytical problems raised by this inflation of the role of the trade unions in the transition to socialism.' ('G. D. H. Cole in the Stage Army of the Good', *Society for the Study of Labour History, Bulletin* 28, spring 1974.)
[75] R. Hyman, *Industrial Relations: A Marxist Introduction*, 1975, p. 60.
[76] *Guild Socialism Re-Stated*, p. 138.

designed to illuminate essential principles, not a finished structure; for the society of the future would be the product of a complex process of social change in which many influences would play their part. An ideal was useful in so far as it clarified principles and enabled us to act better in the present. To more general charges that a Guild society would be impossibly complex, Cole—like the Webbs—would point to the infinitely more chaotic complexity of capitalist social organization. To charges of utopianism, Cole would argue that the Guild idea was an expression of tendencies already discernible in the present and, therefore, essentially practical.[77] To charges that Guild Socialism expected effortless victory, Cole could point to his anticipations of a vigorous struggle with capitalism. If Guild Socialism is to be effectively assessed and criticized, it must at least be presented in its original complexity and not merely in a received version whose defects are already identified.

It has already been suggested that Cole's discussion of social change, with its attempt to show the complementarity of the evolutionary and revolutionary positions, provides a major clue to the fundamental nature of his Guild Socialism, from which both its strengths and weaknesses derived. In Cole's hands, Guild Socialism became an intellectual magnet, attracting to itself an ideological assortment which it claimed to embrace and reconcile. If the language of balance and conciliation was so characteristic of Guild Socialism, it was because the commitment to synthesis was so imperative. In terms of personnel, the motley composition of the Guild movement has often been noticed; yet this finds its true explanation in the motley composition of the Guild idea itself. In so far as this provided the attractive foundation for a broad, non-sectarian movement of the left it was a source of strength; but in so far as it represented an intellectual amalgam capable of instant disintegration into its constituent elements at the first real challenge it provided a major source of weakness. Hence the decisive impact of the Russian Revolution on Guild Socialism, producing Cole's intricate exercise in synthetic artistry designed to demonstrate the complementarity of the weapons in Guild Socialism's armoury.

Yet the Russian Revolution served to expose all the latent tensions and disagreements within the Guild movement which no ingenious synthesis could ultimately reconcile. Even so, Cole's own response to

---

[77] This claim is characteristic of much utopian thought, of course. It is discussed briefly but interestingly by A. Arblaster and S. Lukes in the Introduction to their utopian anthology, *The Good Society*, 1971.

the Russian Revolution was to occupy a middle ground from which to engage in dialogue with both critics and enthusiasts in an attempt to keep the Guild movement intact. On the one hand, therefore, he suggested a basic identity between the Guild and Soviet ideas, whilst on the other hand he conceded that 'there are comparatively few of us whom Moscow in its present mood would not wish to send to join Mr. Henderson and Mr. Thomas in the lowest inferno'.[78] In general, he was content to ask questions and seek information about developments in Russia, from both a critical and sympathetic perspective. Sometimes he came close to suggesting a basic antagonism between the self-governing ideal of Guild Socialism and the communists who, 'in disciplining the workers for revolution . . . are in danger of constructing a Society based, not on freedom but on subordination'.[79] At the same time, he offered broad support to the Russian Revolution and was hopeful about its future development. Above all, however, he insisted on the futility of domestic attempts to imitate the Russian example—and on the harmful effects of an erroneous Moscow policy which sought to encourage such imitation. Russian experience would doubtless offer lessons for both emulation and avoidance, but 'assuredly no amount of study of what has happened in Russia will absolve the British Labour movement from the duty of thinking out and formulating its own policy to suit the conditions not of other countries but of this country'.[80] Cole's occupancy of the middle ground with respect to the Russian Revolution was his attempt, ultimately unsuccessful, to hold together that coalition both of men and ideas which his Guild Socialism essentially represented. He was both gradualist and revolutionary; both for the Revolution and against it. Here, then, was one expression of an ambiguity basic to Cole's wider Guild Socialist position.

It was an ambiguity born out of synthesis. This becomes strikingly clear when the leading elements in this synthesis are themselves examined. For example, it was as a hybrid that Cole initially presented the case for Guild Socialism, for its essence was announced as a reconciliation of the insights of syndicalism and collectivism. The same approach informed much else in Cole's statement of Guild Socialism. He was committed to an active democracy, yet recognized the need for expertise and leadership. He favoured decentralization, yet was alive to considerations of economic viability and political efficiency. Hence he

---

[78] 'Guilds at Home and Abroad,' *Guildsman*, Feb. 1921.
[79] *Guild Socialism and Communism* (op. cit.).
[80] 'What We Want To Know About Russia,' *New Statesman*, 1 May 1920.

was not simply the apostle of small groups; rather, 'the presupposition is always in favour of the least centralized form of administration which is economically practicable'.[81] He was the enemy of bureaucracy, but defended the role of central officials, not least in the trade unions.[82] He made the exercise of will central to social change, yet acknowledged the conditioning framework of the material world. He proclaimed the power of spontaneity, but insisted on the necessity of a learning process. He hoped for a revival of craftsmanship, but defended machine production. He embraced the spirit of medievalism, but was ultimately a modernist. His pluralism found a place for the institutional expression of a general will. His commitment to a unified social order was rooted in diversity. His communitarian ideal was ultimately individualist. Indeed, the diffusion of power inherent in a Guild society was seen by Cole as chiefly valuable as a guarantee of individual freedom. 'If the individual is not to be a mere pigmy in the hands of a colossal social organism,' wrote Cole, 'there must be such a division of social powers as will preserve individual freedom by balancing one social organism so nicely against another that the individual may still count.'[83] Cole frequently presented the notion of a 'balance of powers' as the key Guild principle, not least because of its beneficial implications for individual freedom. Yet the concept of 'balance' was basic to Cole's Guild Socialism in a more general sense, for it was designed both to balance a range of ideas and to create a social structure in which legitimate claims to power were balanced and reconciled. Here was a definitely Aristotelian approach, for a unity was to be created out of diversity and a social order to be created which was a synthesis of a range of ideas and interests. In conception and purpose, Aristotle's 'polity' and Cole's Guild Socialism had much in common. Above all, they represented considerable enterprises of intellectual and sociological synthesis. When Bertrand Russell described Guild Socialism as 'the best practicable system'[84] his use of an Aristotelian idiom well illustrated this synthetic character of the Guild idea.

Thus Cole embraced gradualism and revolution; collectivism and syndicalism; medievalism and modernism; localism and centralism; democracy and organization; spontaneity and preparation; idealism

[81] *The Future of Local Government*, 1921, p. 85.
[82] See *World of Labour*, p. 265.
[83] *Self-Government in Industry*, p. 139.
[84] B. Russell, *Roads to Freedom*, 1918, p. 13. Similarly, K. C. Hsiao (*Political Pluralism*, 1927, p. 237), wrote that: 'Mr. Cole's pluralistic state would simply seem to be Aristotle's practically best state in its modern dress.'

and materialism; individual and community; nationalism and internationalism; unity and diversity; Morris and Marx.... The catalogue
is not exhaustive, but nor is it intended to demonstrate that Cole's
Guild Socialism was merely founded upon a series of contradictions.
Yet the tensions were evident enough, as phrases like 'stable revolution'
and 'scientific Utopianism' amply indicate. In Cole's hand, Guild
Socialism became something of an intellectual umbrella for socialists, a
mansion with many rooms. Everything could be accommodated, balanced and reconciled. Guilds and the state, industrial and political
action, evolution and revolution—all came together in Cole's giant
synthesis. Even the pattern of ownership under socialism was presented
as essentially flexible, for Cole urged the need 'at all costs (to) avoid
becoming narrow doctrinaires and applying our theories in the spirit of
the Inquisition'.[85] His socialist society would be minimally monolithic,
hence his socialist theory was only minimally rigorous. Its synthetic
character made it both attractive and vulnerable. His own eclecticism
lay at the heart of Guild Socialism itself. This was also the perceptive
verdict of a former Guild Socialist who moved over (temporarily) into
official Communism: 'Even at the risk of seeming unduly personal,'
wrote William Mellor, 'I must stress the part played by Mr. Cole in
Guild Socialism; for if one can understand his psychology, one can
understand the real failure of the Movement to which he belongs.'[86] It
was Cole's mixed intellectual parentage, the tensions and ambiguities
which have been traced in his thought, which go far to explain the
compromise basic to the Guild Socialist position.[87] His eclecticism
required him to employ his formidable intellectual agility in defending
a broad middle ground on which the Guild Socialist compromise was
founded. Sorel denounced 'the reconciliation of contraries in the
equivocations of the professors',[88] a phrase which captures a good deal
of the nature of Cole's Guild Socialist enterprise.

It was a difficult middle ground to defend. It was difficult institu-
tionally, for Cole expected much of a trade union movement whose
defects he documented so forcefully. Whilst stressing the sterility of
trade union leadership, therefore, he also attacked those unofficial
elements who threatened the existing structure of trade unionism. He
was thus left with a weak middle position whose programme consisted

---

[85] *Chaos and Order in Industry*, p. 196.
[86] W. Mellor, 'A Critique of Guild Socialism', *Labour Monthly*, Nov. 1921.
[87] 'They began as compromisers and they have been compromising ever since.' (ibid.)
[88] G. Sorel, *Reflections on Violence* 1908; trans. T. E. Hulme, 1950, p. 123.

of 'constitutionalising the shop stewards'.[89] He was enthusiastic about
the control demands of the unofficial shop stewards' movement, but
refused to throw over the official movement in favour of independent
rank and file organization. His position on this issue, with all its
consequent difficulties and frustrations, was later to be paralleled in the
political field by his attitude to the Labour Party and its own 'unofficial'
movements. His position was also difficult intellectually, for it involved
an attempt to reconcile a range of ideas which were ultimately irreconcilable. That difficulty reflected itself in a Guild organization com-
prising both Christian medievalists and Marxist revolutionaries—an
organizational expression of an eclectic doctrine. For some, like the
young Victor Gollancz, the Guild idea appeared as an attractive extension of liberalism.[90] For others, like Bertrand Russell, it seemed to offer
simply the least harmful and dangerous of political doctrines.[91] For
some, it promised a revival of craftsmanship and spiritual values; for
others, a revolutionary strategy for the industrial working-class movement. Guild Socialism was a coalition of men because it was an amalgam of ideas. It proved an attractive coalition in a particular political,
economic and intellectual environment, but a necessarily fragile one as
soon as that environment began to change. Cole found himself increasingly isolated, as he always expected that he would.[92] Yet faced
with a Guild movement finally divided between official Communism
and apostles of the spirit he still argued, typically, for a policy which
was 'not either of the extremes, but is equally not a compromise
between them'.[93] Guild Socialism disintegrated with Cole still
struggling to maintain his coalition intact.

For Cole it was a genuine coalition of ideas, not least because it was a
product of his own eclecticism. It is in this light that both the strengths
and the weaknesses of Guild Socialism can best be understood. Yet if
the eclectic character of Cole's socialism has to be emphasized, so too
does its hard centre. That hard centre consisted of a conception of an
active, self-governing community which informed Cole's whole
presentation of the Guild argument. The two parts of this conception

---

[89] *An Introduction to Trade Unionism*, p. 57. See Hinton (art. cit.) for criticism of Cole on this.

[90] Gollancz described his embrace of Guild Socialism whilst 'investigating simultaneously every
possible method of socialist reconstruction, in an effort to discover whether any of them might
perhaps prove consistent with my liberal faith'. (*My Dear Timothy*, 1969, Penguin edn., p. 249.)

[91] See B. Russell, 'Why I Am A Guildsman', *Guildsman*, Sept. 1919.

[92] 'All Gaul was divided into three; but Guild Socialism, if it splits at all, will probably be much
more fissiparous.' (*Guildsman*, June 1920.)

[93] *Guildsman*, Nov. 1920.

stood together. For Cole, Guild Socialism was crucially a theory of democracy, a statement about the exercise of will, the mechanisms of control and the distribution of power in society. As such, Guild Socialism could fairly claim to have put the issue of control and the problem of power on the agenda of British socialism. For Cole, it was also essentially a theory of community, a statement of that socialist society rooted in active fellowship which had been his earliest socialist conception. Even the campaign for Guild Socialism—the 'movement' to its participants—seemed to offer a foretaste of the vitality and comradeship which would distinguish a Guild society. That society would not merely provide a democratic organizational structure, nor merely recognize legitimate claims to a share in control. Rather, it would mean a spiritual revolution, a change of heart, a release of the capacity for active fellowship—a new man. It was from this perspective that Cole found statist and distributionist doctrines inadequate; and found the ultimate justification for Guild Socialism. In this sense, too, Cole was both a romantic and a genuine utopian. To regard him primarily as a theorist of the state or of democracy is to miss the extent to which he was struggling for a theoretical and organizational expression of a conception of life under socialism. If his theory was eclectic, it was also founded—like that of his mentor, William Morris—upon an inflexible conception of the nature of life in a socialist society. 'The Guild System will bring Morris into his own', wrote Cole: 'under Collectivism, he would be remembered only as a quite unpractical Socialist who was so little "in the swim" that he refused to join the Fabian Society.'[94]

[94] *Self-Government in Industry*, p. 234.

PART TWO

Beyond Guild Socialism

VI

Industrial Democracy and the Guild Idea

HITHERTO IT has been possible to trace Cole's development in fairly strict and self-contained theoretical terms. Although it has been necessary to indicate those elements in the intellectual and social environment which had important consequences for the development of his particular theory, that theory could largely be analysed in its own terms. Guild Socialism could be seen as the product of a period of considerable speculative freedom, not least in politics, aided by social and economic developments which produced consequences for the world of labour favourable to the propagation of the Guild idea. Inside this intellectual and social framework Cole could concentrate on the statement and elaboration of his Guild Socialist doctrine, a process which reached its climax by 1920. It was a period of intellectual and industrial experimentation, receptive to a social theory with an industrial focus. Hence it is as social theorist that Cole should primarily be regarded, as he regarded himself, during these years.

By the early 1920s, however, the situation had changed dramatically—and with it the nature of Cole's intellectual enterprise. There was the disintegration and collapse of the Guild Socialist movement, of course, but this should be seen more as symptom than cause. In essence, the political and economic environment had changed in ways which served to erode the basis of Guild Socialism. The Russian Revolution exposed the tensions inside the Guild movement; whilst the formation of the British Communist Party finally destroyed it. That destruction was made easier by the sharp downturn in the economy in 1921 after the brief post-war boom, which served to force the trade union movement back to a defensive role, abandoning industrial action for control for political action for the mitigation of economic distress. The impact of this changed environment on Cole's intellectual development was decisive, for his commitment to relevancy produced important shifts in his thinking. Above all, however, it was the *nature* of Cole's theoretical and political activity which underwent the most major shift. After 1921, he has to be regarded much less as abstract social theorist and much more as programmatic social and economic engineer. He now confronted a world very different from that in which Guild Socialism was born and developed, in which the industrial labour movement was weak and vulnerable, unemployment widespread, political Labour established as a party of government, official Communism established as the revolutionary alternative. In many respects it seemed a much less flexible historical situation, inimical to further excursions in the theory of socialism.[1]

Thus the early 1920s does mark a point of real disjuncture in the development of Cole's thought. The disintegration of the Guild movement into its constituent parts dealt a damaging blow to any further development of the Guild idea, while the collapse of the unofficial control movement within industry deprived the Guild scheme of its organizational agency. Cole was stranded, both theoretically and organizationally—a condition which, in a fundamental sense, was to persist for the rest of his life. The confident unity of theory and practice embodied in the Guild movement was never to be recaptured. One immediate and negative indication of this loss of confidence was the dramatic decline in his published output. Not until 1929 did he produce another major work of social and economic analysis, instead confining himself mainly to weekly journalism. If the drop in volume was significant, so too was the change in content. Social theory was replaced by social and economic history, biography and economics. As an intellectual, in the 1920s Cole came firmly down to earth. As a socialist intellectual, he abandoned high theory for concrete analysis and practical problem-solving. This process can be examined partly in terms of his continuing conception of Guild Socialism, partly in terms of his shift to new areas of interest and partly, too, in terms of a more general revision in his theory of socialism. The process gets underway in the 1920s, with Cole struggling to come to terms with a new and unfavourable environment, and produces a comprehensive restatement of his socialist position in terms of these new conditions in the years that followed. This chapter examines the fate of his democratic theory of Guild Socialism during this period.

By the spring of 1922 Cole was writing of 'the completeness with which the offensive in industry has passed from the workers into the employers' hands.'[2] The onset of slump and unemployment marked the

---

[1] As Cole later recalled: 'I found myself in a difficult position in the post-war years. . . .' (Foreword to B. Pribićević, *The Shop Stewards' Movement and Workers' Control* 1910–1922, 1959.)

[2] 'A Word to the Engineers', *Labour Monthly*, Mar. 1922.

end of the forward movement in trade unionism, symbolized by the collapse of the Triple Alliance on Black Friday. The British labour movement had largely missed its real opportunity for aggression in 1919 and 1920, whilst by 1921 the prospect was again of 'some years' during which it would be 'kept definitely on the defensive'.[3] This central fact provides the framework for the final demise of Guild Socialism, both as organized movement and as coherent doctrine. Just as it had derived much of its vitality and influence from its consonance with developments in the industrial world, it now took its decline from the same source. Cole was always very clear that industrial control movements during this period found their origins not in the various theories of control but in the facts of industrial life at the time. Indeed, this was to be his historical verdict on the wartime shop stewards' movement.[4]

Yet Guild Socialism could, and did, claim credit for its part in turning mood into theory, aspiration into concrete demand. It could point to the adoption by leading trade unions (especially the miners and railwaymen) of programmes containing a control commitment on Guild lines; it could point to a Labour Party constitution which now linked public ownership with democratic control; and it could point to a political atmosphere and vocabulary which now found a leading place for the question of the control of industry. Moreover, it could fairly claim to have succeeded in its objective of challenging a traditional conception of nationalization in the name of democratic control, and to have seen the justice of that challenge accepted by bodies, such as the I.L.P., who had been the apostles of the traditional view. Thus the young Attlee, embracing the Guild position as a valuable corrective to collectivism, declared that 'no form of society will be satisfactory that leaves the worker a wage-slave'.[5] In similar vein, the *New Leader* in 1923 compared Snowden's motion in the House of Commons on the abolition of the capitalist system with a motion on the same lines moved by Keir Hardie at the turn of the century: 'the new point in Mr. Snowden's motion is the significant stress on "democratic control". We have learned our lesson as much from the inspiration of the Guild movement

[3] 'Black Friday And After', *Labour Monthly*, July 1921.
[4] See his *Workshop Organisation*, 1923, p. 2.
[5] C. Attlee, 'Guild v. Municipal Socialism,' *Socialist Review*, May 1923. Of Cole, Attlee said: 'I freely confess that he has caused me, like many others, to revise my previous views as to the future industrial structure of society.' (idem.) (See W. Golant, 'The Early Political Thought of C. R. Attlee,' *Political Quarterly*, July–Sept. 1969.)

as from the errors of bureaucracy in Russia.'[6] Indeed, a full inventory of the influence of Guild Socialism would be long and various—embracing the interest of Lenin, the influence on continental socialists like Otto Bauer, and manifold estimates of the probable future of G. D. H. Cole.[7]

Fortunately, no full assessment of the influence of Guild Socialism is required here. What is required, however, is some analysis of the response of Cole to that erosion of support for Guild Socialism produced by organized labour's retreat to a defensive position in the face of economic depression. One response was to insist on the continuing validity of the Guild analysis and programme in the face of developments in industry and politics. Thus the experiments with working guilds, especially in the building industry, were applauded and defended by Cole, though he was not directly involved with them and was very cautious about their survival prospects in a capitalist environment.[8] He regarded them as useful primarily for their confirmation of Guild Socialist arguments about the desire and capacity of workers for democratic organization, and about the quality of work produced under democratic conditions. They could not inaugurate a Guild society, nor could they survive without such a society; but they were valuable as example and inspiration.

Just as the working guilds attracted the attention of Guild Socialists in the early twenties, so too did the development of fascism in Italy. An analysis of the British response to early Italian fascism reveals the extent to which it received a warm welcome in diverse quarters. Not without cause did an Italian correspondent to the *New Statesman* in 1924 notice and regret 'the strange admiration which so many English papers and English people show for Fascism....'[9] It is scarcely surprising that Guild Socialists, casting their eyes around for social experiments on guild lines, should have looked with special interest at the nature of Italian fascism. Did it represent the sort of decentralized, self-governing social and economic structure which formed the basis of Guild Socialism? Both then and since there have been those who have

[6] 'A London Letter', *New Leader*, 23 Mar. 1923.

[7] On Lenin, see N. Carpenter, *Guild Socialism*, 1922, p. 116. For Cole's influence on Bauer, see the article by M. Croan in L. Labedz (ed.), *Revisionism*, 1962. C. P. Scott regarded Cole as the 'genuine British Bolshevist' (*The Political Diaries of C. P. Scott, 1911–28*, ed. T. Wilson, 1970, p. 333), while Northcliffe contemplated a future under Cole's premiership. (W. Hard, 'Northcliffe Personally', *New Republic*, 23 Aug. 1922.)

[8] On the working guilds, see F. Matthews, 'The Building Guilds', in Briggs and Saville (eds.), *Essays in Labour History*, Vol. 2, 1971.

[9] G. Salvadori, 'Fascism and the Coming Italian Elections', *New Statesman*, 1 Mar. 1924.

wanted to argue that it did represent just this. Thus Ulam suggests, absurdly, that it is the 'irony of history'[10] that Guild Socialism came nearest to realization in fascist Italy. Some Guild Socialists certainly embraced fascism and attempts were made, notably by Odon Por, to interpret fascism in Guild Socialist terms. In his books, *Guilds and Co-operatives in Italy* and *Fascism*, both written in 1923, Por set out as 'neither Fascist nor Bolshevist, but Guildsman'[11] to demonstrate that fascism was a revolutionary doctrine of functional democracy which was best understood in Guild Socialist terms.

It is necessary to say something about Cole's position on this matter. Unfortunately, the historical record is obscure and elusive, at least until the end of that phase of Italian fascism marked by the murder of Matteotti in 1924. Yet some evidence does exist, although confused and even contradictory. For example, Cole allowed one of his articles to appear as an appendix to that book by Odon Por which contained the claim that 'fascism desires to respect the social aspirations of Labour'.[12] At the same time, Por's work was favourably reviewed in the journal edited by the Coles, whilst associates from this period testify to Cole's interest in—even attraction to—the theoretical basis of Italian fascism.[13] However, it is equally clear that Cole in no sense embraced fascism. He wrote virtually nothing about it, so that a viewpoint can be culled only from occasional remarks. As evidenced by his response to the Russian Revolution, Cole's belief in national particularity made him unlikely to want to embrace or import foreign doctrines of any kind, or even to devote a great deal of attention to them. At a time when evidence and opinions about both Russia and Italy were confused and contradictory, Cole's own position reflected this uncertainty. If there is some evidence to suggest a sympathetic interest in the theoretical origins of Italian fascism, there is more explicit evidence to suggest a much more critical stance. Thus in 1923 Cole confessed himself 'much in the dark' about fascism; but on the basis of what he knew he felt able to say that 'the Fascist Corporations have nothing to do with "workers' control": they are agencies for the preservation of capitalism through social peace and reformist concessions to the workers. In the long run, they are likely to achieve no more than previous attempts to reconcile

[10] A. Ulam, *Philosophical Foundations of English Socialism*, 1951, p. 90.
[11] O. Por, *Fascism*, 1923, p. 18.
[12] Por, *Guilds and Co-operatives in Italy*, 1923, p. xvii.
[13] John Parker, M.P. recalls Cole's 'initial sympathy with Mussolini's corporate state which came out in the discussions of the Cole group. He saw it as a development of Sorel possibly leading to a form of socialist syndicalism'. (Letter to author, Apr. 1973.)

the irreconcilable'.[14] It is difficult to be conclusive on this, not least because of Cole's own confessed ignorance and uncertainty about the early nature of fascism. Perhaps it is only a minor footnote in intellectual history anyway, though responses to other and different intellectual systems and political creeds can prove a revealing test for any theorist. Certainly Cole's continuing evaluation of Marxism, or his analysis of Soviet Communism, were to provide important insights into his own developing position, particularly during the 1930s—just as they did for Laski, Strachey and many others.

In the 1920s, however, Cole's focus was firmly domestic. For some years he endeavoured to keep Guild Socialism alive as an idea even after its death as a movement, pressing its analysis in relation to contemporary events. Throughout 1923 and 1924 he struggled, with his wife, to maintain a journal, *New Standards*, which could provide Guild Socialism with a continuing voice in an unfavourable climate. It was a voice which addressed itself primarily to the political development of Labour and to the effects on the labour movement of the economic situation. In none of this was there any further development of Guild theory; merely the reiteration of its leading ideas, though in less confident tone than previously, in relation to contemporary events. Beyond this, there was a preoccupation with the needs of working-class education: an explicit recognition that support for the Guild idea needed rebuilding from the bottom. More generally, there was a deliberate flexibility about the organizational form of a Guild society. Cole showed little tendency to erect a defensive wall around his Guild scheme, but was instead emphatically tentative. He insisted that actual social forms were the product of social development, that a diversity in social ownership patterns was both probable and valuable, and that a relevant social theory would have constant revision as its essence. 'We cannot boldly say that we know now what is the only right form for Guild organisation', he wrote in 1923: 'we are still experimenting, and, I hope, learning from our experiments.'[15] The first results of this learning process, with important consequences for the democratic content of Guild theory, emerged during the 1920s—and were given full statement in Cole's *The Next Ten Years in British Social and Economic Policy* (1929), his first major piece of social analysis and argument for almost a decade.

In a fundamental sense, the decade of the 1920s has to be regarded as

[14] 'Guilds at Home and Abroad', *Guild Socialist*, May 1923.
[15] 'Next Steps in the Guild Movement', *Guild Socialist*, June 1923.

Cole's revisionist decade, during which many essentials of his original Guild theory came under scrutiny and modification. This process did not produce its mature results until 1929, but was in evidence much earlier. It reflected itself in his response to events and in his continuing analysis of the nature and prospects of the labour movement. It reflected itself, at a personal level, in a retreat to an academic tranquillity. The famous 'Cole group' at Oxford, initiated at this time, provided an ideal sounding-board for revisionist ideas. Those ideas related both to the definition of the socialist goal and to the method of its achievement. They represented a development in Cole's thought which was more than a mere shift of emphasis and which came close to eliminating part of the balance necessary for a sensible extremism. It was a development, moreover, which had important consequences for the democratic theory of Guild Socialism.

Cole's revisionism was founded upon the dissolution of the old certainties of the Guild period. He did not formally abandon Guild Socialism, but it now assumed the status of a desirable socialist end-state, distant from the immediate realities of labour politics. It was this breakdown in his own comprehensive socialist theory which he transferred to his analysis of the general condition of the British labour movement at this time. He sought to suggest that the whole traditional structure of socialist ideas was in ruins, leaving British socialism groping for a new synthesis, a new principle of unity. State socialism had dissolved under challenge from the Guild idea, but the latter had failed to win acceptance for its own system. The effect was that socialism was 'still no doubt a faith: but it is, like the faith of some modern Churchmen, a faith that has discarded all its doctrines—a disembodied faith in the soul of a dead idea.'[16] A significant indication of this disembodiment was to be seen in the policy deliberations of the I.L.P., which revealed the lack of any distinct theoretical perspective. Just as socialism had become diffused over a wide area of thought, it also now drew upon an equally wide area. The essential feature of British socialism, therefore, was that it had become 'eclectic and accommodating',[17] losing its old theoretical coherence. This was the analysis which Cole pressed throughout the 1920s, but it reveals more about his own evolution than that of British socialism itself. In many ways, the old certainties remained remarkably intact in this period (too intact perhaps), requiring an event of 1931 proportions to challenge them. 'There is upon us a

[16] 'English Socialism in 1924', *New Statesman*, 6 Sept. 1924.
[17] Ibid.

time of transition in ideas,' wrote Cole in 1924, 'when party labels mean ever less, and men uneasy in old faiths cling to them only in default of new.'[18] As a statement of the general condition of British socialism this was inaccurate; but as an indication of the particular disposition of Cole himself at the time of the decomposition of Guild Socialism and the arrival of the first Labour government it is both significant and revealing.

The transitional character of Cole's own socialism at this time, the product of an increasing scepticism about some of the confident system-building of Guild Socialism, is well illustrated by his response to contemporary events. The style was more tentative; the content more equivocal. Yet the direction of his thought was clear, involving a reconsideration both of the agency of socialist change and of the nature of that change itself. As such, it involved important modifications of his earlier treatment of industrial democracy and the nature of trade unionism. One indication of the magnitude of the change and the direction of his response was revealed in 1924 when he came to revise his *Introduction to Trade Unionism*, which first appeared in 1918. The original version was dominated by a confident belief that the aspiration to industrial control provided the defining characteristic of the nature and history of the trade union movement, a belief which shaped his account of the movement. By 1924, however, the style was cautious and the content descriptive. Whilst he still declared a belief that workers' control must remain the essential animating idea of trade unionism, this was now quickly stated as 'a personal view'[19] and was not explored.

His advice to the trade unions on their appropriate response to the economic environment of the 1920s revealed a similar and dramatic shift of ground. Gone was the Guild Socialist insistence that the trade unions must avoid any cooperation with the employers which did not promise an instalment of control; in its place came a belief that the trade unions shared an interest in the achievement of industrial efficiency. The young Cole would have laughed 'Mondism' out of the window, but now he accepted the merits of this attempt at industrial cooperation and defended the participation of the trade unions in it. His rationale was simple: the general strike weapon had exposed the limitations of mass industrial action, the condition of socialist advance was the return of a Labour government, the unemployment and inefficiency which

---

[18] Ibid.
[19] *Organised Labour*, 1924, p. 151.

characterized the British economy produced evil consequences for the working class which it was in its interests to avoid. This meant that the trade union movement 'cannot . . . wash its hands of responsibility for the efficiency of industry, even while it remains under capitalist ownership and control'.[20] It was claimed that this did not involve a permanent reconciliation with capitalism, merely a temporary accommodation for defined ends. The labour movement had a clear interest in industrial prosperity and, therefore, also in the re-organization necessary to bring this about. Hence the correct course was to 'offer, without disarmament or pretence of friendship of any kind, the participation of the Trade Unions in making industry thoroughly efficient'.[21] The implications of this view of trade unionism for the larger question of industrial versus political action will be examined in the next chapter, as will Cole's developing conception of state activity which made such activity the necessary precondition for the establishment of democracy in industry. Yet it is already clear that Cole had travelled a long way from that Guild position which made the demand for control the central purpose of trade unionism and which would contemplate only those forms of workshop participation in capitalism which gave genuine control without responsibility.

Addressing a Fabian audience in 1929, Cole declared that 'Socialism had need of both poets and sober prose writers but in present circumstances the latter were the more essential'.[22] Certainly his own abandonment of socialist poetry for sober socialist prose at this time was both conspicuous and self-conscious, with the needs of the times invoked as defence and explanation. Although his ambitious exercise in socialist prose at the end of the decade seemed to mark a sudden and dramatic shift of position which embraced both form and content (and was greeted as such), it has been possible to identify its origins as a process stretching over a span of years. Throughout the 1920s Cole could be seen grappling, often uneasily, with a number of ideas and strategies, then struggling to piece them together into some sort of coherent approach and programme. Not until the end of the decade, however, did a new confident unity begin to dispel tensions and uncertainty, as the pieces seemed finally to fit together and to point the way

[20] Ned Ludd (pseud.), 'The Issues at Edinburgh', *New Leader*, 16 Sept. 1927. On Mondism itself, see G. W. McDonald and H. F. Gospel, 'The Mond-Turner Talks, 1927–1933: A Study in Industrial Co-operation,' *Historical Journal*, Vol. xvi, 1973.
[21] Ibid. See also 'The Mond Conferences and Their Outcome', *Highway*, Oct. 1928.
[22] 'The Plain Prose of Socialist Policy', Fabian Lecture, 17 Oct. 1929. Report in *Fabian News*, Dec. 1929.

towards a new conception of socialist advance.[23] Thus *The Next Ten Years* represents a considerable theoretical landmark in his development.

Above all, perhaps, it revealed quite the extent to which Cole had come to revise many of the assumptions which had been basic to his Guild Socialism, despite his continued assertion of the essential rightness of the Guild position. It was, however, an explicit revisionism, for he recalled the growing doubts and uncertainties, the sense of hollow repetition of stale phrases, which culminated in this 1929 book; and it was his own record of this process, which clearly illuminated the direction and nature of the change involved. His explanation and justification were particularly interesting, for they turned on an appeal to the developing external environment which any socialist theory had to confront. He contrasted an environment of stable capitalist prosperity characteristic of the pre-1914 world, which allowed socialism to develop largely as 'an exercise in fantasy',[24] with the harsh realities of a declining capitalism symbolized by chronic unemployment. Cole was critical of those who, when faced with this changed environment, either abandoned politics for that cultivation of the self which so distinguished the intelligentsia of the twenties[25] or were content to repeat hallowed formulae which bore ever less relevance to the urgent problems requiring solution. He now portrayed Guild Socialism as a typical product of the former secure world of capitalist prosperity, whereas a contemporary socialism had necessarily to be more practical in its concerns if it was to prove its relevance to the realities of economic depression. In essence, then, socialism had to change because its setting had changed. If some theoretical purity was lost, much practical relevance was gained. Cole wanted to suggest a natural evolution of socialism from a propagandist to a programmatic stage, for socialism was now demanded 'as men call for water in a burning house', which necessarily makes us 'far less likely to grumble if only muddy water can be got'.[26]

Yet Cole's own revision went deeper than this. Not merely did he immerse himself in muddy water as a labour of necessity, but denied the

[23] Cole wrote to Clifford Allen (15 Aug. 1928) that his intellectual labours were 'bearing fruit with almost disconcerting abundance . . . I'm in the thick of a big book on Labour Policy . . . and I believe it is going to be damned good. Certainly, it is in a different street from anything on Labour I have written for a good many years past.' (Letter in possession of Margaret Cole.)

[24] *The Next Ten Years in British Social and Economic Policy,* 1929, preface.

[25] Thus Cyril Connolly's remark that, in the 1920s, 'politics consisted of an occasional walking tour in Albania'. (Quoted in N. Wood, *Communism and British Intellectuals,* 1959, p. 103.) Cole attacked this sort of 'conscious evasion of social realities'. (*Next Ten Years,* p. 15.)

[26] *Next Ten Years,* preface.

cleanliness of the sort of water he had earlier purveyed. In other words, Guild Socialism was not merely inappropriate in the world of 1929, but wrong absolutely in some of its most fundamental assumptions, not least in those which buttressed its argument for industrial democracy. For example, it was wrong in its suggestion that the character of work would be radically transformed in a democratic industrial structure, as capitalist coercion came to be replaced by a motive of free communal service. Instead, it was now clear that most work would remain as obligation and much as drudgery, despite all social engineering, and that any suggestion to the contrary had simply been 'our particular form of cant'.[27] Cole remained as graphically damning as ever about the routinized boredom of modern factory life, but not only did he now accept the inevitability of much of this but even accepted the Webbian argument, which he had previously attacked with such vigour, that the worker would seek to realize in his leisure what he lacked at his work and that the means to this realization would constitute his leading political demand.[28]

Guild Socialism was further wrong, it was now said, in its conception of the democratic inclinations and capacities of ordinary people, leading it to construct a social structure founded upon an erroneous belief in a continuously active citizenry. Surveying his Guild writings, Cole perceived them, correctly, as 'dominated by the idea of government as a moral discipline',[29] an approach which he was now anxious to discard as hopelessly unrealistic. The whole elaborate edifice of Guild democracy therefore crumbled in face of the discovery of the limited democratic inclinations of the ordinary man, a discovery to be accepted as natural rather than mourned as regrettable. Indeed, it was Guild Socialism which now was judged to have been rooted in the most unnatural foundations, whereas 'the great strength of Conservatism' was that it had 'never made the mistake of supposing man to be continuously an active political animal'.[30] If conservatism avoided this mistake, so too did Fabianism of course, as evidenced by Cole's espousal of an 'economy of effort' in social organization, a good Fabian principle which warned against the unnecessary proliferation of democratic machinery at the expense of leadership and expertise, for 'society must economise the efforts which it demands from its citizens in the

[27] Ibid., p. 16.
[28] See ibid., p. 103.
[29] Ibid., p. 160. The Guild scheme was now described as 'a politically minded person's Utopia'. (ibid., p. 161.)
[30] Ibid., p. 18.

exercise of the art of government'.[31] It is important to appreciate quite the extent of Cole's recantation in this respect, for it led him to strip democratic theory of its participatory dimension, to suggest that democracy could exist without representation (even that social energy can be dissipated by representative institutions), and to insist on the necessity of expert direction of much of social and industrial life. Even Beatrice Webb was moved to comment on the 'apparent sneers at Democracy'[32] which she detected in Cole's *Next Ten Years*!

The magnitude of the change involved was clearly seen in Cole's new sketch of the machinery of industrial democracy, which was designed to be compatible with the expert direction of industry. It centred on a system of works councils with limited powers over work organization and payment, involving no claim to general industrial control. It was presented as a realistic response to the sort of control which was actually wanted by the worker rather than ordained by a normative social theory. Its essential purpose was to provide workers with 'every chance of making their own claims and criticisms effectively heard',[33] a nice Webbian formulation. If this proposal illustrated the magnitude of Cole's theoretical shift, the origins of that shift were to be found in the dissolution of fundamental assumptions already noticed. But where, in a philosophical sense, did Cole now stand? What new theoretical yardstick did he introduce as a basis for social action? He provided the answer without being much interested in the question.

In his study of Harold Laski, Herbert Deane describes Laski's theoretical position at this same period in terms of a 'socialised Benthamism',[34] a phrase which exactly captures the essence of Cole's own position. Both Cole and Laski sought to give a positive social content to the maximizing principle of utilitarianism in the form of a programme of state action. Cole was now content to adopt the happiness of individual men and women as both the supreme good and the guiding purpose of political action, with the provision of happiness viewed from an orthodox passive and distributionist perspective against which (like the younger Mill) he had formerly rebelled. He was not concerned to explore the theoretical credentials of a socialized utilitarianism, however, but merely to assert that 'there is a great deal to be said for "the greatest happiness of the greatest number" as the supreme maxim for

---

[31] Ibid., p. 170.
[32] *Fabian News*, Dec. 1929.
[33] *Next Ten Years*, p. 163.
[34] H. Deane, *The Political Ideas of Harold J. Laski*, 1955.

Industrial Democracy and the Guild Idea 117

political conduct'.[35] Irrespective of its philosophical difficulties, it seemed to provide an attractive and useful basis for a radical political programme.

Its adoption by Cole symbolized his repudiation of his earlier emphasis on the character of the democratic process and his embrace of the nature of the policy product. In simplest terms, what mattered now was not how a thing was done but that it was in fact done. The explanation for this replacement of a theory of the democratic process by a calculation of policy consequences was to be found in Cole's conception of the need for immediate action to achieve economic recovery and reorganization. Such action seemed to require firm political leadership and the exercise of industrial expertise untrammelled by cumbrous representative machinery. Defending this approach, Cole declared his belief that the present generation did not care 'for the forms of democracy in the Victorian sense of the term' and that 'if people who knew their own minds assumed power and accomplished something they would not encounter much opposition...'.[36]

It is necessary to place this revision of Guild democratic theory in the context of Cole's economic preoccupation at this time, which will be discussed more fully in a later chapter. Partly, this preoccupation served simply to shift his interest away from the organization of the workplace to the organization of the economy as a whole. More particularly, however, his actual economic programme aimed to secure broad economic control without an elaborate network of bureaucratic nationalization, towards which he remained scarcely less well disposed than previously. As Guild Socialist, he used to distinguish (and prefer) socialization to nationalization in the name of democracy; now he made the same distinction (and preference), but only to demonstrate the primacy of social control over public ownership. He remained as unenthusiastic as ever at the prospect of a leviathan socialist state bogged down in the work of detailed administration,[37] but now found the antidote to this not in a system of functional democracy but in a conception of general economic control which avoided the snares of ownership and administration. Socialism

[35] *Next Ten Years*, p. 19. It seems that Gaitskell had some influence on Cole's thinking on this matter at this time, with Cole being persuaded to the view that 'one must ... always come back to the happiness of the individual'. (H. Gaitskell, 'At Oxford in the Twenties', in Briggs and Saville (eds.), op. cit., 1960, p. 14.)
[36] 'Nationalisation Old and New', Fabian Lecture, 22 Feb. 1929. Report in *Fabian News*, May 1929.
[37] See *Next Ten Years*, p. 134.

should not think in terms of particular, or even universal, national-ization, but in terms of the achievement of a controlling force in economic life. This involved a socialization of the 'key positions' in the economy, a phrase reminiscent of the 'commanding heights' of a later revisionist period in Labour history (associated with Cole's former pupil, Hugh Gaitskell), with the form of such socialization being open and flexible. Since the aim was simply to ensure a compliance by industries with the requirements of a general economic policy in the public interest, it was unlikely that traditional nationalization would be either necessary or appropriate.[38] Cole suggested a public control of investment which would ensure both a broad economic control and a degree of direct public control of industries which received investment funds.

In terms of the organization of a socialized economy, Cole rejected both direct civil service control and elaborate representative control in favour of a scheme of coordinated industrial commissions, whose independent and responsible status—subject to a general economic control and scrutiny by the state—would reflect the fact that industry was 'essentially an affair of experts'.[39] Thus, when Herbert Morrison announced his plan for London Transport, Cole welcomed it as an example of this new socialism of public boards with large autonomy in place of the old conception of direct state or municipal ownership.[40] He had ceased to demand an extensive machinery of internal democracy for socialized industry; but he still sought a form of socialization which gave considerable industrial autonomy and avoided the snare of bureaucratic state control. The public corporation model, in some form, seemed to meet these requirements.

In a fundamental sense, however, the form of socialization was no longer Cole's primary concern. Much of his easy revisionism, his ready abandonment of traditional assumptions, derived from this central fact. His concern at this time was not so much to demonstrate the errors of rival socialist theories as their essential irrelevance to the immediate situation confronting the British Labour movement. Thus the different

---

[38] Ibid., p. 134.
[39] Ibid., p. 136.
[40] See 'London Traffic and the New Socialism', *New Statesman*, 11 Oct. 1930. Morrison's Bill may have given 'a considerable shock to many sections of Labour opinion' (A. H. Hanson, 'Labour and the Public Corporation', in his *Planning and the Politicians*, 1969, p. 143), but clearly not to Cole. For the place of this Bill in the evolution of Labour policy, see G. N. Ostergaard, 'Labour and the Development of the Public Corporation', *Manchester School of Economic and Social Studies*, Vol. xxii, 1954.

conceptions of the structural form of the socialist future contained in the Webb scheme for a social parliament or in his own Guild plans were now pronounced 'equally beside the point'.[41] What mattered was to provide a short-term economic programme for a potential Labour government. Such a programme should be compatible with a longer term socialist evolution, but should not be designed for the sake of that evolution. Cole stated this position bluntly: 'We cannot ... afford to subordinate immediate claims to the achievement of Socialism.'[42] In other words, the future of socialism was tied by Cole to the ability of the Labour movement to provide a practical and relevant response to the economic crisis of capitalism.

This, then, was the context in which Cole distanced himself most sharply from the democratic theory of the Guild period. Yet his new position was not free from tension and ambiguity. It is significant, for example, that his thought found a new assurance only when confined to a contemplation of the 'next ten years'. If the systematic integrity of Guild Socialism could no longer be sustained, there was no easy attachment to a rival system either. Cole preferred to suspend any further explorations into the theory of socialism for the economic duration, restricting himself to the formulation of a programme for economic recovery. Yet the very notion of such a suspension, coupled with the requirements of a recovery programme, necessarily involved some basic theoretical revision. For example, it involved—as seen in this and subsequent chapters—a statement about the prospects for socialism, a new attitude to the state, a modification of democratic theory and a new conception of parliamentary Labourism. Yet Cole refused to concede, even to discuss, the permanency of such theoretical revision, producing that impression of disjuncture in his thought, the sense of operating at two distinct levels, which always remained such a distinctive feature of his thought. Thus, he argued the case for a recovery programme whilst insisting that there could be no satisfactory solution to unemployment without a fundamental system-change. Equally, he made the state central to the operation of his economic programme whilst continuing to assert its limited place in social theory. He accepted the requirements of a parliamentary road to socialism whilst retaining a deep scepticism about its feasibility. In a wider sense, he continued to defend that community theory of society which had

[41] *Next Ten Years*, p. 156.
[42] Ibid., p. 157.

provided the basis for his Guild Socialism even when he could no longer give it systematic structural form.[43] Much of this tension derived from the dilemma of a utopian socialist who both confronted an environment inimical to utopianism and was impatient to contribute to the solution of immediate economic problems. In so far as this dilemma continued beyond the 1920s, so too did the tension and ambiguity in Cole's socialism.

If the 1920s represented the period of major revision of the democratic theory of Guild Socialism, the decade which followed preserved that revision by neglect. Cole's attention remained firmly fixed on the pressing problems of that troubled decade (the economy, fascism, socialist strategy) and he showed little inclination to return to the themes of the Guild period. Indeed, this was true of the labour movement as a whole in the 1930s, so much so that 'the doctrine of workers' control became attenuated, and the continuity of its influence was seriously threatened'.[44] Labour certainly gave much attention to nationalization in this period and, under the influence of Herbert Morrison, elaborated its conception of the public corporation model; but, despite some residual opposition which demanded a greater role for representatives of the workers, there was little critical debate about the form that socialization should take. The eyes of Labour, like those of Cole, were now firmly fixed on other things.

Yet the events of the 1930s did throw up evidence about the human condition which seemed to make further dents in the fabric of assumptions upon which Guild democratic theory had been built. Above all, the psychological foundations of the Guild argument seemed to look rather flimsy when set against the experience of the 1930s. No longer was it possible to erect a comprehensive social theory upon an untested set of assumptions about human motivation. Particular attention was given to the psychological environment in which the fascist appeal gained ground, with emphasis on the role of fear and uncertainty in mobilizing people for a cause which promised positive, confident solutions to complex problems. In fact, Cole's early discussion of fascism tended to treat it as an essentially activist rejection of a passive parliamentarism, raising important problems about the psychology of activism and the techniques of mobilization. He began to stress the need for the democratic movement to counter fascism by its own

positive programme of mobilization.[45] Before long, however, he was
less impressed with the ability of fascism to stir people to political
activism than concerned with the implications of this ability for conventional assumptions about social theory and organization. Thus his
earlier declaration of his 'trust' in human nature was replaced by a
concern with the psychological foundations of mass movements, for
contemporary evidence had demonstrated the existence of 'deep
irrationalities in the human mind',[46] demanding a reconsideration of
many varieties of traditional social theory. He had always acknowledged the importance of the psychological dimension of politics (usually with a laudatory nod in the direction of Graham Wallas), but now
he demanded the development of a more systematic social psychology—for 'more than anything else, we need to-day a clearer appreciation of what men are like'.[47] Without fuller knowledge of this kind, he
now believed, it behoved us to be cautious in our theoretical constructions. Thus fascism seemed to have knocked another nail into the
coffin of Cole's Guild democracy.

Although further discussion of Guild Socialism was notably absent
from Cole's thought in the 1930s, his occasional attention to Guild
themes was distinguished by a tendency to operate at two distinct
levels. On the one hand, he declared himself an unrepentant Guild
Socialist—even if 'I cannot, nowadays, be quite so cheerful and
confident a Guild Socialist as I used to be'.[48] He continued to insist on
the need to avoid bureaucracy and to transform the character of work;
and continued to make a system of industrial self-government and
functional devolution central to his discussion of the nature of a mature
socialist society. Yet all this was now offered perfunctorily as a long-
term statement of socialist intent; and, even at this level, there was no
further discussion of the substantial modifications he had introduced
into Guild democratic theory in the late 1920s. On the other hand,
however, he was now much less concerned with the nature of a
developed socialism than with the content of an immediate, transitional
socialist programme.

At this level, the Guild position suffered two critical modifications. In
the first place, the need to establish rapid and comprehensive socialist
economic control took precedence over the early establishment of an

[45] *A Guide to Modern Politics* (1934) was described as 'a realistic study of political dynamic' and of 'the "technique" of political co-operation'. (P. 10.)
[46] 'Freethought and the Struggle for Peace and Freedom', *World Union of Freethinkers*, Sept. 1938.
[47] 'The Changing Economic Order', *Science and Society*, Feb.–May. 1937.
[48] 'Guild Socialism Twenty Years Ago and Now', *New English Weekly*, Sept. 1934.

elaborate system of workers' control. 'When we have got our schemes of socialisation into working order,' he wrote, 'we can begin rapidly to devolve responsibility within them; but we cannot afford to risk failure and confusion by trying to be too "democratic" at the very start.'[49] In terms of the machinery of socialization, Cole now explicitly favoured the public corporation model, with a system of dual directorates designed to reconcile expert management with democratic control at the national level (whereas Guild Socialism sought to combine, not merely reconcile, the tasks of management and representation); whilst at a lower level a start was to be made with a system of workshop committees and works councils with limited, but growing, powers.[50] All this was a long way··from Guild Socialism, of course, though Cole emphasized that his concern was only with the character of a transitional period. The second fundamental modification of Guild Socialism, recorded more fully in the following chapter, related to the achievement of socialism itself. No longer was the industrial sphere the decisive arena of struggle; and no longer were the trade unions the decisive agency of socialist advance.[51] Instead, it was now clear 'that socialisation must come as a political measure, rather than as a product of direct action in the industrial field'.[52] In other words, the political victory of socialism was the first priority, for it was the precondition for the appropriate organizational development of a maturing socialist society. It alone could provide the framework within which a system of industrial and functional democracy could be established. Thus Cole (like Laski) had moved to a position which made the achievement of a system of socialist pluralism dependent upon the prior, political achievement of a general socialization.

In general, therefore, the 1930s saw Cole profoundly uninterested in any further critical consideration of Guild theory, with his energies directed towards more pressing concerns. When he did join the discussion on the form of socialization he insisted that his proposals related merely to a transitional period. Yet no attempt was made to relate such transitional proposals to the larger framework of Guild

---

[49] *Socialist Control of Industry* (Socialist League, 1933).

[50] See 'The Essentials of Socialisation', *Political Quarterly*, July, 1931; and *Workers' Control and Self-Government in Industry* (ed. with W. Mellor, New Fabian Research Bureau, 1933).

[51] 'In these days Socialism cannot be founded on a Trade Union basis only.' (*What Marx Really Meant*, 1934, p. 173.)

[52] *Principles of Economic Planning*, 1935, p. 336. Elsewhere he wrote: 'The industrial part of workers' control can come only when we have already won the political part.' ('Workers' Control', *Railway Service Journal*, Apr. 1934.)

theory and, as they stood, they departed little from the mainstream of contemporary Labour thinking on the model of democracy appropriate to socialized industry.[53] Finally, in so far as his discussion of industrial democracy tended to separate present proposals from future objectives, it was wholly typical of the wider character of his thought in this period. It was evident, for example, in his discussion of economic planning; and in both areas his attention alternated, often uneasily, between the nature of a mature socialist society and a rather different description of immediate socialist objectives.

Yet the 1930s did not mark the final abandonment by Cole of the Guild conception of socialist democracy. Indeed, the last twenty years of his life, which have a broad unity in this respect, may almost be described in terms of a return to first things—though a return inevitably affected by the enormity of intervening experience. Themes and ideas which were central to his Guild Socialist thought, but which suffered neglect thereafter, again came to occupy a leading place in his statement of socialism. He justified the intervening neglect (both at the time and subsequently) as, above all else, the necessary consequence of the impact of prolonged economic depression on the organization and spirit of the British labour movement. His own response to this situation had been to immerse himself in these same economic preoccupations. As depression gave way to recovery, as the state declared its responsibility for full employment, and as the foundations of welfarism were laid, it again seemed possible to turn to more fundamental socialist concerns. In academic terms, Cole's transference from economics to the Chair of Social and Political Theory at Oxford at the end of the war symbolized and reflected this shift of emphasis. In socialist terms, however, it could not merely be business as before.

On the one hand, all that the 'Thirties' represented had to be digested—everything from fascism to Keynesianism—before a new socialist theory could be constructed out of the old; whilst on the other hand, socialism now had to confront an international environment dominated by Soviet–American antagonism. If Cole's thought is approached in this way—as a return to earlier concerns subject only to the force of these powerful constraints—we come close to its essential spirit and purpose in its final period. It was a purpose, moreover, which again had the problem of democracy at its centre. For some two decades after the early 1920s, Cole's thought had shown little interest

[53] The classical statement of that model is to be found in Herbert Morrison, *Socialisation and Transport*, 1933.

124 *Industrial Democracy and the Guild Idea*

in continuing the discussion of democratic theory and organization. There was, as has been seen, his partial retreat from earlier positions in the late 1920s and, in the 1930s, his diffident contribution to the debate on the structural form of nationalization. In general, however, during this whole period the issue of socialist democracy was deliberately filed away in favour of more pressing concerns. Not until the early 1940s were the files again re-arranged.

Writing in 1941, Cole described his essential wartime purpose in terms of an attempt to persuade socialists 'to think supra-nationally, to think democratically, and to think realistically'.[54] Later chapters explore the other terms of this statement, but it is the injunction to 'think democratically' which provides the most significant indication of the developing character of his socialist thought in its final period. Above all, it provides a framework which organizes and explains much else in his thinking. At one level, his demand was for a democratic war effort, involving a vigilant parliament, the exercise of necessary controls through local and voluntary agencies, the assertion of neighbourhood and workshop democracy, and a vigorous process of wartime discussion and debate—in which the Labour Party should be central—designed to keep the democratic spirit alive. More significant than these actual proposals, however, was the general conception which informed them. Cole regarded the war as the inevitable progenitor of an immensely strengthened state machine which would be available subsequently as the powerful instrument of whichever force and creed commanded it. It would be available both for socialism and for a quasi-fascist state controlled capitalism. It was this fact which led him to insist on 'the devastating perils of State control without democracy'[55] during the war and on the need to get the wartime state machine into the right democratic hands, lest it should emerge from war ripe for use as the instrument of a fascist totalitarianism—or as the agent of a merely bureaucratic socialism. Yet if the war served to intensify the need to democratize an increasingly powerful state, it did not originate or exhaust that need. Rather, it simply provided a telling illustration—and acceleration—of an existing tendency. Here we come to the heart of his socialist analysis at this time, which focused on the inevitable accretion of state power and on the establishment of the apparatus of socialism irrespective of ideological considerations. The machinery of socialism would come 'as a derivative of the new age of

[54] *Europe, Russia and the Future*, 1941, p. 172.
[55] *The War On The Home Front*, Fabian Tract 247, 1939.

concentrated technical power', which meant that 'the question is, not whether the State is to control, but how, and to what end'.[56] Hence the necessity for socialists to think seriously about the problem of democracy.

Certainly Cole himself devoted much thought to it. His vocabulary becomes dominated by the language of size, in which 'hugeness' takes pride of place as the defining characteristic of the modern world.[57] It is important to stress, against those who insist on depicting Cole as the utopian protagonist of a smaller and simpler society who never came to terms with the sheer scale of modern civilization, that it was precisely his recognition of the inevitability of larger units (both economically and politically) which prompted his concern with a democratic theory which both accepted this fact and developed a response to it. In other words, it was necessarily the age of hugeness, the era of the leviathan; the task for socialists was to accept and capture the leviathan—and to tame it in the interests of democracy. Internationally, Cole's sweeping commitment at this time to giant, supra-national units will be noticed later; whilst, domestically, he presented the increasing concentration of economic life as the necessary product of advances in science and productive technique which were required to improve material living standards. In each area, however, he sought to provide a democratic antidote to these huge political and economic units.

Domestically, therefore, it was necessary for socialists to work out a democratic basis for the political and economic leviathan which they were destined to create. Yet why, according to Cole, was this so necessary? Why could not the socialist leviathan simply take care of itself, distributing its fruits efficiently and justly? In answering questions of this kind, he returned to themes and arguments which had been basic to his statement of Guild Socialism. Democracy recognized the right of citizen participation in social decisions; and democratic activity was itself an exercise in creativity and self-expression for the individual. From these twin foundations he could expand on the democratic case: there must be democracy in small things if there was to be democracy in larger ones; there could be no substitute for an active democracy in a mechanical and remote parliamentarism; economic efficiency required a set of incentives and motives which only a democratic organization of

---

[56] *Great Britain in the Post-War World*, 1942, p. 11.

[57] 'We must, if we are to find a decent way of living under the technical conditions of our time, at once accept hugeness as the environment of the coming society, and find means of not being drowned in it.' (*Europe, Russia and the Future*, 1941, p. 77.)

work could provide; democracy had to be rooted in the activity of the functional and local group, not in the atomistic passivity of the isolated individual—and so on. If all this sounded like vintage Guild Socialist stuff Cole was happy to describe himself as 'an ancient, unrepentant Guild Socialist', whose essential message to the socialist movement was that 'the danger, the appalling danger, that is facing us to-day is that in making our escape from capitalism we shall run right into the arms of bureaucracy masquerading as popular control'.[58] His own response to this danger, therefore, was to press a doctrine of radical democracy on the socialist movement in much the same way as he had done a generation previously. He also returned to a familiar social theory as a setting for this democratic doctrine: his Inaugural Lecture at Oxford in 1945 resumed his attack, suspended a quarter of a century earlier, on a monistic political theory preoccupied with the state and its sovereignty, offering instead a wider social theory rooted in a conception of pluralism which would be 'the central inspiration of everything I have to say as occupant of this Chair'.[59]

In some respects, however, Cole's democratic pluralism now revealed a significant change of emphasis, even of content. In terms of emphasis, his argument for democracy now depended much more than previously on an analysis of the dangers inherent in social atomism which cut the individual adrift from close participation in group life. Under the impact of fascism, Cole had discovered the phenomenon of the 'mass society', that favourite concept of political sociology, which isolated men and women from their social environment and converted them into objects of manipulation by movements and ideologies which promised them a home and a cause. Here was the real problem of man face to face with hugeness, alone against the great leviathan. In pressing this analysis, Cole called psychology to the aid of sociology; for when man was denied democratic involvement in an immediate and familiar social environment, he was 'flung back merely on his unreasoning and amoral under-self, which is ruled by appetite, and is capable of believing anything that will serve its appetitive ends'.[60] By contrast, an actively democratic group life provided man with a secure social and psychological anchorage. Cole advanced this as a clear lesson of fascism

---

[58] *Co-operation, Labour and Socialism*, Blandford Memorial Lecture, Nov. 1946. See also, 'What Socialism Means To Me', *Labour Forum*, Oct.–Dec. 1947.

[59] *Scope and Method In Social and Political Theory*, Inaugural Lecture, Oxford, Nov. 1945.

[60] 'Leviathan and Little Groups', *Aryan Path*, Oct. 1941. The vision of this 'underman' came to haunt Cole's thought at this time. Above all, he presented fascism as founded upon the discovery of 'this terrible underman'. (*The Intelligent Man's Guide To The Post-War World*, 1947, p. 244.)

and of war, and made it central to his statement of the case for a social order rooted in a small-group democracy which 'will not desert little men forlorn and alone in a world whose hugeness leaves them shuddering and afraid of the dark'.[61] It was noticed earlier that the first psychological lesson drawn by Cole from fascism had cautioned him against any confident commitment to an active democracy; yet that same psychological lesson was now harnessed to a sociological argument for a participatory democratic pluralism.

If this approach produced some shift of emphasis within Cole's democratic argument, there was also a similar shift (which reached the borderline of emphasis and content) in his conception of the appropriate democratic structure. The starting-point, however, was both clear and familiar: a genuine democracy had to be rooted in the life of small groups. 'In this age of hugeness', he wrote, 'we must still find means of resting our society on a foundation of small groups, of giving these small groups a functional place in our society, of integrating them with the larger organisations which are indispensable for modern living, of encouraging a continual development of new groups responding to developing needs, and, last but not least, of countering every tendency towards bureaucratisation of this quintessential group life.'[62] Already there is a clue here to some change in Cole's position since the days of Guild Socialism; for instead of embracing existing functional groups as the basic democratic units he now wrote of groups being 'given' a functional status inside a democratic structure. In fact, the functional principle could no longer be said to be integral to Cole's democratic theory—except in so far as groups could be described as functional to the operation of a democratic society.

An important consequence of this theoretical shift was seen when Cole came to define the key groups from a democratic point of view. He focused on where men live and where they work as the essential social units, the twin foundations for a democratic social structure. The emphasis on the workplace, of course, had been central to the Guild position; and Cole continued to stress its importance. Yet even in this respect, he wanted to introduce some significant modifications to his earlier theory. For example, it was now stated categorically that producer cooperation and workers' control could not create or preface socialization, but could only be a consequence of it.[63] He had already

---

[61] *Great Britain in the Post-War World*, p. 153.
[62] *Europe, Russia And The Future*, p. 166.
[63] See *A Century Of Co-operation*, 1944, p. 292.

committed himself to this position in the 1930s, as was noted earlier; but he had avoided any rigorous discussion of the matter then and it was now simply treated as axiomatic. Furthermore, he was no longer prepared to make the trade unions the agency of workshop democracy, regarding them as too remote from the immediate work situation and with a distinct and continuing function to perform; preferring, instead, to think in terms of the erection of a new set of democratic groups rooted in the workplace. Here, too, was a major departure from that original position which sought to convert the trade unions into self-governing producer Guilds; but again Cole offered no real analysis of those factors causing him to abandon his original conception. However, his new position found somewhat more explicit statement, as will be seen shortly, when in the 1950s he again attempted to sketch a structural form of industrial democracy. The evidence provided by his renewed interest in democratic ideas in the 1940s simply suggested that any new projection of industrial democracy on Guild lines would involve a system of worker representation independent of existing trade union organization.

There was a further departure from original Guild democratic theory at this time. It was seen how, in Cole's hands, Guild theory had launched a vigorous assault on the Webbian attachment to territorial, geographical democratic units, which were seen as much inferior from a democratic point of view to the application of the functional principle which established the primacy of democracy in industry. Now Cole moved much closer to the Webb position, emphasizing the democratic importance of the neighbourhood group and devoting much time to a discussion of the sort of physical environment in which neighbourhood democracy might flourish. In the later stages of the Guild movement, Cole had begun to turn his attention to the relationship between a Guild industrial system and a re-organized local government, but now he openly affirmed the democratic parity of workplace and neighbourhood. Indeed, at times he seemed to suggest that neighbourhood had become *more* important than industry for the establishment of a democratic community.[64] He demanded housing development which provided the physical conditions and facilities for an active communal life (and was damning about the sort of suburban jungle which made such life impossible); and was lyrical in his embrace of a 'community poli-

---

[64] Describing the essence of Guild Socialism, Cole said that: 'workers' control in industry is only one aspect, and perhaps nowadays not the most important'. ('Community-Making', Fabian Lunch, 26 Feb. 1945, Cole Collection.)

tics' whereby people came to exert control over their immediate physical and social environment. Linking workplace and neighbourhood, he wanted a democratic system rooted in street and factory 'soviets', for these provided the small-group territorial and economic foundations for a wider democratic society. Despite all modifications, therefore, in this central respect he reaffirmed his earliest conception that democracy had to be built from the bottom, not the top. That bottom had now been broadened, but it still consisted of a group life which incorporated 'the essential qualities of unmediated, direct democracy based on personal contact and discussion, and on close mutual knowledge and community of small-scale immediate problems'.[65]

So here was Cole, in the middle of a world war whose issue remained in the balance, advancing 'hugeness' as the critical problem of the hour and pressing a radical democratic solution. He was impatient with those who described the war as being waged *for* democracy, when their conception of democracy amounted only to a formal parliamentarism in which politics remained the preserve of the politicians. If hugeness was inevitable in the post-war world, it would require an active face-to-face democracy to humanize it. It is important to emphasize Cole's conception of the essential trend of social development, for it influenced so much else in his thought. On the one side, he saw (and accepted) the increasing scale of political and economic organization as the condition of economic rationality and political cooperation. Domestically, this meant an increasingly powerful state machine; internationally, perhaps, a super-state. On the other side, he saw the decline or eclipse into respectability of those institutions and associations (the trade unions, the nonconformist chapels, the cooperative movement etc.) which had diffused a habit of democratic fellowship throughout wide sections of the community, leaving the individual increasingly alone and isolated in face of the new leviathan. It was a bleak and dangerous prospect, requiring bold and imaginative remedies.

Cole's sense of the sterility of the existing political landscape, including that part of it dominated by the Labour movement, in face of this critical challenge made him deal lightly with old allegiances. For example, he was now impatient with the restrictive and bureaucratic mentality which distinguished much of the trade union movement; and

---

[65] *Europe, Russia And The Future*, p. 172. Hence Cole, unlike many post-war 'new democrats', did not seek to use his analysis of fascism and its socio-psychological foundations to prove the need for a more elitist and less activist conception of democratic theory. See G. Duncan and S. Lukes, 'The New Democracy', *Political Studies*, Vol. xi, 1963.

was scornful of the paralysis of will and imagination which seemed to afflict the Labour Party, some of which he now attributed to its dependence on trade unionism. Indeed, so urgent was the need for a new movement which was alive to the essential trend of social development, and so unlikely was the prevailing political framework either to recognize the need or to respond to it, that he suggested the necessity to go 'outside politics'[66] in the search for solutions. By this, he meant a return to the active democratic fellowship of the group, the only sure foundations for a wider democratic society. It was necessary to develop the *spirit* of democracy at group level, the belief that the active exercise of will could tame the modern juggernaut, before a more elaborate democratic structure could be established. This, at least, was Cole's response to the democratic idleness enforced by the wartime political truce.

There is, then, clearly some justice in presenting Cole's thought in the war and post-war period in terms of a return to earlier concerns. If answers seemed more elusive than in the Guild period, many of the questions were strikingly similar. Above all, there was the definition of the relationship between the necessary hugeness of contemporary forces and the need for democratic social control as the quintessential problem of the twentieth century. The problem was easier to identify than resolve; and it remained to be seen whether a democratic sentiment could be converted into a concrete programme for a democratic social structure. Yet Cole had certainly found a new democratic energy which asserted that people would advance towards a socialist civilization 'not by turning their back on the juggernauts that ride over them, but by facing manfully the task of bringing these monsters under collective, democratic, Socialist control'.[67] This was the approach which dominated his socialist thought during the last decade of his life—a period when he could be described as 'still the most creative thinker in the Labour movement'.[68]

According to Bernard Crick, the distinctive feature of socialist literature in the 1950s was its fragmentation, its lack of that 'comprehension' which should be basic to a socialist theory; instead, there was just 'stuff woven for a decade not a season'.[69] If this indictment has to be qualified in some respects, its general accuracy is clear. The 'revisionists' certainly made the theoretical running as the decade progressed, but only

---

[66] *Great Britain in the Post-War World*, p. 165.
[67] 'A Socialist Civilisation', in *Programme For Victory*, Fabian Society, 1941, p. 187.
[68] R. H. S. Crossman, Introduction to *New Fabian Essays* (3rd edn., 1970), p. v.
[69] 'Socialist Literature in the 1950s', *Political Quarterly*, July–Sept. 1960.

to announce that the future of socialism was that it had no future. The left seemed able only to mount a series of responses, to affirm its belief in the challenged orthodoxies—and to announce its 'Conviction'. As the representative of the I.L.P. tradition, Bevanism was strong on sentiment but weak on theory. Just as this had earlier guaranteed the intellectual hegemony of Fabianism within the Labour Party, with the I.L.P. relegated to the role of an ineffectual permanent opposition,[70] it now allowed the intellectual ascendancy of the New Fabians. If Cole preferred to 'stand aloof' from Labour's internal quarrels in these years, it was because the issues seemed really to be 'secondary and . . . [to] threaten the solidarity of the workers' movement for no sufficiently good reason'.[71]

Certainly Cole was a 'fundamentalist' during this period, but it was a fundamentalism which transcended the ideological confines of Labour's internecine strife. He was impatient with revisionists and Bevanites alike. The latter scarcely got beyond the level of negative, instinctive response—and were innocent about the state of the British economy; whilst the former had thrown away socialism in a 'panic against totalitarianism'.[72] Cole's own fundamentalism involved an attempt to define a new direction for democratic socialism both domestically and internationally. Domestically, this meant confronting the problems posed by the welfare state and the mixed economy; internationally, it meant confronting the problem of the relationship between communism and social democracy. In two long pamphlets devoted to these problems (*Is This Socialism?*, 1954, and *World Socialism Restated*, 1956,) Cole provided a challenging contribution to the 'future of socialism' which contrasts sharply with other contemporary offerings of British socialism. Indeed, in his attempt to give content and direction to the non-communist left (and this was the enterprise which provided the theme for the last decade of his life), he aimed at just that 'comprehension' of analysis which was absent from much contemporary socialist writing. These same years saw the appearance of his vast and (the word seems unavoidable) monumental *History of Socialist Thought*, which also sought to comprehend the totality of socialist experience. It is clear that Cole's final years were a period of considerable intellectual vitality, during which he both looked to his own past concerns and,

---

[70] See T. Nairn, 'The Nature of the Labour Party', in P. Anderson and R. Blackburn (eds.), *Towards Socialism*, 1965.
[71] 'Socialism and the Welfare State', *New Statesman*, 23 July 1955.
[72] 'Twentieth Century Socialism?', *New Statesman*, 7 July 1956.

in so doing, anticipated some of the central concerns of the socialist future.[73]

This was particularly evident in Cole's increasing preoccupation with the problem of socialist democracy. When, in 1951, he described British socialism as having 'drifted into a position in which nobody feels any enthusiasm for further nationalisation'[74] (with 'nothing much left to be done, along the established lines'), he was not merely describing an electoral mood but also expressing his own disillusionment. He drew up a catalogue of the failings of the sort of socialism practised by Labour's post-war Government: its brand of nationalization was incapable of stirring the energies and enthusiasm of producer or consumer; the public corporation model, deceptively attractive at its inception—not least to Cole himself, as was seen earlier—turned out to be 'a bad cross between bureaucracy and big business',[75] and, in general, Labour had fallen 'victim of the tendency towards centralisation and authoritarian control which it should have been its mission to fight: it could see the evils of Fascist or Communist authoritarianism, but not the bureaucratic mote in its own eye'.[76] In both language and substance, this indictment reached back over nearly half a century to the Guild Socialist critique of Labour's original Fabianism. Cole's new prescription also contained a familiar ring: the only alternative to a centralized authoritarianism was 'to diffuse power, to fling power and responsibility into many hands...'.[77] Power should be diffused to producers in a system of industrial democracy; diffused to consumers through a new machinery of consumer representation; and diffused geographically in a reorganized and regionalized system of local government. In all this, it is possible to write of Cole's return to first things. Indeed, in his statement of the need to 'bring together *within the Labour Party* those who believe that democratic Socialism requires not a concentration, but a diffusion of responsibility and power',[78] there was clear evidence of a desire to re-create something akin to the old Guild movement itself.

Cole's italics, however, indicate that much had changed—both in

---

[73] 'The New Left has often been tempted to claim him [Cole] as a patron, but perhaps it would be more accurate to say that we have caught up with him, about fifty years late.' (Peter Sedgwick, 'Liquidating the Thirties', *New Left Review*, Jan.–Feb. 1961.)

[74] 'Shall Socialism Fail?' II, *New Statesman*, 12 May 1951.

[75] Ibid.

[76] Ibid.

[77] 'Shall Socialism Fail?' I, *New Statesman*, 5 May 1951.

[78] 'Shall Socialism Fail?' II, *New Statesman*, 12 May 1951.

the environment confronted by a new Guild movement and in his own response to it. There was Labour's domination of the British left; a politically conservative trade union movement; and a decline of interest on the part of both the industrial and political wings of the labour movement in questions of industrial democracy and control. This last point has a particular bearing on any consideration of Cole's thought in this period. In 1948 it would have been possible to interpret half a century of Labour thinking on this matter in terms of the progressive triumph of a centralist definition of democratic control. One contemporary survey did just this; and concluded that 'during the last decade the Labour party has abandoned the goal of workers' control'.[79] Nor did the situation alter very much during the following decade. In 1959, almost in the month of Cole's death, C. A. R. Crosland could introduce a discussion of industrial democracy and workers' control by saying that 'today one scarcely hears a whisper of these matters at Labour Party or Trade Union Conferences'.[80] In these circumstances, therefore, it is broadly accurate to present Cole as a voice in the wilderness during these years. Indeed, he clearly regarded his own work in this way. Writing about his forthcoming book on *The Case For Industrial Partnership* (1957)—described as 'an attempt to apply some of the old Guild Socialist ideas to present conditions'—he remarked that he was 'hoping to get some notice taken of it, but not very confidently'.[81] This background is important, for it had a marked effect on Cole's approach. No longer was it a matter of attempting to press a particular philosophy and programme of industrial (and social) democracy on a 'world of labour' already receptive to the general principle, but of attempting to re-establish the credentials of the principle itself.

Much of Cole's argument followed familiar Guild Socialist lines. It sought to present democracy as a comprehensive social doctrine; to emphasize the human benefits of democratic activity and the costs of passivity; to establish the centrality of participation at work to a wider democratic vitality—and so on. At bottom, it sought to make the question of *status* basic to the socialist position. 'This matter of status appears to me to be of fundamental importance', he wrote; so that the

[79] R. Dahl, 'Workers' Control of Industry and the British Labour Party', *American Political Science Review*, xli, 1947.

[80] C. A. R. Crosland, 'What Does The Worker Want?' *Encounter*, Feb. 1959; reprinted as 'Industrial Democracy and Workers' Control', in his *The Conservative Enemy*, 1962. For dissenting voices cf. R. Harrison, 'Retreat from Industrial Democracy', *New Left Review*, July–Aug. 1960; and D. Butt, 'Workers' Control', *New Left Review*, July–Aug. 1961.

[81] Cole to E. P. Thompson (n.d., 1957; letter in possession of Margaret Cole).

socialist commitment to equality was essentially 'a matter even more of social status than of the abolition of differences of income.'[82] It was upon this foundation of status that he erected a conception of industrial 'partnership'[83] which contained the twin Guild claims to industrial maintenance and to democratic control. As with Guild Socialism, too, this control had to begin at the bottom not at the top; on the shop-floor not in the boardroom. It was because the argument about industrial democracy had ignored this central fact that the Guild Socialists had 'stood somewhat aloof'[84] from demands for trade union representation on the boards of socialized industries. In fact, it has been seen that this was not the only reason for Cole's own aloofness on this over the years.

If much of this was orthodox Guild Socialism, however, Cole's position now contained important departures from Guild theory—departures already hinted at in his previous glancing reference to these matters. The whole balance between industrial and political action had changed: industrial self-government would come as the product of a political socialism committed to the diffusion of power. The trade unions, originally conceived as central both to the achievement and structure of a Guild system, were now relegated to a subsidiary role in the advancement of industrial democracy and entirely dispossessed from any place in the developed machinery of workers' control. Cole now gave a good Webbian definition of the function of trade unions, confining them to an essentially defensive role which meant that 'if they became participants in industrial management, (they) would in effect cease to be trade unions'.[85] Industrial democracy would require a separate machinery of worker representation. Declaring himself a proven friend of the trade unions, Cole was now severely critical of them. He attacked a bureaucratic leadership which was firmly centralist, suspicious of workers' control and antagonistic to workshop autonomy. Although suggesting a number of decentralist remedies for the malaise and atrophy that he detected, he remained

[82] *The Case For Industrial Partnership*, 1957, p. 7. For a more extended and rigorous statement of socialism as 'equal respect', see S. Lukes, 'Socialism and Equality', in L. Kolakowski and S. Hampshire (eds.), *The Socialist Idea*, 1974.
[83] Cole admitted to some hesitation in choosing the word 'partnership' rather than 'control'; but his choice derived from 'an increasing awareness that the word "control" bears quite a different meaning in French and indeed in other languages from that which I associated with it primarily in English. What one means is in French "gestion" rather than "controle"'. (Letter to G. Ostergaard, 17 June 1957; in possession of Margaret Cole.)
[84] *An Introduction To Trade Unionism*, 1953, p. 231.
[85] *The Case For Industrial Partnership*, p. 15.

deeply pessimistic about the condition of trade unionism—and of a trade union-dominated Labour Party. He summed up their contemporary state as the 'great negation'.[86] Certainly it was a gloomy environment in which to seek to inject a new democratic dynamic.

In general, Cole's new version of Guild Socialism was simply more cautious than its predecessor. Gone was the confident system-building and the bold construction of an elaborate machinery of producer and consumer democracy; in its place, only a statement of principles and some indications of the direction of advance. In effect, Cole was now prescribing for a situation in which radical movement towards industrial democracy was simply not on the foreseeable agenda. Hence his desire to offer reassurance that some democratization of the workplace would not react adversely on the quality of leadership or on industrial efficiency, or interfere with managerial prerogatives over high policy. His focus remained firmly on the workplace, where he argued for the democratic election of supervisory personnel, the internal regulation of work and discipline and the collective labour contract. When he looked beyond the workplace, it was only to make specific suggestions—for example, for a public director on the boards of capitalist concerns, or for a regional consultative machinery for socialized industry—not to sketch an extended representative structure. 'Guild Socialist though I am,' he now wrote, 'I do not believe it to be practicable to leap straight from capitalist control of industry to any substantial form of democratic workers' control.'[87] Hence Cole confined his attention largely to the foundations upon which a more comprehensive system of industrial democracy could later be constructed. Central to these foundations was an established machinery of joint consultation, which he made the cornerstone of his immediate programme. Of course, consultation was not control, although he did suggest that it represented something 'corresponding to a stage of political development in which representative institutions existed without responsible government',[88] which later developed into more positive forms of participation and responsibility. Clearly an industrial equivalent of this political evolution was envisaged, and he urged the trade unions to extend the range of their collective bargaining to areas normally restricted to joint

[86] 'The Great Negation', *New Statesman*, 14 Nov. 1953. See also, 'The Labour Party and the Trade Unions', *Political Quarterly*, Jan.–Mar. 1953.
[87] 'Workers and Management in the Nationalised Industries', *Co-operative Year Book* 1951.
[88] 'Management and Democracy', *British Management Review*, July 1950.

consultation. In this way, he saw a means of 'advancing beyond joint consultation to joint decision'.[89]

It can scarcely be claimed that Cole offered a theory of workers' control in this period. What he did offer was a restatement of some essential principles and the outline of an immediate strategy. This left a considerable theoretical vacuum, devoid of any conception of the time-table of advance or of its nature. Instead, there was just the assumption that, once initiated, the movement towards full industrial democracy would take on a powerful dynamic of its own. Furthermore, much of his argument seemed to suffer from this lack of a systematic frame of reference. It was not clear, for example, how far the conception of industrial 'partnership' was realizable under capitalism or required comprehensive socialization; or how a system of joint control would work which had to reconcile the need for an assumption of responsibility by the workers with the avoidance of a partnership with capitalism. In general, Cole's thinking on these matters was now loose and unfinished. It made only modest claims for itself: in a hostile environment it sought to revive a principle and to indicate some first steps towards its realization. The principle was the key. It stood for a conception of democratic, classless fellowship which contrasted sharply with a socialism of mixed-economy welfarism or of bureaucratic nationalization. In defining this as the central problem of socialist advance, Cole suggested that the Labour movement had arrived at a turning-point in its development which required a return to fundamentals. Invoking Beatrice Webb's division of political temperaments into the (anarchist) 'A's and the (bureaucratic) 'B's, he conceded that the 'B's had hitherto enjoyed a clear ascendancy within the Labour movement. The necessary and valuable product of their activity was the welfare state and nationalization: the triumph of the 'B' mind. The task now, however, was to move on from mere provision to the discovery of the means to stimulate a democratic activism; and 'this is precisely what the "B"s are temperamentally unfitted to do by themselves: only the "A"s, held in check by the "B"s, can do it in any effective way'.[90] The only alternative to a new fundamentalism of this

---

[89] *The Case For Industrial Partnership*, p. 45. Despite his denial that he was suggesting 'any natural law whereby the one must develop out of the other' (*The National Coal Board*, Fabian Society, 1948, p. 34), Cole's argument on the relationship between consultation and control seemed to leave little alternative. In fact, there was 'a third option: that the whole pantomime would be seen to be very largely an irrelevance, and ignored by the workpeople'. (K. Coates and T. Topham, *The New Unionism*, Penguin edn., 1974, p. 207.)

[90] 'What Next? Anarchists or Bureaucrats?', *Fabian Journal*, April 1954.

Industrial Democracy and the Guild Idea 137

kind was to 'rest content with what has been achieved and to give up trying to establish a socialist society'.[91]

At the same time, Cole sought to establish the theoretical and historical credentials of his own brand of 'A' socialism—a socialism which stood outside the clash between communism and social democracy. It was this enterprise which provided the internal unity in his thought in this final period, bringing together his reconstructed democratic socialism and his record of international socialist development. 'To my mind,' he mused just before his death, 'there have always been two fundamental cleavages in Socialist thought—the cleavage between revolutionaries and reformists, and the cleavage between centralisers and federalists.'[92] The former division had received most attention, of course, but it failed to comprehend a tradition of socialist thought within which Cole wanted to locate himself. This was the 'federalist' tradition of libertarian, de-centralist socialism which had played the role of permanent opposition inside both socialist theory and practice. It stood outside the conflict between the giants of world socialism, revolutionary communism and parliamentary social democracy, both of which 'regarded increasing centralisation of power as an unmistakable characteristic of progress, and regarded themselves as the destined heirs of capitalist concentration and of the centralised power of the modern State'.[93]

Cole's *History of Socialist Thought* may (and perhaps should) be read as a long essay in retrieval: the retrieval of a valuable and neglected tradition of 'federalistic' socialist pluralism. His rehabilitation of Fourier, his defence of Proudhon against Marx, his account of Bakunin and the First International, his embrace of Kropotkin, his attack on the rigid centralism of German Social Democracy, his rescue of William Morris: all this, and more, formed part of his retrieval of a motley historical tradition. It was a tradition, moreover, to which Guild Socialism—now judged to have made 'the outstanding contribution to new non-Communist theories of Socialism during and immediately after the first world war'[94]—could be readily assigned. At the very end of his life, Cole claimed to find support for this tradition in a developing automation which offered the prospect of a reduction in the scale of

---

[91] *Is This Socialism?*, *New Statesman* Pamphlet, 1954.
[92] 'Socialism: Centralist or Libertarian?' (MS in Cole Collection). This piece was written to introduce an Italian collection of Cole's work (*Studi Sul Socialismo*, (ed. C. Doglio), Florence, 1959). It also appeared in *ISSS Information* in two parts in 1959.
[93] *A History of Socialist Thought*, Vol. III, Pt. II: *The Second International 1889–1914*, 1956, p. 970.
[94] Ibid., Vol. IV, Pt. I: *Communism and Social Democracy 1914–31*, 1958, p. 25.

138   *Industrial Democracy and the Guild Idea*

industrial organization, a 'retreat from bigness'[95] which opened up new possibilities for the 'federalists' of socialism. If the phase of mass-industry was over, then so was the era of mass-democracy; and this would mean that the tradition to which Guild Socialism belonged could no longer be dismissed in the glib language of technological determinism.[96] 'I hope and believe,' he wrote, 'that the time is coming when the libertarian tendencies in Socialism will be enabled to reassert themselves with growing strength, and when the bureaucratic tendencies will be correspondingly weakened. I am not a Syndicalist; but I believe none the less that Syndicalism had hold of an important element of the truth which has been grossly underrated by the politicians of Communism and Social Democracy alike. . . .'[97] In thus grappling with the contribution of syndicalism to a theory of socialism, Cole ended his political life as he had begun it. It may plausibly be suggested that, in this respect and in a very different environment, his thought had come almost full circle.

[95] 'Retreat From Bigness', *New Statesman*, 22 Mar. 1958. Cole declared himself 'in hopes to-day that this phase of social evolution is drawing to an end'. (Foreword to B. Pribićević, *The Shop Stewards' Movement and Workers' Control*, 1959.)

[96] Guild Socialism had been dismissed by Dahl, for example, as 'technologically an obsolete doctrine at the time of its formation'. ('Workers' Control of Industry and the British Labour Party', *American Political Science Review*, xli, 1947.) By 1975, however, Sir Frederick Catherwood, chairman of the British Institute of Management, could announce that giant factories would soon become extinct 'like the dinosaur', a view which echoed Cole's conception of future industrial development. ('Outsize Factories Will Die', *Guardian*, 17 Jan. 1975.)

[97] 'Socialism: Centralist or Libertarian?' (op. cit.).

VII
Political Action and the State

THE LAST chapter attempted to trace the changing content of Cole's theory of socialist democracy in the period following the collapse of the Guild movement—and to put these changes into a contextual and chronological setting. The present chapter complements this account by looking at Cole's changing conception of socialist method during this same period, for original Guild theory was no less distinctive on method than in substance. It is necessary to examine Cole's continuing treatment of the relative merits of political and industrial action and, therefore, of the role of the state. His position on these matters during the Guild period has already been extensively examined. It was noted then that his position was always sensitive to the pressure of events, shifting the balance in his thought between industrial action in the workplace and political action through the state. It was noted especially, however, that such a balance always existed, never resolving itself into either a pure economism or the political embrace; but that his mature position during the Guild period, while still upholding the traditional Guild insistence on the centrality of industrial action, also strongly defended a complementary role for a socialist politics—not least to counter the corporatist ambitions of post-war capitalism. This, then, is the starting point for an examination of the development of his thought on this matter in the long period after the collapse of the Guild movement itself.

The Guild movement had disintegrated as economic depression reimposed its discipline on the world of labour, causing the labour movement to look increasingly to political action to redress the industrial balance. A distinctive period of labour history seemed to have ended, as was widely recognized at the time. 'For some time to come,' wrote Cole in mid-1921, 'it seems probable that the main noticeable activities of Labour will have to lie in the political field.'[1] As the industrial labour movement was weakened, the focus turned to the

---

[1] 'The Swing of the Pendulum', *New Statesman*, 16 July 1921. Beatrice Webb also recorded that 'the pendulum was once more swinging back to political action'. (*Diaries 1912–24*, ed. M. I. Cole, 1952, p. 211; dated 27 June 1921.)

rising fortunes of political Labour, culminating in its formation of a
minority government in 1924. It was this process which Cole scrutin-
ized from a Guild perspective, insisting on the modest rewards to be
expected from parliamentary activity, but demanding that such activity should at least contribute to the development of the wider socialist
movement.

On the formation of the first Labour government the editors of *New
Standards* announced that their hearts 'obstinately refuse to be
uplifted'.[2] The government should do something for the poor then get
defeated quickly; for at least that would serve to clarify the issues. If
Cole found it easy to give loyal support to MacDonald it was precisely
because of a limited belief in the efficacy of the whole enterprise he was
engaged upon. He claimed that the essential Guild argument on the
question of method was no less valid now that Labour was a party of
government than when it was an insignificant parliamentary minority:
namely, that 'Socialism will be built up, not by even a Government with
a real majority behind it, but by the creative action of the workers
outside Parliament and outside politics in the narrower sense of the
term'.[3] This fact provided the crucial yardstick against which the
parliamentary activity of Labour had to be judged. Did such activity
contribute to the development of consciousness and will amongst the
working class? Did it act as brake or spur? From this perspective it
became clear that 'the first duty of a Labour Government is not to
achieve Socialism, or alter this or that part of the social machine, but to
do everything it can to stimulate among its followers the will to, and the
capacity for, power.'[4] This is why the question of workers' control must
be such a priority, for it was decisive for the development of consciousness and the will to power. By 1924 the control demand had
slackened off, with Labour preferring to postpone it to an indefinite
future in favour of more immediate reforms. For Cole, this could only
have disastrous consequences for the development of socialism and
constituted a major indictment of the tendencies at work inside the
parliamentary movement. He declared himself as adamant in 1924 as
in 1914 that he would 'sooner see the Labour Party not propose
nationalisation at all than propose nationalisation in bureaucratic
terms'.[5]

[2] Editorial, *New Standards*, Feb. 1924.
[3] Editorial, *New Standards*, Mar. 1924.
[4] 'Labour Government and Workers' Control', *New Standards*, Oct. 1924.
[5] 'About Nationalisation', *New Standards*, July 1924.

Thus Cole's initial response to contemporary events and tendencies following the formal demise of the Guild movement was to continue to press a Guild analysis of socialist method, just as he sought (as seen in the preceding chapter) to keep intact the substance of Guild democratic theory. The central event was the political preoccupation of the labour movement and it was this which required analysis from a Guild perspective. Thus Cole warned of the modest dividends and large dangers to be expected from parliamentary activity, insisted on the continuing primacy of industrial action in the achievement of socialism, and demanded that the essentially auxiliary role of the political movement should be evaluated in terms of its contribution to the will and consciousness of its mass following. For Cole himself, such an evaluation was necessarily critical, especially with respect to the minority Labour government of 1924. Yet if it was important to dampen the political euphoria of the labour movement, it was also necessary to respond to its industrial plight. No longer was it possible simply to urge the centrality of the control issue on a trade union movement forced onto the economic defensive. Cole continued to present control as the animating idea behind trade unionism and to stress the necessity for the sort of organizational preparation which recognized this, but now it was also vital to mount a more immediate defence operation for the trade union movement. Thus his industrial journalism in the early 1920s, particularly in the *New Leader* and *New Statesman*, was concerned above all else with the analysis of the contemporary industrial scene and with the advocacy of an intelligent militancy on the part of organized labour in defence of wages and hours. He argued that the trade union movement should organize for united resistance, should not leave the organization of the unemployed to the Communists, and should demonstrate to the government its firm resolve. If none of this had much to do with encroaching control on Guild lines, Cole's answer would be that it was necessary to hold the line now in order that it might again be pushed forward later. This was an answer which hinted at the style of his later reconsideration of socialist method.

In the later stages of Guild Socialism, Cole was already beginning to suggest the need for substantial flexibility, even important modifications, in the statement of Guild theory. This flexibility has already been noticed, but in one area (the working guilds) it particularly suggested a changing conception of socialist method. The experience of the working guilds had raised the problem of the supply of capital in a direct and acute manner. For Cole, this meant the beginning of a reconsideration of the role of the state, for he declared himself convinced that 'we cannot make the big Guild we want until we can command State aid in the provision of capital for Guild development'.[6] To command such aid involved a capture of the state by the workers, thus pushing Cole towards a wider reconsideration of the role of political action. At the same time, his last major piece of Guild Socialist writing, *The Future of Local Government* (1921), also involved a rehabilitation of the regionalized state in a Guild society. It was now suggested that the evils of nationalization could be offset by regionalization, that a reorganized local government had a vital role under Guild Socialism, and that 'the objections which apply to the highly centralised national State need not apply in the same way to smaller bodies exercising jurisdiction over more manageable areas, even if these bodies reproduce to some extent, on a smaller scale, the structure of the State itself'.[7] From a number of directions, therefore, the way was prepared for a wider reconsideration of the role of the state and of political action.

The developing situation of the early 1920s could only hasten this process. Economic slump and unemployment, with their consequences for the morale and aspirations of the labour movement, highlighted the need for a socialist economic policy. The collapse of the trade union offensive exposed all the old weaknesses of will and organization inside British trade unionism, a profoundly depressing spectacle for those people, like Cole, who had pinned their hopes on the industrial triumph of socialism. Thus the collapse of the Triple Alliance on Black Friday was seen as a sad demonstration that 'neither in leadership nor in vigilance among the rank and file is the British Labour movement yet ready for the assumption of power, or for the critical struggle with the forces of Capitalism.'[8] The easy optimism of the immediate post-war period was now replaced by a much more cautious estimate of the state of the labour movement. Nor was Cole immune from the prevailing tendency to seek to redress the industrial balance through an increasing emphasis on parliamentary politics. If he refused to join wholeheartedly in the political euphoria, he did concede a much larger role to political action than hitherto. In the early days of Guild Socialism such a political role was accepted; then it was largely denied; then it was again promoted to an auxiliary status; but by the early 1920s it can be said to have been awarded a position of full complementarity

---

[6] 'Guild Prospects in Engineering', *Guild Socialist*, Jan. 1923.
[7] *The Future of Local Government*, p. 176.
[8] 'Black Friday And After', *Labour Monthly*, July 1921.

with industrial action in Cole's thinking. He now looked forward to a 'real working combination of the political and industrial resources of Labour'.[9]

If the industrial malaise had put political action firmly on the agenda, however, Cole confronted a socialist political scene which seemed already rigidly polarized between an irrelevant 'revolutionary' Communism and a tepid parliamentary Labourism. If Cole's industrial base had gone, there seemed no natural political home for him either. Not in the ranks of British Communism certainly, already staffed by many former Guild Socialists. His judgement, both contemporary and retrospective, was that the formation of the British Communist Party along lines directed by Moscow represented a setback for British socialism. He was consistently emphatic about the unoriginality, futility, divisiveness and sheer irrelevance of a British Communism which was 'drifting aimlessly "leftwards", in the direction of a Bolshevism in which it does not believe'.[10] At the same time, however, there was the spectacle of a Labour Party hot in the pursuit of respectability but tepid in its attachment to socialism. It, too, seemed to be drifting, but towards a parliamentary definition of socialism, the implications and content of which had never been properly worked out.

By the early 1920s, therefore, Cole found himself increasingly isolated, both theoretically and organizationally. The demand for workers' control had receded as economic depression worked its effects on a labour movement which looked increasingly to political action. The Guild movement had collapsed, its rump taken over by the Communists. The political world of the left seemed to have frozen, divided between a feeble parliamentarism and a hopeless revolutionism. Cole continued to press the relevancy of the Guild analysis, with appropriate modifications, in these changed conditions, but already there were signs of a more fundamental shift in his thinking. He had always presented Guild Socialism as a reconciliation of the evolutionary and revolutionary perspectives in the form of a policy of 'positive piecemeal transformations',[11] but the prospects for such a policy now seemed dim. He warned of the consequences if this attempt to construct a new society from within the structure of the old should fail: 'If a Movement like the Guild Movement cannot succeed, then the conclusion I should

[9] 'The Swing of the Pendulum', *New Statesman*, 16 July 1921.
[10] 'Communism and Labour Policy', *New Statesman*, 7 Aug. 1920. Cf. W. Kendall, *The Revolutionary Movement in Britain 1900–21*, 1969, where (p. 302) the foundation of the Communist Party is judged 'an historic error on the grand scale'.
[11] Ibid.

draw would be that you have just got to "bust up" capitalism.'[12] In fact, as will be seen, this was a conclusion which Cole himself emphatically did not draw.

One conclusion which Cole did draw from the demise of Guild Socialism, however, was the need to direct his energies to other things. In the 1920s he has to be described much less as theorist and propagandist, much more as scholar, historian, educationalist, economist and teacher. In many ways this shift may be seen as a response to necessity: if history could no longer be made it could at least be written. Hence, too, his immersion in the work and organization of adult education, for this path remained open when others seemed to have closed, at least temporarily. Certainly he managed to distance himself with both speed and rigour from the historical experience of Guild Socialism, able to subject it to dispassionate analysis. This capacity for objective analysis in the wake of Guild Socialism's demise, a capacity to 'recount the facts, and not to moralise over them',[13] could be taken as evidence of his early abandonment of a Guild position.[14]

Yet it was not simply a case of a retreat into educational work as a consequence of the collapse of the Guild movement. Rather, it was the assertion of an existing belief that a Guild society would require a preparatory and educative process before the assumption of industrial control by the workers could be made effective. In other words, an educative process was conceived as an essential part of Guild Socialist method, not least because of the idealist and voluntarist character that Guild theory was seen to assume in Cole's hands. The experience of the demand for workers' control made by sections of the labour movement in the immediate post-war period seemed to emphasize this need for a vigorous educational offensive amongst the workers before such a demand could be made successfully. The collapse of labour's industrial offensive revealed a movement without an idea, without a diffused consciousness. For Cole, the remedy was a 'real working-class education', in which every section of the labour movement would become 'a centre of Socialist planning and discussion',[15] with strategy emerging as the product of conscious rank and file decision. Cole's own activity was an attempt to press this remedy on the labour movement. If labour was to demand control in industry and beyond, it must develop 'new

---

[12] 'Guild Socialism', in R. W. Hogue, (ed.) *British Labour Speaks*, New York 1924, p. 255.
[13] *Labour in the Coal-Mining Industry*, 1923, p. xii.
[14] Cf. H. P. Rathbone, 'The Collapse of the Cole Industry', *Labour Monthly*, Dec. 1923.
[15] 'Black Friday And After', *Labour Monthly*, July 1921.

standards' of its own, involving the primacy of an educational process. It must take seriously the business of education for socialism. In practical terms, this meant support for all those bodies which provided education for the workers, irrespective of their ideological differences. Cole devoted much time and energy to the demonstration of the futility of sectionalism in the provision of workers' education in the face of the common task. If his own activity centred on the W.E.A., this did not prevent much critical comment on the structure and organization of that body.[16]

Although Cole's antipathy to educational sectionalism made him ill-disposed to wage a campaign for a 'pure' education on W.E.A. lines against the propagandist schools, preferring to support all types of educational provision for the workers, he nevertheless retained a clear conception of the difference between education and propaganda—and of their respective values. At a personal level, he found in the W.E.A. an arena of intellectual freedom, a scope for unorthodoxy, which the more propagandist schools would deny him. At a general level, he defended the value of education over propaganda, or at least the primacy of the former over the latter from a working-class point of view. He was sensitive to the distortion of what he regarded as the true function of education. In many respects he was an educational radical,[17] yet his conception of the nature and purpose of education was firmly traditional. He was impatient with the 'sheer nonsensical obscurantism' of those socialists who wanted to discard the existing state provision of education as mere capitalist education; for when some of the substance of this charge was admitted it remained 'a great truth that biased education—even education with the most wrong bias—is far better than no education at all, if it is done with a reasonable degree of competence'.[18] Here was that attachment to an educational ideal which allowed Cole to spend a happy teaching life in England's most conservative seat of learning.

At one moment in the 1920s his hopes for workers' education seemed destined to receive a decisive endorsement by events, changing the course of his own career in the process. The central event was the offer by the Countess of Warwick of her residence, Easton Lodge, to the trade union movement for educational purposes. This fact is relevant to

---

[16] 'I'm in the W.E.A., not so much for what it is, as for what it might be.' (*New Standards*, May 1924.)

[17] Certainly in the context of British socialism. See R. Barker, *Education and Politics 1900–51*, 1972.

[18] 'Educational Ideals', *New Standards*, Sept. 1924.

an understanding of Cole's wider theoretical development for it brings together and highlights many of his leading beliefs about the central place of education in the evolution of the labour movement towards socialism. The Easton Lodge scheme seemed to provide an opportunity for the working-class educational bodies to transcend their sectionalism in the cause of a genuine workers' college, backed by the resources of the whole trade union movement. At Easton Lodge an educational community would be formed, a foretaste of the society of fellowship to come, where the vital preparatory work for a successful advance towards socialism would be done. In urging generous support for the scheme, Cole reminded the trade union movement that 'we are seeking education for a great object—for nothing less than the creation of new society in which the workers will rule'.[19] He threw all his energies behind the scheme, busily sketched out a curriculum for the new college, and was widely tipped as its first principal.[20] When the scheme finally came to nothing—wounded by the internecine strife within working-class education, killed by the retreat of the T.U.C. in the aftermath of the General Strike—he was bitterly disappointed. Easton Lodge had seemed to provide a hopeful antidote to the collapse of Guild Socialism, a constructive response by the labour movement to its gloomy industrial prospects in the world of the 1920s. When this hope also collapsed, Cole's plans for the labour movement suffered another major disappointment. It, too, helped to shape the course of his own thinking in the late 1920s, proving further reason for a reconsideration of socialist method.

Cole's distinctive contribution to working-class education in the 1920s (and beyond) lay primarily, of course, in the historical field. This is not the place to attempt a full assessment of Cole's history *qua* history, but it is necessary to say something about its relationship to the structure of his socialist thought. Above all, this is necessary because Cole himself recognized such a relationship, having a firm conception of the role of historical education in the development of the labour movement. If his historical writing was scholarly it was also committed, as evidenced especially in his spirited biographical studies of Cobbett and Owen. 'Every historian has a bias,' he wrote, 'and it is legitimate to prefer the bias of Cobbett to the bias of Macaulay or Trevelyan.'[21] That

[19] 'Easton Lodge: The Plea of An Enthusiast', *Labour Magazine*, Sept. 1926.
[20] There is an interesting file of correspondence etc. about the Easton Lodge scheme in the Cole Collection.
[21] *The Life of William Cobbett*, 1924, p. 421.

good history could also be good pamphleteering was a view firmly upheld by Cole, and practised too. If Cobbett's historical writing was defective it was because it did not 'live up to its bias',[22] a test which Cole set out to overcome in his own work. Not only did he have a clear conception of the nature of historical writing, however, but also of the purpose of history itself for the labour movement. In essence, it was the function of a comprehensive social history to arm the worker with that sense of his own past which would create a confidence to make his own future. So vital was this historical dimension that Cole wanted a body of teachers and students who would 'go forth to preach the gospel of social history to every worker'.[23] His own activity in the 1920s put him in the vanguard of such a body. It had to be a genuine gospel, however, not a propagandist imitation. Although he insisted on the necessary bias of all history, and was adamant about the centrality of social history in the development of working-class confidence, he would countenance no attempt to force the historical record into a particular mould of ideological interpretation. If he emphasized the contribution of Marx to the development of a unified social historical approach, he rejected any crude reduction of history to satisfy the appetites of simpler Marxists.[24] For Cole, good history was also good propaganda.

Indeed, the main criticism of Cole's historical work is that it was insufficiently interpretative. Its characteristic merits were an encyclopaedic ordering of the material, a factual reliability, a lucidity of presentation and a sanity of judgement. His *Short History of the British Working-Class Movement* and *History of Socialist Thought* fully reveal these merits at work. His more detailed studies, especially *Chartist Portraits* and *Attempts at General Union*, build upon these considerable merits to provide a pioneering contribution to an understanding of the complexity of personality and locality in one particular period of labour history, thus providing 'a point of departure for more recent historical

[22] Ibid.
[23] 'The Importance of History to the Workers', *New Standards*, Mar. 1924. Cf. Gail Owen, 'G. D. H. Cole's Historical Writings', *International Review of Social History*, Vol. xi, 1966. This is a useful bibliographical guide to Cole's historical writings (and to their critical reception), but, because the author misses his very clear conception of the relationship between history and socialism, it is wrongly asserted that Cole was 'never able to resolve the conflict within himself between the propagandist and the scholar'.
[24] See 'A Word to Max Beer', *Labour Monthly*, Nov. 1922; and his review of R. P. Arnot's *The Miners: Years of Struggle*, *Economic Journal*, lxiii, 1953, where he writes that 'when the full history comes to be written objectively it will hardly be in such colours of black and white as suit Mr. Arnot's purpose'.

research'.[25] In a more general sense, Cole may be regarded as the outstanding pioneer of the remarkable development of the discipline of 'labour history' in Britain in recent years. Yet his work had characteristic defects too. Its encyclopaedic sweep and massive volume seemed too often to inhibit any real attempt to stand back from the accumulated material, to organize facts into tendencies or to float interpretations. Particularly disappointing in this respect was his *History of the Labour Party From 1914*, a book which offered the opportunity to organize direct experience into a coherent analysis of the modern British Labour movement. Instead, it emerged as a chronicle which was both eminently sensible in its particular judgements (largely reproducing Cole's attitude to events as they had happened) but curiously flat in its general approach. Only rarely did his historical writing blend chronology and interpretation to real satisfaction. Some of his retrospective essays and lectures in the last decade of his life achieved this, perhaps because the demand for compression in this sort of activity necessitated a separation of the essential from the inessential. Of his book-length studies, perhaps only his *Life of William Cobbett*—generally acknowledged as his best single piece of historical writing—really succeeded in welding together narrative and interpretation. The presentation of Cobbett was vivid; but no less impressive was the analysis of Cobbett as the crucial transitional figure in the development both of British society and of the British labour movement.[26]

The content of Cole's historical work reveals much that is relevant to an understanding of his socialist thought, though usually this is implicit rather than explicit. His history has been described as 'essentially Marxian';[27] but this is a description which, except in the very loosest sense, is highly misleading. It would be more accurate to describe his history as essentially social-democratic. This can be illustrated in a number of ways. For example, if Cole agreed with Marx that capitalism was a necessary and progressive phase of economic evolution, he consistently rejected any attempt to write economic history in terms of increasing working-class impoverishment. Furthermore, if economic determinism allowed some scope for human actors, Cole's history—like his Guild Socialism—allowed them large and often decisive

[25] Asa Briggs, Introduction (p. ix) to new edition (1965) of *Chartists Portraits*, 1941.
[26] The importance of Cole's treatment of Cobbett is recognized and discussed by M. J. Wiener, 'The Changing Image of William Cobbett', *Journal of British Studies*, Vol. xiii, 1974.
[27] Gail Owen, 'G. D. H. Cole's Historical Writings'.

scope. It is enough to record his string of biographical portraits to register this point.[28] Above all, perhaps, Cole's history focused not on the developing character of capitalist exploitation but on the progressive development of the labour movement and its increasing ability to win a foothold in state power. Bernstein had prefaced his revision of Marx by describing a historical process in which 'in all advanced countries we see the privileges of the capitalist bourgeoisie yielding step by step to democratic organisations';[29] and Cole's own presentation of the historical record implied a very similar standpoint. In both cases, the treatment of history carried with it a clearly reformist perspective. Finally, Cole's history deliberately eschewed the universal historical sweep of Marxism and emphasized instead the limitations imposed by particular social and cultural settings. This was also important, as will be seen in a later chapter, in Cole's delineation of a democratic socialism distinct from Marxism, but it was forever present in his writing of history. For example, in describing the formation and development of the Labour Party he grounded his account in the social, economic and cultural context of British society so that 'in retrospect, it looks as if the Party had, by sheer force of circumstances, to develop in its own peculiar way'.[30] In general, therefore, Cole has to be regarded as a sensible, partisan historian of social democratic persuasion.

To return to the main concern of this chapter: it became increasingly clear that adult education and labour history could provide no real substitute for an explicit reconsideration of socialist method in terms of the environment confronted by the labour movement in the 1920s. In 1920 Cole had described a Europe tottering on the brink of class war,[31] with a weakened and discredited capitalism vulnerable to the confident advance of the powerful forces of labour. By the end of the following year, however, he was busy documenting the tide in reverse and pointing the implications for British labour. His central message in the changed situation, in which the revolutionary moment had passed, was the sheer futility of a domestic revolutionism subservient to foreign precept and example which necessarily divorced itself from the industrial and political realities which confronted the British labour movement. The Labour Party was silly to invoke a revolutionary threat to its

[28] 'Unlike some labour historians, Cole did not underestimate the personal element in labour history.' (Asa Briggs, op. cit., p. vii.)
[29] E. Bernstein, *Evolutionary Socialism*, 1889, preface (trans. E. Harvey, Independent Labour Party, 1909, p. xii).
[30] *British Working Class Politics 1832–1914*, 1941, p. 10.
[31] *Chaos and Order in Industry*, 1920, p. 8.

own moderation; the Communist left was wedded to a revolutionary posturing which guaranteed its irrelevancy. 'To anyone who knows anything of the elements of which the British Labour movement is composed,' asserted Cole, 'the British revolution is a bogey of the most unconvincing sort.'[32] For Cole, therefore, the first requirement for relevancy in the immediate post-Guild period was the recognition that British labour confronted a non-revolutionary situation, both in terms of its own consciousness and organization and in terms of the continued strength of capitalism. Such a recognition was not necessary previously, as evidenced by the history of Guild Socialism itself. Once made, however—and the situation in the early 1920s seemed to require it—it became the central conditioning fact for social democratic thought in Britain. If Cole was emphatic in forcing this recognition of the non-revolutionary situation of British labour, his own later thought represented a long struggle with the dilemma for socialism created by just this recognition.

Not only did the absence of a revolutionary road to socialism seem to be a fact of political life for British socialists in the early 1920s; so too did the hegemony of the Labour Party. Just as Cole emphasized the former, he also accepted the latter, albeit without a great deal of enthusiasm. It was necessary for socialists to operate within a political environment dominated by the twin leviathans of official trade unionism and official Labour. Cole was impatient with those groups who tried to evade the consequences of this central reality. Thus the belated adoption by the I.L.P. of a Guild programme was greeted by Cole not with enthusiasm but with sober reflections on the necessary eclipse of the old socialist groups in face of the dominance of Labour. In future, such groups as the I.L.P. (and the National Guilds League) would rise and fall according to circumstances, feeding their contributions into the wider Labour movement. Here Cole was not merely stating a political fact, but suggesting a deeper truth about the place of socialism itself inside this movement. It would be a subsidiary place, for 'in this country above all, doctrinaire Socialism is a political impossibility, and experimental Socialism alone acceptable even to the organised working-class'.[33] There could be no ideological socialist party, only an opportunist and pragmatic Labour movement to which socialists would make their own

[32] 'Nonsense About Revolution', *New Statesman*, 10 Dec. 1921. The Communist Party did not have 'brains or influence enough to subvert a molehill'. ('Left-Wingers and Communists', *New Statesman*, 3 Oct. 1925.)
[33] 'The Position of British Socialism', *New Statesman*, 20 May 1922.

distinctive contribution. If Cole was critical of Labour's ability and personnel, he gave willing assent to its evolutionary and undoctrinaire programme, a necessary product of its transition from a pioneering and propagandist beginning to its present occupancy of a central role on the parliamentary stage. He now even advised the Labour Party to avoid 'scenes' lest it incur the taint of Bolshevism! As Guild Socialist, Cole had proclaimed the bankruptcy of Labourism: now he anounced its hegemony. The world of labour had become the world of Labour. The change was symbolized at a personal level in a letter to Arthur Henderson in 1923: 'If I can be of any use to the Labour Party, I'm willing to do all I can to help. It looks as if all help would soon be needed.'[34]

The events of the 1920s seemed to confirm this sort of assessment and to emphasize the inadequacies of the Guild conception of socialist advance. In fundamental respects, the General Strike provided the labour movement with its central experience during this period, upon which many different analyses could be constructed. It could be regarded as the harbinger of a revolutionary potential within the British working class, checked only by a reactionary trade union leadership. Alternatively, it could be welcomed or mourned as the final telling confirmation of the futility of industrial action for the political achievement of socialism.[35] Cole's response was surprisingly equivocal, for here was the form of action prescribed by Guild Socialism and still recommended by Cole to the labour movement in the early days of the depression as the appropriate defensive strategy against attacks on its wages and hours. At one level, of course, Cole's support for the Strike was unquestioned: he defended its essential rightness and threw himself into its organizational work. Yet he liked to proclaim the justice of every strike, reserving his criticism for the realm of strategy, so it is necessary to probe a little deeper.[36] What emerges is a distinct lack of enthusiasm at the prospect of a general strike, grave forebodings about its likely outcome and a genuine desire to find an honourable way out. His commentary on the Strike was marked by an impatience with the obstinacy and stupidity of all parties to the dispute and a desire to break

[34] Cole to Henderson, 13 Dec. 1923 (Transport House). Henderson replied: 'I much appreciate your willingness to help the Party in the future'. (14 Dec. 1923, ibid.)

[35] Beatrice Webb, of course, welcomed it as marking the end of 'a proletarian distemper . . . the death gasp of that pernicious doctrine of "workers' control" . . . .' (*Diaries 1924–32*, ed. M. I. Cole, 1956, pp. 92–3; entry for 4 May 1926.)

[36] E. A. Radice, a member of the 'Cole group' at this time, recalls Cole's fondness for proclaiming that 'every strike is right'. (Conversation with author, 11 Oct. 1972.)

through the cumbrous machinery of representative government to impose the sort of settlement which was agreed upon by all men of goodwill. The Strike was pronounced as devoid of all economic or political advantage.[37]

In part, Cole's argument was based upon tactical considerations of course. A general strike initiated when trade unionism was weak and vulnerable could be no more than a gesture of despair, best avoided if possible. Yet the argument was more substantial than that, for the 1926 General Strike coincided with that more general reappraisal by Cole of the state of British socialism already noticed. As such, it seemed to mark the end of a definition, both for Cole himself and for a whole tradition of industrial action. Merely to ascribe the failure of the Strike to an alleged betrayal on the part of the T.U.C. was for Cole both absurdly inaccurate and an evasion of the Strike's real. lesson. That lesson was stated bluntly: 'no matter how strong Trade Unionism may be, it cannot, by the use of purely industrial methods, hope to stand up directly to the power of the modern State'.[38] A general strike with a revolutionary purpose might well be a different matter, of course, but in 1926 the workers were conspicuously devoid of such a purpose. The Strike had provided a fine demonstration of working-class solidarity, had purged the memory of Black Friday, but its main effect was to demonstrate that mass industrial action of this kind could be contained and broken by the resources of a modern state. Its importance, therefore, was to force a reconsideration by the labour movement of the respective merits of industrial and political action, for 'the General Strike bubble has been pricked and there is no likelihood of any attempt to employ this double-edged weapon again, in the same way, for a generation to come at least'.[39] Cole pronounced this conclusion with as much relief as Beatrice Webb and the leaders of official Labour. The events of 1926 had served both to nourish growing doubts and to point the need for a major reconsideration by the labour movement of its strategy and purpose.

For Cole, this involved a reappraisal of the assumptions and activities of the trade unions. No longer could he embrace them easily as the key agency of socialist advance, wresting industrial control from capitalism in the workplace, with other forms of action relegated to an essentially auxiliary role. A changed political and economic environ-

---

[37] 'Where We Stand in the Coal Crisis', *New Statesman,* 17 Apr. 1926.
[38] 'Some Lessons of the Late General Strike', *New Statesman,* 19 June 1926.
[39] Ibid.

ment had forced new issues to the fore, demanding new and different responses. If economic depression served as the occasion and justification for this revision, its origins went deeper. It involved a basic reconsideration of the method of socialist advance. In the aftermath of the General Strike such a reappraisal was inevitable, a fact welcomed by Cole who used the opportunity to press a new conception of trade union purpose. In 1916 Beatrice Webb had wondered when the Guild Socialists would 'realise the weakness of their chosen instrument',[40] and she found her answer, in Cole's case, barely a decade later. The centrality of state power in the achievement of social change was now accepted as the defining framework of socialist activity, shifting the emphasis away from the industrial arena. Therefore the socialist capture of state power, envisaged by Cole in parliamentary terms, became the necessary precondition for the achievement of workers' control in industry. What this meant was that the trade unions could (and should) be moderate industrially whilst radical politically. At issue here was a whole conception of the method of advance from capitalism to socialism and also of the means of improving working class conditions under capitalism. If Cole's prescription represented 'the definite ending of an epoch in Trade Union history',[41] an epoch in which he had been a central figure, then he now accepted and welcomed this fact.

Having established the centrality of political action, Cole turned his attention to the content of a socialist political programme. Here, too, revision was the order of the day. His sense of a theoretical crisis at the heart of British socialism, a dissolution of traditional assumptions, has already been noticed. By the late 1920s, however, his concern was less with the celebration of uncertainty than with the positive formulation of a coherent political programme rooted in a new conception of socialism itself. In one fundamental respect, at least, he embarked on this enterprise by adopting part of that dominant theoretical tradition inside British socialism whose crisis he had announced and which he had formerly decisively rejected—namely, the emphasis on the state. Much of his Guild Socialist activity had been concerned with the demonstration of the state's false ascendancy in political theory and the particular sterility of its domination of British socialist theory. Indeed, he had been emphatic on the need for Guild Socialism to develop an alternative political theory of its own if state socialism was to be

---

[40] *Diaries 1912–24*, ed. cit. p. 58 (entry dated 4 Apr. 1916).
[41] 'Trade Unionism and the Future', *New Statesman*, 15 Sept. 1928.

effectively challenged. However, when in the 1920s he began to think out the ingredients of a socialist programme which had the state at its centre, this process was matched by no elaborate revision of state theory. In this respect, Cole's evolution differed markedly from that of Harold Laski, whose similar and contemporary shift from a pluralist to a collectivist perspective had a firm and conspicuous theoretical anchorage. Just as Cole's adoption of a pluralist political theory had—unlike Laski's—been the product less of academic excursions into the theory of the state than of the needs of a political programme, so his abandonment of that theory had a similar character. Its origins were clear, however—a growing realization of the limitations of industrial action, an acceptance of the central role of state power in the promotion or obstruction of socialism and, above all perhaps, a determination to mobilize the state in a programme of economic recovery.

This last point is critical, not least because it is sometimes missed in the intellectual history of the period. If an explanation is sought for the revival, albeit unheralded and undramatic, of a collectivist social thought in the 1920s amongst people and groups who had earlier set out to challenge it, then one essential ingredient of such an explanation is to be found in the pressing demands of an economic environment where the state alone seemed capable of action. Certainly for Cole this was decisive, producing a demand for state action unmatched by any coherent revision of state theory. This lack of theoretical revision, if unsurprising, is unfortunate and unsatisfactory. Having developed a set of propositions about the nature and status of the state in a comprehensive social theory, involving a statement about its relationship with capitalism and its role in the transition to socialism, Cole proceeded to construct a programme of state action which rested upon an undiscussed denial of these very propositions. There was only a statement of the key role of the state in the economic system, the fact that 'at countless points, business policy and State policy intersect, so that it becomes the obvious interest of both employers and workers to control the State',[42] but this was not much to set against the sort of social theory he had developed earlier.

For Cole, however, it was no longer a time for social theory but for political and economic action. He therefore addressed himself to the task of formulating a socialist political programme. If it was a revisionist programme, it involved a revision both of Guild Socialism and

[42] *Industrial Policy For Socialists*, I.L.P., 1926, p. 4.

of Fabian collectivism. The central problem and goal was defined as the transference from capitalist to socialist hands of the key areas of economic control. This involved an identification of the source of capitalist power and of a strategy for its capture which entailed a fundamental departure from a Guild Socialist position. Thus, although the workshop remained the arena of direct capitalist exploitation, Cole now declared that 'it is not in the factory or workshop that the controlling forces of modern capitalism are to be found'.[43] He was now concerned to stress the complex interdependence of the modern capitalist system in terms of its control of production, distribution and exchange, its mechanisms for resource allocation and for the supply of capital and credit. In other words, it was necessary to see capitalism as a whole if an effective socialist strategy was to be developed, to see it as a system, whose vital arteries could be identified and attacked in a coherent way. Only if those arteries could be brought under the control of a general socialist economic policy could particular problems (workers' control, unemployment etc.) be dealt with satisfactorily. If a departure from Guild Socialism was involved here, some major revisions of traditional collectivism were necessary too. No longer was it possible to present socialism as the culmination of a series of particular nationalizations, for that was a conception which failed to understand the systematic character of capitalism. Above all else, it was necessary to achieve a socialist control of investment and allocation decisions in the economy, thereby winning a direct ability to shape the course of economic policy as a whole. This meant a revision of socialist strategy and priorities which gave central importance, for example, to the socialization of banking and finance rather than to the nationalization of traditional industries. Indeed, socialism could no longer be synonymous with nationalization, whilst the attention of socialists should shift from the fact of ownership to the forms of economic control. Such an approach was so fertile with possibilities that Cole could even 'conceive of the State being enabled to call the tune without nominally nationalising any industry at all'.[44]

In the space of a few years Cole had clearly travelled a long way. At the beginning of the decade there was the commitment to industrial action, the indictment of the capitalist state, the essential limitations of parliamentary politics—and all the rest. Then came that loss of certainty, sustained by events, which he presented as a general crisis of

[43] Ibid., p. 5.
[44] 'Concerning Nationalisation', *New Statesman*, 21 July 1928.

theory and direction inside British socialism. Out of the uncertainty slowly emerged a new conception of socialist advance, occasioned by a determination to find a relevant socialist response to economic crisis. Here we find Cole lecturing the left on the responsibilities of political power, advising the trade unions to seek an accommodation with capitalism and urging that the success of socialist demands (e.g. the 'living wage') required a serious exploration of the facts of life of British capitalism. If the abandonment (or suspension) of much of Guild Socialism was involved here, there was no easy embrace of Fabianism either. The particular achievement of workshop control was now presented as the product of a general socialist economic control; but that general control was to be achieved outside the assumptions of traditional state socialism. In the aftermath of Guild Socialism Cole had come to believe that British socialism needed a fundamental revision; by the end of the decade he again felt confident enough to define the direction that such revision should take.

The expression of this new conception came in 1929, with the publication of *The Next Ten Years in British Social and Economic Policy*, Cole's first major book since the stream of Guild Socialist works had dried up at the beginning of the decade. It was an important book, both for Cole's personal evolution and for its place in the wider tradition of British socialist thought, though its uninspiring title did much to disguise its significance. It was the product of a process of reappraisal, during which fundamental assumptions were revised and traditional theories tested against events. All the dimensions of Cole's thought and activity which may be traced during the 1920s—his increasing distance from Guild Socialism, his immersion in the problems of the economy, his attempt to sketch a new socialist programme—were reflected and brought together in this new big book on socialist policy. It seemed to represent a dramatic act of conversion on the part of a leading left intellectual, the abandonment of a militant creed of industrial control for a cautious programme of political moderation. As such, it received both the enthusiastic welcome accorded to a new convert and the charges of betrayal which accompany suspected ideological defection. There was agreement about the nature and direction of Cole's theoretical development, however, summarized in a typical review headline as 'Cole's Return to the Fabians'.[45] The Webbs were happy to witness this return to the fold of Fabianism's *enfant terrible*, marred only by a

---

[45] *Labour Monthly*, July 1929. In another review, Laski described Cole as having 'moved from a somewhat dryly doctrinaire Guild Socialism back to a Fabian outlook, parts of which have been

belief that his theoretical excursions into the wilderness had served to mislead a whole generation of potential Fabians, producing a vacuum in organization and ideas which Cole himself had now to begin to fill.[46]

But was it a return to the Fabians? Or, a more interesting question, was it *just* a return to the Fabians? Certainly there were those who found in Cole's new position ample confirmation for their view that, even as a Guild Socialist, he had never ceased to be a Fabian. It was possible to find in his statement of Guild Socialism those elements—the retention of a community control, the provision for consumer representation, the emphasis on technical expertise—which seemed to indicate the pervasiveness of a Fabian parentage which now produced its authentic offspring in the shape of Cole's 1929 book. Thus, his old Guild antagonist, S. G. Hobson, could cite the book as clear evidence of an ultimately political cast of mind which had earlier prevented him from embracing a genuinely industrial doctrine.[47] Yet Cole's book had a severely limited purpose, complicating any attempt at theoretical identification. If its title was uninspiring, it was also accurate, for the aim was not to carry forward the theory of socialism but to provide the Labour movement with an immediate political programme. Cole was impatient with the arid theoretical controversies inside the Labour movement which centred on 'the respective virtues of Rightness and Leftness in the abstract',[48] when Labour's urgent need was for a concrete and immediate programme. Indeed, so anxious was Cole now to banish theoretical discussion that he suggested an agreement upon fundamentals inside British socialism, an obsolescence of the old controversies, which opened the way to an agreed practical policy which was free from 'the dead lumber of assumptions and traditional beliefs'.[49] He was so full of the need for Labour to do something (particularly about unemployment) that he was contemptuous of those who were content merely to say something.

The programme outlined in *The Next Ten Years* has to be understood

modified by the influence of Mr. Keynes'. ('If G. D. H. Cole Were Premier', *New Leader*, 7 June 1929.) Hugh Gaitskell hailed the book as 'the most important contribution to Socialist thought published since the war'. (*Highway*, Nov. 1929.)

[46] A. L. Rowse recalls Beatrice Webb putting this point of view to him strongly. (Conversation with author, 7 Dec. 1972.) Introducing Cole to a Fabian audience in 1929, Beatrice said she 'largely agreed' with his latest book. (*Fabian News*, Dec. 1929.)
[47] S. G. Hobson, *Pilgrim to the Left*, 1938, p. 188.
[48] *The Next Ten Years in British Social and Economic Policy*, 1929, p. 421.
[49] Ibid., p. 422.

in this light, for its practical bias made Cole careless of theoretical barriers and uninterested in theoretical problems. No longer was he concerned to debate the nature of the state, for example; merely to outline a programme of state action.[50] That programme was designed both to provide emergency action on unemployment and to suggest a longer term strategy for economic recovery and stability. Moreover, the socialist content of this proposed policy was argued very much in terms of its contribution to the solution of these problems of capitalist instability. The economic content of the programme will be discussed in the next chapter; but it is necessary here to say something about the relationship between this economic programme and Cole's conception of socialist advance. He insisted that such a relationship necessarily existed, since the causes of economic instability sprang directly from the essential nature of capitalism. He was prepared to concede that capitalism might well survive if it could guarantee a stable prosperity,[51] but regarded such a guarantee as impossible because of its fatal inability to harmonize production and consumption. For this reason alone, therefore, it became necessary to inject a decisive element of socialism into economic life in order to achieve what capitalism could not. This approach conditioned the nature of the socialism involved, for the essential aim was to replace a dominant capitalist 'tone' in the economy by a dominant socialist tone. It is this approach, too, which therefore makes it necessary not merely to catalogue Cole's abandonment of much of Guild Socialism but also to record his revision of fundamental tenets of Fabian collectivism. 'What really matters', he declared, 'is not ownership, but control of policy',[52] a statement which expressed the key idea behind his formulation of the 'new socialization'.

But was this 'new' socialism really socialism at all? In many respects it differed little from the contemporary movement amongst progressive Conservatives and interventionist Liberals which sought to stimulate capitalist recovery by a more positive state role in the reorganization of industry. As such, its emphasis on social control could be viewed as an important stage in socialism's embrace of the 'mixed' economy.[53] At least classical Fabianism, whatever its limitations of conception and defects of strategy, defined capitalism in terms of its private approp-

---

[50] It was accurately observed that Cole 'does not seem much concerned with the character of the State so long as it acts'. (*Labour Monthly*, July 1929.)

[51] *Next Ten Years*, p. 103.

[52] Ibid., p. 142.

[53] And was so viewed; see Barbara Wootton's review, *Economic Journal*, Dec. 1929.

riation of the fruits of industry and sought, via collectivism, to expropriate the appropriators in the public interest. Hence the question of economic ownership must be central to any socialism which had a clear conception of the source of generation of social wealth. Cole accepted this analysis of capitalism, and with it the need for a direct attack on capitalist appropriation, but offered an alternative prescription. Instead of ownership, he proposed a radical programme of taxation—notably drastic inheritance taxes—to drain off the proceeds of capitalist accumulation. Taxation was presented, again in the style of a more modern revisionism, as the proper successor to traditional nationalization in the socialist armoury. 'Let the State control the nation's industries,' he wrote, 'and it need not care who owns them, as long as it has the unfettered power of taxation in its hands.'[54] An eventual transference of ownership would be involved, of course, as taxation completed its work of expropriation, but Cole was full of the advantages of this new road to socialism. It offered the possibility of immediate economic control without all the disadvantages of old-style nationalization. Not only did it enable Cole to retain a Guild Socialist antipathy to nationalization, but also to deploy in its favour some of the virtues previously claimed for Guild Socialism itself. For example, his taxation strategy amounted to a new version of encroaching control, which was claimed to possess all the benefits in terms of the diminution of transitional dislocation once claimed for its Guild predecessor. It completed Cole's statement of the new socialism, designed to reconcile immediate economic action with a wider socialist purpose, which gave to his thought an assurance and a system absent since the days of Guild Socialism.

Although it has been possible in this and the previous chapter to portray Cole's socialism in the 1920s in terms of a process of revision (of both content and method), he was never forced to think critically about the sort of social framework which made such revision both necessary and possible. In other words, he was able to present a reformist programme as a temporary labour of necessity, even as a suspension of theoretical activity. After this time, however, not least because of the experience of the second Labour Government, he was forced to think out the implications for socialism of a non-revolutionary situation. Instead of a tacit revisionism, he began to define the conditions for a positive socialist gradualism.

[54] *Next Ten Years*, p. 143. Cf. the similar argument of C. A. R. Crosland, *The Future of Socialism*, 1956.

Here was that search for a third way, a radical gradualism, a 'sensible extremism',[55] which provided the defining characteristic of his future activity as a theorist of social democracy. In the 1930s, certainly, it was the nature of this search which lay at the heart of his many preoccupations and which must be basic to any analysis of his theoretical development. If it was a decade which dealt hard with social democracy, it was also a decade in which Cole began, for the first time, to think seriously about the definition, content and strategy of a democratic socialism. In 1929 it had seemed enough to prescribe a practical programme for a Labour Government, despatching copies to Labour leaders like MacDonald and Snowden (who promised to read it after the election!), without any more fundamental consideration of the nature of socialist advance. Within a year or two, however, the situation had changed dramatically. Events and temperament ·combined to move Cole away from a deliberately untheoretical 'practical' socialism towards a serious statement of the conditions of socialist advance in a particular sort of social and political environment. To some, this meant simply Cole's emergence as the chief apologist for a vacillating social democracy; whilst to others it meant that he had become too little sensible and too much extreme—indeed, that he was even 'the greatest enemy of freedom alive in this island'.[56] One thing, at least, was clear: if a sensible extremism was a nice phrase it was thereby a no less difficult enterprise.

It is necessary at this point to say something about the general character of Cole's activity in the 1930s, for it reveals a good deal about its theoretical substance. Above all, perhaps, he again felt that he had something to contribute to the socialist argument in Britain. After the relative quiescence and deliberate tentativeness of the previous decade, his work in the 1930s was both confident and encyclopaedic. In volume alone, it easily submerged the mountain of words poured out earlier in the cause of Guild Socialism. Its spread was simply bewildering, passing effortlessly from a discussion of historical materialism to a critique of the gold standard, from an account of the mysteries of Chinese politics to advice on the best methods of pig feeding. There was a rationale behind this prodigious output, for he proclaimed the necessity of a diffused understanding in a complex world if the correct political choices were to be made. He was committed to the notion of an informed citizenry as the necessary basis of a democratic politics,

[55] Cole's phrase. See *Some Essentials of Socialist Propaganda* (Fabian Tract 238, 1932, p. 18).
[56] St. John Ervine, *Time and Tide*, 24 Nov. 1934.

and was impatient with those disciplines (of which economics was by far the worst offender) which seemed determined to inhibit wide understanding by ·means of an exclusive vocabulary and method. Cole's belief was that 'most things which it is important for ordinary people to know—though not quite all—can be stated in untechnical language.'[57] He was therefore a convinced popularizer, even at the cost of much wearisome effort and toil. His succession of 'guides' in which the 'intelligent man' was navigated safely and with often breathtaking lucidity through the contours of world history or the intricacies of economic crisis were the products of this conception. They decorate—or litter—the intellectual landscape of Britain in the 1930s.

In works of this kind exposition and interpretation, analysis and argument, were closely interwoven. Yet they were untypical of much British socialist thought in the 1930s in their painstaking concern with concrete and detailed examination of the phenomena upon which theory had to be built.[58] It would be difficult to claim the 1930s as a creative period for socialist thought in Britain, yet it was certainly—at least in British terms—a distinctly theoretical era. The experience of the second Labour Government, world economic crisis, the rise of fascism, developments in the Soviet Union (and much else besides) seemed to many to provide the materials for a systematic theoretical response. Strachey's elegant presentation of a Marxism for Englishmen and Laski's global propositions on the nature of capitalist democracy distinguished a decade which has been described in terms of a general 'retreat from intelligence'.[59] The description is unfair if it seeks to deny that events themselves seemed to supply ample complementary evidence for a coherent theoretical response on the part of intelligent men, but clearly has merit if it seeks to indicate that this theoretical activity was often accompanied by a suspension of critical spirit and a scant regard for difficult evidence.

Cole was distinctive in his deliberate avoidance of such high theory. Indeed, he regarded the contemporary world as subversive of traditional categories of thought ('you cannot fit the Third International into the framework of Victorian political theory . . .'[60]) and inimical to

[57] *The Condition of Britain* (with M. I. Cole), 1937, p. 20.
[58] It is salutary to recall that, despite the mythology of the Red Decade, the 1930s was 'a decade in which the impact of the entire British Left on practical problems and immediate events was virtually nil.' (B. Pimlott, *Labour and the Left in the 1930s*, 1977, p. 1.)
[59] H. Deane, *The Political Ideas of Harold J. Laski*, 1955, p. 218.
[60] 'The Approach to Politics', *Highway*, Nov. 1931.

the early formulation of new grand theory. The complex, dynamic reality of the contemporary world was announced as the only reliable textbook of political theory.[61] It was that reality in its many aspects that Cole endeavoured to probe. Above all, he wanted to ask questions—about the crisis of capitalism, about the nature of fascism, about Marxism, about contemporary social structure—even though the evidence was often complex and the answers elusive. In the 1930s it is in relation to *events* that Cole's own theory has to be examined. His conception of the state, or of liberty, or of the nature of man, found expression not in theoretical tracts but in his response to events and to theories about events. From this process a distinct theoretical perspective did emerge, though itself complex. In terms of the concern of this chapter, the central event was undoubtedly the life and death of the second Labour Government, for it was this which crystallized Cole's developing conception of socialist method.

The experience of the second Labour Government and the manner of its downfall in 1931 provided the decisive formative episode in the development of British socialist thought in the 1930s. It was an episode fertile in lessons of various kinds. Thus it was possible to focus on a betrayal by leadership; or to portray political Labour as having strayed too far from its trade union leash; or to emphasize the machinations of the bankers; or to suggest more fundamental lessons about the nature of social democracy and of the socialist transition. For John Strachey, for example, 1931 represented a classic case-study of social democracy in action, when it had either to perform its historic task of doing the dirty work of capitalism or leave the political stage—though, in fact, British Labour managed to do both. The events of 1931 taught 'the lesson that social democratic gradualism was bankrupt'.[62] By contrast, there were those who, having poured their wrath on MacDonald or the bankers, looked forward to better things next time round. Cole adopted neither of these positions. He refused to subscribe to scapegoat explanations, preferring to write of MacDonaldism rather than MacDonald and insisting that if there was dictation by the bankers it was because the Government had 'asked to be dictated to'.[63] Above all, he stressed the necessity of regarding 1931 as the end of a definition. If he did not follow

[61] 'Current politics, including, of course, current economics, is nowadays the best introduction to Political Theory'; so that 'you will get more out of Laski's little book on *Communism* than out of his massive *Grammar of Politics*, and more out of the newspapers than out of Bosanquet or T. H. Green'. (ibid.)
[62] J. Strachey, *The Coming Struggle For Power*, 1932, p. 318.
[63] 'Was It A Bankers' Conspiracy?', *New Statesman*, 29 Aug. 1931.

Strachey in an indictment of a whole social democratic tradition, he did demand a reconsideration of that tradition's central assumptions. Hitherto British socialism had assumed 'that the capitalist cow was still a good milker',[64] whereas capitalist crisis had now exploded this assumption, leaving British socialism clinging to an obsolete concessions policy with no developed alternative. Cole proclaimed the necessary end of that social reform socialism inherited from the Liberal tradition and looked forward to the emergence of 'a new kind of gradualist Socialism'.[65] His own work was an attempt to define the content of this new conception.

It is significant that Cole was announcing the end of a definition for British socialism long before the final débâcle of 1931, an event which he regarded as the depressingly inevitable confirmation of his own thesis. He had never seemed entirely at home in his 1929 role as self-appointed policy-maker for a reformist Labour Government, so that when that Government rapidly sank into malaise and inertia he seemed to gain a new intellectual vigour. Thus in Labour's grim winter of 1930 he was able to tell Beatrice Webb that he was 'bubbling with ideas just now'.[66] He responded to Labour's policy vacuum by initiating discussions amongst 'loyal grousers' in the movement, whom he organized into a Society for Socialist Inquiry and Propaganda (S.S.I.P.), with the aim of thinking the Labour movement out of the intellectual cul-de-sac in which it found itself. At the same time he presided over the reincarnation of the Fabian Society as a research organization (N.F.R.B.), designed to complement the activities of the S.S.I.P. in the provision of Labour with an intellectual general staff, so that the task of learning the 'lessons of 1931' could be begun already in 1930.[67] It was in the context of these organizations and their activities that Cole's attempt to re-define the content and strategy of British socialism took place. The enterprise encountered suspicion and irritation from official Labour until its fall from power and electoral humiliation in 1931. Consequently these events were greeted by Cole not with despair but with a sense of 'elation and escape',[68] involving the abandonment of one definition and an opening towards a new one. At a personal level, he experienced a sense of release from a reformist

---

[64] 'What the Labour Movement is Thinking', *Week-End Review*, 20 Dec. 1930.
[65] Ibid.
[66] Cole to Beatrice Webb, 9 Dec. 1930 (Passfield Papers).
[67] See R. Eatwell and A. W. Wright, 'Labour and the Lessons of 1931', *History*, 63, 1978.
[68] 'The Old Labour Party and the New', *New Statesman*, 14 Nov. 1931.

perspective to which he had become a reluctant recruit in the 1920s following the collapse of Guild Socialism. The collapse of that perspective itself in 1931 was embraced by Cole as an opportunity for Labour to 'now stand, as it has never in effect stood before, for socialism as an immediate political objective'.[69]

Many people in the Labour movement expressed relief at the events of 1931, regarding the episode as a welcome and necessary clearing of the decks, both in terms of policy and personnel. It was an opportunity to set out again with an improved boat and a new crew. Cole shared much of this same mood and expectation. Indeed, it provided the basis for his essential treatment of 1931 as the occasion for a reformulation of a social democratic tradition rather than for its abandonment. At the same time, however, he was more distinctive in his insistence that such reformulation must be rooted in an acceptance of 1931 as an example rather than an event, a culmination rather than a betrayal. This was the theme which dominated his thought and writing in the early 1930s, as he insisted that only an analysis of that ideology whose defects became so apparent in 1931 could provide the proper foundation for a new ideological perspective. A better boat and new crew were not enough: also needed was a clearer sense of destination and a more sophisticated compass.

Cole's first task, then, (to exhaust an ailing metaphor) was to describe and indict the set of assumptions which left the Labour movement stranded in 1930 and dashed against the rocks in 1931. Hitherto Labour had assumed 'both the stability and the "squeezeability" of capitalism',[70] allowing a concessions policy to be successfully pursued whilst a series of separate nationalizations worked its cumulative effects. Here were the component assumptions of the sort of gradualism which had been Labour's working philosophy. Cole wanted to argue that both assumptions were now clearly false. Thus, on the one hand, he treated 1931 as final evidence that (in his favourite metaphor) the capitalist orange could no longer be squeezed. Labour under Mac-Donald had been rendered impotent when capitalist crisis had robbed it of its central principle of action. A crisis for capitalism was necessarily a crisis, rather than an opportunity, for British socialism because of its adherence to an obsolete concessions policy. Here was the essential meaning of 1931, for when a capitalism which was no longer expansive and progressive could yield no further concessions, even having to

[69] 'A Socialist View', *Economist*, 17 Oct. 1931.
[70] Ibid.

reclaim some previous ones, British socialism was presented with a crucial dilemma. It had either to submit to the requirements of capitalism, in the hope that a concessions strategy could be successfully resumed at a later date—the MacDonald option—or it had to reject such a course, even though it was the logical outcome of its own past thinking. Thus, although the bulk of the Labour Party refused to follow MacDonald, the fact remained that 'within the assumptions on which they had previously been acting they were without an alternative policy to that which they had rejected'.[71] If capitalism could no longer be squeezed, nor could its stability be assured either. Labour had adhered to an extractive policy of social reforms and a conception of nationalization by instalment whilst treating capitalism as a constant, as something which would continue to function normally in face of Labour's inroads. Here was another traditional assumption which Cole was anxious to demolish. He expounded the 'paradox of interventionism',[72] whereby Labour's concessionary policy of limited intervention was seen to depend for its success on a thriving capitalism, the very condition which such interventionist tampering with the free operation of the profit system necessarily impaired. Here, too, the events of 1931 served to highlight this paradox at the heart of Labourism. Moreover, a policy of progressive nationalizations, like that of concessionary social reforms, could not assume the continuance of an otherwise stable capitalist environment; for it would both have effects on that environment and elicit a response from it.

It was for these reasons, then, that Cole sought to present 1931 as the end of a definition. Essentially, it was a definition of the nature of the socialist transition. By demolishing the assumptions at its centre, he wanted to ensure the abandonment of that conception of evolutionary gradualism which had dominated Labour's thinking. Merely to state the conditions for a successful gradualism was enough to demonstrate its impossibility. Above all, gradualism would have to confront the effects on capitalism of its own activity. At some point this would produce a crisis situation in which old-style gradualism would either have to capitulate or turn itself into something else. A gradualism which was prepared only to tinker with capitalism would succeed in eroding capitalist efficiency without replacing it with anything else. Cole's statement of this position was both vigorous and convincing, whilst much later evidence could be adduced in its favour. Yet if

[71] *The Intelligent Man's Guide Through World Chaos*, 1932, p. 611.
[72] 'The Labour Party From Within', *Nineteenth Century*, Oct. 1931.

gradualism was to be abandoned, what was to be the alternative? Cole's argument seemed almost to have been designed to prepare the way for an affirmation of a revolutionary perspective (and certainly could contribute much to such a perspective), whereas its real intention was rather different. Indeed, his position on this matter did much to distinguish and define his role as a theorist of social democracy. Instead of old-style gradualism he offered new-style gradualism, presented as a response to the problem of radical social change in a particular type of social and cultural setting. 'The question which Communists seem never to have thought out,' he wrote, 'is how Marxism ought in the twentieth century to be applied in those countries which are already equipped with liberal-democratic Constitutions, and have already large middle classes exercising the predominant influence in their political affairs.'[73] Cole's own constant concern was precisely to formulate a socialism appropriate to societies of this type. His new-model gradualism of the early 1930s was intended as just such a formulation—and distinguished by its twin foundations from that traditional gradualism whose limitations had been so conspicuous in 1931.

In the first place, it was necessary to devise a strategy which would overcome those inherent limitations of mere interventionism which he had so forcefully documented. Such a strategy had to be rooted in an acceptance of the idea that partial intervention, excursions into the periphery of capitalism, would only dislocate one sort of economic system without inaugurating a new one. Thus, in place of a gradualism of piecemeal instalments, Cole urged the necessity of 'a frontal attack upon the key positions of capitalist society'.[74] This notion of a frontal assault became central to the Cole vocabulary at this time. Capitalism would not be eroded; it must be toppled, swiftly, decisively and constructively. If the attack must be frontal because of the necessary defects of a more oblique approach, the problem remained of defining those key capitalist positions against which a frontal assault had to be directed. Cole was clear about this too, for he emphasized the essential irrelevance of selective nationalizations of manufacturing industry at an early stage when the first task was to get the financial arteries of capitalism into socialist hands. In concrete terms, this would involve the immediate socialization of the Bank of England and the joint stock banks, along with the other financial institutions concerned with the

---

[73] *The Intelligent Man's Review of Europe To-day* (with M. I. Cole), 1933, p. 672.
[74] *A Plan For Britain*, Clarion Press, 1932.

supply of capital and credit. To this list Cole would also add a socialized transport industry and those institutions concerned with the control of overseas trade; the whole package designed to oust capitalism from its critical areas of economic power and to provide a nucleus of social control which would both keep the economic system running and open the way towards more extensive socialization and towards comprehensive economic planning.

Two features of this programme deserve notice at this stage. Firstly, while Cole had begun to insist on the primacy of socialized finance long before the events of 1931, particularly in terms of its contribution to a recovery programme, the experience of the Labour Government did much to emphasize the centrality of financial institutions in the political economy of capitalism. Above all, after 1931 a preparedness to socialize the joint stock banks—a policy briefly embraced at Labour's 1932 Conference—became almost the touchstone of socialist seriousness.[75] Certainly this was Cole's view, not because of a 'bankers' ramp' reflex after 1931 but because banking was regarded as the pivot of the economic system and thus central to any real advance towards socialist economic control. Either the state would control the bankers or the bankers would control the state: this was the kernel of Cole's argument in 1931 and beyond. He continued to defend this position, making it integral to his argument for national planning, long after 1931 had receded from immediate memory and when many people in the Labour movement had begun to suggest that a socialized central bank alone would provide a Labour government with sufficient financial control for its economic purposes. He remained attached to a view 'that any Socialist Government which is not prepared to tackle thoroughly the question of the banks cannot be a Government that means seriously to advance towards Socialism'.[76] A second feature of Cole's programme for a frontal attack on capitalism was its insistence that it should not be sidetracked by the demand for immediate social reforms. This was presented as a logical corollary of the strategy of frontal attack. The aim was to mount a determined offensive to secure social control of the key areas of economic power, not to continue a concessions policy by other means. It was a strategy which 'quite deliberately subordinates the getting of immediate social reforms, however desirable, to the laying of the foundations for a constructive Socialist system'.[77] Social reform

---

[75] See 'A Socialist View', *Economist*, 17 Oct. 1931.
[76] (Ed.), *What Everybody Wants To Know About Money*, 1933, p. 512.
[77] *The Need For A Socialist Programme* (with G. R. Mitchison; Socialist League, 1933).

must, therefore, not be the chief appeal to the electorate; rather, social reform must be presented as conditional upon the establishment of socialist economic control. This was likely to prove the hardest lesson for the Labour movement to learn, yet was a necessary implication of this new conception of strategy.

Here, then, in the doctrine of frontal attack on key capitalist institutions, was a central pillar of Cole's new gradualism. Its other main pillar was a natural consequence of this same doctrine, for it was not enough to devise a socialist strategy which escaped the limitations of traditional gradualism without also giving some thought to the mechanics of its application in a concrete social and political context. In other words, how could British socialism launch such an offensive within the confines of an ancient parliamentary system of government? The question was fundamental to Cole's position, for there was little advantage in having documented the inherent limitations of interventionism and having formulated an alternative if there existed no agency for its implementation. In general, Cole accepted the need to recognize the fact of a non-revolutionary situation (above all, as he liked to put it, because the British working class had much more than their chains to lose); yet if a 'frontal' socialism proved impossible because of the nature of British parliamentarism, could it expect a future only of political impotence? The answer of Cole (and others) to this question provoked a controversy which stretched far beyond the confines of the Labour movement. Indeed, it raised issues which have allowed serious liberal minds to cite this episode in British socialist history as this country's nearest approach to a 'fulfilment of Mill's prophecy'[78] about the perils of majoritarian tyranny.

It is important to be clear that, in so far as the 'lessons of 1931' for the Labour movement related mainly to the problems of economic strategy and political method, the revisions in the latter were the necessary product of the new requirements of the former. The distinctive merit claimed for the new economic strategy was that, unlike the old gradualism, it proposed not a series of isolated and uncoordinated forays into capitalism but concerted action designed to transform the basis of the economic system 'at a blow'. This process could be likened to a military advance, with 'the element of simultaneous movement on a wide front and the seizure and consolidation of key positions'[79]—a decisive break

[78] J. W. N. Watkins, '*John Stuart Mill and the Liberty of the Individual*', in D. Thomson (ed.), *Political Ideas*, 1969, Penguin, p. 157.
[79] *The Need For A Socialist Programme* (op. cit.).

with the sort of gradualism which was content to lay siege, take pris-
oners and pick off occasional stragglers. Yet this familiar gradualism,
whatever its limitations from the point of view of an early achievement
of socialism, did correspond very nicely with the requirements of the
British parliamentary system. That system had evolved a deliberately
ponderous and time-consuming procedure which made it difficult to
act quickly or to legislate on more than one thing at a time; exactly those
attributes which seemed designed to subvert the conception of a rapid
socialist transition developed by people like Cole and bodies like the
Socialist League in the early 1930s. One response to this situation
would be to announce the inherent impossibility of a parliamentary
road to socialism and to explore other possibilities. Indeed, this was
basic to Cole's own earlier Guild Socialist position. His personal antipathy to parliamentarism has already been noticed; not only did it
sustain his Guild Socialism but—more important for present purposes—it helped to shape his later conception of the political machinery appropriate to an effective socialist strategy. During the 1920s,
whilst moving back into the mainstream of Labour politics, he already
provided indications that he was aware of Labour's need to confront
this central problem at an early stage;[80] while even during his brief (and
reluctant) period as a parliamentary candidate he could not resist
telling his electors what a miserable business parliament was.[81]

After 1931, therefore, it was unsurprising that Cole took the lead in
coupling a new socialist strategy with a radical reconsideration of the
role of parliament in the transition to socialism. His own background
and disposition gave him a licence in this matter which went beyond
that enjoyed by such figures as Cripps and Laski who, although
engaged in the same enterprise, were ultimately inhibited by their
attachment to a somewhat different tradition.[82] Cole's starting point
was the belief that the present parliamentary system was 'an admirable
instrument for the preservation of Capitalism'.[83] It was a system rooted

[80] Cf. *Industrial Policy For Socialists,* 1926, I.L.P., p. 31.

[81] He tells his electors: 'I regard parliamentary politics as a demoralising business, in the sense
that it is very liable to undermine the faith of those who successfully engage in it in the
practicability of really drastic measures of social change. . . .' (*King's Norton Labour News,* July
1930.)

[82] A. H. Hanson writes that: 'It is doubtful if the constitutional consequences of Mr. Cole were
generally understood in the League or in the Party, but his views . . . represent the most extreme
expression of constitutional radicalism to emanate from a prominent Labour party member
during this period of vigorous internal controversy.' ('The Labour Party and House of Commons
Reform', in *Planning and the Politicians,* 1969, p. 65.)

[83] *A Plan For Britain,* 1932.

in pre-democratic assumptions, inimical to rapid legislative change and designed for a party system whose protagonists shared a fundamental community of interest. So unsuitable was such a system for radical social change that an effective transition to socialism was 'utterly impossible within the traditional limits of parliamentary procedure'.[84] The lesson of this for Cole and the Labour left in the early 1930s was not that parliament should be abandoned or by-passed, but that it should undergo a procedural revolution designed to make it consonant with the requirements of socialism's new economic strategy.

The details of such procedural change were often left vague, but its purpose and essential principles were clearly stated, most starkly by Cole himself. Above all, the transition to socialism required a parliamentary procedure which allowed many things to be done together and which shifted the detailed responsibility for many areas of social and economic life away from parliament towards a number of working bodies. To meet the first requirement a general Enabling (or Emergency Powers) Act was proposed, giving sweeping powers of socialization in accordance with the needs of a socialist economic plan, with compensation claims postponed for later consideration by a special tribunal. The passage of such an Act would be prefaced by the abolition of the House of Lords. The need for this sort of emergency legislation was argued in terms of the crisis situation necessarily produced by the arrival in power of a serious socialist government, a situation requiring drastic action if wholesale dislocation was to be avoided. The left liked to cite the Defence of the Realm Acts of the First World War (and, later, the emergency legislation of the National Government) as precedent for its plans in this matter, for 'the coming to power of a determined Socialist Government will constitute an emergency fully as serious as the war, and calling for no less extensive governmental powers'.[85] The second main procedural requirement of the socialist transition involved a sharp reduction in the parliamentary workload. Here the proposed rule was that parliament would confine itself to the principles of legislation and final accountability, while the real task of administration and application would devolve upon a number of statutory commissions able to operate flexibly and swiftly in their particular areas of social and economic specialism.[86] With a

[84] Ibid.
[85] *Socialist Control of Industry* (Socialist League, 1933).
[86] 'The Method of Social Legislation', *Public Administration*, Jan. 1931.

greater use of orders in council and departmental regulations, the stage was set for the rapid establishment of the essentials of a socialized economy. Thereafter socialist thought could address itself to the organizational problems of a mature socialist society.

Much of the discussion inside the Labour left, particularly in its early and formative phase at the beginning of the decade, which produced this sort of programme for the socialist transition took place under Cole's presiding spirit. It also took place behind closed doors, where unlikely men whispered dangerous thoughts and doubted the wisdom of making them public.[87] Even so, this exercise in constitutional revolution created a magnificent political storm. Labour's enemies, seizing upon choice phrases from tribunes of the Socialist League, were able to raise the cry of 'democracy versus dictatorship'. In turn, this sent spokesmen for official Labour scurrying to their pens to compose new declarations of their faith in the institutions of parliamentary democracy and to dissociate themselves from those who suggested that the British parliamentary system might be less than ideal as a vehicle for socialist advance. Finally, the Communist left was able to embrace social democracy's plan for a strengthening of the state machine as telling confirmation of its degeneracy into social fascism.[88] For his part, Cole provided plenty of ammunition for those wanting to cast him for a central role in a modern demonology. In private discussions he urged the need for public honesty about the nature of a socialist programme, for it was less important to avoid frightening the electorate than to begin the task of educating them for socialism. Thus, his private declaration that a Labour government 'must set out to be as much of a dictatorship as is necessary and that is likely to be a good deal'[89] found ample echo in his published work. A string of quotations could be assembled to demonstrate the extent of his departure from the canons of parliamentarism: there could be no place for an elaborate talking-shop in the building of socialism; no limits imposed on the dictatorial powers that might be required during the transitional emergency; no security for any institution or value which impeded the achievement of socialism. If the transition was to be constitutional, it would nevertheless be

[87] For example, Attlee's suggestion that the S.S.I.P. should train people to take over command positions within the armed forces. (*S.S.I.P. Monthly Bulletin*, August 1932, Cole Collection.)

[88] Cf. R. Bassett, *The Essentials of Parliamentary Democracy*, 1935, for an orthodox Labour response to the ideas of the Socialist League. The Communists attacked the 'Cripps-Cole school of so-called "dictatorship"' as an 'essential part of the road to the fascist dictatorship'. (*Labour Monthly*, Oct. 1933.)

[89] Memorandum, Apr. 1932, Cole Collection.

revolutionary, for it would 'remove from individuals what they are accustomed to consider inalienable rights, destroy concepts which they thought to be fundamental, and set up as the basis of society a new series of ideas.'[90]

Once again Cole had found himself isolated, defending a precarious and vulnerable intellectual compromise. In this instance, however, it was an isolation disguised by a particular and temporary conjunction of events. 1931 and its aftermath produced a climate favourable to a fundamental reconsideration of socialist purpose and method inside the Labour movement, along the lines already indicated. The disastrous end of one definition seemed to have created a dynamic and flexible historical situation producing a free market in ideas and organizations which promised a new and radical beginning for British socialism. For one short moment it seemed that the Labour Party as a whole was prepared to accept a 'loyal grouser' version of the lessons of 1931.[91] Yet, of course, it was not. As the decade developed, with 1931 absorbed, the old guard back into parliament, the trade unions tightening their political grip, the traditional balance of power inside the Labour Party re-asserted itself—with fatal consequences for the sort of socialist strategy developed by Cole and others at the beginning of the decade.[92] Far from having marked the end of a definition, 1931 took its place as a sad episode in British socialism's continuing definition of its own activity.

Yet was it naïve of Cole to expect anything else? In crucial respects it surely was, for ultimately his own position was politically untenable. Having moved uneasily inside the social democratic tradition by the end of the 1920s, the events of 1931 seemed to provide him with an opportunity to remake that tradition in ways that would remove its past limitations. Cole's own analysis of those limitations was brilliant and enthusiastic, as was his conception of the priorities for a new socialist economic strategy: the difficulties began when he attempted to define the political conditions for the success of the new strategy. Affirming his loyalty to Labour as the mass party of the working class, his programme

[90] *The Need For A Socialist Programme* (op. cit.).

[91] For example, at the 1932 Leicester Conference; after which Laski wrote to Cole that: 'you in particular, and S.S.I.P. in general, deserve warm congratulations for Leicester. Clearly for the first time you have got socialism moving in the party.' (Letter, 10 Oct. 1932; Cole Collection.)

[92] So that the S.S.I.P. turned out to have been merely a group 'whose short career coincided with a brief moment in Labour Party history when left-wing ideas were respectable' (B. Pimlott, 'The Socialist League: Intellectuals and the Labour Left in the 1930s', *Journal of Contemporary History*, Vol. vi (1971) p. 15). Further discussion of the S.S.I.P. (by Margaret Cole) and the Socialist League (by Patrick Seyd) is to be found in A. Briggs and J. Saville (eds), *Essays in Labour History, Vol. III: 1918–1939*, 1977.

nevertheless required that Labour should become a political party of a different kind. Parliamentarism could only work if Labour remained a party of the traditional type; socialism could be won only if Labour rejected the traditional assumptions of the parliamentary system: much discussion—and confusion—in British socialist thought in the 1930s turned upon these central propositions.[93] For his part, Cole was both clear and frank about the political implications of his new socialist strategy, announcing that if British socialists 'ever come to the point of returning to office pledged to carry out their new and more radical policy, they are likely to find that their political methods will have to approximate more closely than they at present imagine to those of Fascism and even Communism'.[94] In other words, Labour would have to appeal to the electors on a platform of 'dictatorship'—an absurdly naïve suggestion from someone with Cole's understanding of the ideology and composition of the British Labour movement.

Here, then, was the isolation and paradox of Cole's position. The future of socialism was tied to Labour's transformation into the sort of political entity it had never been and, perhaps, could never become. Cole would not carry his programme outside the ranks of Labour, while the fate of the Socialist League showed the dismal prospects for such a programme within the Labour movement. As a Guild Socialist, Cole had offered the paradox of 'stable revolution'; while now, as social democrat, his no less paradoxical offering was of 'constitutional revolution'. Both positions were attractive, vulnerable and, ultimately, isolated. His constitutional revolution, however, did represent a genuine attempt to think out the conditions for radical socialist advance in a non-revolutionary situation. As such, it may be regarded as a first answer in his continuing search for 'a third policy which is neither Social Democratic Parliamentarism nor Communist Revolutionism'.[95]

Not merely was it a first answer, however, but also Cole's essential answer to the problem of socialist method in the post-Guild period. Its development has been traced in the 1920s, involving an increasing

[93] The left tended to argue that parliamentarism could no longer work because it depended upon a community of interest between the major parties which no longer existed. At the same time, however, the left also tended to attack Labour for its failure to renounce a community of interest of this kind. For criticism of Laski along these lines, see R. T. McKenzie, 'Laski and the Social Bases of the Constitution', *British Journal of Sociology*, iii, 1952.

[94] *The Intelligent Man's Guide Through World Chaos*, p. 613. It has rightly been observed that this entire line of argument 'rested on the twin assumptions of capitalist sabotage and Socialist integrity'. (J. Jupp, 'The Left in Britain: 1931 to 1941', M. Sc. thesis, University of London, 1956, pp. 327–8.)

[95] Ibid., p. 607.

willingness to turn to the state for solutions to pressing economic problems, a disillusionment with the trade unions as agencies of socialist change, an acceptance of the centrality of political action in capturing the state for socialist purposes—and an acceptance of Labour's hegemony on the British left. Both Cole's moderate programme of 1929 and his radical programme of the early 1930s were rooted in this set of assumptions about method, which continued to dominate his thought for the rest of his life. If he sometimes anticipated a revival of rank-and-file militancy within the trade unions (as he did during the Second World War), he never again sought to make them central agencies for the achievement of socialism. Instead, he continued to acknowledge the constraints imposed on their activity by a capitalist economic environment and urged on them the need to be both moderate industrially and militant politically.[96] His earlier 'economism' had never been unqualified; but now he declared open war on it. Similarly, if he was often prepared to concede to the Marxists the possibility of a revolutionary moment in the transition to socialism (and the defects of parliamentarism), this did little to weaken his advocacy of a vigorous constitutionalism as the normal form of socialist political action in the capitalist democracies. This assumed that the capitalist state would ultimately prove receptive to a strategy of this kind, though Cole did not confront directly this question of the nature of the state under capitalism. However, an answer was implied in his treatment of labour history and was made slightly more explicit when (as a later chapter will show) he came to revise Marxism in the direction of a democratic socialism which, in both method and content, was presented as the necessary and appropriate product of a particular type of society.

The chief consequence of the conception of socialist method sketched by Cole in the early 1930s and reiterated thereafter was to make the Labour Party central to his activities and expectations. At the time of the formation of the British Communist Party in 1920 Cole had dismissed the possibility of a real revolutionary politics under British conditions and had accepted the inevitability of Labour's domination of the British left—and never saw any reason to revise these judgements subsequently. Thus Labour commanded his loyalty because of its status as the mass party of the working class; and he regarded its left wing as the only available arena for a realistic socialist politics. His loyalty was never uncritical, of course, and there were moments (particularly during the popular front period, when he declared his 'sense of

[96] See *What Is Wrong With the Trade Unions?*, Fabian Society, Tract 301, 1956.

the deep and utter rottenness of the present Labour leadership'[97]) when a breaking-point was almost reached. Yet it is significant that such a point was never in fact reached. Rather, Cole was always critical of those organizations and activities (the Socialist League, the I.L.P., the Unity campaign) which threatened to bring themselves into direct conflict with official Labour. Even when he supported these groups on policy, he dissented from them on strategy. He developed a conception of socialist strategy which involved the acceptance of a pressure group status within a framework of loyalty to the wider Labour movement. He regarded S.S.I.P. as an organization exactly of this kind.

In this context, it is interesting to note the development in Cole's thought from a Guild Socialist position which paid little attention to the organizational and leadership problems of forging a socialist party out of a mass movement to a position which not only accepted the centrality of a socialist political party but also which, in relation to the British Labour Party, demanded the creation of a disciplined 'party within a party'[98] as the appropriate organizational vehicle for socialism. Cole was not so innocent as to believe that activity of this kind would not at times fall foul of official Labour, despite all protestations of loyalty. What he did maintain, however, was that it was the duty of British socialists to avoid giving the Labour leadership any unnecessary excuse to expel them; that expulsion not resignation was always the proper course; and that in the event of such expulsion the first duty was to get back inside at the earliest possible moment. 'I propose to go on working inside the Labour Party until I am kicked out'[99] announced Cole at a time of maximum antagonism with the leadership; and this was always his practical political prescription for British socialists. He never found it a satisfactory position; but equally, like Tawney, Laski and many others, he never found a satisfactory alternative to a 'sensible extremism' of this kind.

[97] 'Unity and the People's Front', *Labour Monthly*, Mar. 1937. Another moment of despair with Labour came in 1950 and involved both domestic and international policy. Cole resigned the chairmanship of the Fabian Society and withdrew from the preparatory discussions for *New Fabian Essays*, after contributing a memorandum which declared that 'the Labour Party has no programme that is worth a straw, except defence of the Welfare State'. ('Notes on the Long-Term Politico-Economic Outlook', Memorandum, Sept. 1950. New Fabian Essays material, Cole Collection.)
[98] 'A Critique of British Communism', *This Unrest*, 1933. This conception of strategy was spelled out in his articles, 'If Socialism Is To Come', *Adelphi*, May and June, 1933.
[99] *The People's Front*, 1937, p. 335.

VIII
Economics: Capitalist and Socialist

GUILD SOCIALISM had little serious economic content. There was much concern with economic structure, but little with economic theory or policy. Indeed, it was assumed that if the correct industrial structure could be established then economic policy would largely take care of itself. There was no real discussion of the role of the market under capitalism or of alternatives to the market under socialism. Antipathy to the state inhibited a thoroughgoing economic collectivism, but also prevented any rigorous discussion of those issues of economic coordination and allocation to which a comprehensive socialist theory must address itself. Similarly, if Guild Socialism gave casual assent to the economic theory of Marxism, this simply provided an economic underpinning for its own theory of exploitation which was always stated in essentially human terms in relation to authority structures at work. As final illustration of the disposition of Guild Socialism in this matter, it is only necessary to recall Cole's tendency to suggest that there was something rather vulgar about economic preoccupations in face of the central issue of industrial control and that the Guild system would bring with it a release from such preoccupations.

Against this background, Cole's economic thought in the post-Guild period takes on a particular interest. Partly, this interest derives simply from an examination of his developing concern with economic problems, beginning in the 1920s and continuing thereafter. The social philosopher became the economist, an evolution which reveals much about the changing emphasis within his wider conception of socialism. Partly, too, Cole's economic thought has a special interest because it typifies a basic characteristic of his socialist thought as a whole. This is the characteristic of dualism, the tendency to work at two levels in the presentation of argument or the formulation of theory. This was noticed in his discussion of industrial democracy and it will be suggested as a central feature of his thought. In relation to his economic thought, this tendency is always present. It leads him to combine a reformist interest in immediate economic problems with a more fundamental interest in the economics of socialism. An examination of his economic thought has, therefore, to address itself to both these levels—and to the problems involved in this sort of bifocalism.

It was the impact of economic depression on the control movement inside trade unionism in the early 1920s which forced Cole to face the realities of economic life. It seemed a sharp and bitter lesson in the vulnerability of the labour movement to external economic forces. All his espousal of the primacy of will and organization seemed to dissolve against the facts of economic life. 'The fact of facts in the industrial situation to-day is the return of unemployment', he announced in 1921; so that 'the task of tasks for the Labour Movement is to find a remedy.'[1] His instant remedy was to revive the Guild demand for industrial maintenance. Basic to the Guild scheme, though not much worked out, was the idea that the Guilds would be responsible for their members in good times and bad. Unlike capitalism, the Guild system would ensure that the worker was not simply discarded when trade was bad. This aspect of Guild Socialism, though integral, was never central to the presentation of the Guild argument and its elaboration never undertaken with any rigour. However, with the return of mass unemployment in 1921 the consequent weakening of the movement for industrial control seemed to provide an opportunity for a shift of emphasis inside Guild Socialism towards its commitment to industrial maintenance. Certainly this was Cole's initial response to the arrival of the economic slump, involving an attempt to sustain the relevance of the Guild position in unfavourable circumstances. Thus by late 1921, noting that 'the present is a sufficiently depressing time at which to write about any movement for industrial emancipation', he declared that 'here and now, the most important thing for the public to grasp about Guild Socialism is its positive suggestion for dealing with unemployment.'[2]

Unemployment was seen as important to Guild Socialism for two main reasons. Firstly, it was necessary to show that Guild theory had a relevant response to this central fact of working-class life. Secondly, it was necessary to check the development of unemployment if the labour movement was not to suffer such an erosion of strength and confidence that would prevent it from pushing forward with the demand for industrial control. The policy of industrial maintenance seemed to meet

---

[1] 'Down With Unemployment', *Guildsman*, Jan. 1921.
[2] 'The Aims of Guild Socialism', *Time and Tide*, 28 Oct. 1921.

these requirements. It could be presented as a key element in a Guild society, already exemplified in the contemporary behaviour of the building guilds, a pointer to a society without the fear of unemployment. At the same time, it could also be presented as the central demand on the employers here and now, both as a right ('it is not a State charity that we are demanding, but an industrial right'[3]) and as an antidote to unemployment (a stimulant to working-class purchasing power). The demand was addressed not to the state but to the employers, with maintenance to be administered through the machinery of trade unionism in a way which would encourage labour's confidence and potential for control.

Of course, the demand was futile, in so far as capitalism could not concede it. It was also spurious, in so far as it was never clear how individual guilds would be able to fulfil it either. It was valuable only in a propagandist sense, for capitalism's inability to guarantee maintenance could serve to expose it in the eyes of the workers and strengthen their resolve to win industrial control. Thus when Cole put industrial maintenance firmly in the forefront of Guild Socialism's immediate programme it represented his final attempt to interpret and respond to the economic crisis of capitalism inside an explicitly Guild framework. When it proved irrelevant as a viable economic strategy, he began to move outside that framework in his search for economic solutions. His rationale for this departure was simple enough. An aggressive, control-minded labour movement could only flourish in a stable economic environment; such an environment no longer existed; therefore it was necessary for those who wanted further advance towards workers' control to press a remedy for the slump and unemployment which presently made such advance impossible. If this was the rationale from a Guild Socialist perspective, however, it did not provide a total explanation for Cole's increasing attention to economic policy. Not only did mass unemployment represent a major obstacle to any movement for industrial control, it was also an evil whose eradication was of paramount importance in its own right. As will be seen, Cole's anger and impatience at the failure of governments to tackle unemployment in a determined fashion took its inspiration from both these sources.

But if a remedy for unemployment had to be found, where should the search begin? This was a difficult question to answer, as the gloomy record of governments and economists in the 1920s amply demon-

[3] *Unemployment and Industrial Maintenance*, N.G.L. pamphlet, 1921, p. 5.

strates. The economists seemed lost in a remote world of trade cycle theory, where formal analysis seemed to triumph over the need to develop a practical response to chronic unemployment. As such, much economic discussion seemed frankly irrelevant.[4] At the same time, governments seemed wedded to a financial and monetary orthodoxy which could not distinguish cyclical from structural unemployment, could not countenance the use of countercyclical budgetary policy, and which seemed to rely on a strategy of resolute inactivity in the hope of an eventual revival in world trade.[5] It was a difficult question for socialists too, of course, for if unemployment was an essential characteristic of capitalism a natural corollary would be that it was incapable of solution without a more fundamental social transformation. Whether by conviction or by default, therefore, socialists of different persuasions could also unite on a policy of inactivity sanctioned by the prevailing orthodoxies. It will be necessary to say a little more about this later.

Cole found such inactivity intolerable. If his own search for a remedy for unemployment brought no immediate results, he was relentless in his opposition to quack remedies. In a situation where the refusal to act, in the expectation of external revival, or action designed only to force down the level of wages, in the hope of restoring Britain's competitive position, seemed to represent the sum total of the collective economic wisdom of governments, Cole found ample scope for his dissenting economics. Beginning early in 1921 and continuing throughout the decade, his industrial journalism, particularly in the *New Statesman*, represented a sustained critique of prevailing economic orthodoxy in relation to the analysis and treatment of unemployment. Above all, he attacked those exponents of 'economy' who failed to recognize 'the fallacy of the supposition that a general reduction of wages offers a short and safe cut to industrial prosperity'.[6] The only sure effect of a policy of wage-cutting would be to diminish aggregate demand in the economy through its impact on working-class purchasing power and so intensify economic depression. Cole poured scorn on a political economy so lost

---

[4] 'The study of economics was drawn along by the logic of its own development, largely uninhibited by considerations of relevance, and argument was conducted for argument's sake.' (K. Hancock, 'Unemployment and the Economists in the 1920s', *Economica*, Vol. xxvii, 1960.)

[5] See K. Hancock, 'The Reduction of Unemployment as a Problem of Public Policy 1920–29', *Economic History Review*, Vol. xv, 1962–3.

[6] 'Must Wages Come Down?', *New Statesman*, 5 Feb. 1921. Similarly, 'the destruction of the workers' purchasing power is surely an odd way of meeting a slump which arises from a shortage of economic demand for goods'. (*Out of Work*, 1923, p. 67.)

in abstractions that it produced policy consequences for unemployment which defied common-sense.

In an important sense, it was common-sense which provided the cornerstone of Cole's approach to economics. It seemed silly to tackle unemployment by cutting demand; silly to hope for a revival in world trade instead of recognizing the necessary decline of Britain's traditional export industries; silly and irrational that there should be unemployment at all when there existed so much unmet demand. It was this sense of the monstrous irrationality of an economic system which met need with unemployment which made Cole impatient of the economic orthodoxies. Instead of wage-cutting there should be wage-stabilization; attacks on the dole replaced by guaranteed maintenance; government economy abandoned in favour of a bold and comprehensive scheme of industrial development. How would such a programme be financed? Cole pointed to the cheap money and abundant labour situation produced by depression, suggested a development loan to utilize this idle money for constructive work and reminded the deflationists that 'the balancing of the Budget is not everything'.[7] It is not suggested that his programme emerged as the product of a rigorous economic theory, for it did not. Rather, it took its practical proposals from the radical public works tradition, given classical statement in the Minority Report of the Webbs, which marked the beginnings of a countercyclical approach to the treatment of unemployment. The proposals of the Minority Report represented the decisive answer to governmental inactivity, and 'we shall have to come back to them now—to their main principles at any rate, if not to all their details'.[8] Throughout the 1920s, therefore, Cole was the apostle of a big public programme for the provision of work, organized and financed by central government in a way which would overcome the limitations of more traditional exercises in public works. The programme appeared in various names and forms, but in general it represented Cole's central contribution to the policy debate on unemployment during the 1920s.

It is necessary to say something about the sort of economic theory which could issue in this approach to economic policy. One thing is clear: Cole had little interest in, or aptitude for, economic abstractions. His writings are studded with broadsides at the algebraic economics of the professors, which continued unabated after he joined their number.

[7] 'The True Political Economy', *New Statesman*, 21 Jan. 1922.
[8] 'The Moral of Poplar', *New Statesman*, 10 Sept. 1921.

He was concerned to probe the assumptions behind the formulae, to stimulate a critical approach to the economics of the textbooks, and to demonstrate that universalistic formulations were rooted in a particular set of economic assumptions.[9] In a very fundamental sense, Cole did not *like* economics. His economic preoccupations following the collapse of the control movement inside trade unionism should be seen essentially as a labour of necessity, justified only by the impact of the economic environment on the fortunes of the labour movement. An economist *malgré lui*, therefore, Cole's theoretical economics were largely derivative, even when his policy recommendations were radical and suggestive. He required an economic theory which would reconcile a radical critique of the system contradictions inside a capitalist economy with a practical approach to the treatment of unemployment.

Cole found such a theory in the work of J. A. Hobson, that heretic amongst early century economists, whose ideas were 'received in respectable economic circles with almost universal cries of execration and horror'.[10] Cole always enjoyed pointing to his good heretical credentials in this way. Hobson's analysis of the maladjustment between saving and spending under capitalism, whereby a maldistribution of purchasing power caused saving to outstrip demand in times of boom and so inducing slump, was to provide the backbone of Cole's own economic thinking throughout the inter-war years. Hobson's 'under-consumption' or 'over-saving' theory had great virtues in Cole's eyes. It sanctioned the necessity of maintaining working-class purchasing power in times of depression; it focused attention on the need for radical income redistribution if purchasing power was to be stabilized at a high level; it forged an inextricable link between employment and the distribution of income; and it sanctioned a concrete strategy for the treatment of unemployment which was compatible with a more fundamental critique of the nature of capitalism. For all these reasons Cole was vigorous in pressing a Hobsonian analysis of the slump of the 1920s, which was presented as an 'object-lesson in the maladjustment of saving and spending under the conditions of modern industrial

[9] As in his *The Economic System*, W. E. A. Outline, 1927, p. 89.
[10] 'The Economics of Unemployment', *New Statesman*, 16 Dec. 1922. Hobson won belated recognition in Keynes's *General Theory*. Appropriately, Keynes turned to Cole for an obituary piece on Hobson for the *Economic Journal*, in an effort to make 'some sort of amends' for earlier neglect. (Keynes to Cole, 25 Apr. 1940; letter in possession of Margaret Cole.) For a discussion of Hobson, see M. Freeden, 'J. A. Hobson As A New Liberal Theorist', *Journal of the History of Ideas*, xxxiv, 1973.

organisation'.[11] The analysis involved a remedy: not a further attack on working-class incomes but a stimulus to the purchasing power of the workers in order to bring saving and spending into equilibrium.

The major attraction of Hobson's economic theory for Cole at this time was the support it provided both for a systematic indictment of capitalism and for immediate action on unemployment. As such, it provided ideal theoretical equipment for a socialism which also wanted immediate economic improvement. Cole declared himself 'convinced' that there could be 'no full solution of the problem of unemployment as long as capitalism exists'.[12] Such a solution demanded a complete reshaping of the principles of income distribution along lines incompatible with capitalism. It was this agreement on the inability of capitalism to generate sufficient working-class purchasing power to prevent recurrent crisis which allowed Cole to describe a 'close relationship between the theories of Hobson and Marx',[13] in analysis if not in prescription. Unlike many socialists in this period, however, Cole was not content to leave the matter there. Having established the status of unemployment as a symptom of capitalism, incapable of abolition without an attack on the fabric of capitalism itself, it remained to investigate the possibility of ameliorative action in the present. That such action, if possible, should be taken seemed to Cole self-evident in view of the monstrous nature of unemployment. Unemployment caused so much distress, so weakened the labour movement, that 'if there is a way, even under capitalism, of reducing or eliminating trade fluctuations, the workers cannot afford to disregard it'.[14] Cole was adamant that the inability to abolish unemployment within the framework of capitalism should not, and did not, preclude the obligation to search for palliatives. If there were narrow limits to what could be done along these lines, then greater was the need to explore those limits to the full.

Here is the source of that dualism, that sense of operating at two levels, which distinguished Cole's thought. His commitment to a Guild conception of socialism survived the eclipse of the Guild movement, but struggled for reconciliation with a no less determined commitment to proffer relevant analysis and guidance to the labour movement in a changed economic and political situation. Until the end of the 1920s,

---

[11] Ibid.
[12] *Out of Work*, 1923, p. 87.
[13] 'Unemployment' (Syllabus, Labour Research Dept., 1923).
[14] *Out of Work*, p. 52.

when he again attempted to define the nature and purpose of British socialism in a coherent and systematic fashion, this dualism (or bifocalism) reflected itself in considerable tension and uncertainty in his thought. Drawing upon a Hobsonian analysis of the trade cycle, however, he was able to maintain a successful economic dualism which looked to the overthrow of capitalism for the abolition of that income maldistribution which caused slump and unemployment, but which also recommended a positive programme for the mitigation of distress. Thus he was able to argue that there could be no cure for unemployment within capitalism, while at the same time urging a constructive strategy for economic amelioration. In this way, the necessity of socialism and the need for relevant analysis and action in the present were reconciled: capitalism could be both indicted and reformed.

Cole's first post-Guild reform programme for capitalism was sketched out in 1929 in his *The Next Ten Years in British Social and Economic Policy.* His distinctive contribution to the immediate treatment of unemployment was his proposal for a National Labour Corps, a voluntary emergency army of the unemployed to be engaged in socially useful work throughout the country. He canvassed the scheme widely and forcefully at this time, not as a satisfactory long term solution but as a valuable form of immediate action which preferred work to doles and which would have a stabilizing effect on purchasing power and employment. For Cole, the scheme had one over-riding merit: it offered the possibility of *doing* something practical about unemployment, a fact which provided the decisive answer to any doubts and criticisms that the scheme might meet. In its defence, therefore, he insisted that the socialist 'simply cannot, when power comes his way, confess that he has been talking through his hat all these years, and that he, like those whom he has attacked, knows no way of setting the unemployed to work'.[15]

Apart from his emergency scheme, he also suggested a strategy for the treatment of the longer term and structural unemployment which characterized the British economy. Such a strategy was prefaced by a recognition that a changing economic environment demanded a fundamental reorganization of British industry, involving an acceptance of a reduced importance (and rationalization) for the traditional export industries and a stimulation of newer science-based industries. Cole wanted to argue both that there was still no general acceptance of the necessity for this sort of industrial reorganization and that such

[15] *Next Ten Years*, p. 62.

reorganization would not take place in the absence of a consciously directed programme. He sketched the required programme, involving above all else the public control of key investment and allocation decisions in the economy through the device of a state investment board. Cole's aim, then, was to achieve stable economic recovery; this was seen to require radical industrial reorganization; but such reorganization could not be secured by capitalism because of its inability, via market rates of interest, to generate the right amount of saving or to direct investment to where it was most needed; therefore a bold programme of state intervention was required. Here was the essential form of Cole's argument. The remainder of his recovery programme derived from a Hobsonian analysis of the under-consumption origins of capitalist crisis generated by a maldistribution of purchasing power. He suggested a number of proposals, notably in the sphere of redistributive taxation and welfare provision (especially a system of family allowances), designed to effect a drastic redistribution of purchasing power in favour of the poor, thereby erecting a buttress against recurrent economic instability.

Cole's programme was offered to the Labour movement as a recipe both for short-term economic improvement and longer term economic stabilization. It was also offered as an essentially practical and concrete programme, unburdened by tiresome theoretical controversy, which would meet the need for the Labour movement to adopt a positive stance in relation to the pressing problem of unemployment. In effect, Cole demanded the suspension of socialist theory in favour of practical economic action, a position whose value and tenability his own *Next Ten Years* was designed to demonstrate.

This raises some interesting questions about that interpretation of this period of Labour history which has gained the status of conventional wisdom. The interpretation is familiar and essentially simple: the central fact of political life in the 1920s was depression and unemployment; prevailing economic orthodoxy, embraced by the politicians, prevented any constructive governmental response; the challenge to orthodoxy should have come from Labour as the major radical party, drawing upon the economic heresies of Keynes and progressive liberalism; Labour failed to make this challenge, critically during its 1929–31 government; its failure is explained by its attachment to a traditional socialist ideology which could only think in system terms; hence it could offer no policy for the transition, relapsing in practice into the prevailing orthodoxies because of its inability to 'translate

Economics: Capitalist and Socialist 185
moral fervour into constructive policy'.[16] In many respects this account
is unsatisfactory. If not essentially wrong, it is certainly incomplete.
Above all, for present purposes, it ignores the extent to which individuals and groups within the Labour movement during the 1920s did
attempt to develop and press a strategy designed to promote both
economic recovery and socialist advance.

There was the I.L.P., for example, whose difficult relationship with
official Labour at this time has received considerable attention but
whose economic programme has been largely overlooked. Although the
I.L.P. had often failed to relate its conception of the socialist commonwealth to any concrete immediate strategy, creating a policy void
to be filled by others, in the 1920s it did begin to think seriously about
the content of a relevant socialist economic policy. The result was a
radical scheme for income stabilization and redistribution aimed at
boosting working-class purchasing power, the product of an under-
consumptionist analysis of the causes of capitalist crisis which revealed
the authorship of J. A. Hobson, amongst others. Whatever its defects,
the I.L.P. programme represented the sort of approach which was
likely to issue in expansionist policy conclusions and an opposition to
deflationary orthodoxy.[17] Indeed, it is significant that the central
charge made by the Communist left against the I.L.P. at this time was
that its economic programme, the product of its contamination by
progressive capitalist economists, represented an attempt to stimulate
the recovery of an ailing capitalism, in which 'revolution is to be
avoided by giving the workers more purchasing power'.[18] In other
words, exactly the reverse of the charge made against the non-
Communist left by Skidelsky and others.

If the Skidelsky thesis is inadequate with respect to the I.L.P., it is
manifestly inaccurate when applied to G. D. H. Cole. This would not
matter if Skidelsky had confined his argument to the case of the Labour
leadership, where it clearly has much of value to contribute, but he
deliberately wants to embrace—and indict—a whole tradition.
'Neither the Labour leaders nor any established party intellectuals',

[16] R. Skidelsky, *Politicians and The Slump*, 1967, p. xiii. Skidelsky is the major exponent of the view
described here. For further discussion of this view by Skidelsky and D. Marquand, see *Society for the
Study of Labour History, Bulletin* 21, autumn 1970. Also cf. Beer (*Modern British Politics*, ch. 5) for a
similar statement of the system-building of Labour's 'socialist generation'.
[17] Of the I.L.P. Michael Foot writes that 'today their ideas stand the test of scrutiny better than
any other political prescriptions of that era'. (*Aneurin Bevan*, Vol. i, 1962, p. 102.)
[18] Emile Burns, 'The I.L.P. Programme', *Labour Monthly*, Feb. 1926. Similarly, the I.L.P. was
attacked for being 'in full harmony with the Liberal economist, Professor Keynes'. (F. Longden,
Labour Monthly, Jan. 1925.)

writes Skidelsky, 'showed the slightest interest in Keynes or any other progressive economist',[19] a statement which is simply absurd in relation to Cole, who could plausibly be nominated as the party's leading intellectual at this time (as he was by Egon Wertheimer, in his contemporary 'portrait' of the Labour Party).[20] As has been seen, Cole's major preoccupation during this period was the formulation of an economic strategy with which Labour could stimulate recovery and reduce unemployment, with socialism relegated to a second order status. This strategy involved an opposition to further deflation, a bold emergency programme by the state for the provision of work, public control of key investment decisions to promote industrial reorganization and measures designed to stabilize working-class purchasing power at a high level.

If it was the under-consumptionist analysis of J. A. Hobson which provided the main theoretical underpinning for this programme, Cole was happy to draw upon the developing work of Keynes, as a perusal of the bibliographical suggestions appended to his economic pamphlets and syllabi at this time amply indicates. The extent to which Cole's economic programme may be described as Keynesian, or proto-Keynesian, is difficult. Certainly in policy terms there was a broadly similar approach, evidenced by their close cooperation inside Mac-Donald's Economic Advisory Council.[21] There was substantial theoretical agreement too, though the largely derivative character of Cole's economic thought, the emphasis on the policy implications of theory rather than its technical elaboration, makes direct comparison somewhat misleading. In general, it may be said that Cole was 'Keynesian' enough to recognize the significance of Keynes's theoretical economics, to welcome it for the support it lent to his own under-consumptionist analysis and to embrace it for its endorsement of those policies (e.g. a comprehensive public works programme, the socialization of investment) which he was anxious himself to promote. In one major area, however, that of deficit financing, Cole had still to grasp the

[19] Skidelsky, op. cit, p. 43. Both here and in his more recent *Oswald Mosley* 1975, Skidelsky seems determined to establish the myth that, apart from Mosley, the left was economically illiterate until Keynes came along. In fact, discussion within sections of the Labour movement had 'ranged over many of the aspects of what was later to be termed the "New Economics".' (D. I. MacKay, I. J. C. Forsyth and D. M. Kelly, 'The Discussion of Public Works Programmes, 1917–35: Some Remarks on the Labour Movement's Contribution', *International Review of Social History*, Vol. xi, 1966.)

[20] E. Wertheimer, *Portrait of the Labour Party*, 1929, p. 191.

[21] See S. Howson and D. Winch, *The Economic Advisory Council 1930–1939*, 1977.

significance of the Keynesian approach, though here too the deficiency was soon to be remedied.[22]

So damaging is the evidence to his general thesis that Skidelsky seems to have cultivated a blind spot as far as Cole is concerned. This would not matter very much (except to a study of Cole) if an interpretation of an important moment in Labour history was not at issue. Skidelsky's argument involves an attempt to attribute the failure of Labour in office to a utopian British socialist tradition which was unable to supply the intellectual material for a relevant economic programme. If such material, even a genuine alternative programme, *was* available to the Labour leadership then a rather different interpretation of its failure is required.[23] Certainly Cole was engaged throughout this period in exactly the sort of revisionist economic thinking, designed to service the needs of a Labour government, the absence of which Skidelsky is most anxious to demonstrate. It is interesting that the two examples of economic thought cited by Skidelsky as possible sources for a constructive socialist economic programme—the counter-cyclical ideas of the Minority Report and Hobson's underconsumptionism—were central to the development of Cole's own theory.[24]

Not only this, but Cole's contemporary critique of the Labour movement bears a striking resemblance to Skidelsky's retrospective indictment. For example, he greeted the arrival of the first Labour Government with an announcement that the Labour movement had as yet 'not developed that constructive economic policy which is the condition of real political achievement',[25] and a recommendation that it

[22] Cole was not yet clear, despite some unorthodox suggestions, about the role of idle balances as opposed to taxation in the finance of public works. For example, at the time of the 1929 election he branded the Liberal proposals as 'madcap finance', but added that 'this is not meant to suggest that there is not a legitimate sphere for borrowing in the handling of the unemployment problem'. (*How To Conquer Unemployment*, Labour Party, 1929.)
[23] Along the lines suggested by Royden Harrison, 'Labour Government: Then and Now', *Political Quarterly*, Jan.–Mar. 1970. A rather different interpretation has been suggested by Ross McKibbin, who challenges the two key assumptions of the neo-Keynesian approach (namely, that a developed alternative was available and that some countries pursued such an alternative successfully). He concludes that Labour 'did about as well as a "progressive" party could do in a mature capitalist economy that was showing no signs of cyclical recovery'. ('The Economic Policy of the Second Labour Government 1929–31', *Past and Present*, 68, Aug. 1975.)
[24] Skidelsky describes Hobson as 'the only trade-cycle theorist whose analysis and remedies were likely to prove valuable additions to the socialist armoury' (op. cit., p. 31), yet disparages the socialist economist who drew most heavily upon Hobson. At the same time, Hobson himself consistently announced his support for Cole's proposals—as in his review of Cole's *Gold, Credit and Employment* (*New Statesman*, 6 Sept. 1930.)
[25] *New Standards*, Jan. 1924.

undertook a fundamental policy reappraisal on an organized basis. Moreover, when the Liberal Party produced its radical economic programme Cole both welcomed it and offered it as an object-lesson to Labour.[26] 'It would be a public service of the first importance,' he wrote, 'if the Labour economists would get together and ... endeavour to think out their ideas of Britain's economic future on the same scale as the Liberal intellectuals have now attempted.'[27] His own *Next Ten Years* was a conscious attempt to remedy Labour's deficiency in this respect. Finally, of course, Cole actively pressed an expansionist, anti-deflationary economic programme on Labour both in opposition and in office, warning it against an embrace by Treasury orthodoxy and becoming ever more critical as that embrace encountered little resistance.[28] In sum, therefore, whilst it would be possible to describe Cole's theoretical development during the 1920s in terms of a triumph of a practical economic reformism over a socialist utopianism (arguably a too complete triumph), it is simply not tenable to seek to bring it under the umbrella of a directly contrary thesis.

If the effects of depression in the 1920s caused Cole, almost as a labour of necessity, to turn to economics, the economic climate of the 1930s provided ample reasons for a continuation of that preoccupation. World slump, the impact of Keynes, the New Deal recovery experiment, the origins of fascism, the development of planning in Russia: all this and much else besides demanded analysis and interpretation from a socialist perspective. It was a heavily economic decade, in which every serious theorist of socialism was forced to become something of an economist. In the British context, the evolution of John Strachey provided perhaps the best illustration of this on the Marxist side; paralleled by Cole's own work inside the social democratic tradition. Indeed, it might be suggested that the sense of hollowness which pervaded Harold Laski's sweeping pronouncements on the nature of capitalism during this period found at least part of its explanation in his

---

[26] 'Liberalism and the Industrial Future', *New Statesman*, 11 Feb. 1928.

[27] Ibid.

[28] It may be true that it would be 'absurd to portray [MacDonald] as a brake on more adventurous colleagues' (D. Marquand, *Ramsay MacDonald*, 1977, p. 795), but this neglects the availability of an alternative economic strategy within the Labour movement. For example, Marquand concludes that MacDonald's 'greatest error' (ibid.) was to reject the advice of Keynes in August 1931 on currency parity, yet Cole (and Bevin) raised the question of leaving the gold standard in November 1930 inside the Economic Advisory Council, when Keynes was more hesitant (Howson and Winch, op. cit., p. 73).

failure to equip himself with the sort of economic tools which could have given substance to his analysis.[29] For his part, Cole earned his living throughout the decade as a professional economist, a fact which had significant consequences for his analysis of events and for his continuing statement of socialism. Yet his economics were of a distinctive kind—severely practical, concretely rooted and concerned with the products of economic theory only in so far as these seemed able to offer a contribution to the solution of real-world economic problems. From the point of view of economic science Cole was insufficiently rigorous, an amateur who refused to employ an idiosyncratic vocabulary and who, like J. A. Hobson before him, turned to economics only as part of a much wider social concern. The lack of rigour was evident enough;[30] certainly Cole was not in the business of pushing back the frontiers of economic theory, at least in an orthodox sense. For him, all economics was necessarily applied economics, for it found its role and justification only its contribution to the wider task of social organization. Hence his scorn for the 'algebraic sterilities'[31] of those more rigorous economic practitioners who forgot this central fact.

Could capitalism recover? This was the question around which much of the political and economic discussion of the 1930s revolved, embracing all shades of ideological opinion. Whether affirmative or negative, the answer given had important consequences for both policy and theory. It could, for example, provide the basis for a more interventionist 'new Toryism'; or, with Strachey, for a comprehensive Marxism. For the left, of course, it was a crucial question. In John Strachey's own case, for example, it is plausible to suggest that it was his different estimations of the possibility of 'recovery' which provided a major clue to his dramatic political and ideological shifts. So, too, with Cole, whose less erratic theoretical development during the 1930s nevertheless exhibited a continuing concern with the prospects and possibilities of capitalist recovery. That concern has already been charted in the context of the previous decade, with Cole energetically drawing up a recovery programme for a Labour government. By the turn of the decade, however, Labour was in office and recovery on the

[29] In spite of his assertion of the primacy of economic forces Laski 'made no effort to master the modern techniques of economic analysis' with the result that his economics consisted of 'a few Marxist phrases.' (H. Deane, *The Political Ideas of Harold J. Laski*, 1955, p. 192.)

[30] Thus Maurice Dobb wrote that Cole's economic writings 'promise more than they fulfil' and that 'one is left with the sense of a problem greater than the acumen devoted to its analysis'. (*Economic Journal*, June 1935.)

[31] Cole to Beatrice Webb, 18 Feb. 1939, Passfield Papers.

agenda. At least, this was Cole's expectation. That a minority Labour government could not push ahead with socialism was accepted; but what it could, and should, do was to stake its political life on a radical approach to unemployment and monetary management. Throughout the early days of the MacDonald Government this was Cole's insistent demand, as he continued to sketch the appropriate economic strategy for a situation in which 'we cannot afford to let industry remain depressed until we get Socialism'.[32]

During 1930, however, it began to seem that the Labour Government had no more serious political will in relation to capitalist recovery than in relation to the achievement of socialism itself. Thus Cole began to couple the demand for economic action with an increasingly sharp indictment of governmental inactivity. Snowden was too orthodox, Thomas too limited, whilst the Government as a whole seemed committed to an economic policy which consisted only in awaiting the beneficent effects of external forces on the terms of trade. This inability or unwillingness to launch a direct attack on unemployment earned Cole's anger and impatience: 'Cannot Mr. MacDonald snatch a moment from his many other worries,' he asked, 'to realize that, unless he does tackle this issue, his Government is heading for disaster?'[33] Thus, although critical of his secessionism, Cole endorsed the substance of the recovery programme outlined by Mosley in his Memorandum, not least because it represented just the sort of emergency package long favoured by Cole himself. Above all, it offered a decisive departure from the prevailing acquiescence.[34]

Cole's own 'memorandum' at this time may be regarded as his little book on *Gold, Credit and Employment* (1930), summarized as 'a plea for a "managed currency"'.[35] Here he discussed monetary policy in relation to unemployment, proposing an end to the gold basis of the internal issue of currency (though its retention for international payments), so that the supply of currency and credit became a task for internal monetary management in the light of the needs of the domestic productive system and in relation to the international price level. What this meant, in the conditions of 1930, was a release of financial policy from its dependence on gold movements, allowing an expansion of credit

---

[32] 'The Cure For Unemployment', *Everyman*, 10 Oct. 1929.
[33] 'The Ghost That Walks', *New Statesman*, 15 Mar. 1930.
[34] 'I do not agree with the Mosley programme in all its points; but that it is broadly on the right lines seems to me to be abundantly plain.' (*King's Norton Labour News*, July 1930.)
[35] *Gold, Credit and Employment*, 1930, p. 88.

designed to boost the productive system. The effects of depression in creating an abundant supply of cheap money provided an exceptionally opportune moment for such a policy. Yet here was a necessary but not sufficient condition for domestic expansion, for the level of production was determined not by the availability of credit but by the existence of demand. The activation of demand was a task for the state, thus allowing Cole to arrive at the nub of his practical programme in the form of state action both for emergency relief and for longer term economic reorganization. In other words, the sort of programme he had been advocating throughout the 1920s, though now he had a clearer sense of its theoretical credentials.

In this way, then, Cole tied an expansionist industrial policy to a radical approach to financial policy. A vigorous attack on unemployment was seen to depend upon a willingness to throw off those superstitions associated with a gold-backed currency which put domestic industrial policy into a financial strait-jacket. Both finance and industry required 'management', involving a recognition that 'Gold and the City have ruled us all too long'.[36] This statement well indicates the way in which Cole linked the prevailing financial orthodoxy with the bearers of that orthodoxy: a rejection of the former necessarily involved a challenge to the latter. Here was the decisive charge to be made against the Labour Government; for it had rapidly and conspicuously allowed itself to become the victim of orthodoxy and the orthodox, whereas its radical heritage should have made it their resolute opponent in its pursuit of a solution to unemployment. Thus Cole received Snowden's 1931 budget as 'an evident indication that the traditional policy of the Treasury is still supreme. . . .'[37] With Labour in office, the dissenter remained a crank—even if the crank was a member of the Government's own Economic Advisory Council.[38]

Not only did Cole urge a recovery programme on the Labour Government, making its performance in this regard the decisive test of

[36] Ibid., p. 95.
[37] 'Mr. Snowden—Optimist', *New Statesman*, 2 May 1931.
[38] Cole's work on the E.A.C. adds little to our knowledge of his economic thought at this time, though it does provide evidence of his alliance with Keynes. As Skidelsky says: 'The "intellectuals", Keynes and Cole, were soon at loggerheads with the "practical men", Balfour and Cadman' (op. cit., p. 144). Through much of the 1930s Cole sat with Keynes on the E.A.C.'s Committee on Economic Information, a body which could sometimes be aggressive in its Keynesianism. (See its 'Letter to the Prime Minister' on Financial Policy, Feb. 1933, (E.A.C. (E.I.) 42).) The E.A.C. itself was ineffectual, of course, doing no more than 'reflect the divisions of opinion among those who claimed to know what was happening'. (A. Bullock, *The Life and Times of Ernest Bevin*, Vol. 1 1960, p. 439)—and Cole was consistently damning about it.

its success or failure as a government, but continued to press his economic analysis in the environment of international slump which brought down the MacDonald Government. The practical 'Keynesianism' of his economic programme of the 1920s has already been noticed, but in the aftermath of 1931 the inverted commas may be dropped, for he now discussed the economic crisis from a recognizably Keynesian perspective.[39] The international origins of the crisis were analysed, along with the sort of international cooperation (on monetary management and price stabilization) essential for recovery. In domestic terms, the economics of 'economy' were dissected and savaged: parsimony might be a good private principle but it could be a fatal public one; public retrenchment, because of its effects on economic activity, might actually reduce income to the state; if the state did not initiate spending in times of depression the money would not be spent at all; an initial injection of spending would generate additional spendings throughout the economy; because national income was not a fund but a flow of goods and services, saving without spending was nothing but waste—and so on. The analysis was firmly Keynesian, both in its theoretical aspects (deficit budgeting, the multiplier effect) and in its policy implications (mobilization by the state of idle money to provide work and stimulate demand). Thus, surveying the effects of 'economy', Cole was quite clear that it was 'far better (to) incur a budgetary deficit during the emergency than make the budget balance at this cost'.[40]

Over the course of a decade, Cole's practical programme for recovery had changed little, consisting essentially of a comprehensive scheme of state intervention. The real change occurred in the theoretical underpinnings of this programme. It found its first—and continuing—theoretical justification in the under-consumptionist argument, but this was an argument which left many problems unresolved. Central to these was the problem of finance for the proposed scheme of state action. For a long time Cole was both orthodox and hazy on this, content to think in terms of increased taxation and a national development loan. Then came a rather tentative embrace of the role of 'idle balances' and of the possibility, even the desirability, of running a budget deficit. The final breakthrough to deficit financing (and here the influence of Keynes was decisive) may be located around 1932; and

---

[39] As in his *New Statesman* pamphlets on *The Crisis* (with E. Bevin), 1931, and *Saving and Spending*, 1932.

[40] *Saving and Spending*, p. 31.

within a year it was substantially complete.[41] If Keynes owed (and paid) a debt to Hobson, Cole was happy to acknowledge a debt to both.

Does all this mean that Cole in the 1930s has to be regarded as an apostle of capitalist recovery, merely the exponent of a socialized Keynesianism? Not really, for the bifocalism, the sense of operating at two levels, which there has already been ample occasion to notice in his thought re-appears in this context too. In this case, Cole wanted to draw a distinction between the short and long term survival prospects of capitalism. It was in relation to the former that he was prepared to contemplate, even to work for, capitalist recovery. What this approach involved is clearly seen when two classics of the left, Strachey's *The Coming Struggle for Power* and Cole's *The Intelligent Man's Guide Through World Chaos*, both written in 1932, are compared and contrasted. Strachey's book was a powerful and sustained statement of the collapse of capitalist civilization, with the appropriate political moral sharply drawn. By contrast, Cole's *Chaos* was an elaborate guide to the complexities of the world economic crisis, at the end of which two alternative remedies were offered—either the 'restoration' or the 'supersession' of capitalism. The reader was then instructed in the policy implications of whichever course was chosen. Of course, the reader was also influenced in his choice (away from restoration towards supersession), but the style of Cole's presentation is significant.[42] As will be seen, he neither wanted nor expected the survival of capitalism in the long term, but, unlike many socialists of the time, he was actively concerned with the conditions for short-term economic recovery.

If, on a broad perspective, Cole could not be described as an apostle of capitalist recovery nor did he succumb to a theory of imminent and final capitalist collapse. 'I am not going to maintain,' he wrote in 1933, 'that the present world slump is necessarily the death agony of the capitalist system, or that there can be no recovery from it without a change of system.'[43] As the decade developed, he found no reason to abandon his belief in the possibility of short-term recovery or in the sort

[41] Sidney Pollard has written that: 'by the end of 1932 at the latest, all the bricks which went to make the Keynesian employment theory were available and could have been used by the unions, had they been minded to assemble them. Most of them are to be found in that remarkable publication, *What Everybody Wants To Know About Money* . . . under G. D. H. Cole's editorship.' ('Trade Union Reactions to the Economic Crisis', *Journal of Contemporary History*, Vol. 1 (1969), p. 111.)

[42] Cole described his purpose as an attempt to 'set out what is involved in each of these two alternative methods of rebuilding the shattered structure of industrial organisation'. (*The Intelligent Man's Guide Through World Chaos*, p. 628.)

[43] *What Is This Socialism?*, Clarion Press, 1933.

of programme which he had long championed for this purpose. Thus, when it became fashionable on the left to portray fascism as a last desperate political response of capitalism *in extremis*, he denied that fascism was doomed *economically*, suggesting instead that it possessed features (above all, a permanent arms economy) conducive to stabilization and recovery.[44] If the economic collapse of fascism was not inevitable, the evidence of the 1930s seemed to confirm that capitalism in the non-fascist countries was also a more durable and resilient economic phenomenon than many had been willing to concede at the beginning of the decade. Cole therefore found in this evidence confirmation of his earlier disbelief in capitalist collapse: 'the past few years have made it plain,' he wrote in 1937, 'that a good deal more than an economic crisis ... will be needed to shake Capitalism out of the seats of power....'[45]

It was this sort of perspective which provided the basis, and justification, for Cole's continuing concern with the conditions of short-term economic recovery. In essence, such recovery was held to be possible. The concern reflected itself during the 1930s in Cole's response to developments both practical and theoretical. As an example of the former, the New Deal was clearly crucial, for here was a practical recovery programme which provoked sharply different reactions amongst commentators armed with divergent theoretical assumptions—not least on the left. Briefly stated, Cole responded with critically sympathetic support throughout. If he was sceptical about the ultimate ability of the Roosevelt experiment to overcome what he (always) regarded as the abrasive individualism of American economic life, he remained adamant that the experiment itself was firmly on the right lines. Its programme of monetary reflation and demand stimulation represented the only serious attempt anywhere to counter depression and 'there is every reason for the world as a whole to hope for its success'.[46] Not only this, but its success would open up important possibilities for the future of economic organization in a more fundamental sense. If it could achieve a moving equilibrium between productive capacity and consumption then it would really be necessary to acknowledge 'the prospect of a stably revived system of State-

[44] A fascist arms economy could 'escape certain of the disadvantages which normally attend the working of capitalism'. ('The Economic Consequences of War Preparation', in *Dare We Look Ahead?*, Fabian Society, 1938.)
[45] 'Can Capitalism Survive?' (in *What Is Ahead of Us?*, 1937, p. 22.)
[46] (ed.), *What Everybody Wants To Know About Money*, 1933, p. 97.

controlled Capitalism';[47] a revival, moreover, which would have been achieved without the need for a fascist-type abrogation of the traditional democratic freedoms and forms of government.[48] The New Deal posed a decisive question for socialist analysis: could balanced economic development be achieved inside an economic system which left the industrial and financial systems in private hands? Cole remained sceptical about this, though conceding that his scepticism was 'now rather of the long run than of the short run'.[49] That he should have been less sceptical about the short run was unsurprising, for his own economic analysis belonged to a tradition which found its practical expression and vindication in the Roosevelt programme.[50]

Cole continued to press this analysis itself throughout the 1930s reflecting, at a theoretical level, his commitment to economic recovery. The under-consumptionist origins of his practical programme have already been noticed and discussed; and they continued to provide the theoretical anchor for his analysis of the nature of capitalist crisis. Thus the world slump, particularly in its American manifestation, was seen to provide 'a perfect example of Mr. J. A. Hobson's favourite thesis'.[51] With the analysis went the prescription, in the form of proposals for the injection of purchasing power. It is interesting to note that this programme offended not only the canons of economic orthodoxy but also earned the condemnation of all good Marxists. John Strachey, for example—not least because of the decisive role of 'recovery' in the development of his own politics—felt it necessary to devote much effort to a demonstration of the fallacies of Cole's expansionist high-wage economics. Cole was guilty of the 'extraordinary error'[52] of believing that a high wage policy could stimulate recovery, whereas not only Marx but the orthodox economists of the Hayek-Robbins school had conclusively demonstrated that it was only by forcing wages down that capitalism could achieve even a temporary recovery. Strachey evidently felt much more comfortable in his Marxism when in the intellectual

[47] *Studies in World Economics*, 1934, p. 15.
[48] *Practical Economics*, 1937, p. 214 (and Ch. 4, *passim*).
[49] (Ed.) *What Everybody Wants To Know About Money*, p. 113.
[50] As Henry Pelling has written: 'Among . . . Socialists who dared at times to expect well of the New Deal, the exponents of the "underconsumption" theory were the most prominent. These were the publicists who were Keynesian before Keynes. . . .' (*America and the British Left*, 1957, p. 138.)
[51] *British Trade And Industry*, 1932, p. 287. For his part, Hobson described Cole's *Chaos* as the 'most serviceable explanation . . . that has appeared' of the capitalist crisis. (*Economic Journal*, Dec. 1932.)
[52] J. Strachey, *The Nature of Capitalist Crisis*, 1935, p. 336.

company of orthodox capitalist economists than in the company of socialist under-consumptionists. Interestingly, his attempted refutation of the latter also brought him into dispute with fellow Marxists.[53]

For his part, Cole continued to tempt the wrath of both Marxist and capitalist orthodoxy for his espousal of a developing Keynesianism. Of the relationship between Cole and Keynes it has been suggested that there existed 'a genuine clash of intellectual traditions'.[54] This is certainly true, for a utopian socialism confronted a rational liberalism, yet this did not prevent substantial agreement on the theory and practice of capitalist recovery. Cole's review of Keynes's *General Theory* was little short of euphoric: the book was described as 'the most important theoretical economic writing since Marx's *Capital*, or, if only classical economics is to be considered as comparable, since Ricardo's *Principles*'.[55] Only someone unfamiliar with the evolution of Cole's own economic thought would have been surprised by this reception. The central significance of the book from Cole's point of view was that it brought together disparate criticisms of economic orthodoxy under the umbrella of a comprehensive and compelling economic theory, thus serving to 'give the critics of economic orthodoxy solid ground on which they can set their feet'.[56] In other words, Hobson was vindicated and Cole could come in from the cold. Although Cole was soon busy distancing socialism from Keynes, he consistently stressed the significance for socialists of the Keynesian revolution in economic thought. If Keynesianism had ultimately to be transcended, it had first to be absorbed. Above all else, it provided socialist economists and the Labour movement as a whole with impeccable theoretical credentials in their opposition to deflation and in their advocacy of an expansionist recovery programme.[57]

Yet all this leaves one fundamental question unanswered: why did Cole *want* even a temporary capitalist recovery anyway? If he could not subscribe to a theory of impending capitalist collapse, preferring

---

[53] See the controversy between Strachey and Burns in *Labour Monthly*, July and Sept. 1935.

[54] D. Winch, *Economics and Policy*, Fontana edn. 1972, p. 354. Cf. the Appendix on 'Keynes and the British Left in the Inter-War Period'. Winch recognizes that Cole, like Keynes, was 'feeling his way towards a new kind of economics'. (idem.)

[55] 'Mr. Keynes Beats The Band', *New Statesman*, 15 Feb. 1936.

[56] Ibid. Cole's review earned Marxist wrath of course. Described as the 'leading British revisionist' he was attacked for having swallowed Keynes whole, whereas 'the best bourgeois economists . . . are not so easily deceived by the daring innovations that are so attractive to the Coles'. (J. Darrell, 'The Economic Consequences of Mr. Keynes', *Science and Society*, winter 1937.)

[57] For an attempt to arrange a more permanent marriage between Keynes and British socialism, see A. L. Rowse, *Mr. Keynes and the Labour Movement*, 1936.

instead to stress the possibility of recovery, why did he seek to convert possibility into actuality by actively working for such recovery? Was this not a strange role for the theorist of a comprehensive socialism? Cole himself provided no direct answer to questions of this kind, but it is possible to piece together from his work the essentials of an explanation. This explanation seems to contain four leading elements. In the first place, Cole was anxious to avoid the sort of transitional chaos which he associated with the breakdown of capitalism. It will be necessary in a later chapter to say something more about the role of 'chaos' in his thought, but for the moment it is enough to record his belief that the collapse of an economic system was an essentially messy business which it was best to avoid if at all possible. Socialism should be built upon more secure and orderly foundations, thereby also improving the chances of it developing into the right kind of socialism.[58] Secondly, capitalist recovery was held to be directly beneficial to the advance of socialism. 'Socialists who want a "Rooseveltish" policy in this country want it not because they think Rooseveltism as such can succeed in restoring stable prosperity,' wrote Cole in 1933, 'but because a "reflated" Capitalism seems to them to afford a better basis for the building of a Socialist system.'[59] Why this should be so was never made very clear by Cole during this period, but it can be assumed that the argument he liked to employ in the 1920s following the demise of Guild Socialism (viz. that capitalist depression was inimical to a forward movement by labour) continued to apply. In the context of the 1930s, the argument seemed weakly stated: why should not capitalist recovery serve to impede the road to socialism rather than the reverse? A healthy capitalism may prove favourable to the success of reformism or labourism: but to socialism?

A third reason advanced by Cole in support of a recovery programme—and one which grew in importance as the decade progressed—concerned the likely political consequences of capitalist collapse as evidenced by contemporary events around the world. In essence, he regarded such evidence as indications that the collapse of capitalism was more likely to issue in fascism than socialism[60]—a prospect with momentous implications for socialist strategy. Quite simply, capitalist collapse involved too great a risk at a time when the fascist threat was so acute. 'Would any of us,' Cole asked in 1938,

[58] 'Can Capitalism Survive?' pp. 46–7.
[59] 'The Battle of Hastings', *New Statesman*, 30 Sept. 1933.
[60] 'Can Capitalism Survive?' p. 23.

'however keen a Socialist he might be, really welcome another slump, in the hope that it might lead, this time, to an irretrievable capitalist collapse?'[61] His own answer was clear; and certainly the argument employed in its favour was powerful. Yet it left him in something of a political and theoretical dilemma, though he seemed but dimly aware of this. On the one hand, he had denied the inevitability or imminence of capitalist collapse; while, on the other hand, he wanted to suggest that such collapse would have a fascist outcome. Here, then, was a bleak prospect for socialism; not least because so many options now seemed to have closed.

Finally, Cole wanted economic recovery for its own sake. This was a constant and decisive ingredient in his thinking, part of his commitment to a practical relevancy. It involved a preference for employment over unemployment and a determination to work towards this end. It reflected itself in an impatience with the paralysis of imagination and courage in politicians who seemed incapable of positive remedial action in the face of prolonged depression. Even if stable capitalist recovery was impossible (as he believed), a temporary recovery as part of a cycle of booms and slumps was much to be preferred to the permanent depression consequent upon a policy of inactivity. Hence, in the political climate of the 1930s in which socialism was not one of the policy alternatives, the 'unsound' economics of Lloyd George offered more than the policy of drift of MacDonald or Baldwin.[62] Simply, Cole vastly preferred action to inaction and was prepared to respond to a positive initiative (for example, the New Deal) even when doubtful about its ultimate success. Indeed, so important was this attitude in relation to the problem of economic recovery that at times he seemed to confuse *any* action with socialist action.[63]

The economics of recovery was not the only species of 'new economics' which engaged Cole's attention during the 1930s: there was also the economics of socialism. Hence the suggestion that his economic thought has a consistently bifocal character. A twin focus seemed to be necessary in the 1930s because not even the new Keynesianism could take capitalist economics beyond the conditions of short-term equilibrium. There remained the economics of permanent recovery and stability. A correct application of Keynesian medicine could nurse

[61] 'The Economic Consequences of War Preparation', 1938.
[62] 'A Run For Our Money', *New Statesman*, 9 Mar. 1935.
[63] For example, when he exaggerated the 'socialistic' character of the New Deal. ('Has Socialism Failed?', *Saskatchewan C.C.F. Research Bureau*, Sept. 1933.)

capitalism back to temporary health, and might even do so at each subsequent onset of malady; but what it could not do was to remove those sources of recurrent illness which derived from 'the inherent tendency of Capitalism to generate out of prosperity the conditions of collapse',[64] through its inability to harmonize the development of productive potential and consuming power as described by Hobson and Marx. Cole devoted much effort to a catalogue of the absurdity, the chaos, the irrationality, the 'sheer idiocy'[65] of a capitalist system of economic organization which imposed scarcity on a world ripe for abundance. As ever, the vocabulary was significant. Gone now was the sense of capitalism as a system of monstrous injustice; in its place had come an indictment of capitalism as a gigantic muddle.[66] By contrast, socialism stood for rationality—indeed, it *was* rationality—for it represented a coordinated social control of economic life aimed at the maximization of plenty. In other words, socialism meant planning—the incarnation of rationality.

It would be interesting to trace the genesis of 'planning' in the British context. This cannot be attempted here, but a few observations are directly relevant to present purposes. For example, it is often assumed that the language and ideology of planning was a uniquely left response to economic crisis in the 1930s, decisively influenced by the experience of the first Russian Five Year Plan. What this account misses is the fact that the planning movement in Britain was largely a product of 'progressive' capitalists, amongst whom Sir Basil Blackett was pre-eminent, and that it found its continuing expression in explicitly 'centre' organizations like P.E.P. and the 'Next Five Years' group.[67] The importance of all this for the left was considerable, preventing any easy espousal of economic planning without at the same time differentiating its own version from that of the progressive centre. If the left became enthusiasts for planning in the 1930s, it is important to remember that this enthusiasm was tempered initially by a certain

[64] *The Intelligent Man's Guide Through World Chaos*, p. 644.
[65] *Studies in World Economics*, pp. 22–3.
[66] Barbara Wootton noticed this change in Cole's argument: 'Today he writes ... not so much of wrongs as of muddles', which evidenced a 'shift of contemporary interest from the wickedness to the stupidity of our economic organisation'. (*Plan Or No Plan*, 1934, pp. 104–5.)
[67] Presenting the case for planning, Blackett suggested that the Cabinet Room 'ought to have prominently emblazoned on its walls the Hegelian motto "The Altogetherness of Everything"'. (Quoted in J. Strachey, *The Coming Struggle For Power*, 1932, 239.) Cf. A. Marwick, 'Middle Opinion in the Thirties: Planning, Progress and Political "Agreement"', *English Historical Review*, 79, (1964) for a statement of the planning movement as an expression of the 'middle-of-the-road collectivism' of the 1930s.

coolness.[68] Certainly there was much sloppy thinking about planning on the left at this time, not least in suggestions for a Plan on the Russian model (after all, was not the five-year duration of British parliaments a happy coincidence?) which would achieve all the spectacular results of the Russian version in a context where the preconditions for such comprehensive planning were entirely absent. Yet the task for the serious left was the development of a planning argument which recognized that there could be no easy borrowing from Russia and which confronted a political world in which the advocates of capitalist planning were already well entrenched.

'Should we try to capture the cry for National Planning for the Labour Party?' asked Cole in 1932,[69] a question which well illustrates the sort of environment in which would-be planners of the left found themselves. Cole's own answer was in the affirmative of course; and he set out to sell the idea of planning as the cornerstone of a socialist economic policy. What this involved, however, was a sharp differentiation of socialist planning from other, bastard varieties. In Cole's words, it was necessary to 'lay bare the vital differences between Socialist and capitalist projects of economic planning'.[70] To people who admired the achievements of Russian planning, it was necessary to point out that those achievements could not be secured independently of the socialist foundations on which they rested. In general, it was necessary to demonstrate why planning was possible under socialism but not under an inherently planless capitalism. Here was the central theme in Cole's presentation of the case for economic planning. At a time when new forms of semi-public enterprise were appearing and when the state was being called upon increasingly to provide correctives to the maladjustments of capitalism, he stressed the limitations of this kind of national planning. 'A National Plan is one thing when the Government of a country holds in its hands the reins of economic power in every part of the national life,' he wrote, 'and quite another when it is only trying, and feebly at that, to inoculate the capitalist system with little doses of Socialism not strong enough to upset the functioning of things as they are.'[71] Cole's purpose, then, was to emphasize the sweeping extent of public control requisite for effective economic plan-

[68] Thus Strachey warned that 'the talk of order and planning is little more than an elegant intellectual disguise'. (*The Coming Struggle For Power*, p. 241.)
[69] Memorandum for S.S.I.P. meeting, April 1932, Cole Collection.
[70] *A Plan For Britain*, Clarion Press, 1932. Marwick (art. cit.) neglects this socialist critique of the planning movement in his search for 'agreement'.
[71] *British Trade And Industry*, p. 422.

ning. Control over the form and content of production, over allocation decisions between consumption and investment, over the size and direction of purchasing power, over the supply of credit, over the volume and direction of capital spending: all this and more was necessary if the 'reins of economic power' were to be firmly held by government as a precondition of national planning. In Cole's hands, therefore, the case for economic planning could not be stated apart from the case for a comprehensive socialism.[72]

If planning may be regarded as the practical expression of the economics of socialism, it cannot be claimed that Cole carried this new economics very far. In this respect his intentions and ambitions were strictly limited. On the one hand, he wanted to suggest the sort of revolution in economic theory which would provide the foundations for a planned economy. This involved a critique of existing economic theory as a merely descriptive science of the price mechanism, the effect of which was to 'shut up Economics in the coffin of Capitalism',[73] unlike an earlier economics which—as in Ricardo or Marx—thought in terms of a standard of value distinct from price. Cole argued the need for a return to this older tradition, in order to construct an economic theory which dealt with social costs and social utilities in a way which meant 'getting behind prices'.[74] On the other hand, this new economic theory had to be built into the operation of a planned economy. Here again Cole confined himself to a statement of the principles involved in the social valuation of factors of production and related problems; and did little more than sketch an outline of planning machinery. His intention was only to raise the central issues, in terms of both policy and organization, with which a collectivist economy would have to grapple, and to suggest the sort of principles which would be brought to bear in relation to them.

By leaving the argument at this level, however, Cole tended to make it all a little too easy. For example, he indicated the role for a socialist technique of cost-accountancy but without any real discussion of the complexities involved in the application of such a technique. Equally,

[72] It has been suggested that Labour's conception of planning at this time was still as a corrective to the market rather than an alternative to it, and that Labour still did not 'seriously consider the centrally planned economy of Hayek's nightmare'. (A. Oldfield, 'The Labour Party and Planning—1934, or 1918?,' *Society for the Study of Labour History: Bulletin* 25, autumn 1972.) However accurate this may be as a description of official Labour policy, it does not apply to the planning argument of that section of the left represented by Cole.

[73] *Economic Tracts For The Times*, 1932, p. 5.

[74] Ibid., p. 188.

he pointed to the problem of the place of consumer choice in the operation of a planned economy without any real attempt to work this out in organizational terms.[75] More generally, the democratic character of the planning process was emphasized, yet the argument was left at the level of abstraction. In all this, then, Cole was deliberately tentative; for his aim was not to make a plan but to suggest what making a plan would involve. Above all else, it would mean a complete reconstruction of economic science, a task hitherto unattempted. Marx had provided a telling analysis of capitalist economics, yet he 'equally with the other economists, is analysing capitalist society, and is not attempting to construct the Economics of Socialism'.[76] Indeed, he would have regarded such an attempt as utopian and premature. For his part, Cole claimed only to be clearing the foundations for work of this kind, not erecting an elaborate economic edifice of the sort earlier represented, in political terms, by Guild Socialism. Yet just as Guild Socialism had reflected Cole's belief that it was necessary (rather than utopian) to think out the political organization of a socialist society, he now held that it was necessary to develop the positive content of a socialist economics. Here, rather than any preoccupation with the conditions of short-term capitalist recovery, was the real direction for a 'new economics'. Capacity and temperament would combine to prevent Cole himself playing a leading role in the technical elaboration of this economic theory of socialism, though he would doubtless be on hand to document its progress in popular and digestible form. Instead, his own practical economics would cast him as a natural 'planner' in the new society.[77]

After the 1930s, Cole's thought lost its economic preoccupation. Partly, this was simply a response to an environment in which economic problems seemed less pressing than in the inter-war period. Partly, too, it was a reflection of Cole's renewed interest (noticed in a previous chapter) in the concerns of Guild Socialism. However, this new sensitivity to the perils of authoritarianism and the need to formulate a non-bureaucratic socialist programme did have implications for the economic component of that programme. Thus, when (in the

[75] Also, Cole offered conflicting views on the role of consumer choice in a planned economy. At one point he sought to deny that consumer preferences possessed 'a superior validity . . . to collective preferences based on conceptions of social need'. (*Studies in World Economics*, p. 260.) However, elsewhere he warned that 'one of the principal dangers of a planned economy (was) that the power of influencing demand may be so used as to weaken the consumers' power of choice'. (*Principles of Economic Planning*, 1935, p. 230.)

[76] *Studies in World Economics*, p. 246.

[77] 'Having no political ambitions, I rather fancy myself for a place on the National Planning Commission.' (*Socialist Control of Industry*, 1933, Socialist League.)

1940s) Cole developed his conception of 'liberal socialism' (discussed in the next chapter), he rooted it in an economic policy which involved a non-bureaucratic process of partial socialization. He argued that the establishment of monopoly conditions over much of the economy had transformed the political and economic landscape, so that 'the choice is not between competition and monopoly, but between monopoly-capitalism and Socialism'.[78] Yet if it was necessary to escape from monopoly-capitalism, it was also important to avoid a monopoly-socialism. To prevent this, he stressed the need—in the interests of freedom and diversity—not only to encourage many different forms of social ownership but also to preserve a wide and valuable range of small-scale private enterprise. This meant a refusal to elevate nationalization beyond its proper rank in the socialist armoury; and a recognition of a legitimate sphere for the operation of the profit motive. It also involved a willingness, in relation to a broad range of manufacturing industry, to think in terms of a 'mixed' form of enterprise[79]—a suggestion which had incurred much socialist wrath when first mooted by Cole in 1929 in his *Next Ten Years*.

In general, Cole's argument for further state control and socialization now rested on two main grounds. In the first place, it was presented as a necessary corollary of the commitment to full employment. This was elaborated in his little book on *The Means to Full Employment* (1943), in which he gave broad assent to the Keynesian position (stopping only to record its Hobsonian lineage and to regret its terminological difficulties) but drew from it firmly interventionist policy conclusions with respect both to cyclical and structural unemployment. For example, the Keynesian emphasis on the need to maintain levels of investment was used by Cole to justify public control and ownership of the key capital goods-using industries (transport, housing, public utilities), thereby giving the state a direct control of investment levels in these sectors which, in turn, would determine the level of activity in the capital goods-producing industries; thus serving as the major counter-cyclical device. This was presented as the essential condition for an effective public works policy on a continuing basis and the minimal condition for a successful application of the Keynesian analysis to the treatment of unemployment. Cole's second main argument for a radical extension of public control and ownership went beyond the conditions for an effective counter-cyclical policy to an analysis

[78] *Plan For Democratic Britain*, 1939, p. 30.
[79] See *Money: Its Present And Future*, 1944, p. 216.

of the monopolistic, restrictive nature of contemporary capitalism which reflected itself in the phenomenon of structural unemployment, an expression of an inability to utilize resources and maximize production. Instead of monopoly there should be planning, requiring a range of state action from control boards to complete socialization. In all this, however, Cole remained insistent that there should only be sufficient public control to ensure a broad direction of economic activity. Indeed, he was prepared to describe his programme as one of 'half-socialism'—and to justify this in terms of the need to reconcile socialist advance with the preservation of liberal values.[80]

In fact, this 'half-socialism' turned out to be both radical and extensive, involving not only a public responsibility for full employment and a comprehensive system of social security but also a formidable shopping list for early socialization (including steel, shipbuilding, chemicals, heavy engineering, banking and foreign trade, as well as a range of public-utilities) designed to provide the materials for effective-economic planning. Yet the aim was not to socialize as much as possible, but to oust capitalism from its 'citadels of monopoly'.[81] This would leave a wide area of economic activity in the hands of various forms of non-monopolistic private enterprise, regarded by Cole as a wholly desirable arrangement. In all this, then, he sought to argue, firstly, that even a successful application of Keynesian techniques involved substantial public intervention and, secondly, that an advance beyond Keynesianism to effective economic planning required an extensive (though non-comprehensive and non-bureaucratic) apparatus of public ownership and control. The dual focus persisted.

The reformist focus carried with it a pragmatic concern with the condition of the British economy and a willingness to suggest improvements even without its fundamental reconstruction on a socialist basis. This approach had characterized Cole's early statement of an economic programme in the 1920s, had continued through the 1930s and was central to his discussion of economic problems in the post-war period. In this last period particularly, he explicitly refused to dodge the immediate problems of the British economy in framing a socialist programme. He repeatedly emphasized Britain's critical economic position in the international market, reflected in the precarious state of

[80] In 1944 Cole gave as 'the principal reason why it is worth while to try for half-Socialism, in preference to going the whole hog' that 'we could not hope to get whole-Socialism without a struggle in which a good deal of our libertarian tradition would almost certainly disappear'. (Draft Outline for New Fabian Essays project, 1944; in possession of Margaret Cole.)

[81] *A Word On The Future To British Socialists*, Fabian Tract 256, 1942, p. 17.

its balance of payments, and urged the need for a large programme of industrial investment and re-equipment. Nor did he shirk the implications of his economic analysis, for he accepted that the need for investment involved a curtailment of consumption for some years ahead. A further implication of this was that organized labour should not push its wage demands beyond a point at which they conflicted with the requirements of investment or reacted adversely on the comparative cost position of British exports. During this period, in fact, Cole consistently lectured the trade unions on the necessity for a sensible and moderate industrial policy. They should not succumb to the illusion that, in the contemporary international economic situation, higher wages could be won at the expense of profits; nor should they indulge in 'forms of militancy which, in making trouble for the employers, at the same time damage production and worsen Great Britain's position in the world market'.[82] His earlier concern with the requirements for short-term capitalist recovery was now paralleled, therefore, by a practical concern with improvements in industrial productivity and in Britain's international competitive position. This was the reformist focus in action.

Yet the other focus remained active too, despite the small encouragement given to it by the post-war economic environment. At the end of the life of the Attlee Government, Cole had noted 'a growing tendency to confuse state economic planning with Socialism, and thus to produce a diluted socialistic doctrine which is little more than Keynesian Liberalism with frills. ...'[83] His own response to this tendency was less to engage in theoretical debate with the Keynesians than to reformulate a set of fundamental socialist economic principles (notably, in his *Socialist Economics*) designed to illustrate the qualitative distinctiveness of both a socialist economy and a socialist economics. He continued to pay tribute to the achievement of Keynes, not least in providing a respectable academic stick with which to beat the classical economists, and accepted that Keynesianism not only represented an elaborate (and effective) mechanism for mitigating capitalist instability but also could be built upon by the economists of socialism. Ultimately, however, the concern of Keynes and his followers was not with the creation of a non-capitalist economic discipline, which meant that the

---

[82] *What Is Wrong With The Trade Unions?*, Fabian Tract 301, 1956, pp. 5–6.

[83] *Socialist Economics*, 1950, p. 7. Cole added that 'it is hardly too much to say that most of the non-Marxist socialist economists swallowed Keynes whole, and became his most fervent disciples'. (Ibid., p. 49.)

advance they had achieved—significant enough in its own terms—'in no way makes less necessary the formulation of the quite distinct economic theory appropriate to a socialist society'.[84] Cole made no claim to provide such a theory: only to state a set of socialist economic principles (the social valuation of production, allocation and distribution decisions) which should form the basis for a developed economic theory.

At this point it is worth asking what Cole now conceived as the *economic* case for socialism and against capitalism, if a Marxian analysis of capitalism's fatal contradictions was rejected and if a Keynesian ability to offset periodic capitalist instability was accepted. Partly, Cole sought to argue that Keynesianism could only mitigate, not prevent, capitalist instability; that even a successful application of Keynesianism would require not merely budgetary and financial adjustments but also extensive and direct state control; and that in a full employment economy labour could no longer be coerced and a new set of incentives and motivations was required. Essentially, however, his economic argument had returned from its emphasis (in the 1930s) on questions of efficiency and planning—the specifically economic superiority of socialism to capitalism—to an earlier argument which was fundamentally normative, ethical, utopian. Capitalism was indicted for its competitive acquisitiveness, its treatment of labour as a commodity, its destruction of fellowship. Having acquired a fleeting independence in the years of depression, Cole's economics had returned to its original home in morals—'of which socialist Economics is quintessentially a branch'.[85]

It has been necessary to emphasize bifocalism as the distinctive characteristic of Cole's economic thought. On the one hand, this gave a particular strength to his treatment of economic matters. It enabled him (as has been seen) to propose concrete and relevant measures of economic recovery and reform rooted in a considerable understanding of economic theory and practice. It also enabled him to sketch the essentials of a distinctive socialist economics. On the other hand, however, it was an approach which necessarily raised the central problem of the relationship between the two levels (or foci) of his economic thought; and it would be difficult to maintain that Cole either confronted this problem directly or handled it satisfactorily. Rather, he tended to alternate between a reformist discussion of capitalist econom-

[84] Ibid., p. 54.
[85] Ibid., p. 9.

ics and a fundamentalist discussion of the economics of socialism, stopping only rarely to consider the implications of this sort of compartmentalism. In an important sense, therefore, he stood both 'for' and 'against' capitalism (in the way that Miliband has described the Labour Party's relationship with capitalism[86]): capitalism was to be reformed, rescued and transcended—all at the same time. If this reflected his commitment to a practical relevancy, it also introduced a theoretical looseness into his thought. It also served to make his economic thought entirely representative of his socialist thought as a whole.

[86] R. Miliband, *Parliamentary Socialism*, 2nd ed., 1973.

IX
Marxism and Democratic Socialism

THIS CHAPTER and the next have much in common. They both concentrate on the major concerns of Cole's thought in its later stages (from
the 1930s onwards) and both reflect a recognizably similar perspective.
In this period, Cole felt it necessary to define the sort of socialist
tradition within which he wanted to locate himself; to give this tradition
a distinctive theoretical statement in relation to other traditions (Marxism especially); and to define its role within the international socialist
movement (with special reference to the Soviet Union). This last
dimension will be discussed in the next chapter. Here the concern is
with Cole's critique of Marxism and the relationship between this
critique and his own developing statement of a distinctive democratic
socialism. Such an enterprise had not seemed necessary before the
1930s: Marxism had been largely ignored during the Guild period,
while the embrace of a practical reformism in the 1920s had been
unaccompanied by any serious consideration of the larger assumptions
involved in this. The events surrounding 1931 coupled with a new
interest in Marxism jolted Cole out of his theoretical inertia.

If Cole was certain about anything, it was of the 'essential relativity'[1]
of all ideas, theories and institutions. He was an absolutist only in this
attachment to relativism. It reflected itself in his analysis of political
and social theories, in his discussion of the nature of rights, in his
treatment of nation states, in his attitude to political methods—and in
his statement of socialism itself. Nothing was timeless and universal;
everything was historically and socially rooted, requiring analysis and
interpretation in its own terms. This did not preclude judgement,
though it did affect the form and style of such judgement. This
approach was seen fleetingly during the Guild period in Cole's assertion of the necessary link between theories and national traditions. It
became particularly apparent in his treatment of the two phenomena
which came to dominate the attention of the left in the 1930s and
beyond: the theory of Marx and the reality of Russia. Hence the
similarity of perspective in this and the following chapter.

[1] *Some Relations Between Political and Economic Theory*, 1934, p. 11.

In Cole's eyes, Marxism possessed one immediate and immense recommendation, for it was a theory which was founded upon just such a conception of the essential relativism of both social theories and social institutions. As a theory itself, it had as its basis not an abstract doctrine of rights but a concrete historical sociology—the only tenable basis for a comprehensive social theory in Cole's view. His attachment to relativism did not lead him to disparage the search for a comprehensive theory of society (in fact, the reverse), but it did make him insist that such a general theory must have its origins in a concrete historical analysis of social development itself. Here, then, was the distinctive merit of Marxism; a fact which meant 'not that Marxism is necessarily right, but that Marx's method of seeking to formulate a general theory in the light of concrete historical experience is the only legitimate method'.[2] For this reason itself Cole was prepared to subscribe to the Marxian tradition, for it embodied the correct method of social analysis. Yet he was also prepared to subscribe to more than this in Marx, accepting not merely that Marx's method was correct but that the substantive product of that method was 'essentially true'.[3] Hence his frequent willingness during the 1930s to give himself a Marxist label.[4]

Why, then, may we not simply accept this designation and leave it at that? Above all, because Cole himself was not prepared to leave it there. In criticism of Marxism the question is often asked: why is a doctrine which claims that all doctrines are relative not itself relative? It is, of course, a question which has produced a long and intricate controversy both within and beyond Marxism, yet Cole's answer was clear. Marxism was itself relative, for it was the product of a particular time and place and of one stage in the development of social knowledge. For Cole, here was both the achievement and the limitation of Marxism; for it represented the most convincing and comprehensive theory of society, while at the same time necessarily bearing the marks and the limitations of the nineteenth-century social environment in which it was formulated. Just as Marxism was the brilliant product of a historical sociology, that same method should now draw upon a growing body of social knowledge for the creation of a social theory appropriate to the conditions of the contemporary world. That social theory would still be recognizably Marxist, but a Marxism amended and adapted where

[2] Ibid., pp. 80–1.
[3] *The Intelligent Man's Review of Europe To-day* (with M. I. Cole), 1933, p. 824.
[4] Contributing to a 1933 symposium on Marx, Cole wrote: 'To look around on the world of to-day with seeing eyes is to be a Marxist, for Marxism alone explains what is going on.' (*Plebs*, March 1933.)

necessary to make it consonant with contemporary social reality. Indeed, this sort of process was inherent in the Marxian method itself. In Cole's words, 'every Marxist is compelled by his Marxism to be a "Revisionist"....'[5]

Here is the clue to Cole's whole approach to Marx, Marxism and Marxists. It found its first comprehensive expression in *What Marx Really Meant* (1934), a book described by Isaiah Berlin as 'the best large-scale popular exposition of Marxism since Engels'.[6] The title, though revealing, is not quite accurate; it ought to read: *What Marx Should Have Meant*. Under the guise of exposition, Marx was interpreted, amended and revised. The style of the argument made it almost impossible to determine where Marx ended and where Cole began. The result represented exactly that version of Marxism which corresponded with Cole's own tastes and inclinations and which, therefore, allowed him to locate himself at this time within the Marxist tradition. This may be illustrated, briefly, with reference to a series of difficult points which Cole contrived to make both simple and palatable. In Cole's hands, the materialist conception of history became merely the 'realist' conception, thereby removing any hint of rigid economic determinism whilst retaining its antagonism to a Hegelian idealism. A loose determinism was preserved, which indicated only that history was made within a range of objectively available alternatives. Above all, history was made by men—armed with ideas, wills and knowledge. Its outcome was devoid of inevitability; for chaos and the dissolution of civilization were real possibilities and any notion of an inevitable succession of historical epochs was just 'a piece of mysticism'.[7] The reality of class did not destroy or submerge the deeper reality of individuality. The correctness of a loose economic determinism was compatible with an independent and important role both for ideas and for political and legal institutions; thus involving a rejection of 'the absurd mistake of trying to interpret all history in exclusively economic terms'.[8] Not only was there no inevitability about the development of history, there was also no inevitability about that generation of consciousness which transforms a social class into an effective social movement. In other words, men not only make their own history; they can fail to make it too.

[5] *What Marx Really Meant*, 1934, pp. 291–2.
[6] I. Berlin, *Karl Marx*, 1939, p. 252.
[7] *What Marx Really Meant*, p. 21.
[8] Ibid., p. 92.

Now the significant feature of all this was not that it was necessarily untrue to the Marxist original, but that Cole made little effort and felt little need to relate it to the original in any critical fashion. Instead, he simply stated a position as being the authentic voice of Marx; or as what Marx *meant* to say even though the evidence was ambiguous, or as what Marx *should* have said (even though he did not) in the light of his own method of social analysis; or even as what Marx (and certainly a good Marxist) *would* say in the light of subsequent social development. In Cole's analysis all these approaches were inextricably mixed up. Both then and now he would be impatient with those wearisome exercises in textual exegesis designed to show what Marx 'really said'. His aim was to give a meaning to Marxism which would make it a useful tool for analysis and action in the world of the 1930s. The result was an activist, idealist, voluntarist, libertarian, minimally determinist version of Marxism; in fact, a characteristic product of Cole's own approach to social theory.

This did not mean, however, that Cole was prepared to fudge those issues on which he regarded Marx as either inadequate or wrong. For example, the Marxist doctrine of increasing misery was judged to be 'plainly wrong in relation to the facts'.[9] Thus spake Cole the economic historian, aware of the growth in the material living standards of the working class during the capitalist period; but the theorist of socialism also wanted to add an extra dimension to this historical inaccuracy. Invoking one of his arguments for support of a capitalist recovery programme, he suggested a paradox at the heart of Marx's doctrine of immiseration. If capitalism was to be brought to economic crisis by its own internal contradictions, how could an impoverished and demoralized proletariat provide a constructive alternative? In such a situation, not socialism but chaos was the more likely outcome. In this way, Cole suggested that increasing misery was not merely historically false but necessarily false from the point of view of the achievement of socialism; for 'surely the essence of the Marxian conception is that revolutions are made by economically advancing and not by decaying economic classes'.[10]

Cole also had an important quarrel with Marx's historical materialism as a comprehensive theory of social development. Above

---

[9] Ibid., p. 109. This would be Cole's approach to the lively debate among economic historians concerning working-class living standards under capitalism. See B. Inglis, 'The Poor Who Were With Us', *Encounter*, Sept. 1971, for an account of this debate.

[10] Ibid., p. 107.

all, it claimed too much for itself. It claimed to provide an explanation of *all* history when, in fact, it provided only a satisfactory account of the internal development of one particular western civilization. It did not explain the development of other civilizations and certainly failed either to distinguish or explain the impact of one civilization on another, the latter providing an arena for the frequently decisive operation of non-economic forces. In Cole's view, it was this sort of failure to explore or recognize the complexities of the historical process (including a failure to recognize the nature of transitional and hybrid historical periods rather than periods of sharply differentiated forms of class power) which had 'vitiated much Marxist thinking'.[11] Yet even this does not take us to those areas of Marx's thought which presented Cole with his major problems of analysis—and his most significant exercises in theoretical revision. For this it is necessary to turn to the analysis of social classes; and to the implications of this analysis for socialist strategy.

'The history of Western Europe since 1918,' wrote Cole, 'most strongly suggests that, however right Marx was in his fundamental philosophy of history, the practical application of his doctrine needs working out afresh in the light of the present class-structure of Western society.'[12] This sentence provides the essential frame of reference for Cole's central revision (or even abandonment) of classical Marxism. The problem of social classes and social structure absorbed his attention not merely in the 1930s, but also before and after, with continuing and significant consequences for his statement of socialism. His Guild Socialism, for example, was much concerned with framing a strategy designed to appeal to particular and defined social groups; while in the 1950s (as will be seen shortly) he still continued to explore the relationship between socialism and social structure. Indeed, it is possible to suggest that, in academic terms, it was as a sociologist (rather than as economist or social philosopher) that Cole promised most; and that, in political terms, his sociology was consistently integral to his socialism. In the 1930s it was not only integral but decisive, and nowhere was this more apparent than in his treatment of Marx. He made much of the fact that Marx never really carried his analysis of social classes beyond the point reached in 1848 and mourned his unfulfilled promise of a fuller treatment of the nature of social classes in the unfinished third volume of *Capital*. In Cole's view, this meant that the Marxist tradition was

---

[11] Ibid., p. 34.
[12] *Socialism in Evolution*, 1938, p. 146.

saddled with a theory of social class designed for, and appropriate to, the conditions of capitalism in the first half of the nineteenth century and which, therefore, was unlikely to survive intact when confronted with the social changes brought about by subsequent capitalist development. Above all, Cole wanted to focus on two critical features of capitalist development as evidence of the need for a radical revisionism: the evolution of joint stock enterprise and the growth of a new middle class. Together, it was argued, these developments provided a damning case against the Marxist theory of increasing class polarization, with important implications for both social theory and political practice.

The argument about the changing form of capitalist enterprise has become familiar, of course. Cole accepted the argument and suggested some consequences. In essence, Marx had been right about the concentration of control under capitalism (and right about the development of finance capitalism and of economic imperialism), but had been decisively wrong about the concentration of capitalist ownership. The development of the joint stock form of enterprise had managed to combine a concentration of capitalist control with a diffusion of capitalist ownership. Cole did not want to suggest that a 'people's capitalism' had been created by this process; emphatically the reverse, for control remained tightly concentrated. Yet the establishment of the joint stock enterprise as the dominant form of capitalist organization had resulted in a significant broadening of both the economic and political base of capitalism. Wide sections of the middle class (and even a narrow section of the working class) had been provided with a financial stake in capitalism. By broadening its basis in this way capitalism had armed itself with 'a bodyguard of retainers', a development which 'prevents effectively the complete polarization of classes which would result from a concentration of ownership as well as control in the hands of a shrinking class of great capitalist magnates'.[13] In other words, joint stock enterprise provided one important reason why Marx's anticipation of an increasing class polarization, involving a narrowing of the capitalist base and the disappearance of intermediate groups, had not been realized.

Another reason, and here we come to the real and permanent heart of Cole's quarrel with Marx, related to the creation by a developing and technically complex capitalism of a 'new intermediate class',[14] the new

[13] *What Marx Really Meant*, p. 119.
[14] *The Intelligent Man's Review of Europe To-day*, p. 695.

salariat of technicians, administrators and professionals. A concern with the social location and political destiny of this 'new' class runs throughout the whole corpus of Cole's work and exercised a continuing influence upon the shape of his socialist theory. At no time was this more true than in the 1930s and nowhere was it more significant than in its implications for Marxism. To put the matter briefly, Cole challenged Marx's conception of a decaying *petite bourgeoisie*, rooted in obsolete, small-scale forms of production, being progressively squeezed out as class polarization intensified until, finally, the great capitalists confronted the mass proletariat. In Cole's view, the nature of capitalist development had altered this scenario in fundamental respects. Above all, a new *petite bourgeoisie* had arrived faster than the old one had contracted, while in terms of personnel the two groups had close links and similar origins. Joint stock enterprise had done much to bring the older group under the umbrella of capitalism, while the new group owed its existence to the development of large-scale capitalism. In other words, the effect of capitalist development had been to introduce a considerable complexity into the social structure—and not to promote a stark simplification. 'In face of this social stratification,' asked Cole, 'what becomes of the simple theory of the class struggle set out in the Communist Manifesto?'[15] The question was, of course, only rhetorical; for crude analysis confronted complex evidence.

Not only did Cole present an analysis of social class sharply different from that of Marx, but also—and more significantly—he mobilized this analysis for the construction of a radically different conception of socialist strategy. The magnitude of this difference was revealed most dramatically when he argued that, because of the nature of class differentiation and the balance of social forces, the achievement of socialism in the countries of advanced capitalism could no longer be the work of the proletariat alone. A proletarian revolution could only succeed by accident (and at the cost of total social breakdown), while 'the proletariat by itself is not strong enough in any country to win and hold a parliamentary majority, or to carry through the construction of the new system by constitutional means'.[16] (Thus, under the title of 'what Marx really meant', Cole announced the impossibility of proletarian self-emancipation!) In Cole's view, the proletariat needed allies; and it could find them in the ranks of the 'new' middle class. 'An alliance of this sort,' he wrote, 'is the only possible way of achieving

[15] *Socialism in Evolution*, p. 143.
[16] *What Marx Really Meant*, pp. 140-1.

Socialism by peaceful and constitutional means, and probably the only way of averting the spread of Fascist dictatorships.'[17]

This last point was especially relevant in the mid 1930s, for fascism represented the possibility that the *petite bourgeoisie* might rally to the defence of the big capitalists if its status and income was seriously threatened, or even that this class might be able to seize and exercise power in its own right. Thus, according to Cole, the proletariat should actively seek middle-class allies both for the achievement of socialism and for the prevention of fascism. This meant, therefore, a socialist programme capable of attracting allies of this kind, though Cole was adamant that this consideration neither should nor did involve a dilution of policy. Why, then, would sections of the middle class align themselves with the proletariat? Cole's answer (already glimpsed in his presentation of Guild Socialism) was that the new salaried middle class had no intrinsic relationship with capitalism and would respond to the appeal of an economic system which offered efficiency instead of muddle, rationality instead of chaos. Hence the potential attraction of a constructive, competent, planned socialism to sections of the new *petite bourgeoisie*, inducing them to 'revolt against the sheer muddle and waste involved in maintaining the capitalist system'.[18] Indeed, it was plausible to suggest that it would prove easier for socialism to detach and attract these middle-class elements than certain depressed sections of the working class itself.[19]

A central implication of this strategy, bringing Cole into dispute with another canon of Marxism, was that the socialist movement in the countries of parliamentary democracy should avoid the sort of action and rhetoric likely to antagonize its potential middle-class recruits. In a word, the proletariat could not escape the necessity of winning allies by a resort to the language and style of revolution. Did this mean a final rejection by Cole of the revolutionary method in favour of the parliamentary? Did it mean a claim, against Marx, that the state in capitalist democracy was a suitable vehicle for the achievement of socialism? These questions were implicitly raised (but not answered) when, in the aftermath of 1931, Cole announced his programme of 'constitutional revolution'; and they were inevitably raised again in

[17] Ibid., p. 140.
[18] *The Simple Case For Socialism*, 1935, p. 250. Cole also suggested the potential appeal of socialism in terms of 'the itch of the technician or the administrator to clean up this prodigious mess'. (*Socialism in Evolution*, p. 244..)
[19] *The Simple Case For Socialism*, p. 249.

relation to Marxism. In answer to them, he provided only a set of attitudes rather than a developed theory. This was both a major omission and a typical characteristic of his thought.

A serious omission was the failure to undertake any critical analysis of Marx's theory of the state, despite the fact that it was clearly crucial for socialist strategy to decide to what extent democracy had transformed the state from an instrument of class coercion into an agency of social service and whether this process could be carried further. Cole's position on this has to be pieced together from occasional remarks[20]—and, as suggested earlier, from the position merely implied in his historical works. What this did indicate, however, was that he did not make his revision of Marx hang upon the achievements of parliamentary democracy (his lack of love for which has been amply noticed); but rather upon the changes brought about by a developing class structure. Moreover, Cole's revisionism was of an openly pragmatic kind. He did not assert that socialism could be created entirely by a parliamentary gradualism which captured the state machine; for parliament was an alien institution from the point of view of socialism, while capitalism would not simply abdicate at the behest of a parliamentary majority. At some stage, therefore, a revolutionary moment was likely.[21] At a personal level, Cole's distaste for the business of revolution was considerable (never succumbing to those dreams of berets and machine guns which sometimes tempt the powerless intellectual) but he regarded the acceptance of a revolutionary possibility as necessary for a serious socialism. At the same time, however, he wanted to escape from the sterile controversy between evolutionists and revolutionists by means of a pragmatic strategy appropriate to the concrete social environment in which socialists found themselves.

What this meant (and here there were echoes of an earlier 'encroachment' policy) was a parliamentary strategy which would carry socialism as far as possible by this method, even if it could not take it the whole way. Moreover, the extent to which the state would be smashed or captured depended on its particular character in concrete situations; and, in relation to the parliamentary democracies, he suggested that they had states which, 'if they can be seized and con-

[20] See his discussion of the state in *A Guide To Modern Politics* (with M. I. Cole, 1934,) where it was stated that, in the countries of advanced capitalism and parliamentary democracy, 'the State has become in reality an instrument of service as well as of coercion'. (P. 393.)

[21] He frequently declared his belief that 'the Socialist movement will have at some stage to assume a revolutionary form, if it is to succeed in introducing Socialism'. (*The Simple Case For Socialism*, p. 286.)

trolled, there are forces in operation within them that are fully consistent with the purposes Socialists have in view'.[22] In states of this kind, socialists should make full use of the parliamentary method, both because the method promised much (if not everything) and because the balance of social forces ruled out any immediate alternative. Furthermore, there would be no widespread support for an alternative until a radical parliamentarism had been tried and failed—an argument employed by Cole to persuade the revolutionary left to throw its support behind such a strategy. In the immediate situation confronted by the British working class, and without prejudice to later stages of struggle, Cole was clear that 'the right strategy for British Socialism is undoubtedly a strategy of parliamentary action'.[23]

Did all this mean that Cole had managed to turn Marx into 'a dreary Socialist League Fabian'?[24] Not in a direct sense, for he was careful to acknowledge that on central issues (class structure, the state, political method) his own analysis differed sharply from that of Marx. In another sense, however, it is possible to portray Cole as engaged in an attempt to wrest Marx from the Communists and to 'claim' him for social democracy. He was never more scathing than when denouncing the biblical Marxists, those 'theological parrots that screech about the Marxian temple',[25] for their activities served only to make Marxism a more perfect dogma and a less useful guide to action in the contemporary world. To be a good Marxist was to be a permanent revisionist, for if Marx had been right in all essentials about the modern world he would have been wrong to be right. Thus Cole invoked the dialectical method to justify his own revisionism, for the method decreed that it was necessary to utilize Marx in order to transcend him. Not only did the dialectical principle involve an escape from the dogmas of formal logic, but also from the dogmas of formal Marxism. In fact, of course, Cole's appeal to the dialectic was really a piece of casuistry; for his revisionism was rooted in sociology, not dialectics. It derived from a particular analysis of the development of social structure in advanced capitalist societies in the period since Marx. As such, it continued the tradition of Bernstein and, in so doing, explored the void left by the absence (until recently) of a distinctive and relevant Marxist

[22] *What Marx Really Meant*, p. 203.
[23] *Socialism in Evolution*, p. 155.
[24] R. Palme Dutt, 'Marxism in Caricature', *Labour Monthly*, July 1934. Mirsky also described Cole as 'preparing many young people in the art of pot-roasting Marx (or cooking Marx in his own steam in order to de-marx him)'. (*The Intelligentsia of Great Britain*, 1935, p. 217.)
[25] *What Marx Really Meant*, p. 12.

sociology.[26] This analysis could—and often did—provide the basis for a rejection of Marxism. In Cole's case, Marxism was saved by standing Marx on his head. He wrote unashamedly of 'my Marxism'; and to those who declared that this was not the Marxism of Marx his reply was that 'even if that were so, it would not matter, provided that mine was the better doctrine for today'.[27]

It is necessary to link this critique of Marxism with Cole's treatment of the phenomenon which posed perhaps the most critical problems of analysis and action for the left in the 1930s: fascism. What was fascism? How did it arise? Who supported it? What was the correct response to it? These and other questions elicited significant and revealing answers from the theorists of socialism, not least in Britain. It will be suggested here that Cole provided a richer and more convincing (indeed, more accurate) account of fascism than many of his contemporaries on the left; and that it was an account which had many direct consequences for the wider evolution of his socialist thought. Some of these will be the concern of the next chapter; but others are of central importance here. Cole's response to fascism reflected and carried forward his critique of Marxism and played a decisive role in his formulation of a distinctive democratic socialism.

What, then, was fascism? In particular, the key question for socialist analysis, what was its relationship with capitalism? To the Marxist left the answer was easy: fascism was the 'necessary tactic of capitalism in decay' and 'nothing but monopoly-capitalism imposing its will on those masses whom it has deliberately transformed into its slaves'.[28] In other words, a decaying capitalism, threatened both by its own internal crisis and the forces of socialism, had necessarily to cast itself in fascist form in a final, desperate (and, ultimately, fruitless) bid to save itself. This was not an analysis which Cole could accept. He insisted that fascism must be treated as an essentially new phenomenon, posing its own distinctive problems for analysis and explanation. On the one hand, it was not merely a variant of a traditional conservative authoritarianism, while, on the other hand, it was not simply the militia of capitalism. That it had a relationship with capitalism and capitalists, particularly in its

[26] After the early century revisionist controversies 'the whole domain that might have been occupied by a Marxist sociology was in fact taken over by other schools of sociology', with Marxism remaining only as 'a shadowy or unseen protagonist in much of the writing on social stratification or on social change and conflict'. (Tom Bottomore, *Marxist Sociology*, 1975, p. 29.)

[27] *What Marx Really Meant*, p. 42.

[28] H. J. Laski, 'This Bogey of Communism', *Tribune*, 16 July 1937; and his Foreword to R. A. Brady, *The Spirit and Structure of German Fascism*, 1937, p. 11.

early stages, was clear; for if the great capitalists found Hitler distasteful, they regarded him as useful too. Indeed, the central question
posed by the early history of fascism in Germany was 'whether, having
liquidated Socialism, the Nazis are destined to become the tools or the
masters of large-scale German Capitalism'.[29] If this was still an open
question for Cole in 1934, within a couple of years he had arrived at the
essentials of an answer. The way had been prepared by his analysis of
Marxism, in which he had argued that, within a loose framework of
economic determinism, there was ample scope for an independent role
for institutions, movements and ideas.[30] Politics, law, religion, nationalism: all these, and more, could enjoy a considerable practical autonomy, with important consequences for historical development.

Cole's analysis of fascism took advantage of this theoretical flexibility
not merely to separate the fascist movement from capitalism but also to
establish the political and economic primacy of fascism. His account of
German history in the 1930s, therefore, was in terms of the breakdown
of an initial alliance of expediency between fascism and capitalism,
followed by a struggle for supremacy between them in which fascism
emerged triumphant. Capitalism retained its power of subordination
over labour, but at the cost of its own subordination to the fascists.
Thus, to treat fascism as merely the mercenary force of capitalism was
'dangerously to oversimplify',[31] for it had 'become politically an independent force capable of moulding the short-run course of events'.[32] A
failure to recognize this political independence of fascism was not
merely a failure of analysis, but one with important and dangerous
consequences for policy. Above all, to deny the primacy of politics
represented by fascism was to misunderstand the nature of the forces
making for war. The drive towards war came not from a capitalist
search for profits and markets, for the different national capitalisms
preferred to stay at peace; but from a politically independent fascism
sustained by an arms economy and an aggressive nationalism. 'In this
political independence of Fascism lies the chief immediate danger,'

[29] *A Guide To Modern Politics*, p. 197.
[30] *What Marx Really Meant*, p. 91
[31] *Socialism In Evolution*, p. 228.
[32] Ibid., pp. 234–5. Modern scholarship supports Cole's contemporary analysis. See the contributions to S. J. Woolf (ed.), *The Nature of Fascism* (1968), especially that by T. W. Mason, who
writes that: 'the self-destructive measures of the National Socialist system can only be understood
in the context of the primacy of politics'. ('The Primacy of Politics—Politics and Economics in
National Socialist Germany', p. 191.) For an interesting discussion of socialist thought on fascism,
see P. Sedgwick, 'The Problem of Fascism', *International Socialism*, 42, Feb.–Mar. 1970.

wrote Cole: 'World Capitalism, left to itself, would for the present prefer to keep the peace. ... Verily Capitalism has called up devils to put down its enemies; and its devils threaten to tear civilisation to pieces.'[33] Thus fascism provided horrible confirmation of the possibility of an autonomous politics as suggested in his critique of Marxism.

If Cole's analysis of the relationship between fascism and capitalism implied dissent from Marx, so too did his account of the origins and social composition of the fascist movement. While he gave full weight to the attractions for capitalism of a militant anti-socialist movement, he also paid much attention to the legacy of Versailles and to the impact of economic crisis in creating the psychological ingredients for a broadly based and vigorous nationalism. Cole's major concern, however, was with the class composition of fascism, for it was this which seemed to herald the most significant implications for social theory and social strategy—and to confirm the sociological inadequacy of Marxism. He stated the essence of his social analysis thus: 'Both fascism and nazism derive their real strength not from the believers in hereditary autocracy or aristocracy or from the great capitalists who are prepared to assist them in breaking the power of the Socialist movement, but rather from that large section of the community which in the modern world stands between the directors of capitalist enterprise and the main body of the working class.'[34] In other words, fascism was an essentially middle-class phenomenon, embracing many sections of this heterogeneous social group. Yet its driving force came not from the 'old' *petite bourgeoisie* whose decline Marx had charted (though this group rallied to its banner) but from the ranks of that 'new' technically progressive *petite bourgeoisie* which was the distinctive product of modern social and economic development, and which could provide the ingredients for a new and powerful type of social movement capable of capturing state power itself. The emergence of a movement of this kind was seen by Cole as 'a phenomenon of profound significance for the theory of the class struggle'.[35]

In analysing the nature of this significance (and its lessons for action) Cole found himself isolated from the prevailing orthodoxy of the British

---

[33] Ibid., p. 235. For a sharply contrary view, cf. Laski, 'They Go To War In Search Of Profit', *Tribune*, 21 Jan. 1938.

[34] 'Fascism and the Socialist Failure', *Current History*, June 1933.

[35] *Socialism in Evolution*, p. 184. Strachey attacked this analysis of the social basis of fascism: 'The truth is that fascism is always and everywhere the instrument, not as Mr. Cole supposes of the "petit bourgeoisie" using the great capitalists as its unwilling allies, but of the great capitalists using the "petit bourgeoisie" as its dupes.' (*The Nature of Capitalist Crisis*, 1935, p. 347.)

left. Not only did that orthodoxy tend to treat fascism as the essential expression of a contracting capitalism, but it also drew a particular set of lessons from this analysis. For example, it suggested that capitalist democracy would always turn itself into fascism when faced by a serious socialist challenge, producing a necessarily revolutionary situation from which Britain would not be immune. Consequently, there was a tendency to expect (and to see) the development of fascism in Britain and to urge a militant working-class unity to withstand this threat.[36] By contrast, Cole tended to discount the likelihood of a serious British fascism, drawing upon his usual cultural relativism and sense of national particularity to illustrate the absence in Britain of the magnitude of economic crisis or the sources of nationalist sentiment required to fire a powerful fascist movement. His analysis of the rise of fascism elsewhere, however, had taught him that working-class unity provided the surest antidote and the absence of such unity (as in the fatal antagonism between communists and social democrats in Germany) the surest opening to fascism. Yet he differed from many British advocates of 'unity' in insisting that the working-class movement should unite not on a silly and irrelevant platform of revolutionism, which would merely antagonize other social groups, but on a programme of constructive socialism designed explicitly to appeal to sections of that 'new' middle class which elsewhere had been won for fascism. This strategy derived naturally from an analysis of fascism which located its dynamic not in the requirements of capitalism but in the mobilization of intermediate social groups. Here, then, was the 'profound significance' of fascism for socialist analysis and strategy: capitalist crisis and collapse had produced not socialism but its opposite, by activating particular class forces in a new and distinctive type of political formation. The clear lesson for socialism (according to Cole) was that it should devise an economic strategy which avoided the perils of capitalist collapse and a political programme constructive enough to appeal to critical social groups. His 'popular front' programme, discussed in the next chapter, was the practical expression of this analysis.

Fascism also contributed decisively to Cole's developing conception of democratic socialism, for it made him define his attitude to a set of values and practices whose existence he had previously been able to

---

[36] Kingsley Martin, for example, was evidently obsessed by the possibility of a British fascism. On 29 Sept. 1934 he wrote in his diary: 'I see no way of stopping Fascism in this country now' (and added, without irony, 'not even the "NS and N" which is now booming can stop it'). (Quoted in C. H. Rolph, *Kingsley: The Life Letters and Diaries of Kingsley Martin*, 1973, p. 206.)

take for granted. What did fascism threaten which made it necessary
to mount a defence operation against it which even transcended the
normal lines of class antagonism? Cole's clear answer was that it
represented a threat 'against all liberty, all human decency in social
and international relationships, all democracy and, in short, against
the very survival of civilization in Western Europe'.[37] The comprehensive nature of this threat forced him to a conscious awareness of the
nature of this 'civilization' and of his own attachment to it. So attached
was he, in fact, that he was even prepared to suspend the pursuit of
socialism in order to defend it. In pre-fascist days Cole had sometimes
been content with an easy relativism about values (about the nature of
freedom, for example[38]), but fascism did much to endow this relativism
with a tough definitional centre. Unlike Laski, he had always preferred
to stress the incompleteness rather than the hollowness of 'capitalist'
democracy and in this respect, too, the effect of fascism was to concentrate his attention on what an existing democratic tradition supplied rather than on what it failed to supply. Even his deep antipathy to
parliamentarism was replaced by an acceptance of the need to rally to
its defence, for he had come to realize that he 'vastly prefer[red]
parliamentary capitalism to Fascist capitalism'.[39] Furthermore, he was
decisively strengthened in his belief that, if at all possible, socialism
should be constructed upon the foundations of an existing civilization
and not upon its ruins. All this reflected itself in Cole's increased
willingness to emphasize the reality and value of that liberal, democratic, humanist tradition of which he was an essential product.[40] The
aim should be to add to this tradition rather than to subtract from it;
whereas fascism promised to demolish it.

In the aftermath of 1931, Cole had announced that the rapid
achievement of a comprehensive socialism was not merely the most
urgent but really the *only* worthwhile political task. In pursuit of this
end he was prepared to contemplate radical departures from liberal

[37] 'A British People's Front: Why and How?', *Political Quarterly*, Oct. 1936.
[38] For example, in 1931 he had criticized Leonard Woolf's *After The Deluge* for its excessive
concern with individual liberty. Woolf ignored the fact that 'struggle leads inevitably to discipline
and authority' and that liberty only 'gets its chance when . . . the broad form of social life is settled'.
(*New Leader*, 4 Dec. 1931.) Similarly, Cole had written that rights 'have no positive content except
in relation to a particular social context' (*Some Relations Between Political and Economic Theory*, 1934,
p. 21).
[39] 'The Economic Consequences of War Preparation', 1938.
[40] 'We value the tolerance and the half-democracy that we have succeeded in creating under
capitalism, even while we are fully conscious of their limitations.' (*The People's Front*, 1937, p. 330.)

democratic practice. As the decade progressed he discovered a phenomenon which was both different from and worse than capitalism, and which compelled a reconsideration of socialist theory and strategy. It also compelled some re-evaluation of liberal democracy itself. Therefore the 1930s ended with Cole announcing that the correct strategy for socialists was a suspension of socialist activity. It was necessary to stop the ship sinking before it could be sailed in new directions; and so, for socialists, *reculer pour mieux sauter* should be the motto of the hour. They should accept what Cole himself had accepted: that the question of socialism was 'adjourned in Europe pending the issue of the struggle between Fascism and democracy'.[41]

It is important to emphasize the dimension of sheer pessimism in Cole's thought during the 1930s, for it contributed much to his developing statement of democratic socialism. 'Anyone who at this time of day expects to get Socialism easily', he wrote, 'must be utterly blind to the significance of contemporary forces.'[42] The contrast with the easy optimism and spontaneous activism of an earlier period in his intellectual evolution was striking. Events and analysis seemed to force pessimistic conclusions. For example, the experience of Labour's second period of government produced his damning indictment of the limitations of social democratic interventionism. His economic analysis led him to deny the likelihood of early capitalist collapse; while such capitalist breakdown was regarded as creating conditions more favourable to the growth of fascism than of anything else. At the same time, Cole's analysis of the nature of social structure and class differentiation in the societies of advanced capitalism caused him both to reject a revolutionary perspective and to deny that socialism could be achieved without the support of key sections of the middle class. It was this last consideration which contributed to his continuing emphasis that the socialist movement should be demonstrably competent and constructive, for the 'new' professional and technical middle class 'will not face chaos in the pursuit of an elusive ideal'.[43] In this constant concern that the socialist programme should be firmly (and clearly) rooted in a basis of technical and administrative competence, he also revealed his most significant attachment to the credo of classical Fabianism.

The language of 'chaos', which figured so prominently in Cole's work during this period, further illustrated the dimension of deep pessimism

---

[41] *Socialism in Evolution*, p. 196.
[42] Ibid., p. 156.
[43] Ibid., p. 71.

in his thought. At one level, this was simply a permanent concern that the transition to socialism should be accomplished with a minimum of dislocation. As has been seen, this problem exercised and shaped his thought both in its revolutionary Guild Socialist and in its more orthodox social democratic stages. For example, he described (and defended) his recovery manifesto of 1931 as an attempt to 'promote an orderly transition from capitalism to Socialism instead of a plunge into chaos'.[44] This same sentiment (and phraseology) distinguished the whole corpus of his work. Indeed, in one important respect, it would be possible to characterize his theoretical activity as a search for a non-chaotic road to socialism. Partly, this derived from a personal antipathy to all the suffering and dislocation involved in a transitional state of this kind; partly, too, from a belief in the severe disadvantages and defects of a socialism born out of chaos. It was upon the foundations of an existing civilization that socialism should be built, not upon its ruins. Although this conception of the socialist transition continued to distinguish his thought in the 1930s, it was decisively reinforced during this period by a more fundamental and pervasive sense of chaotic possibilities. No longer was it enough to plan for a smooth transition to socialism, but also to recognize that a lapse into chaos rather than an advance to socialism represented a very real possibility for western capitalist civilization. Of course, Cole had always rejected any notion of historical inevitability or succession, but in the 1930s he came to believe that there was 'real and pressing danger of a world collapse into utter planless disorder and despair—a new Dark Age out of which mankind could only hope again to emerge after generations of needless suffering and humiliation'.[45] This same sense of a civilization at risk was widespread in the intellectual history of the period, producing an equally wide variety of responses and consequences. On the left, as with John Strachey,[46] it was often decisive in promoting the embrace of an assuring ideology: but with Cole it merely provided his social analysis with a profoundly pessimistic framework. It also does much to explain his determination to inject a cautionary realism into socialist thought and

---

[44] *The Crisis* (with E. Bevin), *New Statesman* Pamphlet, 1931, p. 43.

[45] *What Is This Socialism?*, Clarion Press, 1933.

[46] For example, Strachey wrote of communism that: 'the essential argument in its favour is . . . that it is the one method by which human civilisation can be maintained at all'. (*The Coming Struggle For Power*, p. 357.) Thus D. Mirsky observed, acutely, that: 'One clearly feels that had there been any possibility of preserving the bourgeois system healthy and progressive, Strachey would not have been for changing it. . . .' (*The Intelligentsia of Great Britain*, 1935, p. 233.) Strachey's later embrace of Keynes fits well with this interpretation.

activity—for nothing less than the survival of a whole civilization was at stake.

It is important to understand just how serious and pervasive Cole held this threat to be. In this respect the tone and content of his thought changed markedly over a short period of time. At the beginning of the 1930s he experienced a great release of intellectual energy as the decline and fall of the MacDonald Government seemed to open up new social-ist possibilities, as the Russian experiment seemed to represent an exciting exception to a bleak world, and as the conception of economic planning seemed to offer a new direction for socialist economic policy. It has been seen how he responded to this environment with a pro-gramme of radical socialism which paid little attention to constitutional and parliamentary niceties. Within a very few years, however, he was anxious to present a very different view of the world, with very different consequences for socialist thought and strategy.

Cole came to see the entire basis of western civilization as threatened on all sides by the forces of darkness, with the human spirit increasingly disciplined by state coercion and ideological conformity. No longer was the nature of the opening towards socialism the first concern, for the growth of fascism (and quasi-fascism) had revealed the precarious status of a set of values—freedom, tolerance, diversity, decency—whose existence he had hitherto assumed as intrinsic to the sort of civilization out of which socialism would be constructed. 'The entire creed of humanistic "liberalism",' he wrote, 'never more than pre-cariously held in Germany, and never held at all in Russia, is chal-lenged out and out by believers in the "Totalitarian State", who are seeking to regiment mankind back into an orthodoxy more rigid and pervasive than that of the "Holy Office", and enforced by hardly less brutal and degrading inquisitions.'[47] The inclusion of Russia in this general indictment was significant, for it indicated just how pervasive he held this threat to a whole tradition of liberal humanism to be. If Russia had to be defended for its socialism, it had also to be included in the general 'totalitarian' tendency of modern life and thought.[48] Here was the central, and terrible, question for Cole at this time: what if the prospect for western civilization consisted only of a choice between rival authoritarianisms, that of the right to maintain capitalism and that of the left to destroy and replace it? If this was indeed the case, then—as

[47] *The Condition of Britain* (with M. I. Cole), 1937, p. 426.
[48] In the West we 'watch the great Russian venture with growing anxiety; for there too we find cruelty and mass-persecution and intolerance'. ('A Disturbing Book', *Aryan Path*, Sept. 1938.)

he sadly recognized—it was certainly 'a poor lookout for those of us who are unable to toe the line to the satisfaction of the side that wins'.[49]

The evolution of Cole's thought in the 1930s, the essential background to his later formulation of democratic socialism, was rooted in this bleak and pessimistic view of the world. Unlike many other socialists, he refused to adopt positions (for example, that fascism was the death agony of capitalism, destined to crumble under its own contradictions) which would have mitigated this general gloom. Instead, he hastened to the defence of a valued and threatened civilization, a process which prompted a more rigorous statement of the libertarian argument than hitherto and which even led him to prescribe a temporary suspension of explicitly socialist activity as the correct socialist strategy. Above all, this gloomy environment induced him to begin to sketch and defend a conception of democratic socialism which avoided both revolutionary communism and reformist labourism. The polarized political world of the 1930s provided an unfavourable climate for a radical social democracy of this kind, making its advocacy a lonely enterprise. In his search for an elusive middle way, Cole found himself isolated from those socialists who, like Harold Laski, had come to view the political world in apocalyptic terms as a choice between fascism and revolutionary socialism. Instead, he continued to insist on the need for a conception of socialism appropriate to the social structure and political traditions of advanced capitalist societies. Such a conception was not offered as a pale imitation of a purer socialism, but as a legitimate and vigorous expression of a distinctive democratic socialist tradition.

In 1939, however, the outlook seemed bleak for Cole's brand of democratic socialism. If it could enjoy release from the sterilities and defeats of the preceding decade, it could not look with great hope on a war which threatened to make a restored capitalism, fascism or communism the only real post-war alternatives. In this dark environment, Cole greeted the arrival of war by re-affirming his belief in another alternative: 'If I do not accept Stalin's answer,' he said in 1939, 'it is because I am not prepared to write off Democratic Socialism, despite all its failures and vacillations of recent years, as a total loss. . . . Democratic Socialism offers the only means of building the new order upon what is valuable and worth preserving in the civilization of today.'[50] It was this conception which he carried into his analysis of the

---

[49] 'Academic and Professional Freedom', *Library Assistant*, Mar. 1936.
[50] 'The Decline of Capitalism', Lecture to Fabian Society, 1939; Cole Collection.

world at war—and which shaped his hopes and prescriptions for the post-war world.

It was during the·war years that Cole first attempted to spell out the nature and credentials of democratic socialism in explicit fashion. The combined effects of fascism, Soviet communism and the war itself had made such an undertaking necessary. His starting-point was an attempt to sketch the content of West European civilization in terms of the growth of a particular 'social morality', from which Nazism was an aberration and which Russia stood almost completely outside. It is significant that Cole described this development of Western civilization not merely in historical, but also in moral terms. He regarded it as a process of moral building, whereby new values were added to old in a way which contributed to moral growth and avoided moral regression. At any one time, it was a moral tradition which had both to be defended and expanded. Certainly Cole defended it resolutely, not merely from the attack by fascism but also from any variant of Marxism which wanted to treat it as an economic derivative.[51] Yet it had to be expanded too, but in a fashion consistent with its own essential principle. For this reason, it was decisively relevant to the problem and prospects of social change. 'In a continuing civilisation,' he wrote, 'changes must be within limits that are compatible with the elasticity of the current social morality—not with that morality as it is, but with it as it can become without destruction of its principle of life.'[52] All this was intended as a preface to his presentation of the sort of socialism which he claimed both incorporated and expanded the moral achievements of Western civilization; and which he described during the war years as 'liberal socialism'.

What, then, was this liberal socialism? Cole provided a working definition: it was 'the Socialism that stands for carrying over into the new society whatever is good and fine in the tradition of the older society that is being displaced, and is also compatible with the new values of the society that is being born'.[53] As such, it was a socialism which refused to condemn an entire civilization because of its pre-dominantly capitalist basis. Rather, it acknowledged and embraced the reality and value of the Western liberal tradition, of which it was itself a product. Indeed, Cole conceded that 'the defenders of capitalism play

[51] See *Europe, Russia And The Future*, 1941, (esp. ch. 7: 'An Excursus on Social Morality') for a full statement of this conception.
[52] Ibid., p. 85.
[53] *Labour's Foreign Policy*, *New Statesman* Pamphlet, 1946, p. 6.

228 Marxism and Democratic Socialism

their best card when they call for its maintenance in the name of freedom',[54] even though this card was not finally good enough to win the game. The question of freedom was central, however, and Cole treated it as such in his presentation of liberal socialism. Was socialism compatible with freedom? No satisfactory answer to this question could be found in that argument which, on the one hand, pointed to the inadequate and sectional nature of freedom under capitalism or which, on the other hand, stressed the expansion of economic freedom under socialism. Of course, there was something in this argument—but Stalin and Hitler together had contrived to make it much less satisfactory than it had seemed only a decade earlier. It was the sense that socialists could no longer afford to fudge the problem of the status of freedom which gave rise to an explicitly 'liberal' socialism, founded upon a recognition that the mere establishment of a socialized economy in no sense resolved the problem of freedom. Russia had shown that social-ism was possible, but had it shown also that it was desirable? Certainly it had become clear 'that social control of the State and the means of production is not by itself enough to ensure freedom in all its desirable forms'.[55]

Cole's liberal socialism was designed to show that a socialism rooted in the Western liberal tradition *would* prove capable of reconciling a traditional set of values with that extension of freedom which derived from a socialized economy. It would be a socialism which valued tolerance and diversity and which hated bureaucratic monoliths. It would be fiercely libertarian and actively democratic. It would (and could) be all these things because it would represent a natural development of Western social morality rather than any sharp break from it. When Cole revived and re-organized the moribund Fabian Society in 1939 he sought to equip it with this sort of liberal socialist philosophy. The new Fabian Society would provide an intellectual home for those socialists who accepted a socialism rooted in the practice of democratic freedom as their only orthodoxy. This involved an oppo-sition to totalitarianism in all its forms, even if a totalitarian system could provide some freedoms which were absent from the Western liberal tradition. In essence, however, liberal socialism stood for the

[54] 'A Socialist Civilisation', *Fortnightly*, Dec. 1940. This article is an abridged and amended version of Cole's contribution, under the same title, to the volume of essays, *Programme For Victory*, Fabian Society, 1941.

[55] *Fabian Socialism*, 1943, p. 37. 'Even in a Socialist society, "after the revolution", there will be an issue to be settled between totalitarians and liberals.' (*The Intelligent Man's Guide to the Post-War World*, 1947, p. 638.)

possibility that a reconciliation could take place between the freedoms evolved by Western civilization and the sort of economic freedoms secured for the masses in the Soviet Union. 'I do not believe these diverse kinds of freedom to be incompatible,' wrote Cole, 'on the contrary, I regard the one kind as the proper complement of the other, and both kinds as realisable within a framework of "liberal" Socialism.'[56]

Previous chapters have recorded some of the policy consequences which flowed from this approach; and the next chapter will look at its international dimension. In domestic terms (and here Cole's focus was explicitly British), it involved a democratic, non-bureaucratic process of socialization. What it did not involve, however, was a comprehensive socialization: that was neither necessary nor desirable. Furthermore, socialization itself would take the form not of civil service bureaucracy but of the public corporation with wide scope for the exercise of managerial initiative and worker participation, along with other forms of municipal and cooperative ownership. This was a programme designed to give a policy content to the philosophy of liberal socialism. As such, it sought to reconcile diversity with social control and to prevent a valued liberal tradition being lost in a drive towards bureaucratic centralism. Above all, it represented a response to the threat posed by the hugeness of contemporary forces to the possibility of a society of democratic fellowship, which 'should make even Socialists wary by now of tearing up by the roots any small man's refuge that is left in a world so ridden as ours by hugeness. It should make them regard the farmer, the shopkeeper, the small manufacturer, not as obstacles in the way of universal centralization, but as valuable checks upon a dangerous agglomerative tendency. Politically, this opens up the possibility of immense innovations. . .'.[57]

It is interesting that, in Cole's case, the driving force for this definition of a distinctive democratic socialism came not so much from experience of 'undemocratic' socialism in the Soviet Union but from experience of fascism in Western Europe. His cultural relativism could accommodate forms of socialist authoritarianism in many parts of the world (as the next chapter will show); but fascism had demonstrated the possibility of a brutal authoritarianism, or a collapse into chaos, in the heart of Western Europe. As such, it was decisive in forcing Cole to

---

[56] *Fabian Socialism*, p. 114. This book contains Cole's statement of the philosophy of 'liberal socialism'.

[57] *Great Britain in the Post-War World*, 1942, p. 12.

define and defend a conception of democratic socialism as the appropriate expression of the liberal humanist tradition of the West. During the war this was described as liberal socialism; after the war, just as democratic socialism. Indeed, Cole's thought in the post-war period was rooted in the attempt to give a philosophy and programme to this democratic socialism.

This was evident in Cole's renewed discussion of Marxism. Indeed, he was regarded by C. Wright Mills as 'the leading man, the most interesting marxist'[58] in British post-war socialist thinking. It would be wrong to conclude from this assessment that Cole wanted to reconstruct post-war democratic socialism on Marxist foundations. Nor did Wright Mills really intend this conclusion, as his own delineation of different Marxist types makes clear.[59] He made Cole (like himself) a 'plain' Marxist: someone who approached Marxism critically whilst accepting it as central to their own intellectual history. Yet even this may exaggerate Cole's affinity with the Marxist tradition in these years. Indeed, it is possible to suggest that, having stood outside the Marxist tradition during the period of Guild Socialism, he embraced that tradition as a 'plain' Marxist during the 1930s, only to distance himself from it yet again thereafter. Striking evidence of this comes from a comparison between *What Marx Really Meant* (1934) and its 1948 successor, *The Meaning Of Marxism*.

In the earlier book, so firmly had Cole planted himself within the Marxist tradition that he made no serious effort to separate his own analysis from that of Marx; and his revisionism was presented as the authentic expression of a living Marxism. In examining this book, it was suggested that it represented an attempt on Cole's part to 'claim' Marx for social democracy. The later book was very different, both in style and content. Cole had now distanced himself from Marx; the tone was firmly third-person. The spirit of the book, too, had changed greatly. In 1934 Cole was content to acknowledge his own debt to Marx and to warn only against a dogmatic Marxism; by 1948, however, he wanted to make his disagreements more fundamental and explicit, for 'in a good many respects my mind recoils from Marxism, as a system'.[60] The earlier criticisms remained—above all, the alleged inadequacy of Marxism in face of the changing structure of social classes; but these

[58] C. Wright Mills, *The Marxists*, Penguin Books, 1963, p. 153.
[59] See ibid. (pp. 95–8) for Mills's distinction between Vulgar, Sophisticated and Plain Marxisms.
[60] *The Meaning of Marxism*, 1948, p. 11.

were no longer presented in the spirit of internal revision but as part of a wider, external democratic socialist critique. There was also more awareness of some problems inherent in Marxism—for example, the mechanics of social revolution, the possibility of an economic system other than socialism replacing capitalism, the possibility of a non-unitary proletariat in power which allowed the continuation of forms of class exploitation; and the experience of fascism was used to explore the weakness of a crude economic materialism. Formerly Cole had sought (in the name of Marx) to present a 'liberal' Marxism: he now launched (against Marx) a sustained attack on anything that smacked of mono-causality, materialism, scientism or determinism.

Above all, however, it was the devaluation of the individual and the elevation of the class which claimed Cole's attention. On this view, the fundamental defect of Marxism was its attribution of reality to classes rather than to individuals. Instead of throwing off Hegelian metaphysics, Marx had 'only substituted a new form of metaphysics, masquerading as science' which had 'the disastrous result of making him think of individuals—of capitalists and workers alike—as abstractions, and of the capitalist class and the proletariat as realities'.[61] Cole devoted much space to a denial of the superior reality of the class to the individual, not least because it was an argument which gave rise to important practical consequences. In his view, it was the devaluation of the individual implicit in original Marxism which provided 'the foundation of much of the ruthlessness and lack of humanism that has characterised the application of the Marxian doctrine'.[62] In other words, Cole wanted to assert a direct line of descent from Marx to Stalin. Together, Stalin and Hitler had clearly done much to shape his mature conception of the 'meaning of Marxism'.

It was a conception which found expression throughout the last decade of Cole's life. Delivering a memorial lecture for Laski in 1951, Cole mounted a powerful attack on the Marxism which Laski was never able to combine with his liberal humanism into a coherent philosophy of socialism. Cole suggested a sharp contrast between an ethical, idealist tradition of democratic socialism and a Marxism which was 'thoroughly determinist in all its aspects',[63] a hangover from a theological worldview. He affirmed his own repudiation of a determinism of

---

[61] Ibid., p. 12.
[62] Ibid., p. 25.
[63] 'Socialist Philosophies and Present Problems', Laski memorial address, Hampstead Town Hall, 3 July 1951 (MS in possession of Margaret Cole).

any kind.[64] What this meant was that democratic socialism, in its search for a philosophical basis (the need for which Laski had always stressed), could find no satisfactory refuge in Marxism—though many, like Laski, had embraced this refuge in the 1930s, only to find it a source of great internal tension thereafter. No longer did Cole want to 'claim' Marx for the social democratic tradition; rather, he expressly repudiated any such attempt. 'I was asked the other day,' he wrote in 1948, 'to write an article to show that the Communist Manifesto of 1848 . . . is in truth a Social Democratic and not a Communist "classic". I declined, for the sufficient reason that no such case could be even plausibly made out.'[65]

Yet the request to Cole had not been unreasonable in view of his treatment of Marx only a decade earlier. Marx also suffered rough treatment in Cole's *History of Socialist Thought* where, in addition to a considerable personal antipathy ('a German of the Germans'[66]), his analysis of capitalist development was pronounced obsolete, while his theory of value turned out to be a 'gigantic metaphysical construction'.[67] Cole had never found much of interest in Marxist economic theory, beyond a critical weapon to be used against capitalist economics, but it now seemed devoid of all relevance. Nowhere was this more evident than in his little book on *Socialist Economics* (1950), which managed to avoid any mention of Marx until the final chapter when Cole, noting the omission, stated simply that 'there is . . . nothing in Marx's writings that has any important bearing on the matters discussed in this book'.[68] Similarly, Cole's analysis of contemporary capitalism was designed to demonstrate the ability of Keynesian techniques to cope with capitalist instability, thereby banishing any (Marxist) expectation of inevitable breakdown.[69] Finally, his exploration of the contemporary structure of social classes, notably in his *Studies in Class Structure* (1955), was organized around a contrast between the

[64] 'I fail to find evidence of *any* general law of historical evolution, and I think belief in such a law is a residue from the religious attitude which attributed its existence to God.' (ibid.)

[65] 'Marx and the Marxists', *Outlook*, Lent 1948.

[66] *A History of Socialist Thought, Vol. II: Marxism and Anarchism 1850–1890*, 1954, p. 310.

[67] Ibid., p. 288.

[68] *Socialist Economics*, 1950, p. 144. Cole added that: 'Marxism and the kind of socialist Economics that is relevant to the constructive problems of a socialist society are on quite different planes.' (idem.)

[69] Cole argued that Keynes provided 'a thoroughgoing rejection of the Marxian diagnosis of capitalism and, as I believe, a correct rejection in relation to twentieth-century capitalism'. (*Capitalism in the Modern World*, Fabian Tract 310, 1957, p. 29.) Cf. 'What Is Happening To British Capitalism?', *Universities and Left Review*, No. 1, spring 1957.

facts of an increasingly complex social differentiation and the Marxist assumption of a progressive simplification.

Of course, Cole remained 'Marx-influenced'; and he continued to declare his adherence to a loose historical materialism. Yet, emptied of so much of its economics and sociology, Cole's Marxism was left only with a partial theory of history which had provided its content in the years before 1914. To a significant extent, therefore, his relationship to Marx had come full circle. It was a relationship in which he distanced himself from key elements in the Marxist tradition. Particularly interesting in this respect was the opening volume of his *History of Socialist Thought*, where the tone of the account indicated considerable regret at the eclipse by Marxism of the lively diversity of early nineteenth-century 'utopian' socialism, not least because the ideological dominance of Marxism forced many varieties of libertarian socialism into the political wilderness. 'Where the "Socialists" had thought in terms of ideals, Marx thought in terms of power':[70] this was the tone of Cole's account of the process. His attitude to Marx in this post-war period gained a special importance since he emerged as the leading socialist advocate of cooperation with the Communists, particularly with those who were trying to liberalize their own parties. The cooperation had to be authentic, rooted in a frank recognition of theoretical differences. Thus to one Communist dissident Cole wrote: 'perhaps I ought to remind you that I do not call myself a Marxist, because I am unable to accept what I believe to be the Marxist fundamental philosophical position.'[71]

This post-war dissociation from Marxism was matched by Cole's continuing concern with the credentials of an alternative tradition—and with its policy implications. Experience of the post-war Labour Government had an important influence on this enterprise, for it was the speed and thoroughness of Cole's passage from support to disillusionment with Labour in these years which provided the essential background for his formulation of democratic socialist programme. A consistent critic of Labour's failure to pursue a socialist foreign policy, by 1948 he was nevertheless prepared to register a highly favourable interim judgement on the domestic record of the Attlee Government. So favourable, in fact, that he felt able to cite the experience of this Government as important evidence against the Mar-

[70] *A History of Socialist Thought, Vol. I: The Forerunners, 1789–1850*, 1953, p. 313. Cf. 'What Is Socialism?' I, *Political Studies*, I, 1953.
[71] Cole to J. Saville, 11 Feb. 1957 (Letter in possession of Margaret Cole).

xist theory of the state. He suggested that the Labour Government had done much to confirm the possibility of a constitutional road to socialism by means of the democratic capture of the state machine; so that the answer to the Marxists was now 'in the facts'.[72] Similarly, his account of Labour Party history since 1914, which appeared in 1948, contained an epilogue on the first two years of the Attlee Government which ended on a decidedly lyrical note.[73] The honeymoon was not to last.

As Labour seemed to expire in office after 1948, Cole came to adopt a more critical stance. His complaint was not that Labour had opted for 'consolidation' (for the economic environment made some consolidation inevitable), but that, in pausing on further nationalization, it showed no sign of pressing on with an alternative programme of radical attack on the structure of capital ownership and class privilege. Nor did Labour seem willing to use the pause for an exploration of alternative forms of socialization, or for a new campaign of socialist education and propaganda designed to stimulate a popular demand for something more than the social service state. Thus the danger was that 'the pause may lead, not to a later advance on an improved basis, but to a lasting loss of impetus, and to an acceptance of a "mixed economy" as a permanent resting-place'.[74] By the turn of the decade the danger seemed to have become reality—and Cole's disquiet turned into despair. Domestically, democratic socialism seemed bankrupt of ideas; internationally, it was the prisoner of a reactionary anticommunism. Democratic socialism was 'stuck': stuck at welfarism on the one hand, stuck in the Cold War on the other. Neither resting-place was acceptable to Cole; and he moved into direct opposition to official Labour on both fronts. It was in this setting, therefore, that he attempted to equip democratic socialism with a distinctive philosophy and programme.

In philosophical terms, Cole continued to build upon the position he had first sketched during the war. This involved a treatment of democratic socialism as the product of a particular sort of civilization; and a view of social development as a process of moral construction. It involved a repudiation of morality as a class-based phenomenon, and a recognition that 'the Socialism that is appropriate for us, as the means of raising the quality of the civilization we have already achieved, must be built upon, and must not flout, the liberal humanistic values that we

---

[72] *The Meaning of Marxism*, p. 195.
[73] *A History of the Labour Party from 1914*, 1948, pp. 477–8.
[74] 'The Dream and the Business', *Political Quarterly*, July–Sept. 1949.

now imperfectly accept and practice'.[75] What this involved, too, was a recognition that other forms of socialism would find no natural home in a civilization of this kind, while this particular form was necessarily non-universal in its application. One implication of this was that there could be no escape from the limitations of democratic socialism into a vigorous communism, for communism was simply not an alternative open to socialists in a society like Britain. Thus 'the question . . . for British Socialists is not whether to go over to Communism, but how to get a new impulse behind their attempt to advance towards Socialism in their own way'.[76] Not only did democratic socialism have its own moral tradition, but its own political tradition too. It inherited an imperfect but valuable democratic structure which it had to complete without destroying. Especially important, it inherited a conception and practice of individual liberty which was not merely a defence of privilege and which it was necessary to incorporate into socialism as a positive commitment to individual diversity. Thus Cole advanced a democratic socialist conception of liberty which was firmly anchored in the individual, not defined collectively in terms of the group or class.[77] When he attempted to reconstruct democratic socialism, therefore, he regarded himself as dealing with a body of ideas which was historically and culturally specific, and which incorporated a distinctive set of political and moral values. At the same time, however, he denied either that this meant any dilution of socialist objectives or that it prevented cooperation between socialists of different types and traditions. Indeed, most of his activity in the 1950s was expressly designed to deny that these were necessary consequences of the democratic socialist position.

Far from involving any socialist dilution, in fact, Cole's restatement of democratic socialism in the years after the Attlee Government sought to release it from its paralysis of will and bankruptcy of ideas by carrying it beyond the confines of the welfare state and mixed economy. At the same time, however, he refused to subscribe to any view which devalued the social and economic gains that had been achieved. Indeed, such a refusal was implied in his statement of democratic socialism itself. In fact, he sometimes lapsed into a complacent optimism (a tendency which claimed many victims in the 1950s) in describing recent social and economic history. This was seen clearly in his 1956

---

[75] 'Socialist Philosophies and Present Problems', 1951.

[76] 'Shall Socialism Fail?', 1, *New Statesman*, 5 May 1951.

[77] See 'Liberty in Retrospect and Prospect', *Rationalist Annual*, 1950; and his 'Western Civilisation and the Rights of the Individual', in *Essays in Social Theory*, 1950.

survey of *The Post-War Condition of Britain*, which made frequent (and favourable) comparisons with the conditions recorded in his similar compilation of contemporary statistics two decades earlier. 'To anyone who accepts social equality as a desirable goal and hates the suffering caused by sheer privation and by the denial of a fair chance,' he wrote, 'the achievement of the past two decades must give immense satisfaction, even if it still falls a long way short of his larger hopes.'[78] Cole detected a fairer distribution of income, a diminution of poverty and a great increase in economic security, along with all the gains in health and welfare which flowed from these economic changes. A later generation, tutored by Titmuss and others, was more cautious in its estimate of the magnitude of the redistribution of economic benefits in favour of the working class in these years; and certainly less optimistic than Cole in its analysis of the social change involved.[79]

Cole's interest in problems of class structure has already been noticed; and this continued into the post-war period. Indeed, his activity in this direction may be regarded as an attempt to equip democratic socialism with a distinctive sociology. Partly, his interest continued to focus on those sections of the 'new' middle-class overlooked by Marx and regarded as critical to social development. If he was not disposed to accept Burnham's managerialism (which he regarded as 'confusing and grossly over-simplified'[80]), he did want to suggest that if these intermediate social groups were not themselves destined to be the heirs of capitalism they could nevertheless decisively affect the nature of the inheritance; and that there was 'a clear similarity between the capitalist class, as it appeared in the earlier stages of its rise to power, and the technical and managerial groups of to-day'.[81] More generally, he wanted to link his discussion of these groups with a more comprehensive analysis of the developing class structure of advanced capitalism. In essence, such an analysis was claimed to reveal a progressive dissolution of traditional class categories and divisions. The picture presented was of an increasingly open and mobile social structure with an erosion of the central agencies of class inheritance. In an ever more complex and differentiated social fabric, social class (never satisfactorily defined by Cole) was becoming a more individual, less structural, phenomenon. In this situation, the term 'middle class' tended to

[78] *The Post-War Condition of Britain*, 1956, p. 438.
[79] For a recent comprehensive account, see J. Westergaard and H. Resler, *Class in a Capitalist Society: A Study of Contemporary Britain*, 1975.
[80] 'The Conception of the Middle Classes', *British Journal of Sociology*, I, 1950.
[81] *The Meaning of Marxism*, p. 281.

become 'a merely descriptive adjective' for ' "middle class" may still be held to exist under such conditions—that is really a matter of words—but a *"bourgeoisie"*, in the sense historically attaching to the term, cannot'.[82]

Much of Cole's contemporary analysis of social structure was decidedly inferior to his historical sociology: limited evidence and a flimsy methodology had to sustain sweeping conclusions, themselves often imprecise. For example, he was so impressed by what he regarded as the increasing democratization of social life that he was led to suggest that, in modern conditions, 'the struggle between classes, though it does not cease to exist, necessarily changes its human character. It becomes more and more a contest, not between unlikes, but of like with like, carried on with more mutual knowledge and understanding'.[83] It is by no means clear quite what this portentous statement was supposed to mean. Yet, in Cole's favour, it can be said that he was attempting to confront a number of problems central to a modern sociology. His questions were suggestive even when his analysis was disappointing. A good example of this was his pioneering essay on *Elites in British Society* which began by raising some leading questions relevant to the sociology of power but then relapsed into a thin analysis of different areas of British social life, finally expiring in a celebration of that diffusion of power, that 'diversity in unity',[84] which was the genius of British pluralism. Here the analysis was simply not strong enough to support its conclusions, and many critical problems of elite theory were avoided. In general, however, it may be said that, having presented democratic socialism as the distinctive product of those societies with a particular type of social structure, he did regard it as necessary to engage in a serious analysis of the distribution, composition and relationship of social classes in societies of this type; to offer, in effect, a sociology of democratic socialism.

Here, then, was the theoretical basis upon which Cole founded his policy proposals in the 1950s. Previous chapters have examined the leading elements in this programme (for example, his renewed interest in participatory democracy), a programme which was designed to revitalize the tradition of democratic socialism and to carry it beyond the confines of the welfare state and mixed economy, the twin pillars

[82] 'The Conception of the Middle Classes.'
[83] *The Post-War Condition of Britain*, p. 43.
[84] 'Elites in British Society', in *Studies in Class Structure*, 1955, p. 144. For more critical analysis of these themes, cf. P. Stanworth and A. Giddens (eds.), *Elites and Power in British Society*, 1974.

upon which it had been left stranded by the Attlee Government. On the one hand, Cole attempted to sketch a genuinely democratic socialist version of a 'mixed' economy conceived as a permanent alternative to traditional nationalization, as 'a highly varied and flexible system of socialised ownership and control',[85] involving producer and consumer cooperation, municipal and public enterprise—and even the continuation of publicly supervised private concerns. As such, it offered a radical departure from the monolithic socialism of large-scale nationalization. On the other hand, his critique of welfarism arrived at similar conclusions about the need for a direct attack on capitalist property in the interests of classlessness and a diffusion of power in the interests of democracy. Socialism *implied* the welfare state but was *not* the welfare state: this was Cole's theme. 'Everywhere the great task that lies ahead of us,' he wrote, 'is that of passing beyond the Welfare State, in which people get given things, to the kind of society in which they find satisfaction in doing things for themselves and for one another.'[86] His actual programme, described in earlier chapters, thus represented an attempt to give concrete shape to this conception of democratic socialism.

The development of Cole's thought which has been traced in this chapter may be regarded as the explication of a position which existed, albeit in undeveloped form, in his earlier Guild Socialist thought. In that earlier period, he sought to present Guild Socialism as the distinctive product of a particular social and ideological tradition and was wary of any easy process of theoretical import and export. Yet it was a distinctiveness rooted in eclecticism: the product might be distinctive but the ingredients were many and various. For a long time, this continued to be Cole's approach. For example, when he accepted a reformist perspective in the 1920s he made no real attempt to define the theoretical credentials of this position; and his loose embrace of Marxism in the early 1930s seemed designed to incorporate it within the social democratic tradition. This chapter has sought to show how this accommodative, eclectic style of thought slowly gave way to an emphasis on the real divisions between theoretical traditions. Fascism was decisive in this; while Soviet communism re-inforced the lesson. Hence he was forced to define the relationship between socialism and an existing liberal humanism and, also, to engage in a more rigorous and critical treatment of Marxism.

---

[85] *Is This Socialism?*, *New Statesman* Pamphlet, 1954.
[86] 'What Next? Anarchists or Bureaucrats?', *Fabian Journal*, Apr. 1954.

Above all, Cole felt it necessary to define a distinctive democratic socialist tradition. He explored its history; defined its values; discussed its relations with other traditions; linked it to particular types of society; endowed it with an appropriate sociology; and gave it a political programme. It is important to understand Cole's emphasis on the distinctiveness of this tradition. He refused to regard it as a pale imitation of a more comprehensive and militant socialism; still less as a retreat into a mild reformism. Rather, it involved a statement about how socialism could and should be achieved in mature industrial societies with a complex class structure and a tradition of liberal freedoms and political democracy—and the form that socialism should take in such societies. Cole's thought reveals the extent to which he was sensitive to the difficulties inherent in a democratic socialism of this kind, not least its endemic tendency to dilution and degeneration; but also that he believed there was no possible or desirable alternative to working within this sort of tradition. Above all, his thought attempted to define the distinctive pedigree of a democratic socialism which was not merely a retreat from Marxism nor an embrace of social democracy. In general, the attempt was successful and its product attractive. Less successful, perhaps, was his parallel attempt to situate democratic socialism in the wider context of international socialism.

X

Nationalism and Internationalism

UNTIL THE 1930s it could hardly be claimed that Cole's thought contained an international dimension. Instead, it seemed deliberately parochial, its occasional international glance designed only to emphasize the 'peculiarities of the English'. This was certainly the tone of his Guild Socialist work. An early syllabus merely posed the problem of internationalism;[1] the answer was implied in the rest of his Guild writings. It was implied in *The World of Labour*, a compendium of international labour developments which emphasized national differences. It was implied, too, in his dismissal of socialist internationalism in the years before 1914; and, later, in his diffident response to the Bolshevik Revolution. It continued into the 1920s, when his focus remained firmly and explicitly domestic. He liked to proclaim his essential 'nationalism' at this time; and, in turn, was often chided for an insularity which found difficulty in transcending the boundaries of territory and culture.[2]

Hence it is impossible to describe Cole's attitude to the developing antagonisms within international socialism during this period, for our only evidence is retrospective, from the perspective of the 1950s. The world of the 1930s ended this easy parochialism. World economic crisis, developments in the Soviet Union, the growth of fascism and, later, the onset of the Cold War forced a wider view. It has been seen how these developments were important in Cole's formulation of a philosophy of democratic socialism; and they were also important in his definition of an international role and outlook for democratic socialism. His attachment to national particularity was not abandoned; rather, as seen also in the last chapter, it was erected into a philosophy and a programme.

A growing regard for the Soviet Union among British intellectuals

---

[1] 'Nationalism and Internationalism, in Relation to Socialism in Europe' (with M. B. Reckitt), 1914–15: Syllabus prepared for Research Group of Oxford University Fabian Society. (Cole Collection.)

[2] Former members of the 'Cole Group' in the 1920s recall this aspect of the group's discussions. (Information to author.)

has been described as 'the most striking feature of the thirties'[3] and certainly this was a phenomenon in which Cole fully participated. Yet he never claimed particular expertise or knowledge about Russia; was never (unlike, say, the Webbs, Laski or Strachey) a leading figure in making Russia respectable or popular; and was never (to beg a lot of definitional problems) a fellow-traveller. However, his support for Russia was both warm and consistent, though not unequivocal. That such support should have been forthcoming from the European left during the 1930s was scarcely surprising, though later commentators have contrived to make it seem so. For example, a picture has been presented of Western intellectuals lured by the appeal of a new Enlightenment; whereas a remark from that antagonist of intellectuals, Ernest Bevin, takes us much closer to contemporary attitudes: 'No country outside Russia appeared to have a policy to-day.'[4]

Cole shared this sort of perspective. He contrasted a coherent Russian planning with capitalist disorganization and pointed to the tremendous economic advance which, against all the odds, had been achieved. He also paid particular attention to a new spirit which he detected in operation inside the Soviet system, regarding this as ultimately of more significance than any institutional arrangement. This was a theme to which he returned time and again in his discussions of the Soviet Union, and in the service of this new spirit he was prepared to forgive much. He announced and applauded 'the widespread consciousness of men and women in Russia that they are fashioning a new world'.[5] Moreover, it was important for socialism in Western Europe that the Russian experiment should succeed. It represented the force of a practical example and—especially vital from

[3] N. Wood, *Communism and British Intellectuals*, 1959, p. 42. Useful material on this phenomenon is to be found in D. Caute, *The Fellow-Travellers*, 1973, although this account is vitiated by its reduction of a complex historical context to a set of 'tribal reflexes' (p. 118). For an incisive critique of Caute, cf. V. G. Kiernan, *Times Higher Education Supplement*, 16 Feb. 1973.

[4] E. Bevin, S.S.I.P. Annual Meeting, May 1932. Report in *S.S.I.P. Monthly Bulletin*, June 1932, Cole Collection. By contrast, Caute (op. cit.) seeks to explain support for Russia in terms of the attraction of a 'new Enlightenment'.

[5] 'The Truth and Russia', *New Statesman*, 18 July 1936. It may be suggested that Cole drew heavily on his wife's impression of Russia gained on her visit with an N.F.R.B. group in 1932. While there, Margaret despatched long letters to Cole about her experiences. In one of these, from Moscow, she wrote: 'Whatever criticisms and faults—and they're plenty, some against Communism, some against Russians—it *is* like a dream coming true. To meet and talk to civil servants and heads of large hospitals, and they talk like the Movement—one keeps forgetting to be surprised, if you understand me, because it comes so natural. One has come home....' (Undated, 1932, in possession of Margaret Cole.) Margaret Cole has recorded how she 'returned to England immensely excited by my Soviet experiences'. (*Growing Up Into Revolution*, 1949, p. 164.)

Cole's point of view—the success of Russian planning would do much to attract the new technical salariat to the socialist cause.[6] In other words, Russia deserved support both for its own sake and for its contribution to the achievement of socialism elsewhere. So strongly did Cole believe this that at times he almost assumed the role of apologist, asserting as a rule of conduct that 'every good Socialist should regard his disagreements with the Russians as quite irrelevant to his desire for their success'.[7]

Ultimately, however, Cole was defender rather than apologist, for the recognition of disagreements marks off the former from the latter. Moreover, he did not cultivate a blindness about Russia, but rather a deliberate realism. If he sought to defend an unpleasant aspect of Soviet life it was not by a refusal to recognize its existence. Although he frequently pointed to the difficulty of getting reliable evidence about developments in Russia amid the welter of conflicting claims, he readily acknowledged the totalitarian discipline of the Soviet system. Indeed, in a piece of remarkable prescience, he announced on the eve of the Webbs' departure for Russia that it would be this aspect of the Soviet system which would attract them to the 'new civilization'.[8] He regarded Soviet totalitarianism as even more comprehensive than that of fascism, for it involved a total subordination of group life; and he recognized the ruthlessness and sheer cruelty characteristic of much of the Soviet system. All of this he disliked and some of it he condemned.[9] In general, however, he was prepared to defend even this dark side of Soviet life. He pointed to the transitional nature of the Soviet system; to the magnitude of its internal task and of its external threat; to the legacy of brutality and dictatorship bestowed by the Russian tradition; and, finally, to an alleged enlargement and re-definition of freedom consequent upon the establishment of socialism. Each of these points really needs amplification and illustration but, for present purposes, it is enough to note that together they allowed Cole to mount a fairly comprehensive defence of the Soviet Union.

Most significant, however, was the style of this defence, for it was this which provided the key to his wider position. Above all, he defended the

---

[6] The success of Russian planning was 'likely to have far larger results than any amount of propaganda in bringing over the technicians to the Socialist side'. (*The Intelligent Man's Guide Through World Chaos*, 1932, p. 515.)

[7] 'Eyes on Russia', *Clarion*, Feb. 1931.

[8] 'The Webbs: Prophets of A New Order', *Current History*, Nov. 1932.

[9] For example: 'The ruthless suppression of the kulaks does seem to me both morally indefensible and also economically wrong....' (*Practical Economics*, 1937, p. 52.)

Soviet Union *in its own terms,* as an attempt to establish socialism in a particular sort of national and social setting, involving a distinctive set of problems and responses. As such, it demanded support and sympathy—and an acceptance that the manner in which it tackled its own problems was largely its own business. To the charge that this stance involved an application of 'double standards',[10] Cole would readily assent, for his declared relativism implied multiple standards. The Soviet Union stood as example, not as model. Indeed, the essence of Cole's argument—seen earlier in his attitude to the Bolshevik Revolution—was that Russian experience was largely irrelevant to the situation faced by socialists in Western Europe. Differences of historical development, economic modernization, social structure and political tradition conspired to emphasize Russian specificity. This meant, for example, that the actual operation of economic planning in Russia was generally 'unfruitful of lessons by which the Western countries can profit',[11] while there were also likely to be profound differences of political method.

It is interesting to note that at a time when socialists like Harold Laski were devoting much effort to a demonstration that there could be no British 'exceptionalism' to the general revolutionary case, Cole was busy documenting the 'exceptionalism' of the Russian revolutionary experience and suggesting a large role for constitutionalism in Western Europe. His central message, in relation both to Marxism and to Russia, was the need for socialism to take a form and a strategy appropriate to particular societies. Hence he could deal sympathetically with Marx and support Russia while attacking official communism; for 'when Russian Communists set out to generalize their experience, and to order Socialists in other countries to follow precisely their example in the sacred names of Marx and Lenin, the inappropriateness of their dogmas to the Western situation soon becomes manifest'.[12] Thus, already in the 1930s, Cole's treatment of the Soviet Union revealed that emphasis on 'appropriateness' which was basic to his formulation of democratic socialism; and which was to become the guiding principle of his international position.

It is again necessary to notice the place of fascism in the development of Cole's thought for, more than anything else, it served to give his thought a genuinely international dimension. The almost deliberate

[10] Caute, op. cit., p. 203.
[11] *Practical Economics*, p. 60.
[12] *Socialism in Evolution*, 1938, p. 151.

parochialism of his early thought has already been noticed; it helped to give a regrettable insularity to British socialism as a whole. In the 1930s, however, all this changed (despite his continued insistence on the importance of national differences), not merely because fascism was a vital European development which forced itself on the attention of socialists everywhere, but also because Cole's particular analysis of fascism stressed its international implications. In fact, Cole became *more* internationally minded than those socialists whose emphasis on the capitalist nature of fascism gave them a more domestic focus. His attention to the nationalist sentiment at the heart of fascism led him to suggest, as early as 1933, that war was a very real possibility.[13] This view was decisively reinforced later in the decade by his analysis of the nature of the fascist arms economy, which revealed 'how completely Nazi Germany has now become a State planned and planning for war'.[14] Nor was Cole slow to work out the foreign policy implications of his diagnosis of fascism, for as early as 1934 he demanded a system of pooled security with Britain, France and Russia as its nucleus, designed to erect a united front against fascist aggression; and it was this same demand which he repeated with increasing vehemence and desperation as the decade progressed.

Yet all this did not leave Cole's international position entirely free from ambiguity. On the one hand, his recognition of the need for determined resistance to fascism had to co-exist, often uneasily, with a deep personal pacifism. 'I refused to fight in the late war, and if there were another war, I should certainly refuse again,' he declared in 1933,[15] but the subsequent course of events (not least in Spain) did much to modify this position. After an intervening period of almost total confusion in which he endeavoured to retain a personal pacifism although pronouncing it 'irrelevant'[16] to practical politics, he arrived at a position which reluctantly acknowledged the existence of a 'duty to try to kill rather than to die'.[17] On the other hand, if he was ambiguous on pacifism, he was even more ambivalent about rearmament. Of course, a similar ambivalence was characteristic of the British Labour movement as a whole at this time. It faced a real dilemma: opposition to

[13] *The Intelligent Man's Review of Europe To-Day*, 1933, p. 650.
[14] *Practical Economics*, p. 117.
[15] *What Is This Socialism?*, Clarion Press, 1933.
[16] *The Simple Case For Socialism*, 1935, p. 101.
[17] 'A Disturbing Book', *Aryan Path*, Sept. 1938. By 1940 Cole could state bluntly that: 'Hitler cured me of pacifism.' ('Some Political 'Isms', B.B.C. Schools Broadcast, 1 Oct. 1940; Transcript in Cole Collection.)

fascist aggression required armaments, yet could the Chamberlain Government be trusted to use these arms for the right purpose? Contrary to that view which sees this merely as a piece of socialist muddle-headedness, it did represent a genuine problem for the left, not least because of the nature of British foreign policy throughout the decade. For his part, Cole was clear that, except in the event of a direct attack on its own interests, British conservatism would not support an international anti-fascist alliance. Thus Chamberlain would 'sooner see Hitler overrun Europe than find himself fighting Fascism as the ally of the Soviet Union'.[18] Cole's personal contempt for Chamberlain was immense and he would not contemplate a rearmament programme under his auspices; indeed, he would 'refuse all collaboration with the present rulers of Great Britain'.[19] At the same time, however, he was critical of the Unity Manifesto of the Socialist League because of its implacable opposition to all rearmament, for he could not 'be a party to creating a situation in which an incoming Government of the Left might find itself unable to resist Fascism'.[20]

Was there a policy which could sustain a logical connection between these seemingly inconsistent stances? In terms of practical politics almost certainly there was not. Yet Cole sought to establish such a connection by insisting, at worst, that support for rearmament should be given only in return for definite pledges about the use to which such arms would be put or, at best, that the existing government should be ousted and replaced by one to whom arms could more reasonably be entrusted. The actual political environment gave little reason to believe that either of these demands would be met, serving to give Cole's opposition to rearmament scarcely more logical or practical foundations than those of less discriminating opponents of rearmament. Yet the agency whereby Cole hoped to give organizational and programmatic force to his demands—namely, a 'popular front'—takes us to the very heart of the impact of fascism on the development of an international perspective in his thought.

Experience of fascism did much to strengthen Cole's belief that the working-class movement should actively seek class allies (particularly from critical sections of the middle class), yet he always linked this prescription for strategy with an insistence that it involved no 'dilution' of socialist policy. Further experience of fascism, however, effectively

[18] 'Dilution? British Labour Must Not Be Fooled A Second Time', *Tribune*, 1 April 1938.
[19] 'The British Labour Movement Today', *American Socialist Monthly*, Feb. 1937.
[20] *The People's Front*, 1937, p. 337.

cancelled this last provision, producing a decisive shift (and illumin-
ation) of his wider position. By 1936 he had come to believe that the
fascist threat had created an international emergency of such acute
dimensions that it required an emergency response. Such a response
involved an acceptance that for the time being the international situation should take precedence over anything else—even over the
achievement of socialism itself. It was the failure of the Labour Party
leadership to accept either the fact of an international emergency or the
need to make an appropriate response to it[21] which led Cole, with an eye
on European example, to advance the cause of a popular front which
would unite all those people who realized the primacy of the international danger in a crusade powerful enough to force a change of
government and a reformulation of foreign policy. It was to be a
crusade not an electoral pact; it was necessary because the Labour
Party had no hope of securing an early electoral victory; and it was to
embrace everybody from Communists to progressive Conservatives.
For present purposes it is less important to document the political
impossibility of this project than to notice its significance for the
development of Cole's thought.[22]

In the first place, the price and pre-condition for an agreed international policy was an agreed domestic policy. Because of the nature of
the political and ideological alliance envisaged by the popular front,
this domestic policy clearly could not be decisively socialist. Instead, it
could only be a social reform programme, embodying the policies of the
'progressive' consensus. So valuable was the prize of an agreed international policy that Cole was more than willing to pay this domestic
price. His dramatic shift of position in this respect was clearly revealed
by his changing attitude to the 'Next Five Years' Group, whose programme contained the essentials of a progressive social and economic
package. Reviewing this programme in 1935, Cole stressed the essential
unworkability of this sort of 'socialistic' reformism which left the central
fabric of capitalism intact: 'I do not believe that the right course in the
immediate future is to work for a Ministry of All the Progressives, that
will get on with the things on which all progressives agree, and leave

---

[21] Cf. Attlee's statement, in 1937, that he would consider a popular front only 'in the event of the
imminence of a world crisis'. (*The Labour Party In Perspective*, 1937, p. 124.)

[22] See *The People's Front*, 1937, for a full statement of Cole's position. L. P. Carpenter, confusing
the united and popular fronts, writes that: 'the People's Front proved incapable of carrying out
Cole's hopes for a socialist society'. (*G. D. H. Cole: An Intellectual Biography*, 1973, p. 192.) Yet this
was never its purpose. For a detailed discussion of this period, see R. Eatwell, 'The Labour Party
and the Popular Front Movement in Britain in the 1930s', Oxford D.Phil. thesis, 1975.

unsolved the major questions about which they differ.'[23] Within a year, however, he had become the apostle of exactly such a Ministry of All the Progressives and wanted to equip it with an economic policy 'not much more to the left of the "Next Five Years" group'.[24] In other words, the fascist threat had so intensified internationally that socialists should be prepared to dilute their programme for the sake of a broad anti-fascist front. Cole was prepared to declare that he was 'far less concerned about the need for passing Socialist measures in the immediate future than about the need for saving democracy from total eclipse'.[25]

Moreover, Cole's sense of the emergency nature of the situation made him refuse to make the achievement of a 'united front' amongst the working class (an official Labour–Communist alliance) a pre-condition for popular front activities. Indeed, he was impatient with the stance of the 'self-righteous minority of Socialist Simon Pures, isolating itself from all contaminating contacts',[26] which continued to purvey both an erroneous analysis of fascism and a dangerously irrelevant conception of socialist strategy. In fact, this whole issue again served to illustrate the necessary fusion of analysis and action. For example, Laski (along with the Communists, until new orders arrived from Moscow) greeted the idea of a popular front by reiterating the incompatibility of capitalism and democracy, by repeating an analysis of fascism which made the international crisis merely the clash of rival imperialisms, and by denouncing any form of class collaboration which involved 'a suspension of socialist principles in the service of socialised liberalism'.[27] It was precisely such a 'suspension' which Cole advocated—not of socialist principles, however, but of immediate demands; and not in the service of a socialized liberalism but to serve the needs of an anti-fascist alliance. It was not an abrogation of socialism for, as Cole insisted, in the British political climate of the late 1930s the early achievement of socialism was simply not one of the alternatives. This being so, it behoved socialists to follow a course which would 'preserve a Britain capable of choosing freely between capitalism and Socialism, and a Europe in which British freedom will be a political possibility'.[28] Thus, not merely had Cole's thought assumed as international

---

[23] 'Chants of Progress', *Political Quarterly*, Dec. 1935. As yet there was 'no sufficient urgency to drive all the "progressives" to huddle together for warmth'. (ibid.)
[24] 'And What About England?', *New Statesman*, 13 June 1936.
[25] *The People's Front*, p. 15.
[26] 'The United Front—And The People's Front', *Labour Monthly*, Jan. 1937.
[27] H. J. Laski, 'Unity And The People's Front', *Labour Monthly*, Mar. 1937.
[28] *The People's Front*, p. 249.

dimension by the end of the 1930s but also, under the impact of fascism, had even given priority to the international situation in the formulation of domestic policy.

The war and post-war years provided ample reason for a continuation of this international preoccupation. If the defeat of fascism removed one area of concern, the development of the Cold War quickly supplied another—and one which raised in acute form the problem of the international role of democratic socialism. Indeed, this attempt to define an international policy for democratic socialism—above all, in relation to other forms of socialism—became a dominant concern of Cole's thought in its later stages.

The year 1939 has good claim to be regarded as the nadir of the social democratic tradition; the climax of a decade in which, in Europe, it had failed to organize effectively against fascism and in which, in Britain, it seemed to have developed into a conservative monolith unable to comprehend the urgent requirements of the international situation. In the years before 1939, Cole had struggled both within and outside this monolith for a popular front programme against fascism; yet by 1939 the struggle had been lost and the monolith had won. The arrival of war at least introduced a new flexibility into the international situation, and provided an opportunity for Cole to prescribe a new international policy for democratic socialism. He could regard the war itself as horrible confirmation of the sort of analysis he had been pressing throughout the decade and could locate its origins in the failure of the European powers (particularly Britain) to organize for resistance to fascist aggression at an early stage. The Nazi-Soviet pact was one terrible result of this failure, a fact which did much to explain, though not to justify, Soviet policy. The war also provided Cole with an emotional release (especially after the removal of Chamberlain), for it enabled fascism to be confronted openly and decisively—and in the name of democratic socialism. Just as he had earlier presented the case for a popular front in terms of the threat to an entire civilization posed by fascism, he could now support the war itself as, broadly, the defence of that civilization against the barbarians.

This position was clearly seen in Cole's pamphlet on *War Aims*, written in 1939, where he proclaimed his attachment to the value-system of Western civilization and indicted Soviet policy precisely because it was prepared to sacrifice that civilization, leaving in its place nothing 'except the smile on Stalin's face'.[29] Inevitably, Cole felt

[29] *War Aims, New Statesman* Pamphlet, 1939.

obliged to explain Stalin's position in terms of the latter's detachment from the Western liberal humanist tradition, which meant that we should not 'expect Stalin to concern himself about the preservation of our values, which are not his'.[30] These values were of deep concern to Cole, however, for as a liberal he wanted to preserve them and as a socialist he wanted to build upon them. In their defence he threw himself into the war effort, demanding a 'war socialism' which would mobilize the entire economy on a war footing and demanding of the wartime shop stewards' committees that they should demonstrate their capacity for industrial responsibility by making themselves the vanguard of productive efficiency.[31] When he advocated a policy of 'war socialism' both the war and socialism were to be the beneficiaries; indeed, their fates were indissolubly linked.

It was during the war that Cole revealed, in striking form, what his conception of a realistic international policy for democratic socialism involved. Above all, it involved a commitment to supra-nationalism. This marked a further development in Cole's own international position. It has already been noticed that his early insularity softened markedly under the impact of fascicm, with his embrace of an energetic internationalism. Yet if fascism was decisive in making him an internationalist, the effect of war was to convert internationalism into supra-nationalism. He could not regard this as a welcome or willing conversion, for he remained more comfortable within a familiar national perspective; yet it was presented as a conversion made inevitable by bitter European experience. The ultimate responsibility for a war which threatened the existence of an entire civilization was attributed to the system of independent and separate nation states. Cole now pronounced that system obsolete and insisted that the fundamental ingredient of the post-war settlement should be 'the entire abandonment of national sovereignty'.[32] It was typical of Cole that, having embraced a new principle, he should press its application with all the ruthless zeal of a convert. In this case, it meant a commitment to a post-war settlement in which a few great states were dominant—perhaps, ultimately, only one. In relation to Britain, this meant that she should become part of a West European political and economic union; and the Labour Party was charged with the task of ensuring that Britain did not contract out of the new Europe. It is true, however, that Cole made the success of this new European state

---

[30] Ibid.
[31] See *A Letter To A Shop Steward*, Fabian Society, 1942.
[32] *Europe, Russia and the Future*, 1941, p. 17.

dependent upon the acceptance of a common social and economic base (viz. socialism)—a condition which came to look increasingly unrealistic as the shape of the post-war world emerged; but this detracted little from his embrace of a supra-nationalism far removed from an earlier Little Englanderism.

Yet it was in relation to Russia and Eastern Europe that the real meaning of Cole's hostility to the nation state was seen most starkly. He recognized that Russia's rebuff of the Nazis would enable her to sweep across much of Europe, swallowing up many small states on the way. Unlike some social democrats, who would doubtless 'hold up their hands in holy horror'[33] at such a prospect, Cole would decisively welcome it. He regarded his personal distaste for Stalin and his works as quite irrelevant to the fact that Soviet communism was probably the only force 'capable of sweeping clean the stables of Eastern and Southern Europe'.[34] Indeed, he declared his readiness to 'go further' in this direction—and here it is necessary to quote at some length to capture the exact note in his position. He would:

much sooner see the Soviet Union, even with its policy unchanged, dominant over *all* Europe, including Great Britain, than see an attempt to restore the pre-war States to their futile and uncreative independence and their petty economic nationalism under capitalist domination. Much better be ruled by Stalin than by the restrictive and monopolistic cliques which dominate Western capitalism. Nay more: much better be ruled by Stalin than by a pack of half-hearted and half-witted Social Democrats who do not believe in Socialism, but do still believe in the 'independence' of their separate, obsolete national States....[35]

There was much more in the same vein from Cole, both during the war and afterwards, when he continued to defend Soviet hegemony in Eastern Europe both as a necessary response to the political facts of life of the area and as the price to be paid for international cooperation with the Soviet Union.[36] However, when the cumulating drama of his own prose carried him to an espousal of a Stalinist sweep through the whole of Europe in preference to a relapse into a tepid and parochial social democracy, he embraced a position which was effectively nullified by

[33] Ibid., p. 15.
[34] Ibid.
[35] Ibid., p. 16.
[36] In 1945 he declared that: 'the condition of our coming to terms with the Soviet Union is, as far as I can see, that we should stop talking poppycock about parliamentary democracy in the Balkans.' (*Welfare and Peace*, National Peace Council, 1945.)

the whole force of his general argument at this time. Nullified because redundant, for he had developed a method of social analysis which erected formidable barriers to a total supra-nationalism of any kind, not least to one under Stalinist auspices. Here it is necessary to return to the sort of relativist approach which (as seen in the last chapter) was basic to his conception of democratic socialism; and which had important implications for his analysis of the international scene.

Above all, it implied a particular treatment of the Soviet Union. This style of treatment had been glimpsed in Cole's discussion of Soviet experience in the 1930s; and it became central to his international argument during the war and post-war period. His starting-point was a belief in the essential unity of different forms of socialism (these differences being explained by the force of particular traditions, cultures and requirements); from which he concluded that it behoved Western socialists to regard with sympathetic tolerance the developing situation in the Soviet Union. While never disguising his own personal antipathy to Stalinism (which came to symbolize for him the horrible triumph of the class category over the individual), he refused to pretend that his own preferences counted for anything when compared with the force of the national imperative. There has already been occasion to notice the way in which he consistently located the more unpleasant features of Soviet communism in the brutal heritage of Russia's czarist past; a method of analysis designed not merely as an exercise in apologia but as an expression of a fundamental national and cultural relativism. Thus, his firm belief was that Soviet communism represented a necessary and appropriate form of government not merely for the Soviet Union itself but also for countries at similar stages of economic development and with similar types of social structure.

Hence Cole's willingness to see a Soviet solution imposed on Eastern Europe; and his constant emphasis on the absurdity of attempts to export the institutions of parliamentary democracy to countries where no natural roots for them existed. His analysis of Germany also reflected this same approach, for he documented the absence of a genuine liberal tradition in Germany which made it likely that 'there is, and can be for some time to come, no possible basis in Germany for a parliamentary regime'.[37] Instead, a Soviet-totalitarian system was suggested as more appropriate to German conditions, a suggestion which Cole decorated with remarks about a German temperament more inherently totalitarian than the Russian, the latter being

[37] *The Intelligent Man's Guide to the Post-War World*, 1947, p. 299.

redeemed by a strain of anarchism only disciplined by the importation of a *German* Marxism.[38] Whatever the merits of this sort of analysis, it is important to record that, in Cole's case, it was founded not merely upon a set of national prejudices (for example, a Vansittart-type belief in German barbarism), but was intended as a realistic response to the facts of national difference. Cole did not *like* Stalinism; did not *want* a totalitarian Germany: but a realistic relativism implied a recognition of their inescapability. At least, that was Cole's belief.

In the case of Russia, however, Cole felt able to state his case for realistic analysis on much stronger ground than that of mere national difference. He sought to explain to the social democratic left that Russia remained an essentially socialist society; and a society which, if it abrogated some liberal democratic values, decisively enlarged and realized others. On the former point, he rejected any suggestion that the Revolution had been 'betrayed' by the present leadership or that a 'new class' of bureaucratic exploiters had developed. In his view, it remained true to its Marxian origins while its internal policy had been 'consistently directed in the interests of the main body of the people'.[39] On the latter point, Cole partly relied on his cultural relativism to demonstrate the absence or devaluation of liberal democratic values in Russia (so that 'a police engaged in espionage causes no such revulsion of feeling in the Soviet Union as it would here; there is no such sentiment as we have against the State's officials opening private letters or studying private bank accounts ...'[40]); partly, too, on a formulation of democratic theory which refused to equate democracy with parliamentarism and which recognized the superiority of the sort of direct and continuous democracy of primary groups represented by the soviets. 'I regard the Soviet system as much more democratic than parliamentarism,' he wrote, 'and I advocate it for a large part of Europe as the most appropriate way of bringing real democracy to power.'[41]

This was the sort of realism which Cole was anxious to inject into the thinking of the social democratic left in Europe. It rested upon a belief in the fundamental unity of communism and social democracy, despite the differences enforced by culture and tradition which reflected themselves in a diversity of socialist method and machinery. In other words,

[38] See Ch. 13 ('Germany In The New Europe'), *Europe, Russia And The Future.*
[39] *The Intelligent Man's Guide to the Post-War World*, p. 799.
[40] Ibid., p. 286.
[41] 'Europe, Russia and the Future: A Reply', *Left News*, Mar. 1942. Cole described the 'doctrinaire "democrats" who mistake a system of parliamentary elections on a popular basis for the quintessence of democracy' as 'the worst enemies the socialist movement suffers from'. (Ibid.)

socialist advance—like all social change—had to be recognized as the essential product of the sort of social environment in which it took place. This recognition carried with it a responsibility for a fraternal tolerance within the international socialist movement. Cole had consistently (from 1917 onwards) urged just this recognition on Moscow; in the wartime and post-war period he pressed it on European social democracy. By emphasizing the possibility of a unity founded upon the acceptance of diversity, Cole hoped to heal what he regarded as the fatal and unnecessary division within international socialism. In pursuit of this end he proposed an application to the international field of 'that spirit of toleration of which Social Democrats make so much in its bearing on domestic political affairs'.[42] It would be a toleration which would accept the need to give a free hand to the Soviet Union in East Europe. For those socialists who thought this price too high, Cole recommended, and provided, a heavy dose of realism.

Thus when, during the war, he began to define a philosophy and programme for what he called 'liberal socialism', he was anxious to equip it with an international dimension. This was necessary, above all, because of the prospect of a post-war world divided up between the contending forces of American capitalism and Soviet communism. For liberal socialists, this prospect had little attraction. 'If America and Russia are henceforward to divide the empire of the world between them,' wrote Cole, 'a good many of us, within whichever sphere our lot may fall, will find ourselves subjected to a form of government with the basic assumptions of which we strongly disagree.'[43] His own response to this situation was to urge, consistently and emphatically, the construction of a 'third force' in Europe, which would offer a 'middle way' (these phrases recur in Cole's writing at this time) between the rigid ideological alternatives represented by the contending forces. In practical terms, this meant the construction of a West European political and economic union, with Britain and France as its nucleus, which would be powerful enough both to withstand dictation from America or Russia and to build a bridge between them. Such a union would form part of a wider conception of international zoning, which Cole embraced as involving both an abandonment of national sovereignty and a recognition of the existence of a number of natural cultural blocs.

In Cole's view, liberal socialism provided the only realistic foundation for a West European bloc, for it reconciled the need for socialism

---

[42] 'Socialism in the World of Tomorrow', *Aryan Path*, Jan. 1946.
[43] *The Intelligent Man's Guide to the Post-War World*, pp. 716–17.

with the maintenance of a traditional value-system, thereby combining
social freedom and social control in a form uniquely appropriate to a
particular civilization. This general conception informed Cole's
approach to foreign policy issues at this time. Wanting a Europe able to
act as the vanguard of world collaboration (and wanting a union of
socialist forces to make this possible), he attacked Labour's foreign
policy for its willingness to line Britain up behind the United States,
both politically and economically, in an anti-Soviet bloc. He demanded
a 'sharp disassociation of Britain from American foreign policy',[44] not
in order that British Labour could attach itself to the Soviet camp but so
that it could place itself at the head of a liberal socialist Europe. His
controversial opposition to the American Loan was one expression of
this conception.[45] As the shape of post-war Europe emerged, however,
his enthusiasm for a European union cooled sharply when it seemed
ever less likely to have a socialist basis and ever more likely to be
organized in the interests of a reactionary Catholicism and of a monopoly capitalism with close American affiliations. Yet ample cause
remained for a virile opposition to British foreign policy.

Much that was unsatisfactory in Cole's thought during this period
derived from the sort of international analysis described here. On some
points, his analysis was simply wrong—when, for example, he
announced the inevitable eclipse of the nation state as a consequence of
war, or when he presented fascism and socialism as the only possible
post-war alternatives. On other points, his thought revealed confusions, even contradictions. In relation to America, for example, he
was so anxious at one stage that Britain should achieve a close
economic relationship with America that he was even prepared to risk a
satellite status; whereas this was exactly the prospect which later
aroused his strenuous opposition.[46] In relation to the Soviet Union, too,
his enthusiasm for a political realism which would give a free hand to
the Soviet Union over much of Eastern Europe was matched by a
contrary indignation at the use made of this freedom.[47] In other
respects, he displayed a deficiency of judgement which almost

44 Ibid., p. 1031.
45 'The Loan, the Present and the Future', *New Statesman*, 5 Apr. 1947.
46 Cf. Cole's advocacy of economic union with America 'at almost any cost' (*Great Britain in the Post-War World*, 1942, p. 68) with his later opposition to 'a satellite Britain, held firmly in the clutches of American capitalism'. (*The Intelligent Man's Guide to the Post-War World*, p. 998.)
47 His enthusiasm has been noted; for his indignation, see his attack on the 'ruthlessness' of post-war Soviet action in eastern Europe and on the 'moral apostasy' of a West which acquiesced in it. (*The Intelligent Man's Guide to the Post-War World*, pp. 1088–90.)

amounted to a political innocence—in his assessment of the internal
development of the Soviet Union (its use of torture, its treatment of
nationalities, the distribution of power etc.), or in his easy anticipation
of a socialist Europe.

Much of the explanation for this sort of poor judgement was to be
found in the looseness of Cole's theoretical analysis. It is impossible to
be happy with a sweeping relativism which had the effect of relegating
much of Eastern and Southern Europe to the dustbin of history (or at
least to the dustbin of democracy and national independence). When it
was a relativism rooted in a realistic recognition of the facts of national
difference it had something to commend it; but when it was founded
upon a mere image of national character, sustained only by the flimsiest
evidence (as when Cole invoked the great Russian novels in demonstration of the essential anarchism of the Russian temperament) it
forfeited all credibility. Moreover, Cole continued to oscillate between
a historical and cultural relativism in relation to all theories and values
and an attachment to a stiff moral absolutism. As a result, it was often
unclear whether he meant to present a particular value as a mere
cultural preference, or whether he intended to endow it with a more
universal and fundamental significance. This lack of clarity probably
reflected Cole's own uncertainty about this; but it produced unfortunate consequences—for example, in his discussion of the status of
liberal freedoms in relation to the achievement of socialism.[48]

Cole's statement of democratic theory was also vulnerable.
So anxious was he to demonstrate the inadequacy of parliamentarism
from a democratic point of view that he tended to forget that this
demonstration alone was not enough to prove the democratic superiority of the Soviet system. Part of the explanation for this was his further
tendency to identify democracy with other states and conditions—
above all, with fellowship, with solidarity, with community—

---

[48] Even within the same book Cole declared that he was 'fully convinced that what matters most
is to eradicate the class system, even if the particular liberties by which I personally set most store
suffer severe damage in the process' (*Europe, Russia And The Future*, p. 17), while later defending a
liberal socialism with the declaration that: 'To repudiate, in the name of Socialism, the ethic
which alone can provide a foundation for the successful working of a Socialist society is a
monstrous heresy.' (Ibid., p. 183.) More generally, cf. the value relativism of his *Inaugural Lecture*
(1945), where he announced that he would not condemn the values of another society 'even if it is
not my "cup of tea"' (p. 11), with his presentation elsewhere, in the form of a personal credo, of a
set of values which were announced as 'good, in a thoroughly and finally objective sense . . . not
merely for us, at the present point in historical development, and not merely in relation to the
particular pattern of living which our civilization has worked out'. (*The Intelligent Man's Guide to the
Post-War World*, p. 38.)

which led him to contrast a passive Western atomism with an activist communal solidarity of the Soviet Union, the latter defined as an expression of an essential democracy.[49]

Finally, it is necessary to record that many of these difficulties in Cole's analysis reflected themselves in his statement of socialism, not least in its international aspects. Above all, he was wedded to a view of socialism as an essential unity, rooted in the acceptance of certain common ends and with differences confined to the level of means—and enjoined by the force of national circumstance. This view failed to recognize the possibility of the negation of ends by means, or to define the key ingredients of a socialist society. It was scarcely enough to embrace the conception of a number of socialisms, unless some real attempt was made to define the common denominator of such a plurality. In general, Cole contented himself with pleas for socialist unity, both domestically and internationally, even though this involved an acceptance of the essential brotherhood of Stalinism and 'liberal' socialism. At times, he seemed anxious to avoid this conclusion;[50] whereas, in fact, his own analysis had left him with no real alternative.

The immediate post-war environment soon dampened Cole's hopes for the creation of a democratic socialist 'third force' in Europe. In consequence, he moved into sharper opposition to official Labour on international policy. In a controversial article in 1951,[51] in which he tried to define a socialist attitude to the developing world situation, he announced his refusal to regard the Korean war as anything but a civil conflict (in which he hoped the North would win), his refusal to support American crusades in defence of reactionary regimes throughout the globe and his own support for China in any war into which Britain might be dragged as a result of American foreign policy. He continued to insist that the task for democratic socialism was to define an international role for itself which would not make it a tool either of the communists or the anti-communists, but which would represent an authentic expression of its own distinctive ideology. At the turn of the decade the prospects, both domestic and international, for a 'third force' of this kind were gloomy indeed. Thus Cole concluded a survey of

---

[49] Hence such statements as: 'But the existence of undemocratic elements in the Soviet Union does not mean that it is not, fundamentally, a democracy.' (*Great Britain in the Post-War World*, p. 113.) Cole's tendency to identify democracy with activity was reflected in his description of Soviet life as 'buzzingly companionable'. (*Fabian Socialism*, 1943, p. 134.)

[50] As in his statement that: 'Even if the totalitarian State is socialist in its basic economic institutions, it will degenerate into tyranny.' ('Leviathan and Little Groups', *Aryan Path*, Oct. 1941.)

[51] 'As A Socialist Sees It', *New Statesman*, 3 Feb. 1951.

half a century of socialist history by saying that, in 1951, he felt 'lonely and near despair in a world in which Socialist values as I understand them are being remorselessly crushed out between the two immense grinding-stones of Communist autocratic centralism and hysterical American worship of wealth and hugeness for their own sake and not as a means to that human fellowship which lies at the very foundation of the Socialist faith.'[52] In this situation, however, his response was not to retreat from internationalism, but to argue that democratic socialism could escape from its post-war impasse only by resolute international cooperation.

Indeed, it was Cole's acute sense of the post-war malaise of demo- cratic socialism and of his own theoretical isolation (charted in the last chapter) which, above all else, prompted his embrace, both practical and scholarly, of a vigorous internationalism during the 1950s. In terms of scholarship, it reflected itself in the writing of his *History of Socialist Thought*: in practical and political terms, in his initiation of the International Society for Socialist Studies (I.S.S.S.). There was, perhaps, a certain irony in view of the almost aggressive nationalism of his early years that it was Cole's 'wonderful spirit of Socialist inter- nationalism'[53] which tended, on his death, to be singled out as his chief bequest to the socialist movement. Naturally, it was his work in the 1950s which was cited as the evidence for assessments of this kind. In fact, as has been seen, an increasingly internationalist perspective can be detected in his thought from the moment, in the early 1930s, when fascism jolted him into a wider awareness. It continued into the immediate post-war world in the shape of his demand that British Labour should take the lead in the creation of a European 'third force' independent of the developing rival blocs.

This was a demand which Cole continued to press later, though in increasingly economic terms as the political development of Europe ceased to offer the prospect of a socialist majority.[54] He also pressed the

---

[52] *The Development of Socialism During the Past Fifty Years*, Webb Memorial Lecture 1951, Athlone Press, 1952.

[53] Julius Braunthal, introduction (p. xiii) to Cole's *A History Of Socialist Thought*, vol. V, 1960.

[54] See *Money, Trade and Investment*, 1954, where Cole suggested an economic partnership between Western Europe and the sterling area to escape American domination, and urged Britain to lead 'a crusade for independence' (p. 412) aimed at the creation of a 'viable "third economy"' (p. 414). Hence the seemingly safe assertion that Cole would 'certainly have been an anti-marketeer' (W. A. Robson, *Political Quarterly*, Jan.–March, 1972) may be wide of the mark. In fact, in 1957 he declared himself 'sceptical' whether the terms of British entry would be economically advan- tageous, though he was 'not unfriendly ... in principle' to the Market. (Letter to V. Dedijer, 18 Mar. 1957; in possession of Margaret Cole.)

need for socialists in Western Europe to disentangle themselves from Cold War containments. For Britain, this would involve a neutralist renunciation of the American alliance, support for liberation movements in all parts of the world and a commitment to *détente* and disarmament. By the mid 1950s, so distressed was Cole both at Labour's domestic timidity and its international inhibitions that he began to stake everything on the revival of a thoroughgoing socialist internationalism. In an article which prompted the formation of I.S.S.S. he wrote: 'I believe that we have reached a point at which there is no prospect of rescuing Socialism from its imprisonment within national frontiers ... except by re-creating an international Socialist movement, not as a federation of national parties, but rather as a crusade of a devoted minority in every country.'[55] Thus he envisaged a World Order of Socialists, whose members would put an international loyalty before their loyalties to their own national parties, thereby seeking to reconstruct democratic socialism on an essentially international basis. But what would such a crusade stand for?

It was Cole's answer to this question which raised a major and continuing problem in his thought. The intention was clear enough, however. The World Order (or I.S.S.S. as it became) was to provide a theoretical and organizational forum for the non-communist left; and a meeting-place for contacts and cooperation with the communists themselves. It was the last part of this enterprise which defined Cole's distinctive concern in this period and brought him into conflict with internationalists of a more restricted persuasion. Yet even his position (as will be seen) was not free from confusions and unresolved ambiguities. 'We must keep on trying to reach out across the iron curtain for means of re-establishing Socialist comradeship':[56] here was the sentiment which provided the framework for much of his activity in the hostile climate of the 1950s. He had consistently sought to 'reach out' in this way in the past, of course, and had agonized over the division within the international socialist movement which had produced such harmful consequences. In the post-war world, however, the division came to seem particularly serious from the standpoint of the non-communist left, which found itself entangled in an anti-communist alliance which ranged it on the side of reaction in so many areas of the world. In Cole's view, democratic socialism had 'allowed itself to be

---

[55] 'The Future of Socialism', II, *New Statesman*, 22 Jan. 1955.
[56] *Labour's Second Term*, Fabian Tract 273, 1949, p. 17.

temporarily diverted into an anti-communist blind alley'.[57] His own activity was designed to extricate it from this diversion and to set it on a more promising—and socialist—course. Clearly, it was an enterprise which raised issues fundamental to a theory of socialism. Above all, was it permissible to base a programme of action on the assumption that an international socialism really existed? Was there a World Socialism to be 're-stated'?

It is useful to sketch the essentials of Cole's approach to this problem as coherently as possible, before its difficulties are examined. In essence, he returned to a familiar social and cultural relativism in stating the case for socialist unity, in which 'Appropriateness is All' stood as his guiding motto. Comparing the philosophical foundations of communism and democratic socialism, he could attribute (and transcend) their differences to the fact that 'the two conceptions are related to two different kinds of society'.[58] One was appropriate to those advanced industrial societies with a heritage of liberal democracy; the other appropriate to those many societies lacking such conditions. Hence the former was constitutionalist and libertarian; the latter probably revolutionary and authoritarian. To deny all support to regimes of the latter type would be to countenance the preservation of reaction in many parts of the world. Once it was accepted that both communism and democratic socialism were essentially parochial doctrines then the way was cleared for fruitful socialist cooperation. This was the approach which always informed Cole's treatment of the Soviet Union: the correct stance was that of critical support. It was necessary for democratic socialists to attack many aspects of the Soviet regime, while embracing it as 'a great and glorious achievement'.[59]

Cole spelled out the implications of this approach for democratic socialists in Western Europe. They should pursue friendly cooperation with the communists, and support all liberalizing tendencies (as Cole did internationally with respect to Yugoslavia, and at home in his support for those dissident British Communists associated with *The Reasoner*). They should give unwavering support to the anti-imperialist movements in the developing world. Above all, they should refuse resolutely to take part in any anti-communist crusade or to denounce socialist regimes simply because of their abuses and imperfections. Moreover, all this could be done without any compromise of basic

[57] *World Socialism Restated*, New Statesman Pamphlet, 1956.
[58] 'What Is Socialism?', II, *Political Studies*, I, 1953.
[59] A *'History of Socialist Thought, Vol. IV. Pt. II: Communism and Social Democracy 1914–31*, 1958, p. 894.

democratic socialist principles. 'I hate the ruthlessness, the cruelty, and the centralised authoritarianism which are basic characteristics of Communist practice; and I do not intend to mince my words in attacking them,' wrote Cole, adding: 'But I also believe in the need for working-class unity as a necessary condition of the advance to Socialism.'[60] This was the position which he continued to uphold when events in Hungary dealt their severe blow to his larger hopes. He denounced the criminality of Soviet action in unequivocal terms; but refused to make it an excuse for anti-communist hysteria and continued to insist on the need to heal the breach in world socialism. At bottom, democratic socialists could ill afford to be self-righteous towards the communists, for 'if they have been helping to build what is, in certain respects, a badly perverted form of Socialism, we have hardly been building Socialism at all'.[61]

All this was a difficult and precarious position to sustain. To many sections of the non-communist left it smacked of Soviet apologetics and provided clear evidence that Cole 'never achieved an objective and detached position between Communism and Social Democracy'.[62] In fact, Cole's argument did possess a considerable and consistent backbone, as has been seen. At the same time, however, it was seriously flawed. Despite all his insistence on the essential unity of international socialism, he never made a critical attempt to define the content of this unity. Indeed, he failed to provide even a definition of socialism itself, suggesting at one point that it could be 'described and characterised, but not defined'.[63] He could define his *own* socialism, but if pressed for an essentialist definition could only point to the complex historical evidence contained in his *History of Socialist Thought*.

Did this mean that socialism was simply a matter of self-designation? Cole really provided no answer to this question, which

[60] *World Socialism Restated* (op. cit.). Similarly, Cole wrote: 'I, myself, am thoroughly anti-Stalinist, but I do not propose to spend all my time fighting Communism. I want to aim at something positive.' ('The Crisis in International Socialism', *The World Socialist*, Feb.–March, 1956.)

[61] 'World Socialism and the Hungarian Crisis', *The World Socialist*, Feb. 1957. Moreover, if the United States had made Hungary the occasion for war with the Soviet Union, Cole would have supported the latter, for 'in the last resort, I am on the side of Socialism against capitalism'. (idem.)

[62] R. H. S. Crossman, 'G. D. H. Cole and Socialism', *New Statesman*, 3 Sept. 1960. Cf. P. Shore, 'The World of G. D. H. Cole', *New Statesman*, 25 Aug., 1956. On Hungary, particularly, Cole's attitude seemed to combine 'a running apologetic for Russian imperialism with an attempt to play the game of "realpolitik"'. (M. Walzer, 'Hungary and the Failure of the Left', *Dissent*, spring 1957.)

[63] 'What Is Socialism?', II, *Political Studies*, I, 1953.

meant that his commitment to socialist unity seemed to lack any hard theoretical centre, a deficiency which his appeal to a cultural relativism could scarcely make good. At one point he did claim, almost as an aside, that public ownership and control were 'the quintessential conditions of a Socialist system',[64] but no attempt was made to say whether these were necessary or sufficient conditions—a critical omission, not least in someone who elsewhere asserted the possibility of a non-socialist succession to capitalism. All these problems were particularly apparent in Cole's treatment of the Soviet Union, which reads as an elaborate series of indictments and reprieves hemmed in by a multitude of equivocations and qualifications. One example will illustrate this. Cole convicted both Lenin and Stalin of a disregard for individuality and personal happiness in their treatment of the Revolution as an end in itself which made them 'guilty of sin against the spirit of humanity';[65] a judgement which was followed immediately by a tribute to their achievements in presiding over 'one of the very few great and admirable events in world history'.[66] Many similar examples of Cole's uneasy embrace of sins and sinners could be given.

What Cole's account lacked was any critical *socialist* analysis of the Soviet Union: his refusal to develop a working definition of socialism and his easy identification of socialism with the Soviet Union had deprived him of the sort of theoretical tools necessary for a task of this kind. Here, it has been suggested, was the real 'gap in Cole's armoury'.[67] Certainly it made his plea for socialist unity seem increasingly hollow, and his own position ever more isolated. By the end of his life, moreover, even he seemed to have accepted the irrevocable nature of the breach between communism and democratic socialism. It was a breach between 'a basic individualism which asserts, and a basic collectivism which denies, the priority of individual values. There is, and can be, no way of transcending this fundamental difference. . . .'[68]

Cole's historical account of socialism merely provided a depressing commentary on the division within international socialism, a division which had ensured the failure of the sort of reconciling position

---

[64] 'Reflections on the Past Twelve Months', MS, 1957; I.S.S.S. material, Cole Collection.

[65] *A History of Socialist Thought, Vol. IV, Pt. II: Communism and Social Democracy 1914–31*, 1958, p. 604.

[66] Idem.

[67] M. Beloff, 'G. D. H. Cole—Secular Saint?', *Encounter*, Feb. 1972. Beloff's attack on Cole is bitter and misguided, not least in its assertion that 'like the Webbs . . . Cole was prepared to take the Soviet presentation of Russia at its face value'. This is simply not true, as has been seen.

[68] *A History of Socialist Thought, Vol. V: Socialism and Fascism 1931–39*, 1960, p. 324.

(symbolized by the 'Two-and-a-Half' International) which Cole had sought to advance. He could do no more than write a retrospective obituary of the 'centre' in international socialism. In terms of prescription, all he could finally offer was a sad plea for peaceful coexistence. He had sought to redress the domestic malaise of democratic socialism through an internationalism which would transcend the internecine conflict of communism and social democracy. The difficulties and defects in his international position have been noted; and, by the end of his life, he was obliged to concede failure. He could only affirm his own conception of a distinctive socialist democracy: it was left to a later generation to attempt to give this conception an international expression.

XI

A Bit of a Puzzle?

Mr. G. D. H. Cole
  Is a bit of a puzzle,
  A curious role,
  That of G. D. H. Cole,
With a Bolshevik soul
  In a Fabian muzzle;
Mr. G. D. H. Cole
  Is a bit of a puzzle.

(M. B. Reckitt, *The Guildsman*, June 1919.)

SPEAKING ABOUT the Webbs in 1956, R. H. Tawney remarked that 'there is a sense in which the fact that they were socialists is less important than the kind of socialists they were'.[1] It is a suggestive remark, not merely in relation to the Webbs but also in its application to the wider socialist tradition. To attempt to organize the many varieties of socialist thought along a single axis (whether that axis is revolutionary and reformist, or Marxist and non-Marxist, or statist and pluralist) is to miss much. It misses the very real complexities of the socialist position, especially those complexities which derive from intellectual origins and cultural location. Evidence of this sort of complexity was noticed in Cole's own comprehensive account of the development of socialist thought, in which the division between communism and social democracy was found inadequate to encompass the antagonism between centralism and federalism. A similar complexity could be charted within British socialism, for in significant respects Owen, Morris, the Webbs, Tawney, Laski, Orwell, Strachey and Cole (to take just some leading examples) clearly represent different *kinds* of socialism, albeit within a single national and cultural tradition. To define their socialism adequately, or to locate it within a wider socialist framework, requires an exploration of intellectual origins and theoretical development which no simple taxonomy can provide. In Cole's case, this study has sought to assemble the materials for such an

[1] R. Terrill, *R. H. Tawney and His Times*, 1973, p. 216.

exercise in socialist 'location'. It should now be possible to say something about the *kind* of socialism that Cole represented.

At one level, his socialism seems only to represent a parade of paradoxes. Indeed, it is both remarkable and revealing that each stage in his intellectual development became the occasion for a new paradox: 'scientific utopianism', 'constitutional revolution', 'liberal socialism' and 'sensible extremism' are just a sample of these Cole inventions. What they reveal is a mind constantly struggling to forge a theoretical and practical compromise amongst seemingly divergent socialist positions. As a result, official Labourism found this enterprise (and its author) elusive and unreliable; while to the revolutionary left it seemed hopelessly eclectic and unsystematic. Thus William Mellor could present Cole as the central representative of a tendency which sought always to 'reconcile irreconcilables', evidence of a mind which was 'not nearly simple enough'.[2] In similar vein, Maurice Dobb could point to the lack of system, of completeness, in Cole's work: 'One feels stimulated to thought yet left with concepts which are vague and imperfectly defined ... and the final conclusions, in the desire to make them plausible, rather too eclectic to have a quite satisfactory ring.'[3] These are perceptive and acute criticisms. There has been frequent occasion in this study to notice the absence of definitional precision and analytical rigour in much of Cole's work: terms and concepts tend to float around within a framework which is only loosely organized. Partly, this simply reflects Cole's lack of attachment to the discipline of a systematic ideology; partly, too, his profound personal antipathy to philosophical niceties.[4]

Yet the failing is a real one, above all because it introduced considerable confusion into his statement of the socialist position. For example, he made democracy integral to socialism, but failed to explore critically its relationship to other ideas and values (liberty, individualism etc.); instead, such problems tended to be resolved by an easy definitional identification. Even the concept of socialism itself escaped critical analysis, which allowed him to proclaim the essential unity of all varieties of socialism but which prevented him from subjecting such varieties of thought and practice to critical or conceptual (as opposed to merely descriptive or historical) scrutiny. This con-

[2] W. Mellor, 'A Critique of Guild Socialism', *Labour Monthly*, Nov. 1921.

[3] M. Dobb, *Economic Journal*, June 1935.

[4] Cole announced it as his 'humble conviction' that 'high philosophy is all rubbish—failure to answer questions which are unanswerable because they are not real questions at all'. ('The New "New Atlantis"', *Fortnightly*, Nov. 1942.)

ceptual imprecision was compounded by his cultural relativism. However salutary this was in illuminating the necessary impact of different cultural patterns on forms of political and economic organization (and in preventing the sort of tension in Cole's thought between Marxism and liberal humanism which was so marked in Laski's), it did tend to suspend critical investigation in favour of a search for 'appropriateness'. It ensured, therefore, that Cole's thought was seriously flawed. It was often unclear whether he wanted to attribute some absolute status to an idea or value; or whether a mere cultural preference was intended. It seems that Cole himself was never clear about this for, in the space of a page, a universal value frequently found itself reduced to the rank of a limited cultural product. In general, it may be said that Cole failed to distinguish between a social-cultural and a logical-conceptual toleration, with the result that his thought exhibited the sort of 'sloppy pluralism' (producing 'an unselective, eclectic, unfastidious mishmash') against which Ernest Gellner has launched such a devastating attack.[5] Always, this sort of sloppy intellectual pluralism produced important tensions in Cole's treatment of ideological and political systems; at times, it even produced some shabby and sloppy apologetics.[6]

However, the real source of the untidiness in Cole's socialist thought lies elsewhere. Mellor was right: Cole's socialism was the distinctive product of a mind which was insufficiently simple. If it constantly reached out to embrace and reconcile competing positions, it was because it stood for too much rather than too little. Its search for compromise, its perennial attempt to forge a centre out of extremes, its paradoxical formulations: all this was the genuine expression of a complex socialism. It was both revolutionary and reformist; practical and utopian; individualist and collectivist; romantic and rationalist; centralist and localist; nationalist and internationalist. It embraced the spontaneity of will but stressed the need for research, preparation and organization; it stood for a democratic activism but also for disciplined and expert leadership; it claimed a historical sociology as the necessary basis for a comprehensive social theory but was itself ultimately normative. Consequently, it was full of internal tensions and ambiguities,

[5] E. Gellner, 'Myth, Ideology and Revolution', in B. Crick and W. A. Robson (eds.), *Protest and Discontent*, 1970.

[6] For example, when Cole, having documented Soviet coercion, warned against the 'deep error' of believing that the Soviet system 'must engender the same consequences as similar forms of government and coercion would involve among peoples reared in the traditions and practices of Western liberal democracy'. ('The Soviet Polity', *Soviet Studies*, ii, 1950–51.)

as it struggled over time to erect and maintain balance, synthesis and compromise. Here is the essential character of Cole's socialism, a character which enabled its balance and emphasis to shift in new directions at different periods (the spontaneous activism of the Guild period, for example, or the rationality of collectivist economic planning in the 1930s) but which never resolved its ambiguities, turned intellectual fragmentation into a tidy whole or transformed an uneasy synthesis into a disciplined theoretical system.

The problem was further complicated by Cole's tendency always to operate at two levels, though often without making clear which level was intended at a particular time. One level was that of the socialist end-state, the principles and problems of a mature socialist society; the other level was that of the here-and-now issues of the socialist means-state, the problems of strategy, policy and organization. Guild Socialism managed, temporarily, to fuse these two levels; but they necessarily reappeared after its collapse. Their existence distinguished (and confused) Cole's thought thereafter, for he wanted both to affirm his continuing allegiance to the essentials of the Guild position while also offering an analysis and programme directly relevant to the contemporary problems of the Labour movement. At times, he alternated between these two levels—not least in his discussion of industrial democracy—as though means and ends could *in fact* be separated in this way. The source of this dualism was a commitment on Cole's part to provide the Labour movement with relevant analysis and service as it confronted immediate problems in an ever-changing political and economic environment. Hence he was constantly ready to shift his emphasis (most notably, in the 1920s from workers' control to an anti-deflationary economics) in response to the pressure of circumstances; and was forever preoccupied with the appropriate 'next steps' in strategy and policy. It may be suggested that this self-imposed obligation to render useful and practical service to the Labour movement imposed severely inhibiting constraints on his activity as socialist theorist. Certainly this was the suggestive verdict of an old Guild Socialist colleague: 'The effort to interpret the policies of emancipation in terms that involve no loss of contact with the lumbering army of official Labour,' wrote Maurice Reckitt, 'has ... made it impossible for him to make the contributions to social synthesis which he might have made if his mind had not been circumscribed by the obligations of such a loyalty.'[7] Yet Cole felt it necessary to be circumscribed in this way,

[7] M. Reckitt, *As It Happened*, 1941, p. 124.

even though it guaranteed a train of frustrations. Wherefore the most elaborate theoretical construction (he might well have asked) if the 'lumbering army'—the agency and object of the whole enterprise—was nowhere in sight?

The complexity of ingredients in Cole's socialism makes it difficult to give it neat summary. The complexity is often missed by those who portray a shift of emphasis, a response to events, as evidence of more fundamental changes in Cole's socialism. This is the case, for instance, with that most familiar evaluation of his development in terms of a process of 'retreat from former Guild Socialist positions'.[8] In fact, both theoretically and organizationally, it is more accurate to portray a re-grouping than a retreat, involving an attempt to hold the line in hostile conditions. A similar tendency to seek to resolve the complexities within Cole's socialism is evident in recent interpretations of the development of his thought in the Guild period. One account depicts this development between 1913 and 1920 in terms of an inexorable evolution from militancy to moderation, involving especially the abrogation of a revolutionary 'economism' in favour of mainstream political action, so that by the early 1920s 'Cole's turn to the Webbian centre of socialist thought was complete'.[9] At the same time, however, another account of this same period discovers an equally dramatic movement in Cole's thinking—though in an exactly contrary direction. On this view, the movement was away from a conception of political action with the state at its centre towards an industrial theory rooted in a thoroughgoing pluralism, so that by 1920 'the political conquest of the state had become a mere residuum in his theory', with the role of political action 'reduced almost to vanishing point'.[10]

Each of these accounts is deficient for the same reason, which explains their ability to offer completely divergent interpretations of the same period based upon a common body of evidence. What each misses is the fact that the final direction of Cole's socialist thought was never 'resolved' in the way they suggest—not in 1913, or 1917, or 1922, or in 1952 for that matter. The real tensions and possible contradictions were

[8] K. Coates and T. Topham, *Workers' Control*, 1970, p. 274.
[9] J. M. Winter, *Socialism and the Challenge of War 1912–18*, 1974, p. 283. However, Winter himself seems confused about the development of Cole's thought. Thus he writes that 'the socialist position which he had begun to build before August 1914 was scarcely recognisable four years later' (p. 143); but later he argues that 'the case for guild socialism which he argued in the four years which followed the armistice varied only slightly from the one he presented in his earlier work'. (p. 281.)
[10] J. Hinton, 'G. D. H. Cole in the Stage Army of the Good', *Society for the Study of Labour History, Bulletin 28*, spring 1974.

always there: between militancy and moderation, between industrial and political action, between the state and pluralism—and much else besides. This may be regarded as an unsatisfactory situation, evidence of a lack of theoretical rigour, but there can be no escape from its recognition into the pretence of a 'final resolution'.[11] There was certainly change and development in Cole's thinking over time, as this study has attempted to show; but it has the character of movement within the framework of a single and durable socialist conception, however complex and untidy.

It is the nature of this socialist conception which indicates Cole's *kind* of socialism. Its essentials were established by the manner of his first contact with the socialist idea. 'Converted by reading Morris's utopia, I became an Utopian Socialist,' Cole recalled in 1951, 'and I suppose that is what I have been all my life since.'[12] In other words, he became a socialist 'on grounds of morals and decency and aesthetic sensibility';[13] and these were grounds which had little to do with Marxism or Fabianism, little to do with a theory of history or a doctrine of economic efficiency—and everything to do with a view of socialism as a transformation of social and human relationships, a new way of living. Initially, Cole found in creative literature, especially poetry, the most appropriate vehicle for the expression of this conception of socialism; certainly there seemed little need for arduous economic or political preoccupations. If he called himself a Fabian at this time, it was because there was no other natural organizational home for a young intellectual socialist. Yet the Fabianism of bureaucratic collectivism fitted uneasily with the conception of life under socialism glimpsed in Morris. A resolution of this tension was suggested by the syndicalism associated with the pre-1914 labour militancy; and then, more satisfactorily, by Guild Socialism. As Cole later described his position at this time, although his socialism had preceded his Guild Socialism 'the familiar brands of collectivist Socialism were somehow things one wanted for other people rather than for oneself' (in order to eradicate the deprivations and injustices of capitalism), whereas the Guild doc-

[11] Winter, for example, detects in Cole's 'abandonment' of Guild Socialism by 1922 'the final resolution of the tension between the militant and the moderate in his thought'. (Op. cit., pp. 282–3.)

[12] *British Labour Movement—Retrospect and Prospect*, Ralph Fox Memorial Lecture, Fabian Special, 1951, p. 4. Thus at the end of his life he could state simply that 'from the day when I first read *News From Nowhere* my socialist convictions have remained firmly fixed'. (*William Morris As A Socialist*, Lecture, 16 Jan. 1957, William Morris Society, 1960, p. 1.)

[13] Ibid., p. 4.

trine 'offered me a kind of Socialism that I could want as well as think right'.[14] Above all, this was because it represented a version of socialism which saw people 'as having personalities to be expressed as well as stomachs to be filled'.[15]

In essentials, Cole always remained a Guild Socialist; and remained the kind of socialist who was attracted to the Guild idea because it offered a practical approximation to the meaning of William Morris. In the lean years after the disintegration of the Guild movement, he was fully prepared to state the socialist argument in other terms (the relevancy consideration again), as his voluminous output between the wars amply demonstrates. Especially was it necessary to construct an economic case for socialism, by contrasting an endemic capitalist instability with the orderly rationality of socialist economic planning. It was also possible to situate this case within a loosely Marxist theory of historical development. At the same time, he was also prepared to tread cautiously with Guild Socialism, even to the extent of putting much of it into cold storage until the political and economic climate again proved favourable to a forward movement in the world of labour—a stance which has been described as 'an agonising lifetime of "Waiting for Godot"'[16]—and to contemplate weakly diluted versions of other aspects of it. However, even when he was presenting the socialist case in non-Guild terms, his argument (the appeal to efficiency, to abundance, to history) was designed only to construct a socialism which was likely to prove attractive to certain social groups (especially to sections of the 'new' middle class) rather than to give expression to the basis of his own socialism. As far as his own socialism was concerned, appeals of this kind were supplementary, an addition—even a bonus; but certainly not integral. Moreover, the essential Cole kept breaking through—to warn against a rigid determinism, to assert the motive power of human will, to expose the normative foundations of political and economic theory, to reject the notion of a science of society ('the deepest insult you can offer me is to call me a "social scientist"',[17]) and to emphasize the extent of the spiritual (rather than merely organizational) transformation involved in the transition to socialism.

[14] 'Guild Socialism Twenty Years Ago and Now', *New English Weekly*, Sept. 1934.
[15] Ibid.
[16] Coates and Topham (op. cit.), p. 39.
[17] 'Bernard Shaw', Lecture at W.E.A. Conference, Oxford, 1 Aug. 1954; MS in possession of Margaret Cole. Evidently Cole was decisive in the British formation of a Political *Studies* Association, unlike the *Science* elsewhere. (Information from Professor W. A. Robson, personal conversation, 8 Nov. 1972.)

All the ingredients that were detected in Cole's earliest formulation of the socialist idea persisted as the organizing concepts in his thought thereafter. Thus socialism remained as the triumph of an idea, not as the victory of a class or the culmination of history. It was simply one of many historical possibilities open to societies; for there could be other successors to capitalism—some known (fascism), some unknown (chaos). Socialism would come (if at all) and should be worked for as a normative impulse, not as a historical imperative. Marxism may be largely true or largely untrue; but ultimately the case for socialism rested on very different foundations. Here, then, was the real source and style of Cole's approach to social theory, though often obscured by the painstaking rationality of his economic and social analysis. This is not to suggest, however, that this analysis was ephemeral for, as has been argued, a good deal of it (the formulation of an economic recovery programme, the critique of fascism, the account of the changing class structure of advanced capitalism) was substantial and suggestive. Yet it is to suggest that the real source and meaning of his theoretical activity lay elsewhere. Asa Briggs has captured the essential Cole: 'He was the Enlightenment on the surface: the Romantic Movement underneath.'[18]

If the style and method of Cole's socialism exhibited this sort of consistency, so too did its content. There were some changes of course, especially at the level of strategy; and sometimes he came to doubt the possibility of elements within his socialism, though not their desirability. In general, however, his socialism retained a hard doctrinal centre. It found its most complete expression, of course, in Guild Socialism. It was a socialism which rested not upon a doctrine of economic efficiency, nor a theory of social justice, nor an economic egalitarianism, nor an analysis of history—but upon a view of power. The character of human relationships was seen as the product of the nature of power in society, polity and economy. Was the exercise of power democratic or autocratic? Was it remote or accessible? Was democracy narrowly political or genuinely social? Was it unitary or functional? The answers to these questions were consistently regarded by Cole as the key determinants of the character of social relationships. They would determine whether there was solidarity or division, willing service or compulsory labour, vitality or sterility, cooperation or competition, freedom or servility, distrust or fellowship. A socialism of this type would not only be sharply different from capitalism, but also from

[18] Asa Briggs, *Listener*, 20 Oct. 1960.

other varieties of socialism; for it would express an equality that was 'not a cold uniformity of rights and duties, but a warm fellowship of mind and habit'.[19]

Democracy, fellowship, community: these are the central terms in Cole's socialist vocabulary. Characteristically, they were given no clear definition, nor were they separated in any satisfactory way. Broadly, however, it may be said that 'fellowship' described the socialist form of social relationships; that 'democracy' described the nature of the exercise and distribution of social power necessary for fellowship; and that 'community' described both the character of the whole conception and denoted the tradition of social thought to which it belonged. Often the meanings were fused in Cole's presentation of them, for they hang together so closely in his statement of socialism. For example, when he wrote of democracy as 'a mental and moral relation of man to man'[20] or as 'a warm sense, not a mere recognition'[21] a deliberate fusion into a comprehensive 'democratic fellowship' was intended. Even so, an elucidation of the usage of these terms in the Cole vocabulary takes us to the heart of his socialist position.

The terms are familiar enough, of course, in the language of socialism; but, in some respects at least, Cole gave them a distinctive content and meaning. Fellowship, for example, as expressed in the sort of social relationships described in *News From Nowhere*, stood as the key socialist principle, from which other principles were derived. Hence it was different from, and superior to, the practical principle of social justice, which was ultimately 'far too quantitative'[22] to serve as the socialist essence. Fellowship *implied* social justice (and the other socialist principles), but the order of derivation was crucial. However, despite its moral basis, Cole (unlike Tawney, who also founded his socialism upon a conception of fellowship) presented this fellowship in a firmly secular idiom, rejecting any religious associations. Indeed, he was consistently hostile to religion of any kind, profoundly uninterested in the state of his soul, impatient with the spiritual introspection of people like Gandhi[23]—and adamant that a true socialist fellowship was ultimately

---

[19] Introduction to William Morris, *Stories in Prose and Verse* (ed. Cole), 1934.

[20] *The Intelligent Man's Guide to the Post-War World*, 1947, p. 38. This section of the book takes the form of a personal credo and is reprinted as 'What I Take For Granted' in *Essays in Social Theory*, 1950, for Cole says he cannot 'express better the articles of my social faith'.

[21] *Europe, Russia and the Future*, 1941, p. 158.

[22] 'Why I Am A Socialist', in *Economic Tracts For The Times*, 1932, p. 323.

[23] Of Gandhi, Cole asked: 'Why could he not stop thinking of his own soul, and lose himself in the things he was striving for?' ('Gandhi, The Man', *Aryan Path*, Jan. 1931.)

incompatible with a religious other-worldliness. It is sometimes suggested that Cole made fellowship central to his socialism because he found the business of actual personal fellowship so difficult. Yet that is too simple. What is true, however, is that he constantly looked to the internal life of the small socialist groups and organizations (whose formation he always found so compulsive) in which he was involved for a foretaste of that life of fellowship to be expected in a mature socialist society. It is possible, of course, that this expectation was itself hopelessly unrealistic, that it sought in politics solutions to problems and conditions which were not fundamentally political, and that it evidenced a romantic style of politics which, as Irving Howe has elegantly argued,[24] carried with it dangerous and disillusioning consequences.

Yet Cole's conception of fellowship was not suspended in a moral vacuum. Here it differed markedly from much of the 'ethical' socialism of the British left (associated with the I.L.P. tradition) which found it difficult to relate its conception of life under socialism to the needs of a political programme—and which, therefore, tended to look on impotently as these needs were met by 'practical men' who did not share the initial conception. So, too, with Tawney, who developed a powerful and coherent moral position but which, because not rooted in an equally coherent strategy and programme for its attainment, tended to lead a free-floating existence with the result that he became, as his biographer says (without irony), the only British socialist thinker of this century who could be 'saluted from every quarter'.[25] By contrast, Cole's socialism of fellowship was firmly rooted in a theory of democracy which involved a fundamental reorganization of power relationships throughout society and economy. Guild Socialism stood as the most complete sketch of what such a reorganization might look like, with 'self-government in industry' as its cornerstone. It was a democratic theory which contained a deep antipathy to the formal machinery of parliamentary democracy and which sought to explore new organizational forms. Furthermore, it was a democratic theory which had a conception of participation and its benefits at its centre: democracy was *activity*, the natural expression of the cooperative impulse of human will. In these respects, too, Cole's fellowship was built upon very different foundations from that of the 'ethical' left, including Tawney, who tended to accept the established machinery of British parliamentary govern-

---

[24] I. Howe, 'What's The Trouble', *Dissent*, Oct. 1971. Howe has an interesting discussion on the 'confusion of realms' which he detects in much radical politics.

[25] Terrill, op. cit., p. 277.

ment and showed little inclination to oppose its passive implications with a theory of democratic participation or socialist citizenship.[26]

Finally, Cole's conception of democratic fellowship has to be located within a community tradition of social thought. It was a conception which found its earliest, and most durable, expression in the political philosophy of Rousseau. It was reflected in Cole's hostility to doctrines of state sovereignty and to mechanistic explanations of social origins and development. It explains his embrace of a solidaristic 'commonwealth' as the setting within which social institutions exist; and helps to explain his cultural nationalism. It involved a belief that there existed in society 'a sufficient foundation of community'[27] upon which a society of fellowship could be built, an approach which made him sympathetic to elements in conservative social thought. Above all, Cole's attachment to a community conception of this kind explains the 'conflict-equilibrium model'[28] which has been noticed as a central feature (and paradox) of his socialist thought. Conflict was necessary to remove the obstacles erected by capitalist autocracy to real community. Cole's eyes were not fixed upon a future of tranquil harmony, for that was an insufficiently vital and active prospect; but they did envisage the actualization of a community consciousness that was already latent and partial. Of course, a position of this kind necessarily introduced tension and paradox into Cole's socialist argument, as was seen in the context of Guild Socialism. For example, it caused him to waver between a thoroughgoing pluralism and the retention of a central organ of community control. It also caused him to *assume* that the establishment of democratic machinery throughout society and the economy would integrate rather than separate, would promote community rather than impede it. Furthermore, Cole's thought has to be set in the whole context of the tension between community and organization in modern social thought (as described by Wolin, for example[29]); for, seeking himself to embrace at least some of the arguments and positions of the organizationalists, his thought came to reflect many of the tensions within this wider tradition.

[26] Tawney 'did not question the viability of parliament, the civil service, or the parties'. (ibid., p. 244), nor did he have 'any special attachment to participation for its own sake'. (p. 181.)

[27] 'Why I Am A Socialist', in *Economic Tracts For The Times*, p. 325. The affinity with this aspect of conservative thought was recognized in Cole's sympathetic treatment of Burke and Coleridge—and even of Filmer's patriarchalism, for 'the least silly part of it is the resemblance drawn between society and the family'. (*Politics and Literature*, 1929, p. 47.)

[28] J. M. Winter, op. cit., p. 109.

[29] S. Wolin, *Politics and Vision*, 1961, ch. 10.

If we are to get at Cole's *kind* of socialism, it remains to identify one other important characteristic of his thought. This may be described as a radical individualism; indeed, it was his own self-description.[30] Here, too, the complexity—the peculiar 'mix'—of his theoretical position is suggested; for, on the one hand, his radicalism derived naturally from that view of power which produced his democratic theory while, on the other hand, his individualism often sat uneasily alongside his commitment to community. Yet if we seek to locate Cole within an intellectual tradition, it is a tradition staffed overwhelmingly by radical individualists. It contains Morris and Whitman, Cobbett and Paine, Belloc and Chesterton: it involves an attack on privilege, a claim to power, a defence of diversity, a pricking of pomposity and a suspicion of experts. Cole explicitly wanted to locate himself within this sort of untidy tradition. Of course, he also wanted to associate himself with other people and other traditions—with Owen, for example, or with Marxism (though Marx was 'more appropriate to wear ... near the brain than the heart'[31])—but his intellectual lineage was clear. He belonged to a radical tradition which fed into socialism. Indeed, he criticized those accounts of the development of socialism which neglected its radical ingredients; and explicitly brought these ingredients under the wing of socialism in his own account of this development.[32]

Moreover, the acid test of radicalism ultimately separated those socialists and varieties of socialism that Cole found congenial from those he found distasteful. It was a test which always saved him from the Fabian embrace, for: 'what was wrong with the Fabians—Shaw, Webb and all—was that they were not Radicals, though they were, no doubt, Socialists of a sort.'[33] It was also a test which conditioned his personal response to figures as different as Lenin and Beveridge, for—however admirable and necessary the work of such men—they were flawed by

[30] Cole wrote: 'I am a radical individualist as well as a socialist; and I am convinced that the Labour Party, if it forgets its radicalism, will speedily lay aside its socialism as well.' ('The Dream and the Business', *Political Quarterly*, July–Sept. 1949.)

[31] 'My Books', *Swinton and Pendlebury Public Libraries Bulletin*, Jan. 1935. Cole here lists the authors 'nearest his heart': the list includes Cobbett, Defoe, Butler, Owen, Bentham, Rousseau, Morris, Whitman and Peacock—a truly mixed bag.

[32] Cole attacked Alexander Gray's, *The Socialist Tradition*, for its neglect of a radicalism which 'flows into the Socialist tradition fully as much as the programme of public ownership of the means of production, distribution and exchange'. ('British Radicals and the Socialist Tradition', *Phoenix Quarterly*, autumn 1946.) Cole's own *History of Socialist Thought* gave ample space to the representatives of radicalism. To Cobbett, in particular, Cole's work was decisive in giving 'a central role in the rise of the British working classes'. (M. J. Wiener, 'The Changing Image of William Cobbett', *Journal of British Studies*, xiii, 1974.)

[33] 'Bernard Shaw' (op. cit.).

their attachment to bigness, power and bureaucracy.[34] If Cole's radicalism saved him from both the Fabian and the Bolshevik embrace (this is the real solution to Reckitt's 'puzzle'), it also produced a passionate hostility to the aristocratic embrace. Socialism did not mix with a divine aristocracy or with a terrestrial one: rather, it was quintessentially both atheist and republican. The virulence of his attack on Attlee's acceptance of an earldom[35] provided just one striking instance of an attitude never far from the surface of his thought, as did his resolute (and conspicuous) refusal to take part in the royalist pantomime of anthems and toasts. He refused to regard such matters as peripheral; for they were important in defining the kind of socialism that was at issue. His own kind (he jested) would allow him to go to the House of Lords only as Lord Water of Closet. Here, then, is another integral aspect of the essential Cole: he was the product and perpetuator of a British radical tradition which incorporated Old Dissent and waged war on The Thing.

Yet if all this reveals something about the content of Cole's socialism, it leaves wide open the problem of method and agency for its achievement. This was a problem with which Cole's thought had constantly to grapple, often uneasily, as this study has sought to show. The problem was obscured during the Guild Socialist period by an encroachment strategy which had the trade unions at its centre (though even then this sort of economism found a residual role for political action); but became acute as soon as the changed conditions of the 1920s demonstrably prevented trade unionism from acting as a socialist instrument of this kind. Having refused to take up the revolutionary option offered by the foundation of the British Communist Party, and having been forced to abandon the prospect of a revolutionary trade unionism, Cole found himself necessarily drawn into the orbit of parliamentary Labourism. In other words, a rigid and revolutionary conception of socialist ends came to co-exist with a flexible and reformist approach to socialist means. He was a revolutionary who wanted to avoid revolution; a reformer who was not a reformist; and a parliamentary socialist who

[34] Cole thought that Lenin 'believed in bigness and power, not only as means of saving the Revolution, but as essential elements in the Revolution itself'. ('The Bolshevik Revolution', *Soviet Studies*, Vol. IV, 1952–3.) With Beveridge, Cole 'always reacted against his way of treating men in the mass too much as sets of lay figures to be moved around, and too little as capable of doing things for themselves in their own way. I dislike bureaucracy: I think Beveridge loves it. . . .' (*New Statesman*, 21 Nov. 1953.)

[35] Cole wrote that he 'used to have some respect for Mr. Attlee; but he forfeited it all when he became an Earl and a Knight of the Garter. How on earth could he wish to be degraded in these ways?' (*World Socialism Restated*, *New Statesman* Pamphlet, 1956.)

had little liking for, or belief in, parliamentarism. It was a position guaranteed to produce a multitude of tensions and frustrations.

In one sense, of course, all this may simply be evidence of Cole's failure to solve the problem of socialist means. Indeed, it has been suggested that he 'could never quite discover where *he* fitted into the scheme of things', above all because he lacked that 'world-historic arrogance of the intellectuals'[36] which would have armed him with a conception of intellectual leadership within a revolutionary party. Criticism of this kind does capture an important aspect of Cole, for—while completely free of the sort of idealization of the manual working class characteristic of some intellectual socialists—he did hold a consistently deferential view of the role of intellectuals, both individually and in groups, in relation to the organized Labour movement. During the Guild period this view reflected itself as a belief in a working-class spontaneity which intellectuals could do no more than rationalize and express; even much later intellectuals were still conceived as performing only a servicing function in relation to the working-class movement. Hence Cole formed close attachment to Labour leaders who seemed willing to be serviced in this way (Arthur Henderson, especially); was ever hopeful about the potential capacity for socialist leadership of other Labour figures (for example, Ernest Bevin at one stage); and was always forming small groups of intellectual socialists to 'influence' the official Labour movement whilst studiously avoiding any tendency to lead such groups in directions liable to bring them into policy and organizational antagonism to the official movement (hence his formation of the S.S.I.P. but subsequent break with the Socialist League). It is possible, of course, that this sort of deliberate humility was founded upon a realistic assessment of the terms and conditions upon which socialist intellectuals could exercise *any* influence on the political and industrial organizations of the working class; but this did nothing to diminish the frictions of an essentially uneasy relationship.

Cole's stance of critical loyalty seemed elusive and unreliable from the point of view of official Labour, while to the revolutionary left it meant that Cole resided in an ineffectual wilderness,

singularly like one of these ancient Hebrew prophets who in the Biblical narrative keep popping up to rebuke and denounce wicked kings, false prophets, backsliders and idolators (such as the throng in parliament that

[36] J. Hinton (op. cit.).

worship the Golden Calf); and who then retire for a season amongst their disciples until the spirit drives them forth again. They horrify the misleaders: but they disappoint the people who are looking for a consistent and continuous lead in struggle.[37]

Yet if Cole's position was difficult, it did represent a practical compromise based upon a number of important considerations. On the one hand, he was distanced from Labour by his revolutionary conception of socialist ends and by his determination to advance rapidly towards them. Furthermore, he had developed an analysis (in the wake of 1931, though it still seems penetrating) of the dilemmas of gradualism—of a mere interventionism which weakened capitalism without replacing it—which carried with it a programme of frontal and simultaneous attack on the citadels of capitalism (and its political machinery) which went beyond anything contemplated by official Labour. On the other hand, however, there were different, and ultimately more powerful, considerations pushing Cole towards Labourism and away from the revolutionary alternative. Above all, there was the belief that in a society like Britain, at least in any foreseeable future, there *was* no revolutionary alternative. This belief was affirmed at the time of the pre-1914 industrial militancy, at the time of the formation of the Communist Party, in the context of the General Strike, during the 1930s—indeed, throughout. It was buttressed by a continuing analysis of the class complexity and economic structure of societies of the British type. Cole was not 'opposed' to revolution (for he often announced the probability of a revolutionary moment at some stage in the transition to socialism), but he did oppose the futilities of a socialist strategy that focused on this revolutionary moment at the expense of concrete and immediate socialist policy. If Cole discovered the dilemmas of gradualism, he also accepted its necessity.

Moreover, Cole *wanted* a radical gradualism to succeed. He wanted it to prove effective in providing solutions to urgent economic problems; and he wanted it to accomplish as much as possible of the socialist transition. Partly, this was a reflection of his own consistent desire to contribute to the solution of contemporary social and economic problems (the relevancy imperative again). More centrally, however, it was a response to his conception of socialism as the product and extension (not negation) of an existing civilization rooted in the values of liberal humanism, a tradition which it would be 'folly to fling ... away or ...

---

[37] R. P. Arnot, 'A Memoir of G. D. H. Cole', *Labour Monthly*, Feb. 1959.

allow ... to be destroyed'.[38] In a basic sense, he liked the civilization against which he aimed his socialist attacks; and liked particularly his own national version of this civilization—as eulogized in a beautiful passage from Morris on the essence of England that he enjoyed quoting.[39] What this meant was that if there was a non-revolutionary road to socialism, involving a minimum of transitional dislocation and the avoidance of a lapse into chaos which would put civilization itself at risk, then such a road should be taken—even if, ultimately, it might not lead the whole way. Yet, as has been seen, Cole's cultural relativism (and, perhaps, a consciousness of the utopian origins of his own socialism) led him to cultivate a deliberate 'realism' about the sorts of disciplined revolutionary methods necessary for the achievement of socialism in less fortunate societies, an aspect of his thought which was always central to his analysis of the Soviet Union but which popped up in many other contexts too—and which, in its crude form, may be rightly criticized.[40] In terms of his own society, however, he accepted both the necessity and desirability of a gradualist strategy.

It was an isolated stance. It was the stance of the non-communist left, the Centre within international socialism, which had been rendered homeless by the split inside the international movement between a revolutionary communism and reformist social democracy—a split which, for Cole, had coincided with the collapse of Guild Socialism. Cole belonged to a Centre which found itself squeezed by the battle of the rival Internationals, unable to accept either the rigid authoritarianism of Comintern policy or the narrowing reformism of parliamentary social democracy, forced further towards reformism than it really wanted to go because of its exclusion from the revolutionary camp, attacked from both sides, its activities always conditioned by the behaviour of the warring leviathans—and reduced everywhere to the role of an ineffectual minority. It was non-communist but not anti-communist; and spent much of its time in a fruitless search for socialist unity. It was, as Cole described his own case, 'a somewhat isolated position, which I have been able to endure the less uncomfortably

[38] 'Western Civilisation and the Rights of the Individual', in *Essays in Social Theory*, 1950, p. 156.

[39] See *Politics and Literature*, 1929, p. 22. Cole says that 'no one ever praised England more to my mind than Morris'. (idem.)

[40] For example, he condemned the lack of realism of the anarchists in Spain during the Civil War, despite his sympathy with their theoretical position. Similarly, despite his dislike of Leninist centralism he agreed that the revolution in Russia would probably not have been saved 'if the libertarians had had their way'. (*Soviet Studies*, Vol: IV, 1952–3.) Hence Beloff could charge Cole with exhibiting 'that kind of insularity which neither expects other countries to enjoy the advantages of one's own, nor feels sympathy for their peoples if they do not'. (*Encounter*, Feb. 1972.)

because I have never allowed myself to become an active participant in politics.'[41] It was a position which, firm in its conception of socialist ends, was flexible in its attitude to socialist means, refusing to regard either revolutionism or parliamentarism as universally applicable (or even mutually exclusive) strategies. When, near the end of his life, Cole described himself as still 'more a revolutionary than a reformist'[42] he accurately identified the nature and isolation of this position. So too, from the distinctive perspective of a Communist ex-Guildsman, did R. P. Arnot: 'Nobody could bet on Cole to be a consistent Right-winger. His daemon forbade it.'[43] Hence the 'Bolshevik soul in a Fabian muzzle', a description which accurately describes neither the soul nor the muzzle but which nevertheless captures this aspect of Cole's complexity.

At the time of his death in 1959, Cole seemed like a survivor from a past age of different concerns, certainly old-fashioned and probably obsolete. The anonymous reviewer of the *Times Literary Supplement* caught this contemporary mood as he asked: 'did Cole ever really come to terms with the age of mass-production, automation and the bomb?'[44] Technological determinism was everywhere, the Cold War had intensified the division within international socialism, the British left seemed theoretically bankrupt, and the demand for industrial democracy was buried beneath both a practical economic meliorism and an influential doctrine (associated particularly with Hugh Clegg) which defined an existing trade unionism, negative and oppositional, as itself the true form of industrial democracy. Within a decade, however, much of this had changed. A new activism in society (symbolized, in France, by the events of May 1968) was paralleled by a new control-minded militancy in industry (symbolized, in Britain, by the work-in at Upper Clyde Shipbuilders). The demand was for 'participation' in society and 'democracy' in industry, terms which were both loosely defined and momentous in their implications.

Moreover, the demand was now seen to involve a departure from the twin monoliths of official communism and parliamentary social democracy. Indeed, important contributions to the developing discussion of

[41] *A History of Socialist Thought, Vol. IV, Pt. II: Communism and Social Democracy 1914–31*, 1958, p. 850. A. J. P. Taylor has described Cole as 'the only Left figure never tinged with communism and yet equally free from anti-communism'. ('A Bolshevik Soul in a Fabian Muzzle', *New Statesman*, 1 Oct. 1971.)

[42] *World Socialism Restated*, op. cit., p. 7.

[43] Arnot, op. cit.

[44] 'The Twilight of Socialism', *Times Literary Supplement*, 5 Aug. 1960.

socialist democracy came from within the Soviet Union itself.[45] The new industrial climate was reminiscent of that situation at the close of the First World War which had ushered in Whitleyism as the official response. It could again be announced that 'we are all industrial democrats now!'[46] Suddenly all the concerns (and even the vocabulary) of Cole and the Guild Socialists came flooding back. As events in the world of labour seemed to suggest new socialist possibilities, there again arose those, like Cole in 1913, ready to service and give content to this new movement. The work of the Institute for Workers' Control and its associates may be seen in this light—as may the critique of this work from the revolutionary left: both bear a striking similarity to the arguments of the Guild Socialist period.[47] At the same time, there has been renewed academic attention to democratic theory and to the issues of participation and alienation. Much of this discussion has been conducted within an explicitly Guild Socialist frame of reference, seeking (and finding) empirical support for a range of propositions (about the possibilities and effects of participation) that Cole could merely state.[48] Indeed, the ideas of Guild Socialism have been judged as still possessing 'extraordinary relevance to discussions of some of the central social issues of our day, such as work alienation, political and social pluralism, and the meaning of democracy.'[49]

What, finally, does Cole contribute to this discussion? He offers a complex inheritance. He offers an approach which is both encyclopaedic and normative. 'A prolific and repetitive writer, he was always in search of new ways of expressing the essential unity of all branches of social study and of finding practical ways in which social

[45] Notably from Roy Medvedev, who argued that the problem of the relationship between Marxism and democracy was the 'real gap in our theory', which a socialist pluralism should fill. (*On Socialist Democracy*, 1975, p. xx.)

[46] K. Coates and T. Topham, *The New Unionism*, 1974 (Penguin edn.) p. 44.

[47] As examples of the work of the Institute for Workers' Control, see Coates and Topham (op. cit.) and M. Barratt Brown, *From Labourism to Socialism*, 1972. For criticism of this work for its 'perilous ambiguity', cf. R. Hyman, 'Workers' Control and Revolutionary Theory', in *Socialist Register*, 1974 (ed. R. Miliband and J. Saville).

[48] See C. Pateman, *Participation and Democratic Theory*, 1970, and P. Blumberg, *Industrial Democracy: The Sociology of Participation*, 1968. Pateman suggests that 'the evidence supports the arguments of Rousseau, Mill and Cole that we do learn to participate by participating ...' (p. 105); and that 'it is the non-participatory role of the ordinary man in the workplace that is a major influence on his whole view of the world'. ('Political Culture, Political Structure and Political Change', *British Journal of Political Science*, Vol. 1, July 1971.)

[49] Blumberg, op. cit., p. 194. Blumberg also discusses Yugoslav self-management within an explicitly Guild Socialist frame of reference (pp. 194–5); and writes that: 'it is not to Lenin, nor to Marx or Engels that the Yugoslavs have turned in the reconstruction of their society. It is really to the kinds of ideas advanced by the English Guild Socialists....' (P. 193.)

knowledge could be applied to good purpose':[50] this is Cole on J. A. Hobson, but it is also pure self-description. The goal was the good life; the means was a comprehensive social study. It was always better to be an 'untidy social moralist'[51] than a spuriously scientific specialist; better, too, for a socialist finally to be a utopian—for, in Kolakowski's words, 'the Left cannot do without a utopia'.[52] Moreover, Cole's approach was rooted in a particular cultural tradition, a tradition 'dosed with eclecticism' as E. P. Thompson has brilliantly described it,[53] which (to follow Thompson) gave to its intellectual products a distinctively English idiom and rooted them in a highly provincial pantheon. As has been seen, Cole was happy to locate himself within a tradition of this kind—and sought both to respond to it and to prescribe for it.

Above all, Cole sought to define a conception of socialist ends appropriate to a particular sort of culture and society (democratic fellowship) and an equally appropriate conception of socialist means (a sensible extremism). Representing in himself a complex unity forged out of the diverse strands within the British radical and socialist tradition, he wanted to weld that tradition to a theory and practice of libertarian, democratic socialism. If it is true (as it is) that, historically, 'democracy for British Socialists has been a second order problem',[54] it is equally true that, but for Cole, it would scarcely have remained on the agenda at all. Similarly, if it is true (as again it is) that in seeking to relate a theory of industrial democracy to a wider theory of social self-management we are dealing with 'a theory in the making',[55] then Cole's conception of a socialist democracy which neither stops at the factory gate nor at the factory exit would seem to offer an important contribution to this 'making'. He gave final expression to this conception in the form of a personal credo at the end of his *History of Socialist*

[50] 'J. A. Hobson', *New Statesman*, 5 July 1958.

[51] *Socialist Economics*, 1950, p. 9.

[52] L. Kolakowski, *Marxism and Beyond*, 1969, p. 91. Cf. Z. Bauman, *Socialism: The Active Utopia*, 1976.

[53] E. P. Thompson, 'An Open Letter to Leszek Kolakowski', *Socialist Register*, 1973 (ed. Miliband and Saville), p. 24.

[54] G. Radice, 'Extending Democracy', in B. Lapping and G. Radice (eds.), *More Power To The People*, Young Fabian Essays, 1968, p. 5.

[55] M. Hirszowicz, 'Industrial Democracy, Self-Management and Social Control of Production', in L. Kolakowski and S. Hampshire (eds.), *The Socialist Idea*, 1974, p. 216. Hirszowicz adds (p. 198): 'It is to the credit of the New Left that they try to discuss the concept of industrial democracy in the wider context of participative democracy: the ideas promoted once upon a time by J. J. Rousseau, J. S. Mill and later on by G. D. H. Cole seem to re-emerge from oblivion as a new device in social and political theory.'

Thought: 'I am neither a Communist nor a Social Democrat,' he wrote, 'because I regard both as creeds of centralisation and bureaucracy, whereas I feel sure that a Socialist society that is to be true to its equalitarian principles of human brotherhood must rest on the widest possible diffusion of power and responsibility, so as to enlist the active participation of as many as possible of its citizens in the tasks of democratic self-government.'[56]

[56] *A History of Socialist Thought, Vol. V: Socialism and Fascism 1931–39*, 1960, p. 337. Commenting on this passage, Peter Sedgwick has said that at the time it was written—and for a long time previously—it could be 'no more than a solitary confession of faith, from a maverick thinker'; whereas now it could be 'inscribed on a banner to which tens of thousands of young Socialists ... would willingly rally' for 'systematic Socialist debate takes place today *within* the boundaries of rejection defined by Cole'. ('Varieties of Socialist Thought', in *Protest and Discontent* (ed. Crick and Robson), 1970, pp. 37–8.)

A select bibliography of the works of G. D. H. Cole

This list is necessarily selective; for a comprehensive bibliography would require a separate volume. All Cole's books are included, except the detective stories. The selection of articles and pamphlets is designed to illustrate the nature of his socialist thought and its shifting concerns over time. Much contemporary journalism, and explicitly educational or historical writing, is therefore excluded; along with his many study guides, syllabuses and reviews.

(A) BOOKS

1910   *Poems.*

1913   (ed.) *Oxford Poetry 1910–13.*
       (ed.) J. J. Rousseau: *The Social Contract and Discourses.*
       The World of Labour.

1914   *New Beginnings and The Record.*
       (ed.) *Oxford Poetry 1914.*

1915   *Labour in Wartime.*
       (ed.) *Oxford Poetry 1915.*

1917   *Self-Government in Industry.*
       Trade Unionism on the Railways (with R. P. Arnot).

1918   *An Introduction to Trade Unionism.*
       The Payment of Wages.
       Labour in the Commonwealth.

1919   (ed.) G. Renard: *Guilds in the Middle Ages.*

1920   *Social Theory.*
       Guild Socialism Re-stated.
       Chaos and Order in Industry.

1921   *The Future of Local Government.*
       (ed.) *The Bolo Book* (with M. Cole).

1922   (ed.) T. Hodgskin: *Labour Defended.*

1923   *Out of Work.*
       Rents, Rings and Houses (with M. Cole).
       Workshop Organisation.
       Labour in the Coal-Mining Industry.
       Trade Unionism and Munitions.

1924 *Organised Labour.*
      The Life of William Cobbett.
1925 *Robert Owen.*
      Short History of the British Working Class Movement, Vol. I.
1926 *Short History of the British Working Class Movement*, Vol. II.
1927 *Short History of the British Working Class Movement*, Vol. III (All three vols.
      published in single volume in 1932 and subsequently).
      (ed.) William Cobbett: *Life and Adventures of Peter Porcupine.*
      (ed.) D. Defoe: *A Tour Through the Whole Island of Great Britain.*
      (ed.) R. Owen: *A New View of Society.*
      (ed.) *The Ormond Poets* (with M. Cole, volumes of selections, 1927–8).
1929 *The Next Ten Years in British Social and Economic Policy.*
      Politics and Literature.
1930 *Gold, Credit and Employment.*
      (ed.) K. Marx: *Capital*, Vol. I.
      (ed.) W. Cobbett: *Rural Rides.*
1932 *British Trade and Industry, Past and Future.*
      The Intelligent Man's Guide Through World Chaos.
      Economic Tracts For The Times.
      Modern Theories and Forms of Industrial Organisation.
      Modern Theories and Forms of Political Organisation.
1933 *The Intelligent Man's Review of Europe To-Day* (with M. Cole).
      The Crooked World.
      (ed.) *What Everybody Wants To Know About Money.*
1934 *What Marx Really Meant.*
      Studies in World Economics.
      Some Relations between Political and Economic Theory.
      A Guide to Modern Politics (with M. Cole).
      (ed.) William Morris: *Stories in Prose and Verse.*
1935 *Principles of Economic Planning.*
      The Simple Case For Socialism.
      (ed.) *Studies in Capital and Investment.*
1937 *Practical Economics.*
      The People's Front.
      The Condition of Britain (with M. Cole).
      (ed.) *Letters from William Cobbett to Edward Thornton.*
1938 *The Machinery of Socialist Planning.*
      Socialism in Evolution.
      Persons and Periods.
      The Common People (with R. Postgate).
1939 *Plan For Democratic Britain.*
      British Trade Unionism To-Day.
1941 *Europe, Russia and the Future.*
      British Working Class Politics 1832–1914.

Chartist Portraits.
My Dear Churchill, and other Open Letters to Persons in Authority (Populus, pseud.).
1942 *Great Britain in the Post-War World.*
1943 *The Means To Full Employment.*
Fabian Socialism.
1944 *A Century of Co-operation.*
Money: Its Present and Future.
(ed.) *The Opinions of William Cobbett* (with M. Cole).
1945 *Building and Planning.*
1947 *The Intelligent Man's Guide to the Post-War World.*
Local and Regional Government.
Samuel Butler and The Way of All Flesh.
1948 *The Meaning of Marxism.*
A History of the Labour Party from 1914.
1950 *Socialist Economics.*
Essays in Social Theory.
(ed.) *The Essential Samuel Butler.*
1951 *The British Co-operative Movement in a Socialist Society.*
(ed.) *British Working Class Movements: Select Documents* (with A. W. Filson).
1952 *Introduction to Economic History.*
1953 *An Introduction to Trade Unionism.*
Attempts At General Union.
A History of Socialist Thought, Vol. I: The Forerunners 1789–1850.
1954 *Money, Trade and Investment.*
A History of Socialist Thought, Vol. II: Marxism and Anarchism 1850–1890.
1955 *Studies in Class Structure.*
1956 *The Post-War Condition of Britain.*
A History of Socialist Thought, Vol. III: The Second International 1889–1914 (two parts).
1957 *The Case For Industrial Partnership.*
1958 *A History of Socialist Thought, Vol. IV: Communism and Social Democracy 1914–1931* (two parts).
1960 *A History of Socialist Thought, Vol. V: Socialism and Fascism 1931–1939.*

(B) ARTICLES AND PAMPHLETS

Pre-1913   (ed.) *The Octopus* (with A. L. Johnston), St. Paul's School, Nov. 1906–June 1907.
(ed.) *Oxford Socialist* (with F. K. Griffith), 1908–9.
(ed.) *Oxford Reformer*, 1909–10.
'The Reform of the Poor Law,' *Middlesex County Times*, Jan.–Feb. 1910 (also pamphlet).
'Oxford Socialism From Within', *Socialist Review*, Dec. 1910.

286 *Bibliography of the writings of G. D. H. Cole*

William Wordsworth, 1911, Oxford.

'Henry James', *The Blue Book*, No. 1, May 1912, Oxford.

1913 'The New Statesmanship', *The University Socialist*, Michaelmas term, Manchester.

The Greater Unionism (with W. Mellor), National Labour Press.

The Tram Strike —A Letter to City and University (with G. N. Clark), Oxford.

'An Oxford Summer School', *The Blue Book*, No. 5, Jan. 1913.

'William Morris', *The Blue Book*, No. 5, Jan. 1913.

'The Revival of Poetry', *Caledonian Jottings*, July 1913.

1914 'The Genesis of French Syndicalism—and Some Unspoken Morals', *New Age*, 5–19 Feb., 1914.

'Fabian Excursions', *Daily Herald*, 10 Feb. 1914.

'The Need for the Greater Unionism' (with W. Mellor), *Daily Herald*, 24 Feb., 1914.

'The Class War and the State' (with W. Mellor), *Daily Herald*, 10 Mar. 1914.

'Guilds and Industrial Change', *New Age*, 9 Apr. 1914.

'Industrial Unionism and the Guild System' (with W. Mellor), *New Age*, 25 June, 1914.

'Nationalisation and the Guilds', *New Age*, 10 Sept.–15 Oct., 1914.

'Socialism Old and New' (with W. Mellor), *Daily Herald*, 3 Oct., 1914

'Freedom in the Guild', *New Age*, 5 Nov.–31 Dec., 1914.

'Scientific Management', *Sociological Review*, Apr. 1914.

'Trade Union and Labour Notes' (with W. Mellor), *Daily Herald*, 1914–18 (regular column).

'At The Sign of The Book', *Highway*, 1914–15 (regular column).

1915 'Conflicting Social Obligations', *Proceedings of the Aristotelian Society*, Vol. xv, 1914–15.

'Democracy and the Guilds', *New Age*, 4 Feb. 1915.

'Trade Union Rules and the War', *Nation*, 27 Feb. 1915.

'State Sovereignty and the Guilds', *New Age*, 15 Apr. 1915.

'The State and the Engineers', *A.S.E. Monthly Journal and Report*, Apr. 1915.

'The Working of the Munitions Act', *Nation*, 4 Sept. 1915.

'Labour and Munitions', *Nation*, 18 Sept. 1915.

'The Munitions Act: A Plea For Reconsideration', *Nation*, 16 Oct. 1915.

Trade Unionism in War-Time (with W. Mellor), Herald Pamphlet.

The Price of Dilution of Labour (with W. Mellor), London.

1916 'The Nature of the State in View of its External Relations', *Proceedings of the Aristotelian Society*, Vol. xvi, 1915–16.

'National Guilds and the Balance of Powers', *New Age*, 16 Nov. 1916.

'National Guilds and the Division of Powers', *New Age*, 14 Dec. 1916.

Safeguards For Dilution (with W. Mellor), Amalgamated Society of Engineers.
The Munitions Acts and the Restoration of Trade Union Customs (with H. H. Slesser), Labour Joint Committee.

1917   'Reflections on the Wage System', *New Age*, 15 Mar.–26 Apr., 1917.
'The Guilds, the State, the Consumer, Mr. S. G. Hobson, and Others', *New Age*, 6 Dec., 1917.

1918   *The Meaning of Industrial Freedom* (with W. Mellor).
'A Second Round with Mr. Hobson', *New Age*, 21 Feb., 1918.
'The Whitley Report', *Guildsman*, June 1918.
'Why the Workers Should Demand Education' (with A. Freeman), *W.E.A. Education Year Book*.
'Trade Unionism and Education', *W.E.A. Education Year Book*.
Why Labour Left The Coalition, Herald Pamphlet.
'Recent Developments in the British Labour Movement', *American Economic Review*, Sept. 1918.

1919   'National Guilds and the State', *Socialist Review*, Jan.–Mar. 1919.
'The Outlook For Guildsmen', *Guildsman*, Jan. 1919.
'Political Action and the N.G.L.', *Guildsman*, Feb. 1919.
'Some Unsolved Problems of Guild Socialism', *Guildsman*, Mar. 1919.
National Guilds and the Coal Commission, National Guilds League.
Workers' Control in Industry, Independent Labour Party.
'Guilds at Home and Abroad', *Guildsman*, Sept. 1919–June 1921 (Regular column).

1920   'Unemployment', *Guildsman*, Jan. 1920.
'Motives in Industry', *Venturer*, Mar. 1920.
'Soviets and Political Theory', *Freeman*, 17 Mar., 1920.
'What We Want To Know About Russia', *New Statesman*, 1 May 1920.
'Collective Contract', *Guildsman*, July 1920.
'"Communism" and Labour Policy', *New Statesman*, 7 Aug. 1920.
'The Communist Party and the N.G.L.', *Guildsman*, Sept. 1920.
'The Control of Industry', *New Statesman*, 11 Dec. 1920.
Democracy in Industry, Manchester University Press.
Guild Socialism, Fabian Tract 192.

1921   'The Meaning of Guild Socialism', *Theosophist*, Vol. xlii, No. 9.
Guild Socialism and Communism (Chinese periodical? Copy at Nuffield College, Oxford).
'Down With Unemployment', *Guildsman*, Jan. 1921.
'Must Wages Come Down?', *New Statesman*, 5 Feb. 1921.
'The Gun That Did Not Go Off', *New Statesman*, 23 Apr. 1921.
'The New Dark Ages', *Venturer*, May 1921.
'The Swing of the Pendulum', *New Statesman*, 16 July 1921.
'Black Friday And After', *Labour Monthly*, July 1921.
'What Is The State?' *Venturer*, Aug. 1921.

'The Coming Wage Struggle', *New Statesman*, 27 Aug. 1921.
'The Aims of Guild Socialism', *Time and Tide*, 28 Oct. 1921.
'Labour in War and Peace', *Fortnightly Review*, Dec. 1921.
Unemployment and Industrial Maintenance, National Guilds League.

1922   'Non-Manual Trade Unionism', *North American Review*, Jan. 1922.
'Building Houses Without Private Profit', *Labor Age*, Jan. 1922.
'The True Political Economy', *New Statesman*, 21 Jan. 1922.
'A Word to the Engineers', *Labour Monthly*, Mar. 1922.
'The Position of British Socialism', *New Statesman*, 20 May 1922.
'Can The Guilds Succeed?', *Guild Socialist*, July 1922.
'The British Labour Movement—A Retrospect', *Labour Monthly*, Aug. 1922.
'The Guild Movement in Great Britain', *International Labour Review*, Aug. 1922.
'The Economics of Unemployment', *New Statesman*, 16 Dec. 1922.
'Workshop and Mine', *New Leader*, Oct. 1922–Apr. 1923 (weekly column).

1923   Guild Prospects in Engineering', *Guild Socialist*, Jan. 1923.
'Next Steps in the Guild Movement', *Guild Socialist*, Apr.–Aug. 1923.
'Workers' Education', *Highway*, Apr. 1923.
'The Leach-Gatherer', *Socialist Review*, June 1923.
'Labour Confers', *New Statesman*, 7 July 1923.
'The Question of the Hour', *New Statesman*, 13 Oct. 1923.
'An Economic Fallacy', *New Statesman*, 17 Nov. 1923.
'What A Labour Government Could Do', *New Statesman*, 15 Dec. 1923.
'For The Unemployed: What A Labour Government Could Do At Once', *New Leader*, 28 Dec. 1923.
'The Crisis in Workers' Education', *Highway*, Winter 1923.
(ed.) *New Standards* (with M. Cole), Oct. 1923–Oct. 1924.

1924   'Guild Socialism', in *British Labour Speaks* (ed. R. W. Hogue), New York.
'The Socialism of Nikolai Lenin', *New Statesman*, 2 Feb. 1924.
'The Chance At The Docks: Workers' Control and Maintenance', *Socialist Review*, Mar. 1924.
'The Debates on Unemployment', *New Statesman*, 31 May 1924.
'English Socialism in 1924', *New Statesman*, 6 Sept. 1924.

1925   'The Labour Party, the I.L.P. and the Trade Unions', *New Statesman*, 11 Apr. 1925.
'A Socialist Dilemma', *New Statesman*, 18 Apr. 1925.
'The Way to Deal with Unemployment', *New Statesman*, 1 Aug. 1925.
'The W.E.A. and the Future', *Highway*, Summer 1925.
'Left-Wingers and Communists', *New Statesman*, 3 Oct. 1925.
William Cobbett, Fabian Tract 215.

'Principles of Industrial Reconstruction', in *The Book of the Labour Party* (ed. H. Tracey), Vol. I.

1926   'Loyalties', *Proceedings of the Aristotelian Society*, Vol. xxvi, 1925–6.
'Where We Stand in the Coal Crisis', *New Statesman*, 17 Apr. 1926.
'Back to the Samuel Memorandum', *New Statesman*, 22 May 1926.
'When Will the Government Act?', *New Statesman*, 29 May 1926.
'Some Lessons of the Late General Strike', *New Statesman*, 19 June 1926.
'The Close of a System', *New Statesman*, 24 July 1926.
Industrial Policy For Socialists, Independent Labour Party.
'Easton Lodge: The Plea of an Enthusiast', *Labour Magazine*, Sept. 1926.

1927   *The Economic System*, W.E.A.
'The Labour Party and the Future', *New Statesman*, 1 Jan. 1927.
'The Strike Inquest', *New Statesman*, 29 Jan. 1927.
'Where Is Socialism Going?', *New Statesman*, 27 Aug. 1927.
'The Communist Doctrine', *Foreign Affairs*, Aug. 1927.
'The New Trade Unionism', *New Statesman*, 10 Sept. 1927.
'The Issues At Edinburgh', *New Leader*, 16 Sept. 1927.
'How To Improve Industrial Relations', *New Statesman*, 10 Dec. 1927.

1928   'Liberalism and the Industrial Future', *New Statesman*, 11 Feb. 1928.
'The I.L.P.', *New Statesman*, 14 Apr. 1928.
'The Policy of Labour', *New Statesman*, 14 July 1928.
'Concerning Nationalisation', *New Statesman*, 21 July 1928.
'The Trade Unions and the "Mond" Report', *New Statesman*, 1 Sept. 1928.
'Trade Unionism and the Future', *New Statesman*, 15 Sept. 1928.
'The Labour Party and the Nation', *New Statesman*, 13 Oct. 1928.
'The Mond Conferences and their Outcome', *Highway*, Oct. 1928.

1929   *How To Conquer Unemployment*, Labour Party.
'Can We Conquer Unemployment?', *New Statesman*, 23 Mar. 1929.
'The Limits of Democracy', *New Statesman*, 1 June 1929.
'Second Thoughts on the Election', *New Statesman*, 8 June 1929.
'Work or Doles?', *New Statesman*, 5 Oct. 1929.
'The Cure For Unemployment', *Everyman*, 10 Oct. 1929.
'Mr. Thomas and the Unemployed', *New Statesman*, 9 Nov. 1929.
'The First Six Months', *New Statesman*, 7 Dec. 1929.
'The Kink in History', *Listener*, 11 Dec. 1929.

1930   'The Old Year and the New', *New Statesman*, 4 Jan. 1930.
'Mr. Thomas and his Colleagues', *New Statesman*, 15 Feb. 1930.
'Trade Unions and the Government', *Clarion*, Feb. 1930.
'The Inner Life of Socialism', *Aryan Path*, Feb. 1930 (reprinted as 'Why I Am A Socialist', in *Economic Tracts For The Times*, 1932).
'The Ghost That Walks', *New Statesman*, 15 Mar. 1930.
'The Limits of Socialism', *New Statesman*, 17 May 1930.

'The Government and the Unemployed', *New Statesman*, 7 June 1930.
'The Parliamentary Impasse', *New Statesman*, 21 June 1930.
'London Traffic and the New Socialism', *New Statesman*, 11 Oct. 1930.
'Thoughts on Trade Policy', *Highway*, Dec. 1930.
'What the Labour Movement is Thinking', *Week-End Review*, 20 Dec. 1930.
King's Norton Labour News, 1930–31 (regular articles).
'The New World and Its Challenge', *Everyman*, 1930 (weekly economic articles).

1931 *The Crisis* (with E. Bevin), *New Statesman* Pamphlet.
'The Method of Social Legislation', *Public Administration*, Jan. 1931.
'Gandhi, The Man', *Aryan Path*, Jan. 1931.
'Eyes on Russia', *Clarion*, Feb. 1931.
'The Labour Party and the Future', *New Statesman*, 14 Mar. 1931.
'William Morris', *Revisions and Revaluations*.
Incentives Under Socialism, Little Blue Book.
'The Form of Socialisation', *New Statesman*, 27 June 1931.
'Was It A Bankers' Conspiracy?', *New Statesman*, 29 Aug. 1931.
'The Old Labour Party and the New', *New Statesman*, 14 Nov. 1931.
'A Socialist View', *Economist*, 17 Oct. 1931.
'Free Trade, Tariffs, and the Alternative', *Week-End Review*, 31 Oct. 1931.
'If Parliament had an Emergency Session', *Today and Tomorrow*, July 1931.
'Time Ripe For New Ideas', *Daily Herald*, 5 Nov. 1931.
'The Essentials of Socialisation', *Political Quarterly*, July–Dec. 1931.
'The Labour Party From Within', *Nineteenth Century*, Oct. 1931.
'The Approach To Politics', *Highway*, Nov. 1931.

1932 *War Debts and Reparations* (with R. Postgate), *New Statesman* Pamphlet.
'Communism For Englishmen', *Adelphi*, Apr. 1932.
'Year XIII or Year XV?', *New Statesman*, 9 Apr. 1932.
A Plan For Britain, Clarion Press.
'The Political System of Russia' (with M. Cole), *American Mercury*.
'The End of the "Labour Alliance"', *New Statesman*, 6 Aug. 1932.
Some Essentials of Socialist Propaganda, Fabian Tract 238.
'Socialism, the Labour Party, and the I.L.P.', *Adelphi*, Sept. 1932.
'Medieval Trade Guilds and the Modern World', *Service*, Autumn 1932.
'The End of the Bourgeois', *Student World*, Oct. 1932.
'The Webbs: Prophets of a New Order', *Current History*, Nov. 1932.
'Why I Am A Socialist', *Adelphi*, Dec. 1932.

1933 *Saving and Spending*, *New Statesman* Pamphlet.
The Need For A Socialist Programme (with G. R. Mitchison), Socialist League.
Socialist Control of Industry, Socialist League.

What Is This Socialism? Clarion Press.
(ed.) *Workers' Control and Self-Government in Industry* (with W. Mellor), New Fabian Research Bureau.
'Freedom and Tolerance', *Ipswich Evening Star*, 4 Jan. 1933.
'Marx', *Plebs* symposium, Mar. 1933.
'A Critique of British Communism', *This Unrest*, 1933.
'If Socialism Is To Come', *Adelphi*, May and June 1933.
'Economics in the Modern World', *Political Quarterly*, Apr.–June 1933.
'Fascism and the Socialist Failure', *Current History*, June 1933.
'The Present Confusion', *New Statesman*, 26 Aug. 1933.
'The Case For Going One's Own Way', *Kensington News*, 8 Sept. 1933.
'Are Public Works Unsound?', *Service*, Autumn 1933.
'Has Socialism Failed?', *Saskatchewan C.C.F. Research Bureau*, Sept. 1933.
'The Battle of Hastings', *New Statesman*, 30 Sept. 1933.
'What is Roosevelt Driving At?', *New Statesman*, 28 Oct. 1933.
'The Problem of the Coal Mines', *Political Quarterly*, Oct.–Dec. 1933.
'Labour's Opportunity', *New Statesman*, 8 Apr. 1933.
'Democracy and Dictatorship', *Highway*, Nov. 1933.
'The Débâcle of Capitalism', in *Recovery Through Revolution* (ed. S. Schmalhausen), New York.
1934 *The Working Class Movement and the Transition to Socialism*, Socialist League.
'Planning International Trade', *Foreign Affairs*, Jan. 1934.
'Socialism and Monetary Policy', *American Socialist Quarterly*, Spring 1934.
'Workers' Control', *Railway Service Journal*, Apr. 1934.
'Freedom in Danger', *Bournemouth Weekly Post*, 16 June 1934.
'Guild Socialism Twenty Years Ago and Now', *New English Weekly*, Sept. 1934.
'Where Does the Labour Party Stand Now?', *New Statesman*, 15 Dec. 1934.
1935 'My Books', *Swinton and Pendlebury Public Libraries Bulletin*, Jan. 1935.
'A Run For Our Money', *New Statesman*, 9 Mar. 1935.
'Planning and the Co-operative Movement', *Co-operative Review*, Sept. 1935.
'A Four Years' Retrospect', *New Statesman*, 31 Aug. 1935.
'Chants of Progress', *Political Quarterly*, Oct.–Dec. 1935.
'Democracy in the Twentieth Century', *Highway*, Nov. 1935.
'Labour Party's Future', *New Statesman*, 23 Nov. 1935.
Planned Socialism: The 'Plan Du Travail' of the Belgian Labour Party, New Fabian Research Bureau.
1936 *Fifty Propositions About Money and Production*, Stanley Nott.
'The No-Sayers', *Bristol Evening World*, 5 March 1936.

'Academic and Professional Freedom', *Library Assistant*, Mar. 1936.
'Can We Abolish Unemployment?' (with Harold Macmillan), *Service*, Summer 1936.
'Planning and Socialism', *New Statesman*, 9 May 1936.
'And What About England?', *New Statesman*, 13 June 1936.
'In Defense of Liberty', *Bacup Times*, 3 Oct. 1936.
'A British People's Front: Why and How?', *Political Quarterly*, Oct–Dec. 1936.
'After Edinburgh', *New Statesman*, 17 Oct. 1936.
'Capitalism At The Crossroads', in *Economics and Law, The Machinery of Social Life* (ed. Chadburn and Collins).

1937   'The United Front—And The People's Front', *Labour Monthly*, Jan. 1937.
'The Disunited Front', *New Statesman*, 23 Jan. 1937.
'The Next Step in the Coal Industry', *Political Quarterly*, Jan.–Mar. 1937.
'The British Labour Movement Today', *American Socialist Monthly*, Feb. 1937.
'Unity and the People's Front', *Labour Monthly*, Mar. 1937.
'The Changing Economic Order', *Science and Society*, Feb.–May 1937.
'Russia's Eight Years', *Tribune*, 7 May 1937.
'The Free Man's Labour', *Northern Daily Mail*, 13 May 1937.
'Can Capitalism Survive?', in *What Is Ahead Of Us?*, Fabian Society.

1938   'Economic Prospects: 1938 and After', *Fact*, No. 11, Feb. 1938.
'Dilution? British Labour Must Not Be Fooled A Second Time', *Tribune*, 1 Apr. 1938.
'Trade Unions and Rearmament', *Labour Monthly*, May 1938.
'A Basis For A Social Crusade', *Fortnightly*, July 1938.
'A Disturbing Book', *Aryan Path*, Sept. 1938.
'Freethought and the Struggle For Peace and Freedom', *World Union of Freethinkers*, Sept. 1938.
'Independent Progressive', *New Statesman*, 19 Nov. 1938.
'The Economic Consequences of War Preparation', in *Dare We Look Ahead?*, Fabian Society.
'Britain's Economic Policies and World Affairs', in *Europe Into The Abyss* (ed. A. Forbath).

1939   'British Capitalism and War Preparation', *Modern Quarterly*, Jan. 1939.
'Nazi Economics: How Do They Manage It?', *Political Quarterly*, Jan.–Mar. 1939.
'Freedom's Garden', *Blackley Guardian*, 25 Feb. 1939.
'Making Democracy Work: Freedom and Citizenship', *Hampstead and Highgate Express*, 10 Mar. 1939.
'The Tutor and the Working Class Movement', W.E.A. *Tutors' Bulletin*, Apr. 1939.

War Aims, New Statesman Pamphlet.
The War On The Home Front, Fabian Tract 247.
'Socialism Is The Only Solution', *Tribune*, 24 Nov. 1939.

1940 'J. A. Hobson': Obituary, *Economic Journal*, June–Sept. 1940.
'This Freedom' (with W. Beveridge), *Listener*, 22, 29 Feb. 1940.
'France and Britain', *New Statesman*, 29 June 1940.
'Paying For The War', *Political Quarterly*, Oct.–Dec. 1940.
'A Socialist Civilisation', *Fortnightly*, Dec. 1940.
'The Decline of Capitalism', in *Where Stands Democracy?*, Fabian Society.

1941 'The Man-Power Problem', *Political Quarterly*, Apr.–June 1941.
'Before Dawn', *New Statesman*, 17 May 1941.
'Another Sort of Freedom', *Hampshire Chronicle*, 26 Apr. 1941.
'Freedom in Chains', *Birkenhead News*, 28 May 1941.
'Leviathan and Little Groups', *Aryan Path*, Oct. 1941.
'The Future of Local Government', *Political Quarterly*, Oct.–Dec. 1941.
James Keir Hardie, Fabian Biographical Series.
'A Socialist Civilisation', in *Programme For Victory*, Fabian Society.

1942 'Europe, Russia and the Future: A Reply', *Left News*, Mar. 1942.
'British Trade Unionism under the Impact of War', *Fortnightly*, Apr. 1942.
'Reconstruction in the Civil and Municipal Services', *Public Administration*, Jan.–June 1942.
'The New "New Atlantis"', *Fortnightly*, Nov. 1942.
'Opinion in the Making', *New Statesman*, 15 Aug. 1942.
'Production Committees', *New Statesman*, 3 Oct. 1942.
A Word On The Future To British Socialists, Fabian Tract 256.
A Letter to an Industrial Manager, Fabian Society.
A Letter to a Shop Steward, Fabian Society.
Take Over The War Industries!, Fabian Society.
Production: A Plan For War Industry, *New Statesman* Pamphlet.
Beveridge Explained, *New Statesman* Pamphlet.
The Fabian Society, Past and Present, Fabian Tract 258.
'Private Monopoly or Public Service', in *Victory or Vested Interest?*, Fabian Society.

1943 *When The Fighting Stops*, National Peace Council.
'Beatrice Webb as an Economist', *Economic Journal*, Dec. 1943.
Richard Carlile, Fabian Biographical Series.
John Burns, Fabian Biographical Series.
'Plan For Living', in *Plan For Britain*, Fabian Society.

1944 'The Future of British Co-operation', *Co-operative Productive Review*, Feb. 1944.
'Co-operation: The Second Century', *Co-operative Productive Review*, Sept. 1944.
'Delegated Legislation', *New Statesman*, 18 Mar. 1944.

'The Impact of Current Economic Changes on Industrial Relations and on the Demand for Labour', *British Management Review*, Vol. v, No. 2.
'The Social Studies in the Universities', *Political Quarterly*, Oct.–Dec. 1944.
How To Obtain Full Employment, Odhams.
Planning of World Trade, Odhams.
'A Better Civil Service', in *Can Planning Be Democratic?*, Fabian Society.

1945 *Scope and Method in Social and Political Theory*, Inaugural Lecture, Oxford.
Welfare and Peace, National Peace Council.
'From War to Peace in Industry', *Political Quarterly*, July–Sept. 1945.

1946 *Labour's Foreign Policy*, New Statesman Pamphlet.
'Socialism in the World of Tomorrow', *Aryan Path*, Jan. 1946.
Co-operation, Labour and Socialism, Blandford Memorial Lecture.
'Socialism and Germany', *New Statesman*, 16 Mar. 1946.
'British Radicals and the Socialist Tradition', *Phoenix Quarterly*, Autumn 1946.
'The National Coal Board', *Political Quarterly*, Oct.–Dec. 1946.

1947 *A Guide To The Elements of Socialism*, Labour Party.
'Sociology and Politics in the Twentieth Century', *Politics and Letters*, winter–spring 1947.
'The Loan, the Present and the Future', *New Statesman*, 5 Apr. 1947.
'Trade Unions, Workers and Production', *Political Quarterly*, July–Sept. 1947.
'What Socialism Means To Me', *Labour Forum*, Oct.–Dec. 1947.

1948 'Democratic Socialism For Europe', *New Statesman*, 17 Jan. 1948.
'Living Together in Europe', *Fortnightly*, Feb. 1948.
Why Nationalise Steel?, New Statesman Pamphlet.
'Marx and the Marxists', *Outlook*, Lent 1948.
'Whither in Western Europe?', *Clarion* (Oxford), Trinity 1948.
'The Teaching of Social Studies in British Universities', *Universities Quarterly*, May 1948.
The National Coal Board, Fabian Society.
British Social Services, British Council.
Europe and the Problem of Democracy, Peace Aims Pamphlet.
'Principles of Post-War Planning and Industrial Reorganisation', in *The British Labour Party* (ed. H. Tracey).

1949 'Trade Unions and Trade Unionists in Britain Today', *Political Quarterly*, Jan.–Mar. 1949.
'Socialism or Mixed Economy?', *New Statesman*, 23 Apr. 1949.
Labour's Second Term, Fabian Tract 273.
'The Dream and the Business', *Political Quarterly*, July–Sept. 1949.
'Technology and the Social Studies', *Rewley House Papers* (Oxford), Vol. III, No. I, 1949–50.

Consultation or Joint Management? (with J. M. Chalmers and Ian Mikardo), Fabian Tract 277.
'To Plan or Not To Plan?' *and* 'Do We Choose The Economic System?', in *Economics, Man and His Material Resources*, Odhams.

1950 'The Conception of the Middle Classes', *British Journal of Sociology*, Vol. i, 1950.
'Liberty in Retrospect and Prospect', *Rationalist Annual*.
'An Open Letter to Members', *Fabian Journal*, May 1950.
'An Open Letter to Members', *Fabian Journal*, Oct. 1950.
'Labour and Staff Problems under Nationalisation', *Political Quarterly*, Apr.–June, 1950.
'The Future of Producers' Co-operation in Great Britain', *Review of International Co-operation*, Apr. 1950.
'The Soviet Polity', *Soviet Studies*, ii, 1950–51.
'Management and Democracy', *British Management Review*, July 1950.

1951 'As A Socialist Sees It', *New Statesman*, 3 Feb. 1951.
'Shall Socialism Fail?', *New Statesman*, 5, 12 May, 1951.
'Co-operation and the State', *Review of International Co-operation*, June 1951.
'Workers and Management in the Nationalised Industries', *Co-operators' Year Book*.
'Nationalised Industries—The Problem of Democratic Control', *Clarion* (Oxford), Oct. 1951.
British Labour Movement—Restrospect and Prospect, Ralph Fox Memorial Lecture, Fabian Special.

1952 'Nationalisation—or Socialisation', *Co-operative Productive Review*, Mar. 1952.
'Education and Politics: A Socialist View', *Year Book of Education*.
'Realpolitik', *New Statesman*, 26 Apr. 1952.
'What Workers' Education Needs', *Fortnightly*, June 1952.
'What Has Happened to Marxism?', *New Republic*, 17, 24 Mar. 1952.
'The Bolshevik Revolution', *Soviet Studies*, Vol. iv, 1952–3.
'Facts of Life for Socialists', *New Statesman*, 2 Aug. 1952.
'After the Shouting', *New Statesman*, 6 Dec. 1952.
The Development of Socialism During The Past Fifty Years, Webb Memorial Lecture, 1951, Athlone Press, 1952.

1953 'Nationalisation—What Next?', *New Statesman*, 31 Jan. 1953.
'The Labour Party and the Trade Unions', *Political Quarterly*, Jan.–Mar., 1953.
'What Is Socialism? I', *Political Studies*, I, Feb. 1953.
'What Is Socialism? II', *Political Studies*, I, June 1953.
'The Idea of Progress', *British Journal of Sociology*, Vol. iv, 1953.
'The Great Negation', *New Statesman*, 14 Nov. 1953.
'Some Advice to the Left', *New Statesman*, 21 Nov. 1953.

1954   *Is This Socialism?*, *New Statesman* Pamphlet.
        'What Next? Anarchists or Bureaucrats?', *Fabian Journal*, Apr. 1954.
        'After the Dock Strike', *New Statesman*, 6 Nov. 1954.
1955   'The Future of Socialism', *New Statesman*, 15, 22 Jan. 1955.
        'Thoughts After The Election', *New Statesman*, 25 June 1955.
        'Socialism and the Welfare State', *New Statesman*, 23 July 1955.
1956   *What Is Wrong With The Trade Unions?*, Fabian Tract 301.
        World Socialism Restated, *New Statesman* Pamphlet.
        'Socialism and the Democratic Control of Industry', *World Socialist*,
        Jan. 1956.
        'The Crisis in International Socialism', *World Socialist*, Feb. and Mar.
        1956.
        'Socialists and Communism', *New Statesman*, 5 May 1956.
        'Twentieth Century Socialism?', *New Statesman*, 7 July 1956.
        'Reflections on Democratic Centralism', *Reasoner*, Nov. 1956.
1957   *Capitalism in the Modern World*, Fabian Tract 310.
        'What is Happening to British Capitalism?', *Universities and Left Review*,
        spring 1957.
        'Reflections on Hungary', *New Statesman*, 12 Jan. 1957.
        'World Socialism and the Hungarian Crisis', *World Socialist*, Feb. 1957.
        'Hungary is the Test', *New Statesman*, 20 Apr. 1957.
        'Wakeful Partners in Industry', *New Statesman*, 28 Sept. 1957.
1958   'Retreat From Bigness', *New Statesman*, 22 Mar. 1958.
        'J. A. Hobson', *New Statesman*, 5 July 1958.
        'Next Steps in British Foreign Policy', *New Reasoner*, summer 1958.
1959   Foreword to B. Pribićević, *The Shop Stewards' Movement and Workers'
        Control 1910–1922*.
        'The Growth of Socialism', in M. Ginsberg (ed.), *Law and Opinion in
        England in the Twentieth Century*.
1960   *William Morris As A Socialist*, William Morris Society.
1962   'Phases of Labour's Development in Great Britain 1914–58', in H.
        Infield (ed.), *Essays in Jewish Sociology, Labour and Co-operation*.
1977   'The Striker Stricken', (1926 operetta on the General Strike) in A.
        Briggs and J. Saville (eds.), *Essays in Labour History*, Vol. 3, *1918–1939*.

Index

Soviet Union, *see* Russia; Russian Revolution
Spanish Civil War, 244, 278n.
Spontaneity, 20–1, 76, 77–8, 98, 223, 276
Stalin, 226, 228, 231, 248–9, 250, 251, 252, 256, 260n.; 261
State, 3, 5, 14–15, 22, 24, 25, 26, 28, 31, 32–49, 50, 51, 52–3, 58, 74, 94, 119, 124–5, 126, 139, 142, 149, 152–4, 158, 174, 176, 191, 216–17, 234, 263, 267, 268
Storrington Document, 40n.
Strachey, John, 2, 3, 6, 92, 110, 161, 162, 163, 188, 189, 193, 195–6, 200n., 220n., 224, 241, 263
Syndicalism, 21, 22, 24, 25, 26, 27, 28, 30, 32, 35, 38, 40, 42n., 52, 55, 56, 73, 74, 76, 109n., 138, 268

Taff Vale case, 15
Tawney, R. H., 2, 3, 6, 44n., 51n., 72, 84, 175, 263, 271, 272–3
Thomas, J., 97, 190
Thompson, E. P., 27, 281
Titmuss, R., 236
Tocqueville, 55
Totalitarianism, 225–6, 228, 242, 251–2, 256n.
Trade unions, 14–15, 17, 26, 27, 29, 30, 31, 43, 44, 57, 62, 79, 84–90, 94–5, 98, 99–100, 107, 112–13, 122, 128, 129, 130, 133, 134–5, 141, 142, 146, 152–3, 174, 205, 275, 279
Trevelyan, G. M., 146

Ulam, A., 109
Unemployment, 6, 106, 112, 119, 142, 155, 157, 158, 177–84, 190, 191, 198, 203

United Front, 175, 245, 247
Upper Clyde Shipbuilders, 279
Utilitarianism, 23, 116–17
Utopianism, 1, 3, 14, 25, 52, 76, 84, 96, 101, 115n., 120, 125, 188, 196, 202, 206, 233, 264, 265, 268, 278, 281

Vansittart, R., 252

Wallas, Graham, 121
Warwick, Countess, 145
Webb, Beatrice, 32n., 55, 61, 66, 77n., 86, 116, 136, 139n., 151n., 152, 153, 157n., 163
Webb, Sidney, 18, 53, 55, 56, 63, 65, 71, 87, 274
Webb, Sidney and Beatrice, 9, 13n., 17, 18, 29, 44n., 51, 52–71, 85, 96, 115, 116, 119, 128, 134, 156, 180, 241, 242, 261n., 263, 267
Welfare state, 131, 136, 175n., 234, 235–6, 238
Wells, H. G., 21
Wertheimer, E., 186
Whitley Report (and Councils), 91, 280
Whitman, W., 274
Wilkinson, E., 92
Wolin, S., 273
Wootton, Barbara, 26n., 199n.
Work, 22, 27, 28, 30, 55, 58, 62–6, 70, 108, 115, 121, 280
Workers' control, *see* Industrial democracy
Workers' Educational Association (W.E.A.), 89, 145
World Order of Socialists, 258

Yugoslavia, 259, 280n.